Anton Pavlovich Chekhov

Poetics—Hermeneutics—Thematics

Edited by J. Douglas Clayton

ꞆℜG

The Slavic Research Group at the University of Ottawa

2006

Library and Archives Canada Cataloguing in Publication

Anton Pavlovich Chekhov : poetics - hermeneutics - thematics / edited by J. Douglas Clayton.

English language proceedings of a conference held December 10-11, 2004 at the University of Ottawa, Ontario, Canada.

ISBN 0-88927-287-5

1. Chekhov, Anton Pavlovich, 1860-1904--Criticism and interpretation. 2. Chekhov, Anton Pavlovich, 1860-1904--Congresses.

I. Clayton, J. Douglas II. University of Ottawa. Slavic Research Group III. Anton Pavlovich Chekhov : Poetics - Hermeneutics - Thematics (2004 : University of Ottawa)

PG3458.Z8A57 2006   891.72'3   C2006-905610-2

Printed in Canada

Anton Pavlovich Chekhov: Poetics—Hermeneutics—Thematics

Contents

From the Editor

2004 was an important year in Chekhov studies, marking a hundred years from the death of the Russian short-story writer and playwright Anton Pavlovich Chekhov. In Canada this date was marked by a workshop which took place at the University of Ottawa on December 10th and 11th. Participants in the workshop came from Canada, Russia, the United States, Germany, Ukraine, Sweden, Israel, and Poland. The present volume is based on the contributions of the participants at the workshop (with some additions) and reflects the variety of issues discussed. For practical reasons, it is divided into two parts—prose and drama. One of the objectives of the workshop was to create bridges between the different scholarly discourses—mainly in English and Russian—focusing on Chekhov. For this reason, and because many scholars working in one language cannot read papers in the other, this volume in English is reflected by a parallel, almost identical publication in Russian, *Chekhovskie chteniia v Ottave*. The intention is to give the widest possible currency to this research, and also to create resonances and hopefully interaction between the two scholarly discourses.

The workshop had as its title and topic (as does this volume) "Anton Pavlovich Chekhov: Poetics, Hermeneutics, Thematics," and sought to focus on the central issues of Chekhov studies, namely Chekhov's revolutionary innovations in the poetics of both the short story and drama, and their reflection in a variety of his works. This topic was dictated by the current state of Chekhov studies, especially in the Russian-speaking world, which has come to focus increasingly on poetics as the key to Chekhov's unique contribution to literature and theatre. As Vladimir Kataev puts it: "Chekhov's poetic system demands different methods of analysis from those applied to works with a traditional poetics that affirm definite objectively limited ('special') ideas."[1] A formidable impetus to this movement to refocus on the poetics of Chekhov's texts was given by the late Alexander Chudakov in his ground-breaking *Poetika Chekhova*, which represented a fundamental departure from the

---

[1]Kataev, *Proza Chekhova*: 151.

ideologized Soviet approach to Chekhov with its insistence on realism and *narodnost'*. Developing the ideas of western phenomenologists, Chudakov insisted on viewing each work as a system, to be approached and analyzed systematically. Chudakov's book, with its methodical approach to the different elements ("layers") of the text laid the foundation for the contemporary study of Chekhov's poetics. Chudakov broke down his analysis into two parts: narrative structure (the subjective early narrative; the objective manner of his middle period; and his late narratives) and the imagined world in Chekhov's works (the physical world; the relation of the *fabula* or imagined sequence of events to the *siuzhet* or surface narrative as it is presented in the text; and the sphere of ideas).

Chudakov's approach and insights are reflected in many of the articles in this collection. It should be noted, moreover, that the approach did not mean, and was not perceived to mean, that each element of the structure of the text should be isolated out and analyzed with no reference to the other elements. As Igor Sukhikh comments, one can observe a "tendency to a clearer and clearer understanding of the integrality and systematic, structured nature of each work, of Chekhov's art, and of the literary process."[2] Going beyond issues of poetics as such, and bearing in mind this notion of the integrality of all the elements in Chekhov's works and the need to see them as a unified system, the topic of the conference recognized that in Chekhov poetics and hermeneutics, i.e., how we understand the text, are interrelated and contingent upon one another. Any reading of the text is conditioned by how the material of the text is organized, and, to have validity, must come to grips with issues of poetics, i.e., the structures that permit and justify such a reading. By the same token, our understanding of Chekhov's poetics is activated, enriched and corrected by the hermeneutic process, for the ultimate objective of a text is to invite interpretation or exegesis, and it is to this end that the poetics of the text is organized. In other words, the poetics is the key to hermeneutic analysis. By the same token, an essential ingredient in any hermeneutic activity is the perception of the predominant themes and their relationship to each other; clearly, both the choice of themes and their

---

[2] Sukhikh, *Problemy poetiki A. P. Chekhova*: 5.

interrelatedness, as well as their function within the larger structure of the work as a whole, are not fortuitous: they are profoundly related to the ideas of the work. Not for nothing is Chudakov's final chapter entitled "The sphere of ideas," for while one must resist the attempt to impose ideas on the text, the texts themselves contain ideas that express themselves on the thematic level among others. It therefore seemed appropriate to include thematics as the third element in the title and topic of the workshop.

Beyond the structural-phenomenological approach as exemplified by Chudakov's book, it is important to acknowledge the importance of the study of language as an element in present-day literary studies in Russia. This is particularly due to, and shaped by, the work of Mikhail Bakhtin. For Bakhtin, the study of language, or "the word," centres on speech genres, briefly described as the discrete word in its social, temporal and spatial context as an element of dialogue. Meaning, that is to say, is always a function of communication, and communication is the context. These issues are the subject of a recent volume by Andrei Stepanov: *Problemy kommunikatsii u Chekhova*. Bakhtinian studies currently centre in the Russian State University for the Humanities in Moscow, and an excellent example of this approach is to be found in this volume in the article by Valery Tiupa. Much has been made of the fact that Chekhov's characters do not seem to communicate, that their "wires are crossed," a notion explored here by Vladimir Zviniatskovsky. This renders the Bakhtinian view of language problematic, since it challenges the notion of communicative speech. Perhaps, as Clayton suggests, the issue is that for Chekhov communication between individuals is as much non-verbal as verbal; silence can mean as much as any statement (and indeed is a statement). Or perhaps it is truer to say that in communication it is not the spoken word that is paramount, but only one level in a complex psychological communicative strategy. Here traditional literary scholarship finds itself in a quandary, since it consists in the analysis of *texts*, and cannot investigate the tantalizingly non-verbal that seems to characterize much of the communication between Chekhov's characters, especially in the plays.

This is not to say that a study of Chekhov's language cannot yield interesting results, since, after all, it is from the material of language that his texts are constructed. Indeed, Chekhov as an innovator of language is an important and promising topic for scholars. As Emma Polotskaya has shown, one of the first people to understand and embrace the innovative nature of Chekhov's language was the poet Mayakovsky in his article "Two Chekhovs" (1914). Mayakovsky rejected all the clichés that had so quickly come to characterize the content of Chekhov's works, affirming that Chekhov's objective as a writer lay not in the content of his works, but in the word, especially in the lexical renewal of language: "Chekhov's language is as precise as 'Hello,' and as simple as 'Give me a glass of water.'" Polotskaya writes: "In the context of Chekhov's renewal of language [...] Mayakovsky pointed to the social conditions that gave birth to this simplicity and precision: 'The dishevelled life of the burgeoning cities that had spawned new, lively people required that to this fast pace he apply a rhythm that would resurrect the word'."[3]

It is precisely the question of Chekhov's language at the simplest level of lexis that suggests a new and promising approach, exemplified in the article by Irina Gladilina in this volume. If information technology initially seemed to promise speedy results in the analysis of the lexical level of a writer's language, Gladilina finds that it is not statistical dominance that determines the importance of any particular lexical item in the writer's vocabulary: such an approach is too simplistic. In other words, here too it is the insight of the scholar that is paramount. Gladilina's experience resonates with that of Savely Senderovich: "The brevity of Chekhov's texts and his compact style of writing go hand in hand with the increased specific gravity of the word taken separately. The specific gravity of the verbal unit is defined by its repetitions, its various synonyms, and the presence of words that are contiguous by virtue of belonging to the same semantic field, and also by the formation in this way of discrete semantic fields and by the intersection of different fields in one and the same elementary lexical component of the text. The fact that the semantics of the text rests on such structures requires the adjustment of

---

[3] Polotskaia, *O poetike Chekhova*: 226.

the reader's eye to the microscopic level..."[4] All this suggests that the construction of a precise description of Chekhov's language, though worthwhile, is a daunting task, since it implies a reconstruction of the entire world-view of the writer as he expressed it in verbal form.

The contributions of non-Russian scholars to this volume exhibit a variety of approaches, centring on the time-honoured technique of close reading of the text. Robert Jackson applies the technique to great effect in his analysis of the story "Small Fry," in which he demonstrates the importance of the religious subtext of the Easter tale. It is attention to the religious subtexts combined with close readings of the works that American scholars have exploited with considerable success, inspired by the examples of Jackson, Senderovich and de Sherbinin. A variation on the theme of close reading can be found in the article by Herta Schmid, who offers a theoretically sophisticated analysis of ecphrasis in Chekhov. Her approach echoes the widespread analysis of ecphrasis in other contexts in western scholarship. Another theme in current American scholarship is the attention to the medical aspects of Chekhov's work, since he was, after all, a doctor. This approach, pioneered by Michael Finke in his recent study *Seeing Chekhov: Life and Art*, is exemplified in this volume by the article by Cathy Popkin's study of the psychological theme in "An Attack of Nerves," which she shows to be a riposte to the commonly practiced "case history" in medical practice of the time. What fascinates in such studies is the dual nature of Chekhov's vision: as a writer, and as a doctor who perceives the pathology of the individual and seeks to find a description that is both accurate and aesthetically pleasing.

In the discussion of drama questions of poetics may centre on plot, rhythmical structure and thematics as is the case of the articles by Vladimir Kataev, Wasilij Szczukin, and others in this volume, but quickly devolve into issues surrounding theatre productions and the specifics of interpretation. This is not surprising—since any dramatic text, at least any dramatic text by Chekhov—is a series of questions or riddles aimed at the director and actors rather than the reader. Here the non-verbal communicative element comes especially into play. Indeed, it

---

[4] Senderovich, *Chekhov s glazu na glaz*: 12.

was partly here that the innovative nature of Chekhov's dramatic texts "set the agenda" for twentieth-century theatre. As Yana Meerzon shows, the poetics of a Chekhov play require rather different analysis than that for a prose text, since the text needs to be translated into a system of theatrical signs that can be read as playing ironically off one another. Meerzon rests her analysis on the praxis of Vsevolod Meyerhold. This process is, however, an unending one, and leads in post-modernism to the deconstruction of the text in a variety of ways. It would be interesting to examine Boris Akunin's *Seagull*, here analyzed by Volha Isakava, as a further extension of the process of analysis described by Meerzon (not to mention the role of Pogrebnichko's productions in this process).

The editor wishes to express his thanks to Professor Andrei Donskov, director of the Slavic Research Group at the University of Ottawa, for kindly agreeing to publish this volume. Thanks are also due to the Social Sciences and Humanities Research Council of Canada and the Faculty of Arts of the University of Ottawa, without whose support this workshop could not have taken place. Thanks also to Ms Dina Austin, who participated in the organization of the workshop, contributed to the preparation of this volume, and designed the cover, and to Ms Elizabeth Mitchell, whose painstaking work on the text of this volume contributed greatly to the final result.

Unless otherwise indicated, quotations from Chekhov are from the Academic edition: Anton Pavlovich Chekhov, *Polnoe sobranie sochinenii i pisem*. 30 volumes, *Sochineniia*, 18 volumes. *Pis'ma*, 12 volumes. Moscow: Academia, 1974–1983. References to this edition are given in parentheses in the text as follows: Works: S; Letters: P. The volume number is followed by the page number as follows: S 8: 500; P 6: 228.

J. Douglas Clayton

WORKS CITED

Chudakov, Aleksandr. *Poetika Chekhova*. M.: Nauka, 1971.
Finke, Michael C., *Seeing Chekhov: Life and Art*. Ithaca: Cornell U.P., 2005.

Kataev, Vladimir. *Proza Chekhova: problemy interpretatsii.* M.: Izdatel'stvo Moskovskogo universiteteta, 1979.

Polotskaia, Emma. *O poetike Chekhova.* 2nd ed. M.: Nasledie, 2001.

Senderovich, Savelii. *Chekhov s glazu na glaz: Istoriia odnoi oderzhimosti A.P. Chekhova.* SPb.: Izdatel'stvo "Dmitrii Bulanin," 1994.

Stepanov, Andrei. *Problemy kommunikatsii u Chekhova.* M.: Iazyki slavianskoi kul'tury, 2005.

Sukhikh, Igor. *Problemy poetiki A. P. Chekhova.* L.: Izdatel'stvo Leningradskogo universiteta, 1987.

The Communicative Strategy of Chekhov's Poetics

VALERY TIUPA
Russian State University for the Humanities

The radical departure from the preceding classical tradition represented by Chekhov's art, the rupture that Vittorio Strada has called "the most profound revolution in Russian literature,"[1] became noticeable to the most sensitive of his contemporaries even during the writer's lifetime. Tolstoy's remark is widely known: "Chekhov created new, in my opinion completely new, forms of writing for the entire world... Chekhov as an artist cannot be compared with preceding Russian writers such as Turgenev or Dostoevsky or with me."[2] However, the total innovativeness and significance of Chekhov's work for world literature only came to be fully felt in the twentieth century. Moreover, this realization grew and became more profound throughout the century, as the features characteristic of post-classical art typical of the new literature became clear. However, even today the challenge formulated by Vladimir Kataev remains pertinent, namely to define "his [Chekhov's — V.T.] role in the shift that took place in Russian aesthetics at the turn of the nineteenth century."[3]

Arguing from the position of neo-rhetoric,[4] the essence of this shift lies in the radical renewal of the communicative strategy of literature. This strategy consists in the basic positioning of the subject, the object, and the addressee of the statement, thus defining the architectonics of the communicative event. Andrei Stepanov, in his study of communica-

---

[1] Strada, "Literatura kontsa XIX veka (1890–1900)": 48.

[2] Quoted from Sergeenko, *Tolstoy i ego sovremenniki*: 228.

[3] Kataev, "Spor o Chekhove: konets ili nachalo?": 7.

[4] Neo-rhetorics, which arose in the 1950s on the ruins of classical rhetorics in the work of A. Richards, Kh. Perel'man, M. Bakhtin and others, is a philological discipline that seeks to study the communicative behaviour of people as "the specific use of language in all spheres of social life and culture" (Bakhtin, "Iz arkhivnykh zapisei k rabote *Problema rechevykh zhanrov*": 236. See also Tiupa, "Ritorika kak uchenie o kommunikativnom sobytii."

tion in Chekhov, arbitrarily reduces the concept of a communicative strategy to the consequences of the author's intention,[5] rather than "the entire communicative chain."[6] Basing his argument on the "thesis of the self-sufficiency of the communicative problematic"[7] in the case of Chekhov, he limits himself to "that aspect of the image of the author that stands behind all the communicative tactics of the text," and goes on to declare: "We can exclude from our examination the narrator-reader aspect of the communication."[8] Hence, his treatment of the communicative event not as a metatextual interaction (coexistence) of consciousnesses, but simply as "the shifting of the speech genre"[9] on the plane of the text. This leads him to come to an extremely doubtful conclusion: "Chekhov's understanding of communication remains in essence skeptical even in stories that unfailingly leave in the reader's mind a bright feeling."[10] In the deepest layer of Chekhov's strategy as author Stepanov discovers "a skepsis as to the very possibility of there existing an adequate addressee," a disbelief in "the possibility of total communication."[11]

Strictly speaking, the category of "strategy" (the highest level of abstraction in the scientific description of any activity) is applicable only to discourse as a whole—the integrative unity of the creative, referent and receptive competences of the given communicative event.[12] A strategy cannot be reduced to a subjectively pursued objective; it is one of the possible paths to this or another objective. Nor is "the literal reproduction of the poetics of an everyday dialogue"[13] a strategy—that is the tactic of the conception of a text. As opposed to a tactic that is formed and controlled by the actant himself, a strategy is only chosen by the actant. Thereafter the freely chosen strategy limits the actant, imposing on him the base parameters of his communicative behaviour (the idea of a certain sort of power of the discourse over the speaker or writer has already become a commonplace in contemporary rhetoric). Of course, a change

---

[5] Stepanov, *Problemy kommunikatsii u Chekhova*: 54–55.

[6] Ibid.: 323.

[7] Ibid.: 19.

[8] Ibid.: 56, 55.

[9] Ibid.: 70.

[10] Ibid.: 335.

[11] Ibid.: 365, 364.

[12] See Tiupa, "Osnovaniia sravnitel'noi ritoriki." *Kritika i semiotika*, No. 7.

[13] Stepanov: 300.

of strategy is almost always possible, but in the area of communication the choice of a new strategy inevitably means the interruption of one statement and the beginning of a new one.

Recently more and more works have appeared that analyze the communicative behaviour of Chekhov's heroes[14] and identify in his works a rhetorical problem of "obstacles that prevent real human contact (but not that revealed in the phenomena of consciousness, in the 'created legend')."[15] These works demonstrate convincingly that the absence of communication comprises one of the key aspects of Chekhov's thematics. Stepanov rightly remarks that "in Turgenev, Goncharov, Tolstoy and Dostoevsky the antagonists understand each other's position [...] they listen and they hear [...]. The first writer to introduce the theme of the break in communication and make it the centre of his art was Chekhov."[16]

The groundwork for this decisive conclusion was laid by Chekhov scholars of the preceding generations, beginning with Aleksandr Skaftymov.[17] I might refer to one of the numerous statements of this kind made by Zinovii Papernyi: "Chekhov rejects the type of conversation between his characters in which their close, direct contact and interdependence can be felt. Dialogue appears not as a coherent verbal mass, not as an argument between characters about one and the same thing. Rather, it is a conversation of the individual with himself."[18] There are reasons for thinking that the overarching task of dialogue in Chekhov is "to confirm the independence of each character vis-à-vis the other, and the autonomy of the vortex of his life in the face of constantly shifting existence."[19]

When one examines a number of situations of "breakdown in

---

[14] These include: Pervukhina, *Anton Chekhov: The Sense and Nonsense*; Jędrze-jkiewicz, *Opowiadania Antoniego Czechowa—studia nad porozumiewaniem się ludzi*; and Stepanov, *op. cit.*

[15] Kapustin, *Chuzhoe slovo v proze A.P. Chekhova: zhanrovye transformatsii*: 73.

[16] Stepanov, "Kommunikatsiia i informatsiia u Chekhova," *Diskurs*, No. 10: 71.

[17] In the world of Chekhov's characters "each among the others is alone. And the relations between them are pointedly depicted in isolation and lack of contact" (Skaftymov, *Nravstvennye iskaniia russkikh pisatelei*: 353).

[18] Papernyi, *"Vopreki vsem pravilam…"*: 191.

[19] Iezuitova, "Komediia A.P. Chekhova 'Chaika' kak tip novoi dramy": 334.

communication"[20] depicted by Chekhov—not only comic ones, but also those that are profoundly dramatic—one is tempted to define Chekhov's poetic overall as a poetics of deaf and dumb discourse. This radical metaphor is not contrived, but suggested by Chekhov's texts themselves. Thus, in "A Woman's Kingdom" the presence of a *deaf and dumb young woman* is highly significant; in "The Student" the widow Lukeria's "expression was strange, like that of a deaf and dumb person"; in "The Archbishop" there is mention of an "silent and somewhat deaf archimandrite," and so on. Here is a characteristic example of "deaf and dumb" discourse in Chekhov: "'Tell me just one convincing thing. Say just one word.' 'One word? Here you are: Tara-ra boomdeay'" ("Big Volodya and Little Volodya"). If we take as our point of departure for all Chekhov's work his youthful drama known as "Fatherlessness," we are obliged to conclude that textually it begins with a truly "deaf and dumb" exchange of remarks between Triletsky and Anna Petrovna:

> "What?
> Nothing…"

Equally typical for Chekhov's characters is Olga's gesture of communicative behaviour in *The Three Sisters* when "going off to her own space behind the screen" she declares: "Stop that. I can't hear you anyway." Such examples could easily be multiplied many times over.

If one pole of the communicative world of "A Woman's Kingdom" is represented by "a deaf and dumb young woman who is ashamed of something and keeps saying 'Bly bly…,'" then the other is occupied by the main protagonist, about whom it is said, "She liked the fact that she could talk so well." However this opposition is only apparent, for Anna Akimovna is herself constantly ashamed of something (her wealth, her inability to run the business, her desire to marry) and her speech, which seems to her to be so felicitous, is completely ignored by her interlocutor, who is pursuing his own self-interest, and thus takes place in a communicative vacuum.

The problem of deaf and dumb discourse is taken up directly in one of Chekhov's last stories, "At Christmas," published on January 1, 1900 in *Peterburgskaia gazeta*. In it the absurd text of the letter, which is

---

[20] Shcheglov, "Molodoi chelovek v driakhleiushchem mire": 23.

intended to establish communicative contact but is unable to do so because of its very absurdity, appears the quintessence of discursive activity. The story begins with the unanswered remark of the scribe Yegor, "What should I write?" The question is vacuous, since Yegor will in any case compose the text of the letter out of the only material that fills his head (fragments of sentences from the military regulations). The story ends with the remark of the nominal addressee of the letter—the doorman at the spa: "Douche Charcot, your Excellency!" This reply to the question of the general is likewise communicatively void, since the general asks the same question every day. Here even the frying pork is endowed with the gift of speech, for it keeps saying "fliu-fliu-fliu." But the text of the letter itself, which is sent with such great difficulty, is no more than a senseless "fliu-fliu" or "bly-bly."

The deaf and dumb discourse of Chekhov's characters testifies to the self-referentiality of their communicative strategy—a strategy of relating the statement not to the generally understood world of common existence, but to an individually understood, subjective picture of the world. As Katya in "A Boring Story" puts it: "You and I are singing in different operas." In Chekhov's world each character usually talks about his own world (even Yegor, the freeloader in the tavern, who clearly speaks from the heart when to the formulae of the regulations in the letter, adds "our prime Internal Enemy is Bacchus"). At times this strategy reaches the ideal of self-communicativeness, as when Rashevich (in the story "On the Estate") talks "delighting in his thoughts and the sounds of his own voice."

However, for Chekhov the self-referential strategy of communication is a represented strategy, not his own strategy of artistic representation. If it were true that "the author's communicative strategy is clearly directed at the introduction of phatics as such into the text for its own sake,"[21] and not in order to form an artistic impression as a projection of readerly competence, then Chekhov's writing would have to be likened to the speeches of Rashevich. Yet the entire poetics of his own texts is based on the actual possibility of mutual understanding and overcoming the lack of communication observed in Chekhov's characters.

Sometimes such moments, through some miracle of communication, become the object of artistic depiction, as in the Christmas story "At

---

[21] Stepanov, *Problemy...*: 297.

Christmas" (which constitutes the "Christmas" nature of the work, for the genre demanded a happy ending to a touching story). Efimia does not read the absurd text of the letter: its first words are sufficient for her, through laughter and tears, to tell her children about their grandmother and grandfather. In the thoughts of old Vasilisa and her daughter the same village life is present, although they perceive it in different tones. The communicative competences of sender and receiver of the wretched letter are not the same, but they are not unfamiliar to each other: they are co-referent, mutually complementary, as is underlined by the "marry-ability" of their addresses to the "Heavenly Lord," on the one hand, and to the "Heavenly Lady" on the other.

Chekhov's artistic discourse is itself couched in a co-referent strategy of relating the statement to the individually significant world of the "other" (the reader, in whom the author recognizes his "personal secret"), but without rejecting his own (authorial) image of the world. The referential function of such a statement is the intersubjective reality of a "dialogue of agreement" in which "the difference and integrity of the voices is always retained" (Mikhail Bakhtin). Unlike a monologic agreement imposed by the creative will and skill of the author, a dialogic agreement is not a "mechanical or logical identification, nor is it an echo: behind it there is always a distance overcome and a coming closer (but not a fusion)."[22]

The simplified mechanism of organization of the statement in a co-referent communicative strategy can be seen in "The Student":

> "I suppose you were at the twelve gospels?"
> "I was," Vasilisa replied.
> "If you remember, at the last supper Peter said to Jesus […] Then you heard, Judas in the same night […] you understand […] he was also warming himself, just the way I am now […] In the Gospel it says: 'And he went forth and wept bitterly.' I can imagine; the quiet, dark garden, and in the darkness the muffled sobs can hardly be heard…"

Ivan's question is in no way intended to elucidate whether the widow is attending the Easter services (he knows this anyway). Through a rhetorical question and also the ensuing: "you remember"; "you heard"; "you

---

[22] Bakhtin: 364.

understand"; and the overlapping of the Biblical and the present existential situations—through all these "devices" the future preacher brings alive in the personal experience of his interlocutor a co-referential space forming (in convergence with his own experience) an intersubjective reality of dialogical agreement. If in Tolstoy's novel *Resurrection* the culminating role is given to the sacred discourse in its authoritarian referentiality, then, on the other hand, Chekhov's student shares with his listener his imaginative response to the text of the Gospel, helping her in turn to form the co-referential image of a mutually imagined reality:

> If the old woman burst into tears, it was not because he was able to talk so touchingly, but because Peter was close to her, and because she was interested in her entire being in what had happened in Peter's soul.

Translated into the language of rhetoric, this explanation attributes the communicative success of the extra-ritual sermon not to rhetorical skill, but to the co-referentiality of the creative and receptive consciousnesses. However, this co-referentiality is strategically inspired by the orator (who represents in his plot behaviour the initiational archetype of the prodigal son), since the situation of Peter denying and then repenting of his denials is close to him existentially, and he himself is involved in it with his entire existence.

Chekhov constructs his own artistic statements in an analogical way, although of course much more skillfully and with more complexity. One might say that Ivan Velikopolsky's narrative of the denial and spiritual torment of Saint Peter is a meta-textual model of Chekhov's own narrative discourse.

It is extremely instructive to correlate the two strategies under discussion in Chekhov's famous trilogy ("The Man in the Case," "Gooseberries" and "On Love"), in which the first two extra-textual narratives produce discord between the interlocutors ("they fell silent, as if angry at each other" after the first story; "they sat in their armchairs at opposite ends of the living room and were silent" at the end of the second), since they are self-referential in their communicative strategy, whereas the third narrative (that of Alekhin) unexpectedly brings them together. Both Burkin and Ivan Ivanych talk about their own interest ("…as if he was asking personally for himself"), and remain deaf to the reaction of their interlocutor ("Well that's from another opera...") so that their addressee is *bored*. Each time the one who has talked himself out goes peacefully to sleep, while the listener, who is dissatisfied with the story, is tormented by insomnia from the "excess of thoughts." Here are the endings of the first two texts:

> From his pipe, which was lying on the table, came a strong smell of burnt tobacco, and for a long time Burkin could not sleep and for the life of him couldn't understand where the terrible smell was coming from.

> The rain beat against the windows all night. ("Gooseberries")

Alekhin's story was a different matter. His characters turned out to be well known to the listeners (which had not been the case in the previous stories) and the theme ("They started to talk about love") and the problematic "of the secret of personal happiness" were of common interest. As a result of the deliberately arising co-referentiality of the interacting consciousnesses (which is stressed at the end of the text) the content of the story in these consciousnesses develops further, and their former discord is overcome. This is underlined in the finale not only by the change in the weather, but also by the different time of day (the two previous tales had been told at night). Here is the final paragraph of "On Love":

> While Alekhin was talking the rain stopped and the sun peeped out. Burkin and Ivan Ivanych went out onto the balcony, from which there was a magnificent view of the garden and the pond, which now gleamed in the sun like a mirror. They admired the view and at the same time were sorry that this man with his kind, clever eyes, who had told them his story with such sincerity, in actual fact was running around here on this vast estate like a squirrel in a cage, and did not occupy himself with science or something else that would make his life more pleasant; and they thought about what a sad face the young lady must have had when he said goodbye to her in the railway carriage and kissed her face and shoulders. They had both met her in the town, and Burkin was even an acquaintance of hers and had found her beautiful.

The question arises as to how Alekhin's story is closer to the authorial strategy of writing in the mature Chekhov than the stories of Burkin and Chimsha-Gimalaisky. I would answer with the words of Vladimir Lakshin; "in refusing to adopt the role of teacher," in the way "Chekhov did not impose any postulate," and "he turned the moral demands first and foremost on himself."[23] These words are entirely applicable to Alekhin the narrator who *individualizes* his own story as a *separate case*, while the first two narrators of the trilogy sharply criticize their characters, decisively generalize and in general to pontificate. Burkin is by profession a teacher, and Ivan Ivanych preaches passionately: "Don't put your guard down! ...don't stop doing good deeds! There is no happiness and cannot be, for the goal of life in my view lies in something more rational and greater" than personal happiness.

The inappropriateness of this sermonizing is subtly revealed by the fact that it is directed at Alekhin, who has worked all day and is just falling asleep from fatigue. However, the train of thought leading to a rejection of this denial of happiness is left for the reader to make independently. If, of course, he is ready for such a train of thought, for which Chekhov's text offers only cleverly implied hints. For example, the two hunters cum narrators comprise a traditionally comic "carnival couple,' which tends in an unobvious but inevitable way to discredit the seriousness of their statements. We recall that Chimsha-Gimalaisky is a "tall scrawny old man with a droopy moustache," while Burkin is a "short fat man, completely bald, with a black beard almost down to his waist." However, these portraits are placed far from each other in the text, and the comedy of their juxtaposition is revealed only after a very attentive reading.

The communicative strategy of Chekhov's discourse, which is directed at the referential competency of the reader, is based on the co-referentiality of the creative and receptive acts. As a result, it may be characterized as a strategy of narrative enthymeme.[24] The reader's instance is included in the communicative event of the work as a nonverbal, cognitive constituent of the text. It is precisely in this way, I would

---

[23] Lakshin, "O 'simvole very' Chekhova": 11.

[24] "Enthymeme" is a term of classical rhetoric, etymologically denoting "that which is in the mind," and used to indicate what is understood as an argument in communicative practice.

argue, that Chekhov lays the groundwork for the postclassical art of the twentieth century.

A precedent for this kind of artistic communication is to be found in Pushkin's *Tales of Belkin*,[25] however, in classical nineteenth-century literature it was not developed in a significant way. Thus Tolstoy, for example, for whom "Pushkin's stories are somehow bare,"[26] in the cunning labyrinths of his "intertwinings" dots all the "i"s himself, not trusting the reader.

The communicative strategy of artistic writing is realized through its poetics. From this point of view, Chekhov's poetics is an allusive one: it does not provoke the addressee into a self-referential reaction (as is the provocative strategy of many works of art of the avant-garde type), but inspires a process of ratiocination in the mental sphere of the addressee. The writer pulls the attentive reader into a captivating game of allusions—a game that is not self-directed, but creates the effect of "light at the end of the tunnel." The reader, like the protagonists in "The Lady with the Little Dog," imagines that "just a little more, and the solution will be found."

In this case the term "allusion" is not to be understood as an elementary reference, but as a rhetorical device of keeping silent: a poetic (extra-logical) enthymeme that engages the connotative potential of language to form, through a cascade of perspectives, an emerging meaning (unlike a ready-made emblematic meaning). We are thus talking not about allusions in a narrow terminological meaning of the word, although these too are used by Chekhov in great abundance, but of an "intertwining of motifs" (not only intertextual, but also intratextual ones) specific to Chekhov's prose, about Chekhov's principles of composition (division into chapters, correlation of framing and inserted texts) and other such features of his poetics.

Let us examine a simple example from "A Boring Story": a chain of bird motifs. It comes into play against the background of Nikolai Stepanovich's unsuccessful attempt to resort to the emblematics of the fable:

> I looked at Gnekker for a long time with contempt and then shot out apropos of nothing:

---

[25] Darvin and Tiupa, *Tsiklizatsii v tvorchestve Pushkina*, Ch. 6.
[26] Tolstoi, *O literature*: 18.

Sometimes the eagle lower than the chicken does descend,
But chickens never never the heights of clouds transcend.
And the most annoying thing was that the chicken Gnekker turned
out to be much more intelligent than the eagle-professor.

Nikolai Stepanovich's exclamation refers us back to his praise of
the *cock* as the bringer of good news, and also to the cock-like arousal of
the professor himself: "I would like to cry out in a loud voice." Even earlier in the text one can evidently encounter the pointless information that
because of his insomnia Nikolai Stepanovich somehow one night "mechanically read through a whole novel with the strange title *What the lark
sang about*." The fact that the title is considered to be "strange" suggests
that it probably is not linked in the character's mind with his own life.
But the reader of Chekhov's text, in whose consciousness the lark is a
"domesticated bird," easily makes the connection between the protagonist's lack of response to the theme of the swallow's song and his confession: "I feel that I no longer have a family and have no need to bring it
back." Finally, in the life of the narrator, a sort of "sparrow's night" takes
place during which he hears to his horror an unknown bird cry: "'Kivi-
kivi' rang out a call in the stillness of the night, 'and I don't know where
it was: in my breast or outside?'" So what kind of a "bird" is he, this famous scientist? An eagle, a cock, a chicken, a swallow, a sparrow, or
some mysterious bird from distant parts (the onomatopoeic sound "kivi"
suggests some exotic, non-Russian avian)? We recall the "eagles and par-
tridges" of Treplev's play in *The Seagull*. Instead of the emblematics of
the fable with its sole correct allegorical meaning we find here a questioning cascade of meanings of personal self-definition without any correct answer provided by the author. Such is the typically Chekhovian
"correctly formulated question" in one of its least noticeable, hardly detectable manifestations.

While not depriving the reader of his independence, Chekhov's
poetics provides him with a sort of cascade of probably meanings, a certain spectrum of permissible, but willful readings which one can characterize as a suggestive, "inspirational" strategy of text production (as opposed to an imperative one). In particular, the division of Chekhov's
works into chapters is a subtle instrument, a sort of "scalpel" of the creative will that appeals to a receptive will. A strong pause at the end of a
chapter creates a semantically intensified place in the text.

The first and second chapters of "The Archbishop" conclude with the identical remark from the eternally dissatisfied Sisoy: "Doan like it!" The third chapter concludes with a remark from his holiness in an opposite mood: "How good!" With this thought he passes away. However the final part of the narrative that follows his death is ambivalent in its emotional mood. This gives rise to a certain field of emotional tonality in which the will of the reader himself is obliged to adopt a position regarding the polar alternatives. Vladimir Kataev considers that on the whole the story is "unendingly sad,"[27] while Vittorio Strada declares that when one reads this "perhaps most perfect" of Chekhov's stories "there is absolutely no feeling of desperation and helplessness."[28] Anatoly Sobennikov, on the one hand, perceives here "the restoration of mankind,"[29] while Andrei Shcherbenok sees the negation of the "illusory substantiation of meaning," since "the artless finale of the story [...] removes the absolute necessity of faith."[30]

The final chapter, and the story as a whole, concludes with words to the effect that the most holy Peter

> has been completely forgotten. And only the aged mother of the deceased, who now lives with her son-in-law the deacon in a remote provincial town, when she used to come out towards evening to meet her cow and join the other women on the pasture, would start to talk about her children and her grandchildren and about how her son had been an archbishop, and then she would talk timidly, being afraid that they would not believe her...
>
> And it's true they did not all believe her.

Let us examine the peculiarities of the narrative in this far from "artless" final fragment of the text. Mariya Timofeyevna is described in an estranged way, as if she were some old woman whose maternity is especially treated, as if we were making her acquaintance for the first time. As if the reader had already forgotten about the characters in the

---

[27] Kataev, *Proza Chekhova: problemy interpretatsii*: 291.

[28] Strada: 61–62.

[29] Sobennikov, *Mezhdu "Est' Bog" i "Net Boga"*: 149.

[30] Shcherbenok, "Rasskaz Chekhova 'Arkhierei': poststrukturalistskaia perspektiva smysla": 119.

story. In this way the personal memory of the reader is placed in opposition to the general oblivion and included in the situation of the choice between belief and disbelief (for "they did not all believe her").

Another strangeness lies in the clear disorder of the verbal tenses: the old woman who "now lives" (the only case in the text of the use of the present tense by the narrator), "used to come out [...] and join"; "would start to talk." The disagreement of the present tense of the subordinate clause with the past tense of the main clause gives rise to a question: what is the state of affairs *now*? But if the reader asks himself this question, then he has to look for the answer in himself: do I personally believe that a life led by someone is not without trace; do I believe in the "substantiality" of its meaning?

All these inspirational subtleties of the narrative, which is always couched in a dialogic way, as opposed to the monologic form of "instruction" (such as, for example the speech of the narrator in the epilogue to *Crime and Punishment*), do not, of course, take away from the general elegiac tone of the finale. However, the author proposes not the melancholic extirpation of a lonely existence, but has a dramatically tense, open ending.

In "The Archbishop" there is a running opposition between two leitmotifs: the crushing walls of the monastery, its ceilings and shutters, on the one hand, and the light, initially of the moon, and then subsequently of the sun, on the other. The ambivalent image of the departure from life of the main protagonist takes place in the midst of this opposition: "He was already unable to utter a word, understood nothing, and it seemed to him that he was already a simple, ordinary man, walking quickly across a sunlit field, and he was now as free as a bird, and could go wherever he liked!" Such a disharmony between the external and internal sides of the process of dying is deeply inspiring. The reader retains the right (or rather, has imposed on him the responsibility) to bring to an independent aesthetic conclusion the artistic situation of an Eastertide death created by the author—an ambivalent situation run through to an equal degree with motifs both of melancholic loneliness and general celebration.

In the light of the strategy deployed by the author in his texts of an inspirational (co-referential, enthymematical) strategy of writing, the openness of his endings, which has long been noted by scholars, deserves special attention. Petr Bitsilli considered this structural peculiarity to be "the main feature" of Chekhov's works: "there is no 'denouement,' 'conclusion' or resolution of the existential drama."[31] The open endings in Chekhov are not relative or chance occurrences, they are probabilistic. Let us recall some of the most significant:

> ... and a feeling of youth, of health, of strength—he was only twenty-two—and an inexpressibly sweet expectation of happiness, an unknown, mysterious happiness came over him little by little, and life *seemed* to him delightful, marvellous, and full of exalted meaning. ("The Student")

> And it seemed that just a little more, and the solution would be found, and then a new and beautiful life would begin; and it was clear to both of them that it was a long long way to the end and that the most complicated and difficult part was only just beginning. ("The Lady with the Little Dog")

> She went upstairs to her room to pack, and the next morning she said goodbye to her family and, full of life and joyful, left the town, *as she thought*, forever. ("The Bride")

The words in italics, which give these endings the modality of a subjective "seemingness," are sometimes interpreted as a gentle author-ial debunking of the lighthearted optimism of the protagonists. This makes the author into the omniscient creator of his world, of the kind found in classical nineteenth-century literature. Yet the creative instance of Chekhov's artistic discourse is differently positioned: it merely eluci-dates a certain spectrum of probabilities for the subsequent development of events. Of course, each of these characters can subsequently be over-come by deep disillusionment and existential failure. But within the lim-its of the text both Gurov and Nadia have already experienced an unex-pected, unthinkably successful meeting and a transfiguration that has changed the course of their entire life. In the life of Ivan Velikopolsky the conversation around the fire is a micro-event, but nevertheless of univer-sal dimensions ("nineteen centuries"). And we have no basis for doubt-ing that the existential changes that have occurred to them are irreversi-

---

[31] Bitsilli, "Tvorchestvo Chekhova: Opyt stilisticheskogo analiza": 205.

ble.[32]

All these "seemingnesses" of open endings that so frequently occur in Chekhov correspond to the "principle of correlation of indeterminatenesses" formulated by the great physicist Werner Heisenberg: the probabilities of the subsequent changes in a situation are not arbitrary (although not definite); they are mutually complementary. Speaking about the "principle of indeterminateness" in Chekhov, Petr Dolzhnikov conceives of it as a referential competence of the text ("the world of Chekhov's works is a world of indeterminateness"), which leads him to assert "Chekhov's skepticism."[33] This is viewing things from the position of classical nineteenth-century poetics. However, if we take into account the subsequent changes in the sphere of literature, then Chekhov's "indeterminatenesses" appear characteristic of the receptive competence of his discourse: the role of the reader here is analogous to the role of the observer in quantum physics. In other words, Chekhov's texts resemble Heisenberg's nature, which, for all its objectivity "appears in the way it does thanks to our way of asking questions."[34]

In simple terms, as Stepanov has shown, the optimistically minded reader is able to endow Chekhov's texts with a positive concluding meaning, and the pessimist with a negative one. This gives rise to the characteristic effect of Chekhov's writing, namely the sense that the author "is carrying on a heart to heart conversation alone with every reader."[35] This explains the highly significant disagreements that occur at times regarding the interpretation of the intended emotional tonality of one and the same text by highly qualified Chekhov specialists. The most characteristic cause is the more than a century-old division into two

---

[32] Wolf Schmid problematizes the nature of the event in Chekhov's prose, writing, for example, about the story "The Student," "an empty bottle, this initial motif that is accentuated through sound repetition, points to a non-event" and "becomes a symbol of apparent enlightenment" (Shmid, *Proza kak poeziia*: 294. And yet, if in the initial sentences of this text the phoneme "u" does indeed dominate, suggesting the depressed state of mind of the protagonist, then in the concluding sentences the phoneme "a" is dominant. The anagrammatical key to this repetition, which signals the change that has taken place, is the word *zaria* (dawn).

[33] Dolzhenkov, *Chekhov i pozitivizm*: 44, 21.

[34] Geizenberg, *Fizika i filosofiia*: 36.

[35] Strada: 49.

camps of the interpreters of the story "Darling." One group reads the story as sentimental in the style of Tolstoy, while the other sees it as an example of Chekhov's sarcasm.[36]

This does not at all mean that in Chekhov's works "there is no room for a fixed meaning,"[37] or that one can read Chekhov as one sees fit. Boris Akunin or Vladimir Sorokin with their variations on themes from Chekhov are by no means true readers of Chekhov: rather they are characters (inasmuch as their absurdist texts are self-referential). For a Text is still far from being Nature. Because of the creative intention of the author producing the text, it has a virtual meaning. In Chekhov this is a certain potential for meaning: a quite definite (and consequently determinable through investigation) correlation of "mutually complementary indeterminatenesses,"[38] which, in Vittorio Strada's words, create "the feeling of a space beyond the plot, a gap behind which the incompleteness of the world might be divined."[39]

Of course, we are not speaking of any possible perspectives of changes "beyond the plot" in the situation that reigns at the end, but only about the scenarios of existential behaviour attributable to the "Chekhovian character." For this reason the outcome of the artistic structures of the mature Chekhov is always "at the same time clear and ambiguous: ambiguous because the pole of the original is positive as regards the unoriginal one (cf. Gurov's "two lives" in "The Lady with the Little Dog"—V.T.), the ethical and intellectual content of both is problematic, and neither protagonists nor narrator is able to solve the problem."[40] The responsibility for its solution is laid at the feet of the reader,

---

[36] Tiupa, *Khudozhestvennost' chekhovskogo rasskaza*, Ch. 3.

[37] Stepanov, *Problemy…*: 358.

[38] The very concept of "indeterminateness" is borrowed not so much from recent physics as from Chekhov himself. In his youthful play [*Fatherlessness*] the writer uses the character Glagol'ev as a mouthpiece to discuss the "one who expresses contemporary indeterminateness" as "the state of our society" and "the Russian writer of belles-lettres" who "feels this indeterminateness," and who "does not know where to settle" (XI, 16). The mature Chekhov did not so much "not know," he evidently did not consider it possible for him to impose his own definiteness on life, which he saw as the self-defining existential choice of each of his characters.

[39] Strada: 58.

[40] Ibid.: 62.

who actually shapes the mental space of life beyond the text through his moral and aesthetic preferences.

The nature of Chekhov's indeterminateness is elucidated in a letter to Pleshcheyev of April 9, 1889. The writer, while demonstrating in his works the extent to which "life diverges from the norm," at the same time admits the indeterminateness of this norm: "The norm is unknown to me, as it is known to none of us" (P 3: 186). Judging by the further context of this famous letter, the only reliable landmark in Chekhov's ontologically indeterminate world is a responsible freedom ("the framework of freedom") of every individual as he determines himself. However, the uniqueness of Chekhov's communicative strategy lies not so much in the mutual freedom of the partners in the communication (which causes so many of his characters not to complete their communicative events), as in the mutual responsibility of this freedom.

Despite the long-standing assertion of Alexander Chudakov, in Chekhov's works nothing is the result of chance. He artfully shapes all the necessary prerequisites for a classical aesthetic completion of the whole. But the author leaves the conclusive act of meaningful completion (the answer to the "correctly asked question") to the reader, calling upon his communicative, aesthetic and moral responsibility. In its most general features this is reminiscent of Socrates' meiotic, for Chekhov's overarching task is to "activate the reader's thought processes, instill in him intellectual urgency about the need to decide the question of life."[41] Indeed, it is not simply the reader who is reading Chekhov's story, but the story itself that is "reading" its reader: the text works as a test.

In conclusion we can say that in the context of nineteenth-century literature fundamentally new relations between the meta-subjective, virtual instances of Author and Reader are established in Chekhov's works. If, as Bakhtin has shown, Dostoevsky's polyphonic novel brought to literature a dialogic relationship between the authorial consciousness and the consciousness of the protagonist, then Chekhov's innovational communicative strategy brought in turn a dialogic openness to the correlation of the authorial and readerly consciousnesses.

Translated from the Russian by J. Douglas Clayton.

---

[41] Linkov, *Khudozhestvennyi mir prozy A.P. Chekhova*: 34.

WORKS CITED

Bakhtin, Mikhail. "Iz arkhivnykh zapisei k rabote *Problema rechevykh zhanrov*," *Sobranie sochinenii*, vol. 5. M.: Russkie slovari, 1996.

Bitsilli, Petr. "Tvorchestvo Chekhova: Opyt stilisticheskogo analiza," *Tragediia russkoi kul'tury*. M.: Nasledie, 2000.

Darvin, Mikhail and Tiupa, Valery. *Tsiklizatsii v tvorchestve Pushkina*. Novosibirsk: Nauka, 2001.

Dolzhenkov, Petr. *Chekhov i pozitivizm*. M.: Skorpion, 2003.

Geizenberg, Werner. *Fizika i filosofiia*. M.: Nauka, 1963.

Iezuitova, Luidmila. "Komediia A.P. Chekhova 'Chaika' kak tip novoi dramy." *Analiz dramaticheskogo proizvedeniia*. L.: Izd-vo Leningradskogo universiteta, 1988.

Jędrzejkiewicz, Anna. *Opowiadania Antoniego Czechowa: studia nad porozumiewaniem się ludzi*. Studia Rossico IX. Warszawa: Wydawn. Uniwersytetu Warszawskiego, 2000.

Kapustin, Nikolai. *Chuzhoe slovo v proze A.P. Chekhova: zhanrovye transformatsii*. Ivanovo: Ivanovskii gosudarstvenii universitet, 2003.

Kataev, Vladimir. *Proza Chekhova: problemy interpretatsii*. M.: Izd-vo Moskovskogo universiteta, 1979.

————. "Spor o Chekhove: konets ili nachalo?" *Chekhoviana: Melikhovskie trudy i dni*. M.: Nauka, 1995.

Lakshin, Vladimir. "O 'simvole very' Chekhova." *Chekhoviana*. M.: Nauka, 1990: 7-19.

Linkov, Vladimir. *Khudozhestvennyi mir prozy A.P. Chekhova*. M.: Izd-vo MGU, 1982.

Papernyi, Zinovii. *"Vopreki vsem pravilam...": P'esy i vodevili Chekhova*. M.: Iskusstvo, 1982.

Pervukhina, Natalia. *Anton Chekhov: The Sense and Nonsense*. New York: Legas Publishers, 1993.

Sergeenko, Petr. *Tolstoi i ego sovremenniki*. M.: V.M. Sablin, 1911.

Shcheglov, Iurii. "Molodoi chelovek v driakhlejushchem mire (Chekhov: "Ionych")." In: A.K.Zholkovskii, Iu.K. Shcheglov, *Mir avtora i struktura teksta*. Tenafly: Ermitazh, 1986: 21-52.

Shcherbenok, Andrei. "Rasskaz Chekhova 'Arkhierei': poststrukturalistskaia perspektiva smysla," *Molodye issledovateli Chekhova*, III. M.: Chekhovskaia komissiia Soveta po istorii mirovoi kul'tury Rossiiskoi Akademii nauk: Filologicheskii fakul'tet Moskovskogo gos. universiteta im. M.V. Lomonosova, 1998: 113-119.

Shmid (Schmid), Vol'f. *Proza kak poeziia*. SPb.: Ina-Press, 1998.

Skaftymov, Aleksandr. *Nravstvennye iskaniia russkikh pisatelei*. M.: Khudozhestvennaia literatura, 1972.

Sobennikov, Anatolii. "Mezhdu 'Est' Bog' i 'Net Boga'..." (O religiozno-filosofskikh traditsiiakh v tvorchestve A.P. Chekhova). Irkutsk: Izd-vo Irkutskogo universiteta, 1997.

Stepanov, Andrei. "Kommunikatsiia i informatsiia u Chekhova," Diskurs, No. 10 M.: RGGU, 2002: 71-78.

————. Problemy kommunikatsii u Chekhova. M.: Iazyki slavianskoi kul'tury, 1998.

Strada, Vittorio. "Literatura kontsa XIX veka (1890-1900)," Istoriia russkoi literatury. XX stoletie. Serebrianyi vek. M.: Progress. litera, 1995: 11-48.

Tiupa, Valery. Khudozhestvennost' chekhovskogo rasskaza. M.: Vysshaia shkola, 1989.

————. "Osnovaniia sravnitel'noi ritoriki," Kritika i semiotika, No. 7 Novosibirsk: Izd-vo IDMI, 2004: 66-87.

————. "Novaia ritorika kak uchenie o kommunikativnom sobytii," Diskurs, No. 7 M.: RGGU, 1998: 64-67.

Tolstoi, Lev. O literature. M.: Khudozh. literatura, 1955.

If You Listened to Me, I Would Not Talk to You: On a Structural Device In Chekhov's Drama

VLADIMIR ZVINIATSKOVSKY
Ukrainian-American Humanitarian Institute, Kiev

> An effective historical consciousness is first and foremost
> a consciousness of the hermeneutic situation.
> —Gadamer

> Now, my dear buddy, there are no roads—people have arrived.
> —Andrei Platonov, *Chevengur*

More than a hundred years ago it was Chekhov who brought literature and theatre to the crossroads of poetics, hermeneutics and communication theory. And it was precisely a hundred years ago that Leo Tolstoy summed up the literary activity of his younger colleague by declaring: "...thanks to his sincerity, he gave the world new, completely new in my opinion, forms of writing..."[1]

While Chekhov was alive Tolstoy had a high opinion of his prose, but thought less of his plays. It is interesting that in the case of the passage just quoted he did not make any reservation, evidently because he included Chekhov's drama in the "new forms of writing" he had created. Doubtless this was because in the case of drama this "new" element made itself felt more vividly and sharply, becoming the manifesto for a certain state of culture in the coming twentieth century, a state that revealed itself among other ways as a certain crisis of the entire system of communication. In order to come to mutual understanding people now needed more and more to identify themselves with something beyond the boundaries of dialogue; yet, without such an at least partial sharing of points of identity, dialogue is impossible even within one national culture.

---

[1] Gromova, *Chekhov i Lev Tolstoi*: 287.

At the same time, art more and more took upon itself the obligations of that identifier located "beyond the boundaries." Hans-Georg Gadamer put it well:

> For a social culture that has fallen away from its religious traditions expects more from art than is in accordance with aesthetic consciousness which takes the "standpoint of art." The romantic support for a new mythology [...] gives the artist and his task in the world the consciousness of a new consecration. He is something like a "secular saviour" [...] This claim has since determined the tragedy of the artist in the world, for any fulfillment of it is only a particular one, and that means in fact its refutation. The experimental search for new symbols or a new myth which will unite everyone may certainly create a public and create a community, but since every artist finds his own community, the particularity of this community-creating merely testifies to the disintegration that is taking place.[2]

In Russia at the beginning of the twentieth century certain artists and theoreticians of art close to Chekhov discussed this directly, for example Vladimir Kign-Dedlov in his book about the Vladimir Cathedral in Kiev. There he wrote about how, in the author's words, "Victor Vasnetsov created the first national shrine in new Russia."[3] Chekhov was invited to Kiev when the work on the cathedral was at its height: "I have shown you," he wrote in a letter of 27 October 1894, "the Vladimir Cathedral with its paintings by Vasnetsov, which I value highly, love very much, and promote as much as I can."[4] In doing so Dedlov viewed Vasnetsov's paintings in the cathedral not in a religious context, but in that of the national discourse, declaring openly that "religion and reality diverge even more than the moral ideal and real life."[5]

Of course, this declaration by Dedlov is entirely on his conscience, and not on that of Vasnetsov. The critic's ability to delight in the artist for reasons quite different from those for which the artist wanted to delight the public were well-known to Chekhov, who, after one journal pub-

---

[2] Gadamer, *Truth and Method*: 79.
[3] Kign-Dedlov, *Kievskii Vladimirskii...*: 5.
[4] Quoted in Bukchin, *Dorogoi Anton Pavlovich...*: 115.
[5] Kign-Dedlov: 42.

lished an article by Dedlov about him, wrote to the editor: "[...] Dedlov's article [...] attributes to me virtues I never had and never will have" (P 5: 56). I might remark in passing that there is a cliché in Chekhov studies about his "modesty" that we are always ready to use to explain remarks of this kind by Chekhov while ignoring their real content. In the case in question it evidently all has to do with the fact that the critic "does not hear" what precisely the writer is "saying."

In the Russia of the time there was a critic and journalist who specialized in analyzing such strident public declarations formulated according to the principle "if you listened to me, I would not talk to you." The critic and journalist in question was Vasily Rozanov whom, incidentally, Chekhov always read with great pleasure. And of course Rozanov could not let pass Dedlov's cry from the soul about "the first national shrine in New Russia." In a review of Dedlov's book he wrote: "Russian man would die of grief and melancholy if one tried to calm him by saying that in his faith he is national and an expression of the national type, and not that in precisely that faith he is close to God. The difference is huge, and so are the problems!" [6]

Chekhov was doubtless acquainted with Rozanov's review and most certainly was in agreement, all the more, since he had already given his answer to one of those "huge problems" that very same year (1894), when he did not respond to Dedlov's invitation and did not go and see the murals in the Kiev cathedral, but instead wrote the story "The Student." One conclusion to be drawn from that story is that Russians believe in Christ not because they are Russian, but rather because they still find a common language and retain a common culture thanks to their belief.

Let us now pursue further the quotation from Tolstoy's pronouncement on the day after Chekhov's death: "[...] the virtue of his work lies in the fact that it is understandable and akin to not only every Russian, but every human being."[7] We recall that this was spoken by an artist who was to the highest degree endowed with the ability to "bring together a following": the neologism tolstovtsy (Tolstoyans) signified not simply a collective "thankful reader," but a new social—and, in essence, religious—union. Yet he made this statement about a writer who had

---

[6]Rozanov, Sredi khudozhnikov: 47
[7]Gromova: 287.

consciously refused to "bring together a following." One is reminded of Belinsky's words about Schiller and Goethe, who valued in each other precisely what each of them was lacking in himself.

Hence Tolstoy already understood well that the "disintegration" of society into different groupings had to be fought not only through the creation of the "best grouping," but through the depiction of the disintegration itself. Chekhov, he declared, "took from life what he saw, independently of the content of what he saw. [...] He was sincere, and this is a great virtue; he wrote about what he saw and how he saw it." [8]

What was totally new about Chekhov's contribution to dramatic form? Abandoning all the structural devices of preceding dramatists (he admitted that his plays were written "despite all the rules"), he turned the plot *line* into a sort of closed *circle*, well known to philosophers as "Schleiermacher's hermeneutic circle." The plot line is a conscious construction, a conscious selection. Chekhov scholars have talked about "the principle of chance" [sluchainostnost] in Chekhov; I would argue that it is better to talk about *wholeness* [tselostnost], in the sense in which Schleiermacher a year before Pushkin was born was already talking about "the endless nature of the whole, where everything is one, and in this general unity man acts."

Let us now examine what Tolstoy said in the year of Chekhov's death: "He recreated to finest detail whatever was preoccupying him at the moment of creation." [9] There are only two things that one can speak about in this way: photography (which can also be creative, but guarantees only authenticity, not wholeness) and responsible artistic creation— responsible in the sense meant by the early Bakhtin: "A whole is called mechanical if the separate elements are joined in space and time only by an external link, and are not imbued with internal unity of meaning. The parts of such a whole may be adjacent and contiguous, but within they are foreign to each other. [...] What guarantees the internal connectedness of the elements of a personality? Only unity of responsibility." [10]

It is particularly interesting to apply this notion of responsibility to contemporary drama—both in the narrow and in the broad sense of the term. In fact its application ought to signify renouncing the "axiom of

---

[8]Ibid.
[9]Ibid.
[10]Bakhtin, *Estetika...*: 7.

audibility," which pre-Chekhovian drama adopted by default. In the conditions of the crisis of the entire system of communication, when no one is responsible for his words, the entity of the drama (which is equivalent to the entity of its author) ought to consist not in the perfection of the plot line, which given the initial conditions does not and cannot exist, but precisely in the responsibility for all the "non-listening" characters, and in the voluntary assumption by not only the author, but also the reader, the audience and the critic of the obligation to accompany each of the characters through the entire closed (hermeneutic) circle of his consciousness. (The particular case of a character who is himself an artist will be examined later.)

Rare is the Chekhovian character who honestly admits (like Ferapont in *The Three Sisters*): "I'm hard of hearing..." In fact they are all (as we are!) "hard of hearing." And rare is the Chekhovian character who would answer honestly (as Andrei does to Ferapont): "If you could hear me properly, I might not have talked to you. I need to speak to someone, but my wife doesn't understand, and for some reason I'm afraid of my sisters..." (S 13: 141). In fact the desire to "speak to someone" *who is a stranger* is a common characteristic of them—and of us all. There are two historical reasons for this.

On the one hand, the mental apparatus of European and in general of western culture was created by the ancient Greeks, who, as we know, were incapable of either thinking or even reading *"to themselves"*—only *aloud*. Thus, the cultural and linguistic apparatus "of thinking" we have at our disposal works to its fullest only in dialogue.

On the other hand, it is best to chat and argue with an interlocutor who does not prevent us from thinking. The ideal interlocutor, the ideal "alien discourse" is the quotation, i.e., something that is at the same time both "verbal" and "wordless" (in the sense of "unreplying"). It is also not bad to have the sort of interlocutor that manifests a sincere and even burning curiosity (like Ferapont) about the three interrelated problems under discussion (these problems are the same for all of us as they are for Andrei Prozorov, namely: I myself, my family, my country). But at the same time it is desirable to talk to someone with an evident defect of hearing, whether physical or otherwise: someone who is hard of hearing like Ferapont, or who is a foreigner who is learning my language and my culture (no doubt this is why it is so pleasant to address an audience of foreigners, where everything is expressed so sincerely).

The last decades of the twentieth century passed under the slogan "dialogue of cultures." This meant that the normal human impulse to talk to someone *foreign* and to find total self-identification in this dialogue with a stranger acquired, because of some global ideological preferences, the status practically of a panacea. Nevertheless, as is clearly shown in Chekhov's stories and plays, what is interesting in the dialogue with a foreigner is in fact *oneself* and not the stranger; the mere presence of some *furrinner* creates that backdrop against which, for example, the Russianness of a Russian is more clearly perceived. For this to happen, one requires, in addition to the stranger, the presence of at least one countryman, whom one can call upon for support and who functions as the true addressee in this pseudo-dialogue of cultures. Of course, the unintelligibility of the foreigner in this dialogue comes not from his not having anything to say, but simply because he does not have by his side another foreigner of the same ilk. Sharlotta in *The Cherry Orchard* remarks: "I want so much to talk, but there's no one to talk to… I have no one" (S 13: 215).

This heroine from Chekhov's last play has frequently been linked with his early story "A Daughter of Albion"; I mention this comic story written by Chekhov when he was twenty-three for the journal *Oskolki* only to draw attention to the fact that he early found the form and the formula for the pseudo-dialogue with a foreigner in the company of a fellow countryman who is in fact the true target of the dialogue:

> The Englishwoman, raising and lowering her eyebrows energetically, quickly pronounced a lengthy sentence in English. The landowners snorted.
> "First time in my life I hear her voice… Some voice, eh? She doesn't understand. Well, what am I to do with her? "
> "To hell with her! Let's go and drink vodka!" (S 2: 197)

The reply "To hell with her" (literally: "Spit!") in the overall context of the story refers to the fishing, but the juxtaposition of a concrete question with a general answer creates an unintentional comic effect: it turns out that Ottsov is suggesting that Griabov "spit" on the Englishwoman, justifying his metaphorical spit on a hermeneutical basis: "No one asked her not to understand! That'll teach those foreigners!" It is precisely after these words that "Griabov took off his boots and his trousers, threw off his underwear, and found himself in Adam's costume" (S 2: 198). The structural principle of dialogue in Chekhov's mature work is here essentially already discovered, but it still allows an unequivocal interpretation, the key word that unlocks the entire interpretation being given repeatedly in the text, namely the cliché "contempt" (S 2: 196, 197, 198) — the mutual contempt of foreigners for each other.

Sixteen years later, in his maturity, Chekhov in the story "A New Dacha" subjects this same cliché-word to linguistic estrangement. The mutual lack of understanding between masters and peasants in the story is about to be transmuted into the usual contempt for foreigners, which is essentially what these "two cultures in one" are. "It will probably end in us feeling contempt for you," says the master to the peasants. But the word *prezrenie* (contempt) turns out to be unknown to the peasants, who do, however, know the word *prizrenie* (care of the aged). "'We'll look after you...' he promised in front of everybody. 'In my old age,'" (S 10: 125) boasts one peasant to another, ingenuously mispronouncing the words of the "good master." Interestingly, this linguistic mix-up makes the story "esoteric," untranslatable not only into foreign languages, but even into the language of the stage: in order to understand the difference between the words, which are pronounced the same, one has to see them written.

In other stories written at approximately the same time, the "esoteric" details, on the contrary, beg to be interpreted onstage. For example, in the story "The Man in the Case" there occurs what is essentially a declaration of love between Belikov and Varenka Kovalenko (who is Ukrainian, i.e., to some extent a foreigner), but the indication that it has taken place is encoded in the following way: "She sang with feeling the song *"Viiut vitry* [Winds are blowing—Ukr.] [...] and enchanted us all— even Belikov" (S 10: 46). For Chekhov's contemporaries the "entrance aria" of Natalka Poltavka (from the new opera of that name by Nikolai Lysenko based on the classical text by Ivan Kotliarevsky) could be heard literally everywhere; it was the hit song of the time. But a few years only had to go by, and the triumphal all-Russian tours by the "Little Russian troupe" of Mark Kropyvnytsky and the brilliant Maria Zankovetska in the role of Natalka would pass into the realm of theatrical legend, and as a result Chekhov's story can only be completely apprehended by someone steeped in Ukrainian culture, for only he would remember from his childhood *"Viiut vitry"* —this lament of the lonely soul. And so that the reader should be in no doubt as to whom this lament was meant for, the author of the story mentions it yet again, telling how Belikov usually spent the time with Varenka: "He would be silent, and Varenka would sing *'Viiut vitry'* to him [...]" (S 10: 47). Here is an example of what she would sing:

> Who can I turn to, and who will caress me,
> Now that the one who loves me is no more...

After that it is easy to see the cause of the truly revolutionary action that Belikov undertakes in response to Varenka's first (public!) performance of her favourite aria:

> He sat down next to her and said, smiling sweetly:
> "The Little Russian language reminds one of ancient Greek in its tenderness and pleasant melodiousness." (S 10: 46)

One might add that the degree to which this declaration was revolution-ary was understandable, again, only to Chekhov's contemporaries. We read only that in the circular "something was forbidden," but for Belikov "this was clear and definite: it was forbidden—and *basta* (S 10: 43). But the "Little Russian language" that Belikov praised was "clearly and defi-nitely" forbidden by the (so-called Valuev) circular. And this first and last time in his life that Belikov infringed the circular constitutes his dec-laration of love to Varenka; in answer to her appeal, and perhaps also in declaration.

Thus we see in Chekhov's prose a tendency that he brought to its logical conclusion in the plays: the less words are pronounced, the more is said in reality. The limit is reached in the transformation of the aria into a musical accompaniment in the scene in the third act of *The Three Sisters* where Vershinin and Masha declare their love for each other:

> Vershinin. [...] *(sings.)*To love all ages must surrender, [tram-tam-tam] ... its impulses are beneficial... *(Laughs.)*
> Masha. Tram-tam-tam...
> Vershinin. Tram-tam-tam...
> Masha. Tra-ra-ra?
> Vershinin. Tra-ta-ta. *(Laughs.)* (S 13: 163–164)

I have never heard in any performance of this scene a *joint* performance by Vershinin and Masha (with Masha standing in for the orchestra) of this aria by Gremin from Chaikovsky's *Eugene Onegin*. How many ways are these *"tram-tam-tam"* and *"tra-ra-ra"* played, and how much has been written about them by Chekhov scholars! Astonishingly, even Natalia Ivanova in a special study of the role of Gremin's aria in the dramatic plot declares firmly that when Vershinin sings the aria, Masha "responds with neither a musical phrase, nor simply with music." And this despite the fact that all the men in the play are ecstatic about her musical talent and her "splendid" piano playing! "She simply answers: *'Tram-tam-tam...'"*[11]

It seems to me that this is all actually very simple: the battery commander lieutenant colonel Vershinin starts to sing the famous aria of a "grey-haired military man" who has also finally "surrendered to love" (none of this, of course, is in Pushkin's text: it had all been thought up by the librettist M.I. Chaikovsky—with whom Chekhov was well acquainted). And Masha very precisely *joins in* when Vershinin sings, or rather *hums a voice accompaniment* (just as she has evidently already before—perhaps more than once—accompanied him "off stage" on the piano).

Andrey's conversation with the deaf Ferapont in the second act and the opera-singing by Vershinin and Masha in the third represent the two poles of a magnet: around the first are grouped the numerous "dialogues of the deaf," while the second attracts the few moments of mutual understanding. If Ferapont listened to Andrey, Solyony to Tuzenbakh, Kuligin to Vershinin, and Natasha had listened to herself, then, of course, they would not talk at all... But do Vershinin and Natasha speak in their only happy scene? No, they sing. Do they listen to each other? Without a doubt.

With what, then, do we have to do here: total mistrust of words? And, if this is the case, then is this a peculiarity of Chekhov alone? Let us consider Dostoevsky—the apparently most verbose and "ideological" writer in the second half of the nineteenth century. In essence the structure of all his novels works in the following way: one of the characters listens to two or more monologues and then immediately starts to *interpret them*, comparing and generalizing; then breaks out in his own mono-

---

[11] Ivanova, "Ob odnom...": 207.

logue, which either leads to action or accompanies it. Thus, for example, if we reduce the plot structure of *Crime and Punishment* to its basic structure, we can say that the action in the beginning of the novel is the *crime*, and the resulting action is the *punishment*—or rather, the self-inflicted punishment of the main character. But in the very first key monologue, when Raskolnikov talks about his sister's decision to marry Luzhin, he equates Sonya Marmeladova's sacrificing herself by working as a prostitute and Dunya's proposed self-sacrificial marriage, *about which he has heard from their mother*:

> So what's going on? I suppose we've decided to share the fate of Sonechka! Sonechka, Sonechka Marmeladova, eternal Sonechka, as long as the world is still standing! But what about the sacrifice— have you both realized exactly what the sacrifice means?... "There can be no talk of love between them," writes Mama. And suppose if, apart from love, there can be no respect either...[12]

Here the word "both" takes on a strange double meaning: in its immediate context it is addressed to Dunya and their mother, but in a more extended context on the level of ideas, it is addressed to Dunya and Sonya. What is even stranger, Raskolnikov basically does not know his grownup sister, while for the moment he is not at all acquainted with Sonya and can judge the ideas of them both *only from the words of others*. To be sure, these others are close to them (the mother of the one and the father of the other), but they, as often happens, perhaps find it more difficult to understand their own children than anybody.

Where then do we find here the ideas coexisting (as some scholars have asserted) on an equal footing in the dialogue? What we have here is not a dialogue of ideas, but a sort of broken telephone! Raskolnikov is the unfortunate victim of this distortion of information for, as often happens with young people, from every communication he immediately makes a generalization, and from every generalization he makes a practical action has to follow.

In Chekhov's plays we also find people the same age as Raskolnikov who would seek through practical action to radically change not only their personal, but also the social situation, putting an end to

---

[12]Dostoevskii, *Sobranie sochinenii*: 5, 49.

"words, words, words" and setting right the time that is "out of joint."

Tatiana Shakh-Azizova finds it "understandable" that when, at the beginning of the twentieth century, Chekhov's plays started to appear on the English stage, there was an "attraction of English 'Hamlets' to the characters in Chekhov's plays"; that is to say, "the main Shakespearean actors in England turned into the main Chekovian actors."[13] However, this fact seems to me to be not quite comprehensible, and requiring an explanation precisely in the context of the situation of the "communicative crisis" at the beginning of the twentieth century.

On the links between Chekhov's plays and *Hamlet* (especially in *The Seagull*) a great deal has been written. But I would like to stress that not only is the principle of having it out with a loved one (in this case one's mother) by putting on a play a Shakespearean device, there is also the Shakespearean principle of solving the "crisis in communication" at the beginning of the seventeenth century. This begs the question: why is Hamlet's death glorious, and Treplev's inglorious? I would like to draw attention to the fact that Treplev condemned himself to death for his careless attitude towards the word, his imprecise use of words, and his unforgivable, for a writer, use of hackneyed words (S 13: 55). Hamlet, on the other hand, had a different attitude towards words, and an indication of this (as far as I know, until now undetected) attitude can also be found in *The Seagull*:

> Treplev. [...] *(Seeing Trigorin walking and reading a little book.)* There goes a true talent; he goes like Hamlet, and he too has a book. *(Teasingly.)* "Words, words, words..." (S 13: 27–28)

One wonders, with what book does Trigorin appear? What book is he reading? The answer becomes clear from the stage direction before Trigorin's following line: *"Writing in the little book."* That is to say: a moment before he was reading his own notebook, and now he is entering in it some observations that have just come into his head.

Thus Treplev's comparison of Trigorin writing in a notebook with Hamlet reading a book does not quite jibe. Let us try to disentangle this.

---

[13] Shakh-Azizova, "...vsiakomu cheloveku voobshche..." *Chekhov i Lev Tolstoi*: 290–291.

Indeed, in scene two of act two Hamlet appears, as it says in the stage direction, "reading"—evidently simply reading some book. But then in scene five of act one Horatio and Marcellus take Hamlet unawares *noting something in his notebook*. Chekhov's biographers have done us a disservice by seeing everywhere in his works the depiction of his own habits. Thus, we have become accustomed to assume that Trigorin's notebook is an autobiographical trait, and that behind it lies a reminiscence of Hamlet's notebook; but in fact it is an important, but deeply hidden, parallel for the understanding of the direct quotations that are directly revealed. Yes, the quotation "words, words, words" is present. But Hamlet, like Trigorin, *writes down* the words, and moreover, interestingly, it is the *words of the ghost* that he writes. Why? Because he is trying to see behind each word the true essence of the concept and to have a responsible attitude towards the use of words—thanks to which he nevertheless establishes the truth (although he began with ghostly words, i.e., literally with the words of a ghost), restores justice and dies like a warrior.

Treplev, on the other hand, before settling his score with life, utters commonplace words that he himself does not understand; he dies like a bourgeois from Kiev, which is what his passport says he is, fussing that no one should meet Nina in the garden, because "that might upset Mama" (S 13: 59)—as if her son's suicide would not upset her! The last word we hear about Treplev is the same as the last about Hamlet— "silence." But in Shakespeare it is the indeterminate silence of nonexistence *after* a definite and responsible word and gesture in existence. In the case of Treplev, it is silence *instead of* an inconsequential and now no longer inconsequential word: Treplev, as it says in the stage direction, "*silently* tears up all his manuscripts and throws them under the table" (S 13: 59). What (recalling the words of Mikhail Bakhtin) "guarantees the internal linkage of the elements of the personality? Only unity of responsibility. For what I have lived through and understood in art I must answer with my life…"[14] And also for what one has not understood.

It only remains to add that the generation of "Russian lads" to which Bakhtin himself belonged, was in fact the first generation raised totally on Chekhov. That same thought that art should not fear life, but rather answer for it, is the very one to which Nina Zarechnaya comes in the finale of *The Seagull*:

---

[14]Bakhtin, *Estetika…*: 7.

I now know and understand, Kostya, that in our work—whether we are acting on stage or writing—the main thing is not fame or glamour, [...] but the ability to suffer. Know how to bear one's cross and believe. I believe and it is not so painful for me, and when I think about my vocation, I don't fear life. (S 13: 59)

Does Kostya hear her? This time I believe he does. But sometimes one hears too late.

Translated from the Russian by J. Douglas Clayton.

WORKS CITED

Bakhtin, Mikhail. *Estetika slovesnogo tvorchestva.* M.: Iskusstvo, 1986.

Bukchin, Semen. *Dorogoi Anton Pavlovich... Ocherki o korrespondentakh A.P. Chekhova.* Minsk: Nauka i technika, 1973.

Chudakov, Aleksandr. *Poetika Chekhova.* M.: Nauka, 1971.

Dostoevskii, Fedor. *Sobranie sochinenii v desiati tomakh.* M.: Goslitizdat, 1957. 5: 49.

Gromova, Lidija. *Chekhov i Lev Tolstoi.* M.: Nauka, 1980.

Gadamer, Hans-Georg. *Truth and Method.* New York: The Seabury Press, 1975.

Ivanova, Natalia. "Ob odnom 'muzykal'nom momente' v p'ese Chekhova 'Tri sestry." *Chekhoviana: "Tri sestry—100 let.* M.: Nauka, 2002: 203–209.

Kign-Dedlov, Vladimir. *Kievskii Vladimirskii sobor i ego khudozhestvennye tvortsy.* M.: Grossman i Knebel', 1901.

Rozanov,Vasilii. *Sredi khudozhnikov.* SPb., 1914.

Shakh-Azizova, Tatiana. "...vsiakomu cheloveku voobshche..." *Chekhov i Lev Tolstoi.* M.: Nauka, 1980.

.

"Words, Words, Words": On the "Emptiness" of Speech and the Fullness of Songs

J. DOUGLAS CLAYTON
University of Ottawa

Chekhov has been associated with many artistic movements and tendencies: realism, impressionism, naturalism and even, as regards his theatre, the absurd. However, all of these labels represent only one aspect of his work, which, in its multi-facetedness, has few parallels in his time. Perhaps the closest analogy among contemporary artists that we can find to Chekhov is the work of the French painter and sculptor Edgar Degas. Degas is falsely seen as the artist who produced pretty paintings and pastels of ballerinas. In fact, far from this popular image, Degas was a restless experimenter and searcher for new insights. His work represents an ideal combination of art and science, a painstaking, scientific inquiry into human and animal physiology. By the 1870s, the invention of rapid-exposure photography made it possible to take photographs of horses galloping (an advance on the old daguerreotype that required several minutes' exposure). This technological invention was exploited by the American photographer Eadweard Muybridge, whose photographs, published in France in 1878 and 1881, inspired Degas. Thanks to this new technology the French artist was the first artist in history to paint correctly the movements of horses.[1] For Degas, painting after painting, sculpture after sculpture represent a restless inquiry into human poses, musculature, gesture. The absolute, scientific, even brutal truth of his observations took him far from traditional art forms. And yet at the same time his work *is* art to the highest degree, the working out of

---

[1] On Muybridge's work and its impact on Degas's art, see Goetz Adriani, *Degas*: 79–80. The invention of the phonograph, which enabled ethnographers to record for the first time the complex harmonies of Russian peasant songs, was to have a similar influence on the music of Stravinsky. See Richard Taruskin, "Stravinsky's *Petrushka*": 90–91.

careful aesthetic principles. Degas represents a balance of art and dispassionate scientific observation.

In Chekhov's case, there is a like balance, but the science is first and foremost medical and psychological rather than physiological.[2] The issue of the relationship between the professions of medicine and writing has long been an object of some interest.[3] John Coulehan, in a discussion of the emotional relationship between the doctor and the patient, remarks: "[...] detachment has long been considered a necessary condition for medical practice."[4] Coulehan then goes on to assert that "the relationship between physician and patient, like that which exists between poet and poetic subject, is at its heart an emotional connection" —a statement with which, in the case of Chekhov, it is perhaps difficult to agree.[5] Although it is difficult to detect such an emotional link in Chekhov, we should never forget that he was trained as a doctor, and that that training included writing case studies of patients. In a short autobiographical piece published in 1900 Chekhov wrote:

> I do not doubt that my medical activities have had a powerful influence on my work as a writer; they have significantly expanded my field of observation, enriched my knowledge, and only people who are doctors themselves will be able to appreciate the true value in all of this; medicine has also been a guiding influence, and I have probably avoided making many mistakes as a result of my close relationship with it. My acquaintance with the natural sciences and the scientific approach has always kept me on my toes, and I have tried, wherever possible, to deal with scientific facts; where that has not been possible I have tried not to write at all. I should point out in this connection that the conditions of creative work do not always allow complete agreement with scientific facts;

---

[2] Chekhov kept up with the latest medical and psychological research and even planned to write a dissertation on the subject of human sexuality. Writing about the story "At Sea," Michael Finke remarks: "had the story not been written some sixteen years prior to Freud's first public discussion of Oedipus and Prince Hamlet in *The Interpretation of Dreams,* one would be sorely tempted to conjecture about Freud's influence on Chekhov" (Finke, "'At Sea'...": 55).

[3] There is a rather unsatisfactory and amateurish study of Chekhov as doctor by John Coope, *Doctor Chekhov: A Study in Literature and Medicine.*

[4] Coulehan, "Tenderness and Steadiness: Emotions in Medical Practice": 222–236.

[5] Ibid.: 225.

you cannot depict a death from poisoning on stage as it happens in real life. But you must be able to sense there is an agreement with scientific facts even when you resort to convention, that is to say, the reader or spectator must realize that it is only convention, but that the author writes from a position of knowledge.[6]

Indeed, in every character portrayal Chekhov shows an acute sense of the pathology of that individual, the interplay of psychological and physiological factors in his or her make-up, so that we may regard his works not simply as fiction, but rather as the transposition of the technique of the case study into the literary world. In a study of the subject, Faith McLellan offers a typology of writer-doctors, and goes on to write: "The second type of literary work is created when physicians write about cases for which they do not have sufficient scientific explanations, or when they have other messages to convey. They may turn to a hybrid form—here, a product of experience and imaginative speculation, in a work that combines factual and fictional elements."[7] The registering of the psychological and medical "symptoms" of individuals takes Chekhov as far from traditional literary forms as Degas was to go in leaving the tradition of academic painting. For this reason, it is difficult to discern in the characters in his plays stock types from the history of theatre; they are all carefully observed individuals with their own individual make-up and pathology.

Moreover, beyond the analysis of individual characters, Chekhov displays a constant and intense interest in the pathology of human relations. If Degas was able to examine the human or animal form in isolation, Chekhov was obliged, given the fact that human psychology does not exist in isolation, but is caught in a complex web of relationships, to study and portray human society in all its frustrating irrationality and morbidity. His representation of sexual relationships is a case in point.[8]

---

[6] Quoted in Bartlett, *Chekhov: Scenes from a Life*: 76–77.

[7] McLellan, "Literature and medicine": 564(4).

[8] There exists no satisfactory account of the morphology of sexual relationships in Chekhov. Virginia Llewellyn Smith mixes Chekhov's work and his biography in an unsystematic and muddled way. One cannot agree with her assertion that his depiction of such relationships was stereotypical because "Chekhov was writing about an idea and not about relationships he himself had any experience to speak of" (*Anton Chekhov and the Lady with the Little Dog*: 210). In fact, it is clear he

For Chekhov the scientist, the sudden and irrational attraction of individuals for each other is inexplicable, a fact of huge interest but ultimately unresolvable; in his plays and short stories it is frequently the motor that drives a comic situation, although that situation always has a dark, disturbing side to it; ultimately, all relationships based on this attraction seem morbid or predatory, and destined to end in failure. As a reader, one frequently gets the impression that Chekhov either does not know the meaning of the word "love," which he hears individuals repeating when subjected to that powerful hormonal attraction, or that he is prepared to give it a radically different definition from the conventional one.

In what follows, we shall examine how this dispassionate scientific interest in human behaviour works out on the level of speech. Chekhov's approach to language was as radical as the other aspects of his art. Here, we see Chekhov the practitioner of a linguistic art challenging the very bases of the material with which he is working. This is logical, since the psychological observations of humanity that underpin his writings imply a rethinking of the nature of language; human beings constantly speak, and Chekhov registers that speech "as he hears it." His characters speak to express themselves, rather than for communication. For Chekhov the Saussurian/Jakobsonian definition of language as a system of communication seems totally inadequate, for it gives rise to the generally held opinion that his characters do not communicate, that they are involved in a "dialogue of the deaf." In Chekhov people never seem to mean what their words ostensibly mean. But that does not mean that their speech is devoid of meaning. Nor does that mean that they do not communicate in oblique ways. Quite simply, the meaning is displaced, somewhere else, and the communication, which at first sight appears not to take place, is located somewhere beyond the verbal flow, in gesture, in body language, in silences, in unspoken interactions. This is why Chekhov's dramaturgy is such a challenge to the theatre director, since the true action of the play is displaced away from the verbal level of the text.

---

was a careful observer of different types of people and relationships. More persuasive is Carolina de Maeg-Soëp's observation: "The mature writer not only examines the causes of lovers' estrangement and misunderstanding, but he also analyses the actual nature of love itself. He suggests that love is an enigma and thus an incomprehensible, inexplicable phenomenon" (*Chekhov and Women*: 302).

The text, the words of the dialogue, thus form a sort of counterpoint to the true action, which can only by divined, imagined, and brought to life by the intuition of the director and the actor. For this reason also the texts, especially of his plays, represent a challenge for the literary scholar, habituated to working *with the text*, not intuitively reading *against* it.[9]

It is often the case that Chekhov leaves "hidden in plain view" hints to the reader of his stories and directors of his plays as to how they are to be read or staged. Yet the metapoetic aspects of his works are perhaps the least explored. In this paper, I seek to examine one metapoetical moment and trace the indications it gives the aware reader, not only as to how Chekhov's texts should be read and presented, but beyond that how his view of language and human behaviour and his poetic mesh with key motifs and images in his artistic vocabulary. The passage I have in mind is that in "The Steppe" in which the Ukrainian Konstantin Zvonyk appears out of the darkness. Zvonyk, who has a gun under his arm and is carrying a dead bird (*drokhva*) he has shot, has a striking smile and constantly talks of how happy he is. He has been married for a month, and his young wife has returned to her native village. Zvonyk relates how he wooed his young catch for three years:

> "Three years I suffered and then finally decided: three times anathema on you, I'll go into town and be a cab driver... So it's not fated! During holy week I went to Demidovo one last little time to have a look at her. [...] I look—she's with the lads by the river," he went on. "A rage came over me... I called her to one side and it must have been an hour that I said various words to her... And she fell in love! For three years she didn't love me, but for the words she fell in love!" "So what words were they?" asked Dymov. "Words? I

---

[9] Thus, when Astrov in act four of Uncle Vania says: "It must be terribly hot in Africa" as he looks at the map on the wall, the content of his words can be understood roughly as "I am so used to looking at this picture. How I will miss it and all the other dear familiar things this winter, now that I have ruined my relationship with you, Vania and Sonia." Sonia's silence at his remark is not a silence of non-communication. In fact, it is highly eloquent: "Yes, I will miss you too. But I am deeply hurt. You have only yourself to blame." In the film *Diadia Vania* (Andrei Mikhalkov-Konchalovskii, 1970), this meaning is communicated by Sonia pointedly looking at the nib of her pen.

don't even remember... How could you remember?" (S 7: 77)

It is simply "words" that seduce the girl. Their sound, their hypnotic appeal. For words she falls in love with Konstantin.

In this passage we find the key to so many of the love affairs described in Chekhov's stories and plays: women fall in love with men because of their speeches. Vershinin's speeches hypnotize Masha in *The Three Sisters*; Astrov's not only have the same effect on Sonya: she even repeats them in *Uncle Vanya*, act one. And it is Trofimov's speeches in act two of *The Cherry Orchard* that convert Anya to a new vision of her future, leading her to declare that the cherry orchard is no longer important to her. However, I would argue that it is not the apparent content of the words—the ideas that they repeat without end—that is the real content. It is almost as if there is hidden in their words (or displaced beyond them) a real meaning that is quite different from the ostensible one.

The focus on "words" in the passage quoted is not fortuitous; it points to the centre of Chekhov's poetic. We recall the final sentence of Mayakovsky's essay "Two Chekhovs": "there emerge the lines of another Chekhov—a powerful, merry artist of the word." Chekhov's poetic, as Mayakovsky demonstrates, is shaped by a radical revision of the poetic language. Chekhov's view of normal, human speech can be summed up in the formula from *Hamlet* (as we know, an especially important text for Chekhov): "words, words, words"—in Russian, "*slova, slova, slova*." This quotation even forms the title of one story by Chekhov. (A simple perusal of the list of titles of Chekhov's words gives an extensive inventory of the motifs that structure his language and conception of the world.) What is important in Hamlet's retort to Polonius is the *emptiness* of words. The words in Hamlet's book are simply words, and nothing more. For Hamlet, words (especially the words of Polonius, his interlocutor, against whom this remark is directed) are empty sounds— the truth, the actual nature of the complex psychological and political situation in which he finds himself, and Polonius's betrayal and insincerity, is elsewhere.

In the same way, the words Zvonyk utters to his future bride have no particular content as far as he can remember. When Dymov presses him for details (as if he needed to discover the secret of Zvonyk's apparent "happiness"), he is unable to remember the content and is even surprised at the question. What he *does* remember is how the words flowed from him: "Then, like water from a spout, without taking a breath: *ta-ta-ta-ta!* But now I couldn't pronounce a one single word like that..." In other words, it is a mystery to Zvonyk himself how the words flowed from him. Their content may have been unimportant, but the result was both desired and unexpected—they won over his bride. In this description we see Chekhov the natural scientist dispassionately dissecting the nature of the sexual attraction between man and woman. For him the words in themselves seem to perform a function analogous to that of birdsong or some other mating ritual. Konstantin's flow of words impresses and somehow pushes over the reluctant bride. The mechanism by which they softened and seduced his bride is mysterious, but it is disconnected from the meaning of the words in any literal "communicative" sense. At the same time, it is clear that the words have a meaning other than their literal one (whatever that is) that is rooted in the moment and the situation, a meaning that cannot be paraphrased.

This disconnect between the sound of words and words of sound and their ostensible meaning finds its incarnation in the numerous places in "The Steppe" and other texts where human speech is not quoted, but represented by conventional sounds, like Zvonyk's "*ta-ta-ta-ta.*" The conventionality of such formulaic representations of words can be read as an extension of the author's evident belief that actually all speech, and indeed all sound, is ineffable, capable of being deciphered from a variety of perspectives. We are reminded of the gunshot/breaking string sound that is present in play after play, assuming an ever greater abstraction and hence variety of possible meanings; such a sound is present in "The Steppe":

> As if because in the gloom the grass cannot see its advanced age, there arises in it a merry, youthful chatter, such as does not exist in the daytime: the cracking, whistling, scratching, the basses, tenors, and discants of the steppe—all is mingled in an uninterrupted, monotonous hum [...] but then from somewhere comes the sharp, alarming cry of an unsleeping bird, or a vague sound resembling someone's voice, like an astonished "ah-ah!" and sleepiness lowers its eyelids. (S 7: 45)

In the second act of *The Cherry Orchard* such a sound is interpreted by one character as a bird cry, by another as a breaking string, by a third as the falling of a bucket down a mineshaft; while for Firs it is the sound that marked the passing of the old ways. The point is that it is all of these—and none. It is sound, abstract, pure and unrepeatable, the ultimate expression of the unique moment.

In "The Steppe" a world is evoked in which all beings and even things make sounds, and all the sounds are of equal value and equally mysterious. The work evokes a radical vision of a non-anthropocentric world where the steppe itself is a producer of sound. Everything lives, and living means noise, self-expression. This becomes evident to the reader in the following passage close to the beginning of the text: "Six reapers stand in a row and swing their scythes, and the scythes merrily flash in rhythm, all together emitting the sound: "*Vzhzhi, vzhzhi!*" (S 7: 17). The fact that the scythes are described as flashing "merrily," as well as the presence of the exclamation point, makes them appear anthropomorphic in a rather traditional sense, although behind them we perceive the expression of the reapers themselves, comically working in unison. In any case, the focus is on the sound, which appears as part of the orchestra of sounds that inhabit the fabulous space of the steppe. This symphony is evoked when the travellers stop to rest and cover themselves from the afternoon sun:

> Silence fell. All that could be heard was the snorting and munching of the horses and the snoring of the sleepers; somewhere at a distance one lapwing cried and now and then the squeak of three snipe rang out, as they flew over to see whether the uninvited guests had left; lisping softly, the brooklet gurgled, but all these sounds did not disturb the silence, did not awaken the stilled air, but on the contrary drove nature into a doze. (S 7: 23)

If, in the description of the noise of the scythes, there had been a possibility of seeing a simple, traditional example of anthropomorphic description of nature, here we sense all the sources of sound—birds, horses, stream, and snoring sleepers—as being all on the same plane of existence. Indeed, the very silence appears as a source of sound—zero sound—along with the stagnant air.

As in this passage, a principal source of sound in the steppe is the birds. Like trees, birds assume an important presence in Chekhov's works; Chekhov clearly knew the birds of Russia and could identify them by their sounds. One of them even offers the equivalent of human speech—the *spliuk*, which cries out in the night: *"Spliu! Spliu!"* (I sleep! I sleep!). But generally it is rather people who are likened to birds, in "The Steppe" and elsewhere. Thus, we are told that Roza replies to Moisei Moiseich "in a thin, turkey-like little voice," a simile that is repeated when father Christopher retorts to Solomon: "I am talking to you like an old man, quietly, but you go bla-bla-bla like a turkey!" (S 7: 40). Likewise, Solomon is described as being "short and hook-nosed, like a plucked bird" (S 7: 81). The implication is clear: for Chekhov people and birds exist on the same plane, and the sounds they emit function similarly as expressions of their presence, with the communicative functions only secondary, if present at all.

If speech does not correspond to any readily decipherable meaning, if it is *zaum*—beyond rational meaning—then it can easily be replaced with a totally abstract sound that will have the same force as "normal" speech, yet contribute a musical element that heightens the subjectivity of all perceptions. This tendency of speech to abstraction is gradated, from elements of real speech repeated more or less with their meaning intact, through to semantically totally empty sounds. A sign of this transition is repetition: double, triple, or quadruple. Indeed, repetition of speech as a general rule is a sign of semantic emptiness and heightened expressiveness.

Thus there are simply doublings of a word, either a real word or an onomatopoeic one: *"Vzhzhi, vzhzhi!"* (already commented on); "Spliu! Spliu!" (the bird-cry); *"Beite ego! Beite ego!"* (literally "Hit him! Hit him!"); "Mama! Mama!" (repeated twice by Egorushka in a rage at Dymov) (S 7: 83). Then there are triadic sounds, which, as we have noted, reflect Hamlet's triadic repetition "Words, words, words": *"Tup! Tup! Tup!"* (S 7: 71; Pantelei's account of robbers); *"Tary-bary-rastabary!"* (S 7: 79; Pantelei while talking about Varlamov); *"Tsyp! Tsyp! Tsyp!*(Auntie calling to her chicks; S 7: 101). Finally there are quadrupled abstract sounds. Notable examples of these, in addition to Zvonyk's *"ta-ta-ta-ta,"* are the speech of Moisei Moiseich and his wife Roza: *"Gal-gal-gal-gal"*(S 7: 39) and *"Tu-tu-tu-tu"* (S 7: 39). I have not found more than four repetitions in Chekhov's texts.[10]

---

[10] Wolf Schmid examines these repetitions in the context of what he sees as the tendency to "ornamentalism" in Russian literature at the end of the nineteenth

Perhaps the most striking example of this tendency to abstraction in Chekhov's language in "The Steppe" is to be found in the description of the storm. The alienation provided by the perspective of Egorushka enables us to see this as a dialogue of titans, expressing themselves in their own version of *zaum*: "*'Trrakh! Takh, takh! Takh!'* sharply rang out the thunder, rolled around the sky, tripped up and somewhere near the front wagons or far behind moved away with an angry, jerky *'trra!..'*" (S 7: 86). Egorushka's only defense against this rage of the "giants" (*velikany*) is to cry a triple formula that is powerful, although also empty of direct meaning: "*Sviat, sviat, sviat*" (literally "Holy, holy, holy"; S 7: 86, 88).

Returning to the passage describing the appearance of Konstantin Zvonyk, we find a further interesting comment by Chekhov on the noises people make. Zvonyk's words have led him to love, and hence destruction. The gun under his arm, and his clean white shirt, are unambiguous. The words "love" and "happiness" (*schast'e*) as they are repeated in this passage are clearly devoid of meaning. Suddenly one after another those present turn to singing: "Dymov propped his cheek in his hand and began to sing quietly some doleful song. Konstantin smiled sleepily and quietly chimed in in a thin voice. They sang for about a minute and fell silent..." (S 7: 77) Then Emelian proposes singing "something divine." Konstantin declares he is not able to.

> They all refused; then Emelian himself started to sing. He started to wave his arms and nodded his head, opened his mouth, and from his throat burst only a hoarse, soundless breathing. He sang with his arms, his head, his eyes, and even with his lump, sang passionately and with pain, and the stronger he strained his chest to tear from it at least one single note, the more soundless became his breathing. (S 7: 78)

---

century. In fact, it is more appropriate to see them as part of a programmatic restructuring by Chekhov of the nature of language as a human phenomenon. Far from having a mere decorative function, these repetitions restate the function of language as not a communicative medium, but a means of abstract self-expression for the characters in the story. That is to say, they have both a narrative and a metapoetic function. At the same time, by reducing actual language to a blur (in the case of Roza's speech), they intensify the perspectivization of the narrative (the sound as heard by Egorushka). See Wolf Schmid, *Proza kak poeziia*: 249–50.

Here, in this extraordinary evocation of a man who adores singing, but who physically is unable to, we find the higher form of sound emitted by man—the beauty of song, as opposed to the emptiness of speech. Here is beauty, fullness of meaning, the expression of the ineffable nature of life. The irony that no sounds come from Emelian—the zero presence of sound—serves only to heighten the sense of those sounds that he hears with his inner ear. Here, perhaps, Chekhov appears to be saying, is the beauty and meaning of sounds that man is capable of, and which express his true vocation, rather than the empty sounds of speech.

WORKS CITED

Adriani, Goetz. *Degas: Pastels, Oil Sketches, Drawings*. New York: Abbeville Press, 1985.

Bartlett, Rosamund. *Chekhov: Scenes from a Life*. London: Free Press, 2005.

Coope, John. *Doctor Chekhov: A Study in Literature and Medicine*. Chale, Isle of Wight, England: Cross Publishing, 1997.

Coulehan, John. "Tenderness and Steadiness: Emotions in Medical Practice," *Literature and Medicine* 14.2: 1995.

de Maeg-Soëp, Carolina. *Chekhov and Women: Women in the life and work of Chekhov*. Columbus, Ohio: Slavica, 1987.

Llewellyn Smith, Virginia. *Anton Chekhov and the Lady with the Little Dog*. London: Oxford UP, 197.

McLellan, M. Faith. "Literature and medicine: physician-writers," *The Lancet*, February 22, 1997 vol., 349 n9051.

Schmid, Wolf. *Proza kak poeziia: Pushkin, Dostoevskii, Chekhov, avangard*. Sankt-Peterbourg: INAPRESS, 1998.

Taruskin, Richard, "Stravinsky's *Petrushka*." In: Andrew Wachtel, ed., *Petrushka: Sources and Contexts*. Evanston, Illinois: Northwestern UP, 1998): 67–113.

A.P. Chekhov: A Lexicographical Theme with Variations

IRINA V. GLADILINA
Tver State University

At the present stage of development of Chekhov studies the absence of a dictionary of the writer's language is a cause for great astonishment, if not regret. Strictly speaking, the huge number of works on A.P. Chekhov's language produced to date, whether large-scale or partial, does not afford an overall picture of the writer's idiolect. The wave of the "lexicological boom" has yet to reach the language of Chekhov's prose, drama, journalistic writings, and letters. In my view this state of affairs cannot be considered normal.

All the preconditions for the creation of a dictionary of the writer's language are present. This concerns not only and not so much the technical means of processing the information, but rather those shifts that have taken place in the contemporary theory and practice of lexicography. The attention of lexicographers, and of linguists in general, has moved from the sphere of language to that of speech: research has begun to focus on the *functioning* of the different linguistic units. Consequently, the linguistic (explanatory) model of dictionary has been replaced by the ideographical one. In the field of literary lexicography these changes have already produced positive results.[1] However, the "breakthrough" in the lexigraphical representation of Fedor Dostoevsky's ideolect does not by any means suggest that a universal method of describing authorial *discourse* has been discovered, since the principles of lexicographical transcription of the authorial idiolect are directly related to the individual attitudes (or intentions) governing the production of text.

Thus, in a traditional description of the meanings of words Chekhov's lexicon would be little different—on the semantic level—from the general usage at the end of the nineteenth and beginning of the twentieth century. And yet it would not at all represent the "language of A.P.

---

[1] See for example *Slovar' iazyka Dostoevskogo: leksicheskii stroi idiolekta.*

Chekhov." Given the author's clearly demonstrated non-ideological stance, Chekhov's discourse dissipates into thin air, once it is abstracted from the domain of the given artistic whole, and its semantics inevitably is reduced to the linguistic meaning as such. Here two crucial questions arise for any researcher conducting a lexicographical analysis: the status of the unit of representation in the dictionary and—directly applying to Chekhov—how to capture and transmit the entire "authorial" meaning, or more precisely, how to explain the process of individual creation of meaning.

Of course, when the dictionary is intended to represent the writer as a particular linguistic personality, by no means do all lexical units fall within the lexicographer's purview; rather, only those that reflect the author's main ideas that form and shape his world and are the concentrated expression of the particularities of the author's language and style—what one might call the key words.

The authors of *Slovar' iazyka Dostoevskogo* made a subtle distinction between two basic functions of the key words, dividing them into two groups: *ideo*glosses and *idio*glosses,[2] whereby the former express themes that are weighty and significant for the world created by the author, and the latter mark the individual authorial devices that serve to incarnate them. Of course, the dictionary of an author should have as its objective the second category of key words: the idioglosses. The question of the composition of the idioglosses is also far from simple, since one cannot limit oneself to mere formal criteria (their frequency, rate of repetition, central character, whether in the generic or chronological sense, and so on), when describing an author's lexicon. It is here that the so-called method of expert evaluation becomes essential in defining the degree to which the selected lexical unit is capable of performing the function of idiogloss.

A dictionary of this type should, in our opinion, also have an explicative character, that is to say, should not be limited to the pinpointing of meanings, their links and the presentation of exhaustive illustrative material, but should also contain some commentary from the researcher that would serve to clarify the place of the given idiogloss in the author's thesaurus.

Let us now examine two autonomous semantic elements that can

---

[2] Ibid.: 122–127.

be seen as variations on the theme of demarcation and particularities of description of the idioglosses in Chekhov's idiolect.

"Grey" (*seryi*) Chekhov

The received image of the artistic space inhabited by Chekhov's characters is habitually associated with the definition "grey." Using the tools developed by contemporary lexicography, let us attempt to define the extent to which this link is justified, and the actual linguistic means used to establish and maintain it. If we take as our point of departure the regular character of this association, then we must view "grey" as an idiogloss in Chekhov's lexicon—that is to say, as a key unit with the potential to reveal to the reader not only *what kind of* world the author is evoking, but also *how* he does so.

Let us turn to the detailed basis for the status of the idiogloss "grey" (*seryi*) in Chekhov's idiolect. The first criterion, though by no means by significance, but rather by established tradition, for the demarcation of one or another word as key is its formal frequency. This criterion is in fact ineffective in determining a key word, since "grey," like any other word that defines colour, has a complex system of figurative meanings, whose number in concrete texts can only multiply. If we nevertheless base our observations on the actual number of instances of the corresponding "graphic chains" (I intentionally avoid here the term "word," since it assumes the inclusion of meaning), then the frequency of the lexeme "grey" in Chekhov's texts is quite comparable with other words defining colour and in no way marks it as a key word in the given series: "green" — 49; "red" — 132; "dark-blue" — 25; "yellow" — 14; "grey" — 58.[3]

Although contemporary lexicographical practice has undergone serious changes in recent decades, it is nevertheless the "captive" of a certain unavoidable convention, being obliged to represent the meaning of a polysemic word as an aggregate of separate but clearly defined lexico-semantic variants. This has the effect of disrupting the principle of the diffusion of meanings of a polysemic word, "which is the decisive

---

[3] The selection of the lexeme *seryi* from Chekhov's works and letters was made from the electronic version: Anton P. Chekhov, *Polnoe sobranie sochinenii: Elektronnaia kniga* («Klassika,» IDDK).

factor defining its semantics. The fact that lexicographic descriptions do not reflect this (and even seek to strip dictionary entries of indeterminate examples) fundamentally distorts the representation of the semantic structure of the words described."[4] Consideration of the principle of diffusion of meaning is particularly significant in analyzing an author's lexicon, since in a literary text there is a conscious emphasis on the *simultaneous* activation of the *entire semantic structure of the word*. One possible way to demonstrate the depth of meaning of a word and account for all its potential semantics in the text is the exhaustive determination of all the existing syntagmatic links of the given lexeme. Moreover, the complete syntagmatics of the word in question allows one to perceive in the dictionary entry not just a naked matrix, but the author himself, and to read the authorial metatext as an uninterrupted continuum.

Let us attempt to interpret the semantics of the lexeme "grey" in Chekhov's idiolexicon on the basis of all the facts of its usage according to the logic of "sketching meaning" (Heidegger). In order to distribute meanings we will for convenience's sake start with the traditional system of meanings of the word as given in an explanatory dictionary of the Russian language.[5] In addition, it seems essential to retain the generic relativity of the word, which appears only in concrete word combinations, since in an idiolexicon words do not exist in isolation, but in direct relation to one another. This includes purely grammatical relations.[6] For comparison's sake, in what follows the syntagmatic series from the literary prose works (PW) and the letters (L) are given separately:

1. Definition of colour: the colour of ash, smoke, admixture of black or dark colour to white.
PW *Grey* (masc. sing.) goose, house, fence, tomcat, cross, circle, cloudy vault, layer (of dust), sugar, snow, cock, fog, background, lab coat, top hat, tea, tongue (from dust); grey (fem. sing.) blouse, chamois, official document, stone statue, horse, material, night, stripe, frame, face (of a cat), dog, salt, shadow, double-breasted jacket, uniform (of high school pupils), church, hat; *grey* (neut. sing.) sea, sky, blanket, cloth; grey (pl.) eyes, twilight, walls.

---

[4] Shmelev, *Problemy semanticheskogo analiza leksiki.*
[5] See for example: Ozhegov and Shvedov, *Tolkovyi slovar' russkogo iazyka.*
[6] For more on this, see Karaulov, *Russkii iazyk i iazykovaia lichnost'.*

L. *Grey* (masc. sing.) purse; *grey* (pl.) eyes, napkins, walls.

The colour, as noted above, is only one of the functions of the definition, which turns out to be directly linked with an emotional component. It has long been noted that a colour is capable of influencing an individual's mood; moreover, each colour has its own semantics. Thus *grey* is first and foremost an unclear, indefinite intermediate shade ("mixture of dark and white"), which gives rise to the perception of the given colour as belonging to the associative series of *indeterminateness, despondency, boredom, melancholy, endlessness.*[7] Chekhov, of course, has in mind all these emotional connotations of the colour grey.

> 2. (Figurative) Morbidly pale.
> PW. *Grey* (masc. sing) (pale grey) colour of skin, appearance; *grey* (neut. sing.) (yellowish-grey) face.

As we see, the syntagmatics of "grey" in the given meaning are quite limited and consistent, the combinations given having a regular character, and when describing a morbid state Chekhov frequently uses the formula "a grey face," or complex adjectives using the first part *grey-* in combination with the words "appearance, face."

> 3. (Figurative) Mediocre, totally unremarkable, evoking no interest, boring.
> PW *Grey* (masc. sing.) city; *grey* (fem. sing.) life, semi-existence, side (of life).
> L. *Grey* (masc. sing.) courtyard, house; *grey* (fem. sing.) life, public, troupe; *grey* (neut. sing.) memory, field.

The instances of usage of the lexeme "grey" in this meaning are few, but it is precisely this, along with "the colour definition / mood" that is crucial for the given idiogloss. The combinations with the word "life" ("The Thief," "Three Years," "My Life," "The Bride") turn out to be key. The expansion of the meaning and its particular role are indicated through quasi-synonymic series, where the secondary semanticisation of words with linguistically different meanings occurs through their contiguity

---

[7] The lexemes given in italics may be considered to be ideoglosses in the formation of which the idiogloss *seryi* plays an important role.

within a limited context. In this sense the idiogloss *grey* plays the role of an attractor, i.e., is the centre of attraction for other words in the text, with which it forms a contextually associative field: grey monotonous life; the bourgeois, kitchen, grey side of life; static, grey, sinful life. In this case the very combination "grey life" as "mere existence, vegetation" stands in opposition to "life itself": "I have the feeling that our *life* has already finished, and that now a *grey semi-existence* is beginning" ("Three Years").

In Chekhov's letters the set phrase *grey circle* is interesting in the meaning under examination. It occurs from the contamination of two semes—"colour" and "mediocrity": "... but now, when instead of literary physiognomies at the head of the journals are stuck some grey circles and dog collars, a predilection for the thickness of the journal does not stand up to scrutiny, and the difference between the thickest journal and a cheap rag is only quantitative, i.e., from the artist's point of view it deserves no respect or attention" (P 1888).

Chekhov likewise uses this combination in the prose, intentionally revealing the link between the first and third meanings of the lexeme "grey": "Life, which I am currently observing through the window of a hotel room, reminds me of a grey circle: there is a grey circle and no shadings, no glimmers of light" ("A Hunting Drama").

4.   (About the weather) overcast
     PW and L. A grey day, grey weather, grey morning.

In this meaning the word is of high frequency both in the literary prose and in the letters with no differentiation of syntagmatic links: these are completely traditional formulae that serve as depictive devices or artistic details—but only within the given artistic entity.

The idiogloss *grey* (*seryi*) is also represented in Chekhov's lexicon by derivatives: *ser, seret'* (to look or seem grey), *sero*. The short-form adjective "grey" (*sero*) plays a particular role in the creation of the "grey continuum" of Chekhov's texts; this is conditioned by its grammatical function as a predicate. In it Chekhov is determining not the visual series and the emotional mood linked to it, but a particular mode of existence. In the text this form is as a rule combined with other similar forms and in this way serves to create a profound image within a limited space and with rather limited linguistic means (the famous Chekhovian brevity):

"Between ourselves: his spouse also drinks. [It's] grey, disgusting, foul" (P 1888); "I have a new lamp, most esteemed Maria Vladimirovna, all else is boring, grey and old" (P 1887); "We arrive at the church. [Things are] grey, petty and boring" (P 1888); "In Moscow there is nothing new. [It's] boring and sad and grey and leaden" (P 1888).

This descriptive device is present also in Lev Tolstoy, but it is precisely in Chekhov that it becomes one of the dominant features of his authorial idiostyle. Laconicism as limitation of the textual space is achieved by means of the simultaneous intersection in the boundaries of one word of several aspects of the perception of the world.

In my view the archetypical meaning of the colour grey as a *mingling* of black to white is important in understanding the idiogloss *grey* in Chekhov's lexicon.[8] Chekhov's world is extremely close to the real one, and his famous avoidance of ideology (read: multidimensionality) is expressed more than anywhere in his use of half-shades. White and black are as it were two extreme points, the absolute plus and minus, the ideal and the anti-ideal, and between them is being, existence, life, in which *mingling* plays a key role. However, in the given case Chekhov does not appear as its bard; on the contrary, an exhaustive analysis of the lexeme *grey* revealed practically no case of a positive evaluation in its use. It seems that the matter lies elsewhere, in that artistic task that the author has set for himself. Thus, in a well-known letter to Suvorin (1888) Chekhov remarks: "You are right to demand from the artist a conscientious attitude to his work, but you are mixing up two concepts: the solution to a question and the correct couching of the question. Only the second is obligatory for the artist." Chekhov simply makes a diagnosis.

"Two in one."

There would be absolutely no contradiction in describing the word in Chekhov (of course, not every word, but those that are significant for the ideas they contain) as a concept. In many terminological treatments the concept is close to the meaning of the word: this, for example, is how Natalia Shvedova defines it: "The concept is the meaning of the word— one or a certain complex of linked meanings—behind which stands a notion relating to the intellectual, spiritual or existentially important ma-

---

[8] See Vladimir Dal', *Tolkovyi slovar' zhivogo velikorusskogo iazyka.*

terial sphere of man's existence." However, closeness does not mean that the concept and the word are identical. One of the defining characteristics of the word in Chekhov is its semantic ambivalence or textual *enantosemia*,[9] and therefore the concept is the sole possible, not contradictory, unit of representation of the idiolect of the author.

It is particularly important to bear in mind the authorial attitude while working on the word. Thus, one of the leading principles of Chekhov's poetics at the end of the 1880s was the attempt to achieve maximum objectivity of narration and the resulting "individualization of every separate event." On the lexical level of the text this leads to *enantosemia*. *Enantosemia* is the "particular, non-productive variety of antonymy consisting in the opposition of meanings (lexicosemantic variants) of a polysemic word; this is the so-called 'antinomy within the word'."[10] It is precisely this device of opposition within the word that characterizes the semantic dominants of Chekhov's texts. Thus, "equanimity" [*ravnodushie*], a key word in his language, is semantically ambivalent. Its semantic ambivalence is achieved through the presence of two semantic levels in the first root: 1. "identity" and 2. "calmness, balance." It is precisely for this reason that the word "equanimity" in the writer's lexicon acquires two antonymic meanings. "Equanimity 1" is "The absence of compassion, inattention to the internal life of the surrounding individuals."[11] This meaning coincides completely with the usual one— "indifference, a detached attitude to people": "...equanimity is the paralysis of soul, premature death"; "...there are people who are completely indifferent [*ravnodushnye*], deprived of all feeling of compassion, but who cannot walk past human grief and intervene out of fear that the individuals in question might be able to manage without them."

A meaning diametrically opposite to the one described above emerges from the positive evaluation of a calm, reasonable attitude to life and people: "Nature is a very good tranquillizer. It reconciles one to

---

[9] Andrei Stepanov points out the homonymy of the Chekhovian sign: *Problemy kommunikatsii u Chekhova*: 110–121. Without contesting this point of view, we assume, however, that in Chekhov the word is not simply subjected to a shift of meaning in the process of communication, but the shift itself takes the form of an opposition.

[10] *Sovremennyi russkii iazyk: Teoreticheskii kurs. Leksikologiia*: 70.

[11] See: Ozhegov and Shvedova, op.cit.: 628.

things, i.e., gives one *equanimity*. And in this world *equanimity* is a necessary thing. Only those with equanimity are able to see things clearly, be fair-minded and work..." (Letter to Suvorin from Sumy, 1889). Here "equanimity 2" is the contextual synonym of "tranquillity," and the latter is the necessary precondition for "fairmindedness." "Equanimity" in this understanding is the expression of the principle of objectivity, and as such expresses the essence of the narrative system of Chekhov's texts of the 1880s.

An interesting and structurally more complex case is opposition on the level of the pragmatic semantics composing a key word. Let us examine a similar case using the example of the idiogloss "talent" in the text "A Dreary Story." "Talent" denotes a key definition of the narrator-character—the distinguished professor Nikolai Stepanovich: "I am hardworking, with as much endurance as a camel, which is important, and *talented*, which is even more important." The image of the central character is founded on this idea, which places him in opposition to his untalented dissector, to his wife, who has become enmired in the petty details of everyday life, and to his foster-daughter Katya, who is unsuccessful as an actress because of her mediocrity.

The usual positive connotations of the lexeme "talent" are self-evident and supported by the link with the concepts "happiness" and "success." Thus, in Dal's dictionary *talan* (a lexeme that shares the same root and is etymologically cognate with "talent") is defined as being synonymous with the series "destiny, fate, happiness, success, profit, gain." Why is it then that a talented scientist encounters failure? Surely talent is the guarantee of salvation? At this point it is appropriate to examine the definition of "talent" given by the character himself. The meaning of the lexeme "talent" in the professor's discourse is significantly broader that the generally accepted semantics ("1. Outstanding natural capabilities, a great gift; 2. An individual with outstanding capabilities").

Moreover, the seme "outstanding capabilities" turns out to be secondary in the case of this character. In the professor's definition the term "talent" contains the following meanings: "independence," "freedom," "constant doubts and searching," "lack of limitation to a narrow professional sphere," "interest in the surrounding world." All these senses perceived by the professor in the concept of "talent" can be summarized into two principal ones: "freedom" and "interest." The latter quite evidently constitutes an opposition to the sense of the term "equanimity."

However, the professor himself does not pass the test of "talented-ness." He descends to complaints and grumbling and ultimately feels total apathy: "Moreover, recently I have felt such *equanimity* to every-thing." The reason for such tragic metamorphoses is self-evident: his tal-ent is narrow and utilitarian in its orientation. The authorial evaluation of such a talent is negative, as the finale of the story confirms.

In 1888, the same year that "A Dreary Story" was written, Chek-hov wrote in "A Fit": "There are writerly, theatrical and artistic talents, but he has a special talent—a human one. He has a subtle, magnificent feeling for all pain. The pain of others annoys him, stirs him up, puts him in a state of ecstasy... the feeling that Vasiliev had when it seemed to him that the question was resolved was very close to inspiration." In this passage we find rather definite lexical parallels with the state of the pro-fessor during a lecture: a voluptuous languor, ecstasy and inspiration. But in the case of the hero of "A Dreary Story" the object of all his spiri-tual efforts is *science*, whereas the hero of "A Fit" experiences inspiration at the possibility of *saving a person.*

The limits of science, however broad they may have appeared to the individual conscience, turn out to be narrower than "true life." A tal-ent that is confined to its "little box" turns into its opposite. We may thus speak of the polarization of meaning on the level of the evaluative com-ponent of the lexical meaning.

Interestingly, the very device of creating textual enantosemia is made explicit by the author in the professor's speech: "... I ride along and out of nothing to do read the signs to the right and left. Out of the word *traktir* I get the word *ritkart*. That would be good as the surname of a baron or baroness: Baroness Ritkart." The professor discovers that a change of perspective effects a radical change in the "picture of the world," and the very *reversibility of the word* points to the possible *variabil-ity of meaning.* It is precisely this authorial strategy that must be taken into account when choosing a unit in the dictionary of Chekhov's idio-lect.

Translated from the Russian by J. Douglas Clayton.

WORKS CITED

Chekhov, Anton. *A.P. Chekhov, Polnoe sobranie sochinenii: Elektronnaia kniga* («Klassika,» IDDK)—electronic source.

Dal', Vladimir. *Tolkovyi slovar' zhivogo velikorusskogo iazyka.* M.: Gos. izd-vo inostrannykh i natsional'nykh slovarei, 1955.

Dostoevsky, Fedor. *Slovar' iazyka Dostoevskogo: leksicheskii stroi idiolekta.* Ed. Iuri Karaulov. M.: Nauka, 2001.

Karaulov, Iuri. *Russkii iazyk i iazykovaia lichnost'.* M.: Nauka, 1987.

Ozhegov, Sergei Ivanovich and Shvedova, Natalia Iu. *Tolkovyi slovar' russkogo iazyka.* M.: Azbukovnik, 1994.

Shmelev, Dimitri Nikolaevich. *Problemy semanticheskogo analiza leksiki (na materiale russkogo iazyka).* Dissertation abstract, M.: 1969.

Sovremennyi russkii iazyk: Teoreticheskii kurs. Leksikologiia. M.: Russkii iazyk, 1987.

Stepanov, Andrei. *Problemy kommunikatsii u Chekhova.* M.: Iazyki slavianskoi kul'tury, 2005.

"Small Fry":
A Nice Little Easter Story

ROBERT LOUIS JACKSON
Yale University

Chekhov's "Small Fry" ("*Meliuzga,*"1885) continues the line of many of Chekhov's early stories devoted to the so-called "little man" that are outwardly funny, comic, satirical, but whose inner lining suggests a more sober, indeed, somber attitude toward this type. At the same time, in its complexity, depth, and tragic-comic vision, "Small Fry" forms a bridge to the great prose and plays of Chekhov's later years.

The action of Chekhov's story takes place in a room of some Moscow firm. Ivan Danilych Nevyrazimov, a poor clerk, is on duty on Saturday and Easter Sunday. Vexed over his not being able to join his comrades for a good time, and in general despairing over his "hopeless situation" in life, he scours his mind for ways (it turns out ignominious ones) to better his situation. He contemplates writing a letter of denunciation of somebody in order to curry favor with his boss, but in the end recognizes that he lacks the ability even to express himself properly. In a fit of anger and disgust, he relieves his sense of misery by swatting a cockroach that is running across his desk, and then tossing him into the flames of a sputtering kerosene lamp.

The family name of the story's hero, "Nevyrazimov," might be translated as "Mr. Nonverbal" or "Mr. Inexpressible" (the term "*nevyrazimye*" may be used colloquially in reference to underwear, thus, "inexpressibles").[1] The demeaning character of this name certainly announces to any Russian reader the comic, satirical, or even burlesque dimension of the story and of its protagonist. Ivan, Nevyrazimov's first name, widespread in Russia, places him in the league of Everyman. At first glance, it would appear that Chekhov is setting up his hero exclu-

---

[1]At the root of this name is the verb "*vyrazit',*" "to express," or "to convey." By affixing "*ne*" (no, not) to the verb and turning it into a noun one obtains "Nevyrazimov."

sively as a comic type, a butt of cruel humor. Yet in fact the comic element in this story comes under the rubric of the Russian saying, "A Russian often laughs when he ought to weep." The comic in this story has a very serious subtext, and the fleeting and very prosaic contretemps of the hero on the Easter holiday stands in contrast to the tragedy and resurrection of the central figure in the Easter narrative: Jesus Christ.

Chekhov fixes his story in the time-frame of the most solemn moment in the liturgical year of the Russian Orthodox Church calendar: the moment of transition from Lent to Easter, more specifically, that moment when the midnight service of Great Saturday (which usually begins at 11:30 p.m.) passes into Easter Matins: a service marking the moment when the Church "passes over" from sorrow over Christ's death and burial to the joy of the resurrection and eternal life. In short, the temporal frame of the story of Nevyrazimov's is enclosed in a religious framework of eternity.

The secular time frame for the story is approximately one hour. The action of the story begins shortly before 11:30 p.m. The clock strikes 12:30 a.m. near the end the story. The clock announces the temporal moment. In the liturgical narrative frame, however, the "eleventh hour" announces the hour of man's salvation. Nevyrazimov's wish to escape his dungeon-like room for a few hours of gaiety, his yearning for salvation from his miserable life, contrasts with eternal salvation announced by the resurrection of Christ.

Thus, on the semantic plane of "Small Fry" we can speak of an implicit dialogue between two narratives: a "low" tragi-comic narrative involving Nevyrazimov's momentary descent in thought into moral-spiritual degradation and a "high" liturgical narrative relating the last moments of Christ's burial and the ensuing resurrection. The highest point of the Orthodox Easter narrative, the resurrection of Christ (in the Orthodox liturgy the period between 12:00 and 12:30 am) coincides with the lowest point in Nevyrazimov's narrative: that moment when he contemplates denunciation as a means of rising on the bureaucratic ladder.

The story of Ivan Nevyrazimov ends on a prosaic and comic note when he swats the cockroach and tosses him into the flames of the smoldering kerosene lamp. He feels better. On the symbolic-religious plane of the narrative it is Nevyrazimov who lands in the hellish fire. Merely from the esthetic point of view the banal, prosaic dimension of the story precludes the possibility of any dogmatic religious statement on the part of Chekhov. The religious subtext of this secular story, however, introduces marked spiritual material into the story.

The word *"meliuzga"*[2] (the Russian title of Chekhov's story) is a collective noun that can be used affectionately or derogatively (or both) to refer to "little creatures": either "little children" or "small animals." It is a word that describes a collection of people or animals, *not* an individual. With its connotations of the small, trivial, and petty, the word *"meliuzga"* can also be used pejoratively to refer to people of a lower social class or status; or to refer to people who do marginal work; or, again, to speak dismissively of people who are presumably lacking in any importance or significance, that is, people for whom the English language has reserved such terms as "nobodies," "nonentities, "small potatoes," or, in the given case, "small fry," or *"meliuzga."* Chekhov's very use of the word *"meliuzga"* as a title lays the groundwork for a tragi-comic approach to his hero and his dilemma.

The petty clerk Ivan Danilych Nevyrazimov certainly belongs to the "small fry." But so, too, does the cockroach that has a prominent place in the story and in its semantic symbolism: seeking to escape the light, the cockroach anxiously and distractedly runs across Neyvrazimov's desk at the beginning and end of the story. Both the clerk and the cockroach lead parallel lives in the relative darkness of the office. At first glance, their specific and general fates appear different; on closer look, however, their lives and destinies turn out to be similar. Unlike Gregor Samsa in Franz Kafka's *Metamorphosis*, Nevyrazimov never literally turns into cockroach but, as the story demonstrates, he lives a "cockroach life": a phrase used by Nevyrazimov that suggests not only a precarious life in the lower depths of the office, but all the emotional peripeteia of a moral-psychological underground. Chekhov's identification of Nevyrazimov with the cockroach at the beginning and end of the story is a somber one. Meanwhile in the body of this story Chekhov discovers the essential dignity of Nevyrazimov, and without compromising the story's fundamental tragi-comic perspective.

"Small Fry" opens with these lines:

"Esteemed Sir, Father and Benefactor!" —a clerk called Nevyrazi-

---

[2] The word *"meliuzga"* derives from *"meluz"* —a small grain; the meal from a coarse grinding; the siftings from the screening of meal.

mov was composing a draft of a congratulatory letter. I wish that this Holy Day [*sei svetlyi den'*—literally, this "bright day"], like many future ones, be spent [by you] in good health and well being. And for your family, too, I wi..."[3]

The lamp, in which the kerosene was already low, was sputtering and stinking from the soot. An anxious, confused cockroach was running [*begal*] across the table near Nevyrazimov's writing hand. Two rooms off from the watchman's room the porter Paramon was cleaning his holiday boots for the third time, and with such energy that his expectorations and the noise of his blacking brush could be heard throughout all the rooms.

"What more should I write to him, the scoundrel," thought Nevyrazimov, lifting his eyes to the soot-covered ceiling. There he saw a dark circle—the shadow of a lamp shade. (S 3: 209)

Even if Nevyrazimov were able to express himself, or come out with his true feelings and thoughts, he is no position to do so. The person to whom he is writing may be a "scoundrel," as he puts it, but he is also, as we learn at the end of the story, his hated boss. The opening formulaic lines of Nevyrazimov's congratulatory Easter letter mask sentiments and a psychology—typically "underground" in the Dostoevskian sense—that are the complete opposite to the mood of "this holy [or bright] day" with its ultimate celebration of the triumph of light over darkness, of spirit over matter, of purity over pollution, and of eternal life over death.

The brightness of Easter Sunday is no more a part of Nevyrazimov's inner thoughts than it is of his immediate surroundings. The black smoking soot of the sputtering kerosene lamp, the appearance of the cockroach, and the disclosure that Nevyrazimov's mood and thoughts are clearly lacking in true Easter spirit serve momentarily to block out the light of the Easter spirit. Nevyrazimov's mind is focused on his idea of sneaking out of his Easter watch and on vile schemes for escaping from his penurious life. In brief, on the eve of Easter Sunday, when the Church passes from mourning the death of Christ to his resurrection, Nevyrazimov is mourning over his "hopeless situation" (*bezvykhodnoe polozhenie*) in his underground, and dreaming of a very different kind of

---

[3] Ellipses in quotations are Chekhov's, except where set off by interpolation brackets, e.g. [...].

epiphany than that celebrated on Orthodox Easter.

The office scene is a dark one. The kerosene lamp is about to go out. Nevyrazimov lifts his eyes to a ceiling black with smoke. There he sees a "dark circle—the shadow from the shade. Below were dusty cornices, and still lower, walls of a bluish-brown color that had been painted ages ago" (ibid.). The watchman's room seems like a "wilderness." In this dark space there is no light, no spiritual heights, no sign of Holy day, but rather a dismal scene resembling some prosaic Dantesque underworld, or Dostoevskian underground. Such a place is a suitable habitation for anxious and unsettled small fry, both people and cockroaches.

The desperate movements of the cockroach on its way across the desk correlate with the movements of the "writing hand" of Nevyrazimov, providing the first hint of the contiguity between the anxious and confused cockroach and the confused and anxious Nevyrazimov. It is Nevyrazimov who compares his situation to that of the cockroach. He feels "sorry not only for himself, but even for the cockroach ..." He reflects: "I'll get off my watch and get out of here, but he'll spend his whole cockroach life here!" (*Ia-to otderzhuriu i vyidu otsiuda, a on ves' svoi tarakannii vek zdes' prodezhurit!* [ibid.]) The story's end gives an ironic twist to this prophecy.

Light and darkness, the sounds and symbols of the sacred and the profane, constantly alternate in Chekhov's story. The sound of the porter Paromon's "expectorations" and of his blacking brush in the neighboring room would seem to fall in with Nevyrazimov's miserable mood, yet Easter's presence cannot be suppressed. Sounds of Easter penetrate the office window: "They [the church bells] are ringing," the porter Paromon, crossing himself, whispers to Nevyrazimov (ibid.). The bells are ringing for the midnight service (*polunoshnitsa*). Neyvrazimov listens at a small open pane in the window: the "paschal ringing" and "roar of the Easter bells" mingle with the rumble of carriages and rush of spring air. "Only the cheerful tenor sound of a near-by church and some loud, shrill laughter stood out in this chaos of sounds."

The Easter bells, the sacred ringing compete with the sounds of the profane, just as the excitement over the *holy day* mingles with the festive spirit of the *holiday*. Nevyrazimov's thoughts are focused on "our crowd" outside on the streets, on gaiety, on the carriages and the lucky people who ride in them.

> "What a mass of people!" sighs Nevyrazimov, as he glances down
> into the street where human shadows flitted one after another past
> burning lamps. "Everyone is running off to the midnight service...
> [*Vse k zautrene begut*] But our crowd, you can be sure, have tossed
> down a few drinks and are doing the town. What a lot of laughter
> and talk out there! I'm the only unfortunate one who's got to sit
> here on such a day. And every year I have to do it!" (S 3: 210)

It is shortly before midnight and people are hastening to attend
the all-important midnight service that will symbolically welcome the
resurrection and the light. Yet the picture of human shadows flitting past
burning lamps—quite a different kind of light than Easter light—is a
Dantesque one. Are these people or fallen souls who are running off to
the midnight services?

In his story Chekhov uses a key word—"*begat'*"—"to run
(about)"—to suggest a dark perspective on the human condition. This
verb may be used to describe repetitive movement in many directions,
such as dashing or scurrying about, or darting back and forth. The verb
"*begat'*" and its cognate "*begstvo*" are used five times in the story: twice
to describe the movements of the alarmed cockroach who is desperately
seeking to escape; once to describe people running off to church services,
and twice by Nevyrazimov as he dreams of escaping from the office (*begstvo*) and then of taking off to America with stolen goods.

The verb "*begat'*" with its idea of running or running about links
Nevyrazimov, the cockroach, with the Dantesque shadows of people on
the streets. Chekhov's use of "*begat'*" brings to mind, finally, an idiomatic expression that is *not* used by Chekhov, but which nonetheless is
relevant to the Nevyrazimov-cockroach theme, one which exists at the
periphery of the semantic field created by the verb "*begat'*." We have in
mind the expression, "*begat' za nachalstvom*," that is, to court, to make up
to, to fawn upon, the authorities. This is precisely what Nevyrazimov is
doing when he writes his letter of congratulations to his boss, or when he
contemplates denouncing somebody in order to curry favor with his
boss.

The Nevyrazimovs and cockroaches and the shadows running
about all fall under the rubric of "*meliuzga*." Chekhov's attitude toward
these "small fry" is reserved. His use of "*meliuzga*" as the title for the
story certainly points to the lighter or comic side of his narrative, yet in

the context of Easter and its underlying theme of redemption, the identification of a broad swath of humanity, at least its "small fry," with cockroaches suggests a darker side to the comedy.

Yet Nevyrazimov is not the only representative of the commonality in the story, and in the final analysis, Chekhov's presentation of Nevyrazimov goes well beyond caricature. The porter Paramon actively enters the story. As a person and type, he contrasts with the shallow and pathetic Nevyrazimov. It is Paromon who first calls Nevyrazimov's attention to the ringing bells: "Holding his brush in one hand, and crossing himself with the other, he stood at the little window and listened... 'They're ringing!' he whispered to Nevyrazimov, looking at him with motionless, wide-open eyes. 'It's begun!'" (S 3: 209).

When Nevyrazimov puts his ear the window and looks out and sees people running off to church, he thinks only of laughter, drink, and a good time. Paromon listens, too, but his "wide-open eyes" announce a sense of wonder and spirituality. He responds with reverence to the pealing bells. He is aware not only of the holiday but of the Holy day and its solemn meaning. Paromonov crosses himself. Nevyrazimov does not.

It is Paromon the "faithful one" (his name derives from the Greek "paramonos," that is, "sound," "reliable," "faithful") who tells the complaining Nevyrazimov that it is his own fault for taking somebody else's place as watchman during the Easter Sunday weekend. Nevyrazimov, however, had wanted to make some extra money. "But who ordered you to make yourself available for the job?" asks Paromon. "Who ordered you to hire yourself out? Zastupov hired you to replace him [...] It's greed." "The devil you say, greed!" retorts Nevyrazimov, pointing to his indigence. Truth lies with both Nevyrazimov and Paromon (S 3: 210). Yet it is no accident that the devil makes his first entrance with Paromon's reference to Nevyrazimov's "greed." The devil will be invoked again in a symbolically decisive way at the end of the story. For the moment, Nevyrazimov explains to Paromon what concretely interests him on this Easter Sunday:

> It would be nice, now, to go with the fellows to the midnight service, and then to break the fast... To have a couple of drinks, have a bite and then roll off to sleep...You sit down to the table, there's Easter cake, the samovar is hissing, next to you is some nice little

piece (*obzheshka*—from the French "objet") ...You drink a glass and touch her on the chin, and it's very pleasant... You feel yourself somebody ...Ah...A wasted life! Now there goes some brazen woman in a carriage, while I'm sitting here stewing in my thoughts...(ibid.)

Nevyrazimov's ideal Easter weekend, like that of the "human shadows" running off to Church, is not entirely split off from Easter. What he wants most of all, however, is to "feel like a human being," that is, to have food, drink, and women. His ideal includes a moment in church, an Easter cake on the table, but these elements are incidental to his everyday material needs and desires.

Nevyrazimov's words—"A wasted life!" (*Propala zhizn'*!)—do not refer the kind of losses that the coffin-maker, Yakov Ivanov, in "Rothschild's Fiddle," discovers at the end of his life. Yakov ultimately realizes that his losses (*ubytki*) are not unrealized material profits, but an unrealized spiritual life. Nevyrazimov is not unaware of his spiritual needs, but the good life he has in mind is largely brought by money and rank: it finds its embodiment in the lady driving by in a carriage.

"Every person has his own way, Ivan Danilych," Paromon remarks a moment later. "God grant it, and you will work your way up in the service and will ride in carriages" (ibid.). Paromon well knows what Nevyrazimov yearns for. Yet his words conceal another thought: *there is the will of God,* but *man is free to choose.* Nevyrazimov makes his choices.

Paramon holds out the possibility that he, Nevyrazimov, might rise in the service and ride in a carriage. Nevyrazimov, however, is realistically and woefully aware of his limitations. He gloomily acknowledges that he'll never rise above his low rank. He calls attention to the fact that he is "uneducated" (*neobrazovannyi*). To Paramon's observation that their boss, a general, is also uneducated, Nevyrazimov retorts that before reaching his rank the general "stole a hundred thousand." And besides, Nevyrazimov adds bitterly, "a person with my looks won't get far! And I have a most vile name: Nevyrazimov! In a word, brother, a hopeless situation [*polozhenie bezvykhodnoe*]. If one wants to live this way, one can, if not, one can go hang oneself..."(ibid.)

"The roar of the bells outside become louder and louder." But the louder the bells, the louder the sound of carriages, "the darker seemed the brown walls and the sooty cornices, and the more the lamp smoked"

(S 3: 210–211). Nevyrazimov's sense of entrapment gives rise to the desperate thought of "just taking off from the office," but "flight" (*begstvo*), he realizes, makes no sense. He concedes that he would only end up in his apartment where everything would be "more gray and worse." The day would only be followed by the "same gray walls, the same hiring himself out for watchman duty and the same congratulatory letters..." (S 3: 211).

Throughout the story Nevyrazimov defines himself through negatives: He is "*Nevyrazimov*" (one who can *not* express himself), "*Neschastlivyi*" (one who is *not* happy or fortunate), "*Neobrazovannyi*" (one who is *not* educated); his situation is "*Bezvykhodnoe*" (*without* a way out). Now, as he sinks further and further into despondency, he finds his situation "*nevynosimyi*," that is, *not* bearable, or unbearable. Nevyrazimov is a zero in his own estimation.

Yet Chekhov glimpses in the banal and pedestrian Nevyrazimov a core decency and spirituality, something that connects him with the true Easter spirit, its spirit of purity and harmony. Beneath Nevyrazimov's desire to "feel like a human being" lies something more than a craving for material values. For a moment Nevyrazimov becomes aware of a life different from the world of rank and carriages.

> The need for a new, better life made his heart ache with an unbearable pain. He passionately wanted suddenly to find himself on the street, to merge with the living crowd, be a participant in the solemn festivities for the sake of which all these bells were roaring and all the carriages were rumbling. He wanted what he once experienced in childhood: the family circle [*semeinyi kruzhok*], the solemn faces of relatives, the white tablecloth, light, warmth... (ibid.)

Nevyrazimov's longing for a better life gives evidence of a primal need to recover the values that shaped his childhood. In place of the "dark circle" (*temnii krug*) on the ceiling, he desires the "family circle" (*semeinyi krug*); in contrast to the cycle of drink, laughter, food, women, sleep, he also yearns for the "solemn faces of people close to him, a white table cloth, light, warmth." What is exemplified in this image is not merely the family, but what in the age-old tradition of Russian Orthodox piety was called the "little Church" (*malaia Tserkov'*). Here the family, the "little Church," is seen as a place for the cultivation of spiritual harmony.[4] Nevyrazimov's recollection of the "family circle"—the sense of cleanliness and light—echoes liturgical themes of Easter matins: "Let us purify our senses so that we may see the unapproachable light of the Resurrection."[5]

Nevyrazimov's passionate desire to merge with the living crowd, to be a participant in the solemn festivities "for the sake of which all these bells were roaring," brings to mind Dr. Dorn's pleasure in wandering about in Genoa and merging with the crowds, merging with it psychically, and beginning to "believe that a world soul is really possible" (*The Seagull*). The experience of merging with the crowd signals a deep and organic quest for something larger than oneself, some world in which one can lose oneself. In "Holy Night" (*Sviatoiu noch'iu*), a work written almost at the same time as "Small Fry," Chekhov's narrator, witnessing the swarms of people moving about the church grounds right after the liturgical signal for the resurrection, observes:

> You could not speak at all of focused prayers. There was no praying at all, but there was a kind of total, childlike, carefree joy, the seeking of a pretext just to break out and to pour oneself into some kind of movement, albeit an unabashed swaying and jostling. (S 5: 100)

In "Small Fry," "Holy Night," and *The Seagull* Chekhov appears to suggest that the exhilaration of the crowd (whether in holiday or Holy day) provides an intimation of a higher spirit, though not a full expression of that spirit. Carefree, child-like joy and Dionysian excitement may be part of, yet still not the essence of, Easter purity and truth. The Ortho-

---

[4] "The family in the old [Orthodox] tradition of piety is called the *little Church*, in accordance with the theological precepts of St. John Zlatoust [St. John Chrysostom, 347–407 A.D], Archbishop of Constantinople. In the family, in the little Church, each of its members is called upon to live in harmony and unison with others, following the Lord's commandments and will of the Heavenly Father" (*Sem'ia po davnei blagochestivoi traditsii [Pravoslaviia] imenuetsia maloi Tsrekov'ou, soglasno bogoslovskoi formule sviatitelia Ioanna Zlatousta, arkhiepiskopa Konstantinopol'skogo. V sem'e kak maloi Tserkvi kazhdyi ee chlen prizvan zhit' v soglasii i edinomyslii s drugimi, sleduia zapovediam Gospodnim i vole Nebesnogo Otsa.*"). Nikitin, ed., *Malaia tserkov'*: 3.

[5] "*Ochistim chuvstva, i uzrim nepristupnym svetom voskreseniia.*" Cf. *Molitvoslov*: 168.

dox Church Fathers at least in one respect distinguished between *holiday* rejoicing and the spirit of the *Holy Day:* "Let us not celebrate in the ancient kvas," exhorts St. Ioann Zlatoust, "not in the kvas of anger and cunning, but in purity and kvas-free truth."[6] "What can be gained from the celebration of Easter in the manner of those who celebrate it only outwardly, but do not heed its inner meaning," asks St. Ambrose Mediodansky.[7] Nevyrazimov, it would appear, finds a union of the Dionysian and Christian spirits in ancient kvas.

Nevyrazimov, one of those dark scurrying shadows, remembers what he experienced in childhood, and in his depths is joined with the Easter spirit. At the same time he remembers something else, something that for him is more potent than childhood experiences.

> He *remembered* the carriage in which the elegant lady had just driven by, the overcoat sported by the executor, the gold chain adorning the breast of the Secretary...He *remembered* a warm bed, a Stanislav medal, new boots, a uniform without holes at the elbows... He *remembered* because he had none of all those things... (my italics—RLJ) (S 3: 211)

Chekhov indicates the obsessive power of Nevyrazimov's desires by repeating the word "remember" three times. Nevyrazimov's recollections, to be sure, are rooted in privation, and a lack of any feeling of identity or sense of social self-esteem, but his lacks find expression (as Dostoevsky so well understood) in an overpowering and disfiguring craving for status and power and their symbols.

Villainous thoughts, fantasies of escape, quickly suppress Nevyrazimov's fleeting yearnings for a new and better life:

> "Shall I steal? [...] Well stealing, of course, is easy, but hiding it is quite another matter...They say you can run off [*begat'*] to America with stolen goods, but the devil knows where this America is! And then in order to steal something you need an education." The bells fall silent. One heard only the distant noise of the carriages and the

---

[6]"*Da prazdnuem ne v kvase vetse, ne v kvase zloby i lukavstva, no v bezkvasii chistoty i istiny.*" Bulgakov, *Nastol'naia kniga dlia sviashchenno-tserkovno-sluzhitelei*: 564.

[7] "*Chto pol'zy ot prazdnovaniia Paskhi tem, koi prazdnuiut ee tol'ko naruzhno, a ne posleduiut vnutrennemu ee znacheniu.*" Ibid.

> coughing of Paramon, while the sadness and anger of Nevrazimov
> grew stronger and more unbearable. In the reception room the
> clock struck 12:30 a.m. "What about a secret denunciation, or some-
> thing? Proshkin informed on somebody, and went to the top..." (S
> 3: 211)

The earlier roar of sacred bells echoed the high Easter spirit, even as
sounds of laughter, the rumble of carriages and the gaiety of street provided a profane counterpoint. Now, as though responding to Nevyrazimov's ignominious thoughts about robbery and denunciation, the bells
fall silent. Is this the moment of silence before the signal of the resurrection? In any case, the mention of the "devil" at this point signals
Nevyrazimov's symbolic moral-spiritual plunge and apostasy—his idea
of denunciation and betrayal, a plunge made at Russian Orthodoxy's
most lofty and solemn moment. The clock that strikes 12:30 a.m. offers a
sharp contrast to spiritual time of resurrection.

The rising tide of the Easter spirit, the symbolic resurrection of
Christ, contrasts with the falling spirit of Nevyrazimov. The opposing
movements *up* and *down* find parodic and paradoxical expression in the
line: *"Proshkin dones i v goru poshel..."* (Proshkin informed on somebody
and went to the top (*"v goru poshel"*—literally, "went uphill," that is,
"went up in the world"). Going to the top in Proshkin's case is also a
"passing through" the moral barrier (the name "Proshkin" echoes the
word *"proshel"*—from verb *"proiti,"* "to pass through").

Proshkin's going *up hill* and Nevyrazimov's thought to emulate
him form an instructive parallel and contrast with both the resurrection
of Christ and Christ's ascension forty days later from the Mount of Ascension (Mount of Olives). Christ ascends to heaven. The heights that
Proshkin reaches and which Nevyrazimov dreams about are in fact on
the symbolic semantic plane of the narrative hellish depths.

A violent sputtering and smoking of a near-empty kerosene lamp
and the re-appearance of the cockroach accompany Nevyrazimov's Ju-
das-like thoughts of betrayal: "The confused cockroach was still running
about the table without finding a refuge..."

The re-appearance of the cockroach signals not only the low point
in Nevyrazimov's descent; it also serves to reassert in an almost burlesque way the comic dimensions of the story of Nevyrazimov. He is a
pathetic, not a tragic figure. The juxtaposition of his "hopeless situation"

with that of the anxious and confused cockroach underscores another fact: "small fry" like Nevyrazimov and the cockroach cannot faintly dream of escape or flight (*begstvo*) from their unfortunate situations, let alone write denunciations of their colleagues:

> It's possible to come up with a denunciation, but how does one compose one! I should have to invent all sorts of insinuations and innuendoes, like Proshkin... And I wouldn't know how! If I tried to concoct something like that I'd be the first to be on the receiving end. What a muddle, the devil take me! (S 3: 211–212)

And Nevyrazimov, wracking his brains to figure how to get out of the trap of his life, focuses on the letter he is preparing for his boss. For the first time in the story the reader learns the identity of the "scoundrel" to whom Nevyrazimov's letter is addressed and the reasons for Nevyrazimov's helpless rage. The story ends with these lines:

> The letter was written to a man whom he hated with all his soul, and feared, from whom already for ten years he had sought a promotion from a sixteen-ruble position to an eighteen ruble one... "Ah... you're running about here, you devil!" With the palm of his hand and a vengeance he smacked the cockroach who had the misfortune to turn up in front of him. "Vile thing!" The cockroach fell on its back and despairingly wriggled its legs...Nevyrazimov took him by one leg and threw him into the lamp. The lamp flared up and began to crackle...And Nevyrazimov felt better. (S 3: 212)

At the beginning of the story the appearance of the cockroach coincides with Nevyrazimov's calling his boss, the "general," a "scoundrel." Now, at the end of the story the mention of his scoundrel-boss again coincides with the appearance of the cockroach.

In Nevyrazimov's bureaucratic universe his boss, the "general," the "scoundrel," is of course the real cockroach![8] In striking the cock-

---

[8]Linguists have advanced different views of etymology of the Russian word for cockroach—"*tarakan*." Chekhov's allusion to Nevyrazimov's boss as a "*tarakan*," and his adept use of the verb "*begat'*," does not rest on linguistic theories. Yet it is of interest that Roman Jakobson understands the Russian word "*tarakan*" as deriving from a pejorative use of the Turkish, "*tarkan*"—"dignitary," "high official," while another linguist considers the word as deriving from the Chuvash "*tar-*

roach ("vile thing!") Nevyrazimov expresses his frustration with his cockroach-boss. However, he is also striking a man who, like himself, is "without any education'"; a person who got to the top by vile means, but a person whose ruthlessness, position, and power he nonetheless envies. *In striking the cockroach and by extension his boss, Nevyrazimov is striking himself.* His disgust with the cockroach hopelessly and helplessly scurrying about in search of a "refuge" mirrors his own self-disgust and sense of impotence. In tossing the cockroach into the flames he relieves himself of his momentary feeling of frustration, his sense of impotence and, in the process, of his own vile intentions. "And Nevyrazimov felt better. "

In the religious subtext of this tale Nevyrazimov, though sinned against, is also a sinner, and his symbolic fate—a mock one, to be sure, in this comi-tragic tale—is to be tossed into the fires. "Ah, running about here, you devil!" (*A, begaesh tut, chert!*), Nevyrazimov exclaims on seeing the cockroach and tossing him into the fires of the lamp. Figuratively speaking, it is the devil that tosses the sinner Nevyrazimov into the fires of hell—upside down, legs wiggling in the air, as in the icon, *Vision of the Heavenly Ladder of St. John Climacus* (*Videnie Ioanna Lestvichnika*).[9]

At the outset of the story Nevyrazimov suggests that he will escape from the office while the cockroach will go on living his cockroach life. The ending of the story witnesses a reversal of that prophecy: it is the cockroach who "gets off duty" by ending up in the flames of the lamp, while Nevyrazimov will clearly be on duty for the rest of his cockroach life.

The conclusion of the story with its premature end to the life of the cockroach brings the reader back to the beginning of the story and to the truncated ending of Nevyrazimov's congratulatory note to his boss. The second sentence in the letter ends with the half-word:"*Zhel*" (I wi..., or, I des...). Nevyrazimov intended to write "I wish you"—followed by a standard expression, such as, "all that is good, all that is best." His "wish," however, was cut off in the middle. The truncated life of the

---

aqan"—"fugitive" ["*beglets*" in Russian]: Turkish "*täz*"—"to run away ["*ubegat'*" in Russian]. See Fasmer, *Etimologicheskii slovar' russkogo iazyka*: 20–21.

[9] For interpretations of the ending of "Small Fry" quite different from my own, see Popkin, *The Pragmatics of Insignificance*: 32; and Freise, *Die Prosa Anton Cechovs*: 26.

cockroach at the end of the story echoes the truncated "wish" of Nevyrazimov's letter. "*Zhel...*" is a symbol of the stunted, incomplete, unfulfilled life of Nevyrazimov. His miserable life is not the life of a *cockroach*, but the *cockroach* life of a man who through a blend of character and circumstance finds himself trapped in a "dark circle," unable to get back to the values of the "family circle," to the family itself, unable to find a refuge or asylum for his needs and satisfactions. Thus the ending of the story brings the reader to the story's point of departure, one that no longer strikes the reader as an entirely comic one.

Chekhov, of course, does not consign Nevyrazimov to heaven or hell. "Perhaps there really aren't any bad people at all among us, but only trashy ones," Dostoevsky wrote in his *Diary of a Writer* (February 1876). "We haven't matured to the stage of bad people."[10] Dostoevsky's remark might have served as an epigraph to Chekhov's story or to this analysis of it were it not for the fact that Chekhov himself is not a moralist or philosopher struggling with the question, "Is man any good?" or suggesting that "If there is no God, all is permissible." In creating his hero, Chekhov neither sentimentalizes him nor turns him into a petty demon. He depicts his life and poses the questions raised by that life.

Nevyrazimov is not a bad man. He is a man swallowed up in the penury and banality of a hum-drum no-win existence. He is a product of the Russian ant-hill bureaucratic state and of the degraded and degrading world of serfdom. At the same time, he is a free man. His tedious life, Chekhov seems to say, will go on for better or for worse, as will the life of those fleeting shadows on the street. What is certain is that in his tragicomic tale, "Small Fry," the author has given evidence of his awareness of the astronomical distance that separates man from the ideal.

WORKS CITED

Bulgakov, Sergei. *Nastol'naia kniga dlia sviashchenno-tserkovno-sluzhitelei.* 2nd edition. Kharkov, 1900.

Dostoevskii, Fedor. *Polnoe sobranie sochinenii v tridtsati tomakh.* L.: Nauka, 1972–1990.

---

[10]"*U nas, mozhet byt', durnykh-to liudei i sovsem net, a est' razve tol'ko driannye. Do durnykh my ne dorosli.*" Dostoevskii, *Polnoe sobranie sochinenii v tridtsati tomakh*: 22:39.

Fasmer, Maks. *Etimologicheskii slovar' russkogo iazyka.* Translated from the German and additions by O.N. Trubachev. Vol. IV. M.: Progress, 1973.

Freise, Matthias. *Die Prosa Anton Čechovs. Eine Untersuchung im Ausgang von Einzelanalysen.* Amsterdam and Atlanta: Rodopi, 1997.

Malaia tserkov'. Nastol'naia kniga prikhozhanina, ed. Valentin Nikitin. M.: Ruskii Mir, 1992.

Molitvoslov. Jordanville, New York: Holy Trinity Monastery, 1976.

Popkin, Cathy. *The Pragmatics of Insignificance. Chekhov,Zoshchenko,Gogol.* Stanford, California: Stanford University Press, 1993.

"Archaic" Constructions in "Ward Six"

VLADIMIR MARKOVICH
St Petersburg State University

S cholars writing about Chekhov's prose have frequently noted the unusual narrative devices in "Ward Six." Abram Borisovich Derman, for example, theorizes that Chekhov used Turgenev's technique as a starting point, and was somewhat surprised to discover in the tale "surveys of the prior lives of the protagonists typical for Turgenev, their detailed psychological characterization, and the unhurried beginning, and in the latter even [...] the old-fashioned suggestion to the reader as if to a living interlocutor to take a stroll with him through the scene of the action."[1] Alexander Chudakov adds to this several important observations regarding the unusual stance of the narrator. For Chekhov's prose of the years 1888–1894 ("Ward Six" was written in 1892) it is atypical for the narrative to contain direct emotional evaluations of what is being depicted. Yet in "Ward Six" (especially the early chapters) the narrator's speech has precisely that characteristic. The signs of the personification of the narrator in the beginning of the tale are unusual and very noticeable, for example his "expressions of his own opinion" (i.e., passages of narrative in the first person singular, references to his own impressions, etc.). It is interesting that the narrating subject found in the first chapters of "Ward Six" is clearly unlike that in Chekhov's later fiction: he considerably exceeds the narrator of the "third period" in the "degree of subjectivity."[2] Thus one cannot speak of a movement forward. Chudakov sums up: "This is not anticipating the future, but rather an unusual recidivism."[3]

The idea of "recidivism" requires further definition, or rather needs to be put in concrete terms. According to Chudakov, in "Ward

---

[1] Derman, *Tvorcheskii portret*: 260.
[2] Chudakov, *Poetika Chekhova*: 76–77.
[3] Ibid.: 77.

Six" Chekhov reverts for some rather incomprehensible reason to narrative forms typical of his work of the early 1880s. It was from that period, Chudakov believes, that those features returned which had already been abandoned in Chekhov's later prose of the late 1880s and early 1890s. Chudakov has in mind the personal tone of the narrative, its emotional colouring, and the active speech behaviour of the narrator as subject. Derman went even further, believing that in "Ward Six" Chekhov reverted to a poetic not at all his own, one that had already left the literature of the period when Chekhov began to write.

Actually, Derman in turn may not have given enough weight to the radical nature of this "back-sliding" to the literary past that he observed in Chekhov's tale. He did not stress that in "Ward Six" it was to the very earliest narrative forms characteristic of Turgenev that Chekhov returned. Apostrophizing of the reader, direct evaluations of characters, emotionally coloured ruminations and comments on the part of the narrator are all used by Turgenev in the late 1840s and early 1850s in *A Sportsman's Sketches*. Later he left all this behind, and by the middle of the 1850s developed a new manner that he considered more objective. In *A Sportsman's Sketches* the subjective activity on the narrator's part is justified in the majority of cases by the fact that he functioned as a personified narrator, playing the role of an eyewitness or even participant in the events depicted. In "Ward Six" one can observe several signs of this stance that shape the form of the tale. For example, in the description of Gromov there are fragments written in the spirit of the judgement of a close acquaintance evaluating the character on the basis of personal observations.[4] But this stance is not maintained to the end: as early as the third chapter it disappears (except for a small case of recidivism at the beginning of chapter five in the description of Ragin[5]). Thereafter the

---

[4] "I like his broad face with its high cheek bones, always pale and miserable, reflecting as if in a mirror the torment of struggle and continual fear in his soul. [...] I like him as a person, polite, helpful, and unusually delicate in his dealings with everyone except Nikita" (S 8: 74).

[5] "They say that in his early youth he was very pious and was preparing for a career in the clergy, and that, upon graduating from high school in 1863 he intended to apply to the theology school, but supposedly his father, a doctor of medicine and a surgeon, laughed at him bitterly and declared categorically that he would disown him if he became a preacher. How much truth there is in this, I

narrator as acquaintance of the participants in the action is decisively driven out by an omnipresent and omniscient abstract narrator placed outside the events who resembles the subject of pre-Pushkinian prose. However, the preceding forms of subjective activity on the part of the narrator are retained (without being justified by his personification) to the very end. In other words, the centre of the narration is occupied by an implicit demiurge, while on the periphery in a series of markers that coincide with the author of "Ward Six" stands Karamzin with his "subjective authorial narrative" (to use Natalya Kozhevnikova's term). However, Derman was probably not wrong in referring to Turgenev, for the devices of the "subjective authorial narrative" first developed in Karamzin's prose were indeed later used in sketches and related narrative genres of the Natural School, to which the Turgenev of *A Sportsman's Sketches* belonged.

They are used in the same way in the initial chapters of "Ward Six," with the difference that the position of the personified eyewitness narrator is not fleshed out, but only imitated temporarily, in order to justify the narrator's leading role in the structure of the narrative and, more broadly, in the organization of the acquaintance of the reader with the depicted world. That role is necessary in the beginning because in the initial chapters, sketch-like structures are dominant. Narratives of the sketch type lack an unfolding dynamic or plot. Sketches are comprised of generalized and hence static descriptions of mores, which means that the depicted object is as immobile as is time itself in the depicted world. The time in which the character-sketches unfold is also immobile, since it involves the exposition of already completed results of observation and analysis. Even the characters' biographies do not transgress this general rule, for they are subordinate to the same generalizing (and hence static) character-sketches, serving only to explain and illustrate them. In the sketch the only dynamic element is the constructive activity of the narrator as he organizes his character-sketches.

This is precisely the situation in "Ward Six," where the activity of the narrator is the only truly dynamic factor over a large part of the tale. The first chapter is comprised entirely of generalized descriptions of the place of the action and the characters. These give an idea of the "aver-

---

don't know, but Andrei Yefimovich himself admitted more than once, that he never felt a calling to medicine and the natural sciences in general" (S 8: 82).

age" existence of the individuals depicted. In the second chapter the narrator introduces the prehistory of Ivan Dmitriyevich Gromov, and by
doing so singles him out from among all the rest. At this point something like a series of events also starts to form when the reader learns
that the habitual norms of this character's life were sharply disrupted
several times. If we accept the opinion of Yury Lotman and his predecessors[6] and view the event as the breaking of an existential norm that defines the usual existence of the character in question, then it would seem
that there are sufficient events here. But the similarity of this expositional
narrative to an event-filled story turns out to be only on the surface, for it
is part of a generalized character-sketch (essentially again a summing
up) as we are reminded by the descriptive characterological fragments
with which Gromov's prehistory is thickly overlaid.[7]

In the third chapter the overall weight of the generalized descriptions is kept to a minimum, the larger part being taken over by the narration of several isolated events (having to do with Gromov's growing
mental confusion). But chapter four brings the narrative back to the task
of sketching those characters not yet described. In this way the reader is
reminded that the story they have been told is part of this initial series of
character descriptions, and not the beginning of any action. The character descriptions continue until we are given at the very end of chapter
four some information that, it would seem, should start the movement of
the plot, namely the spreading of the rumour that Dr Ragin had begun to
visit ward six. The triple repetition of this motif[8] would seem to suggest
its role in forming the plot. But the information about this intriguing vio-
lation of his normal habits (formerly, Ragin never glanced into the psychiatric division) is followed by a generalized description of his life and
thoughts that takes up three whole chapters (five, six and seven). Then,
without any objective plot motivation, the narrator simply "off the top of

---

[6] See Lotman, *Struktura khudozhestvennogo teksta*: 283.

[7] For example: "He was always pale, thin, subject to colds, ate little and slept
badly. From one glass of vodka his head would spin and he would become hysterical. He was always attracted to people, but thanks to his irascible personality
he never became close to anyone and had no friends" (S 8: 76).

[8] "Recently a rather strange rumour went around the hospital. The rumour went
around that the doctor had started to visit ward six. [...] A strange rumour!" (S 8:
82).

his head," as "controller and organizer" introduces one more expositional sketch of Ragin's helper: the young doctor Khobotov. This exposition takes over, and the story of events is unable to get started.

The ninth chapter reverts to the plot development that had been
squeezed out by the sketches, and it seems after all to begin to fulfil its
traditional function of producing conflict (the philosophical argument
between Ragin and Gromov), and it in itself becomes an event. The argument that begins in ward six brings into the open the disruption of
Ragin's normal existence that had formerly been the object of "rumours."
But in the following (tenth) chapter this event is repeated in detail with
the prospect of further repetition in the future (a possibility that is stated
at the beginning of chapter eleven). The sharp disruption of normal existence begins to become the new norm, as much routine as the previous
one.[9] Ragin's arguments with Gromov replace the doctor's daily conversations with the postmaster Mikhail Averiyanovich, and one begins to
have the impression that the tale will never have a real plot.

It is only in chapters eleven and twelve that a breakthrough takes
place, provoked by the appearance of another conflict (this time between
the main character and his environment).[10] A plot finally develops, filling
the last eight chapters. The structure of the narrative changes, coming
closer to the typological features of Chekhov's prose of this period. The
role of dynamic factor previously occupied by the constructive activity of
the narrator is replaced by the unfolding of the plot. The description of
mores that had dominated the time flow in the first ten chapters is replaced by a blow-by-blow time sequence. The depiction of events is limited to the horizon of the main character, most frequently organized
around his internal perspective. Only the last two paragraphs describing
Ragin's funeral are recounted in the form of an impersonal, objective
narrative that describes the scene from without.

---

[9] "He started to visit the ward every day. He would go there in the morning and
after lunch, and frequently the evening darkness would find him in conversation
with Ivan Dmitrievich."

[10] The beginning of the development of the story is signaled here by the information regarding the time of the events described; "One day at the end of June
Khobotov came to Andrei Yefimovich on some business. [...] In August Andrei
Yefimovich received a letter from the mayor with a request to come and see him
on some important matter. [...] A week later it was suggested to Andrei Yefimovich that he take a rest, i.e., retire" (S 8: 104, 106, 109).

Thus the plot develops, but it does so against the background of a massive plotless structure that has already determined the way meaning is to be produced. It is impossible to discard the meaning formed by this structure, for it is inevitably taken into account by the consciousness of the reader as he assimilates the text. There is also one more thing that unavoidably attracts the reader's attention: the plot develops in correlation with the philosophical argument of the two main characters. Of course, this has an impact on the reader's evaluation of the ideas enunciated during the argument and already assimilated by him.

The plotless structure (i.e., the entire system of generalized character sketches, descriptions and biographies) incarnates the idea that the psychology, behaviour and fate of a human being is determined by the objective conditions of the social environment. The narrator sometimes attempts to challenge this idea,[11] but in the absence of any clear alternatives the reader (and here we should recall that we have to do with a reader of Chekhov's time, who needed clear explanations of what was being depicted) was doomed to accept this idea. In the course of the first ten chapters an objective image of the environment is created, describing its impact on the individual and determining the results of its sudden blows and daily pressures. The result is a detailed explanation of two contrasted existential positions that express the main characters' reactions to the monstrous ugliness of the world depicted.

Both reactions turn out to be somewhat inadequate—such is the result of the oppressive effect of the environment. Gromov protests vehemently and goes out of his mind, being incapable of accepting the catastrophic emotional disharmony with reality. Ragin is easily reconciled with the horrors of the existing state of affairs and flourishes amidst them all.

Each of the main characters tries to justify his position using weighty philosophical ideas that are derived from many frequently deeply varying sources. At one pole a hybrid position emerges cobbled out of ideas from the stoics, the cynics and Tolstoy. At the other is an amalgam of motifs derived from various utopian theories—from the concept of progress in the spirit of the 1860s and 1870s to the philosophy

---

[11] This is suggested, among other ways, by the insertion of careful reservations in the description of Ragin's personality quoted above: "they say," "it seemed," "how true this is I don't know," etc.

of Nikolai Fedorov with its idea of victory over death. It is these positions and their underlying bases that clash in the arguments between the
two friends.

Gromov's and Ragin's dialogues are imbued with certain features
generally typical of arguments among Chekhov's characters. On the one
side (that of Gromov) there is a reluctance to participate in the argument,
a nervousness and a certain rhetorical aspect to the polemic. On the other
(Ragin's) side, self-expression and self-justification are more important
than the truth (a frequently encountered feature).[12] However, seen
against the background of the recurring Chekhovian stereotypes, certain
features stand out and sharply differentiate it from most others. The
ideas that clash in the argument are constantly correlated with reality,
which makes them appear as features of that reality and imbues them
with a serious objective significance.

The ideas and the two main characters' attitude to them are tested
by reality, and reality is in turn tested against the ideas and existential
attitudes of the two main characters. In the two first dialogues (in chapters nine and twenty) Gromov seems obviously to be right. He declares
that the philosophy preached by Ragin does not withstand the test of
real violence or real suffering: "You despise suffering, yet all that has to
happen is for you to have your finger squashed in a door, and you
would scream your lungs out!" (104). This is more or less how it happens:

> Andrei Yefimovich lay down and breathed inconspicuously; he
> waited with horror to be hit again. It was as if someone had taken a
> sickle, plunged it into him and twisted it several times in his chest
> and his entrails [...] He jumped up, tried to shout out loud and run
> as quickly as possible and kill Nikita and then Khobotov, the guard
> and the orderly, and then himself, but [...] his legs would not obey
> him; panting for breath he pulled and tore at the dressing gown
> and shirt on his chest, and flopped down unconscious on the bed.
> (S 8: 125)

When the violence reaches the extreme of brutality and cruelty,

---

[12] For an analysis of the typical features of arguments in Chekhov (and in particular the most frequent deviations from the structure of the ideal argument) see
Stepanov, *Problemy kommunikatsii u Chekhova*: 122–143.

Ragin's reactions fully correspond to Gromov's thesis of the normal response of a living creature "to all sorts of provocation." "I respond to pain with shouts and tears, to contemptible behaviour with indignation, to outrageous treatment with disgust. It seems to me that is the essence of what we call life," Gromov insisted. And indeed when Ragin is locked up in ward six for the first time, he behaves almost the same as Gromov.[13]

What is occurring obliges Ragin to recognize the immorality of his attitude to life: "...and suddenly in his head, amidst all the chaos, there clearly flashed the terrible, intolerable thought that it was precisely this kind of pain that these people [the patients in ward six—V.M.] must have felt all these years." We further read: "...conscience, as unyielding and brutal as Nikita, made him break out in a cold sweat from the nape of his neck to the soles of his feet" (ibid.). The doctor's realization most importantly also confirms Gromov's correctness, for the latter had denounced the conformism lurking in his opponent's philosophy.[14]

In short, the reader is struck first and foremost by the reasons that permit one to talk of the "breakdown" of Ragin's philosophy.[15] Ragin's confinement in the ward for the insane, his beating, and then his demise can also be viewed as the reward for his complacency and passivity. However, these conclusions are not all that can be derived from the situation. The last twist in the polemic between Gromov and Ragin (in chapter eighteen) contains some uncontroverted remarks by the doctor, and these interact with the plot to change its meaning somewhat. One of these remarks—in defence of "small fry" philosophizing (already condemned by Gromov and in part discredited by the course of events)— gives an unexpected turn to the entire process of creating meaning in the

---

[13] "'What the devil?' Ivan Dmitrievich shouted suddenly and jumped up. 'What right does he have not to let us out? How dare they keep us here? I believe the law clearly states that no one can be deprived of his freedom without a hearing in court. This is violence! Abuse of authority!' 'Of course it's abuse of authority!' said Andrei Efimych, encouraged by Ivan Dmitrich's shouts. 'I need to leave! I have to leave! He has no right! Let me out, I tell you!' " (S 8: 124).

[14] "A convenient philosophy. You don't have to do anything, your conscience is clear, and you feel yourself to be a wise man. No sir, this is not a philosophy, nor is it thought or broad-mindedness, it's just laziness, hocus pocus, dreamy nonsense" (S 8: 105).

[15] See Tsilevich, *Siuzhet chekhovskogo rasskaza*: 58.

text. Ragin defends the right of the "small fry" to philosophize, basing his argument on the fact that the "small fry" cannot be satisfied in a situation in which "an intelligent, educated, proud, freedom-loving individual, God's likeness, has no other recourse than to be a quack in a dirty, stupid little town, and spend his entire life with jars, leeches and mustard-plasters!" (S 8: 122). Here the concept of "small fry" is replaced by other categories capable of resisting Gromov's views. Clearly, Ragin's arguments can swing the reader in his favour, especially since in the course of the action he himself changes, becoming less and less deserving of Gromov's censorious opinions.[16]

The second unexpected aspect of this stage in the plot is that fact that Gromov's mental illness results from his exhaustion at the struggle with life: "You are intelligent, noble-minded, sucked in good intentions with your mother's milk, but hardly have you begun life than you are exhausted and fall sick... You're weak, weak!" (S 8: 122). It follows that Gromov's madness is something like Ragin's philosophizing—one more defensive response to the debilitating effects of reality.

It is interesting that this view is at least partly confirmed in the course of the action: for Ragin the reasoning conformist (such is his image in the initial chapters) the brutal violence turns out to be absolutely unbearable, whereas Gromov, who constantly experiences tempestuous emotions, continues to live with this situation as he has always lived.

In the course of the argument a paradoxical idea emerges that erases the difference between the opposing positions of the two friends. Both Gromov and Ragin, each in his own way, talk about the difficulty of distinguishing between psychologically healthy individuals and the insane. This leads to another idea, that it is only disturbed minds that are attracted to the "truth" and "the dawn of a new life." On the other hand one can hardly consider mental unbalance an inappropriate reaction to the real state of affairs. Gromov the paranoid goes out of his mind when he concludes that any individual may be deprived of his freedom at any time and without any guilt on his part. And does not the story of Ragin's confinement in ward six not confirm this conclusion? As a result, the image of the world is rendered considerably more complex.

---

[16] On the transformations in the character descriptions of Ragin in the course of the narrative (especially in the final chapters), see Lopushin, *Ne postigaemoe bytie...*: 58–61.

In general, the functions of the two main components of "Ward Six" are quite comprehensible. The plotless structure "loads" the tale with a tendency to an unambiguous representation of the world in which everything is separated out, motivated, and evaluated. The discussions between the two main characters and in particular the interaction of the ideas expressed with the movement of the plot give the tale a different dynamic. Different approaches to what the characters view as objective reality become possible. As this structure with its two components unfolds, it becomes clear why, in the initial chapters of "Ward Six," "archaic" literary forms going back to the traditions of the Natural School are dominant. Chekhov in essence reproduces the structure of certain novels of the 1840s.

The closest work with this kind of structure to Chekhov's tale is Herzen's novel *Who is to Blame?*, the first half of which comprises biographies and character portrayals, descriptions of patterns of life, and so on, whereas the second half is woven out of the interaction between the plot dynamic and the discussions of the main characters. An argument develops against the background of an objective picture drawn by the narration, all the while complicating its meaning.

The interweaving of the conflict between individual and environment presented in part one and the dialogic conflict developed in part two gave *Who is to Blame?* the necessary generic characteristics of openness, internal dynamics and open-endedness. Chekhov too strove for open-endedness and internal dynamics in the depicted world. Consequently he "novelized" his lengthiest tales, giving them "marginal" and "hybrid" generic characteristics so that they occupy a somewhat indefinite place between "large" and "small" epic forms. The use of constructions of this type clearly goes back to the tradition of the novelists of the 1840s.[17] It is however hard to understand why, in order to "novelize" the

---

[17] On this subject it is worth noting that the rationalizing nature of the traditionally used constructions is even increased in Chekhov. In novels of the Natural School the dialogical nature of the conflict underlined the fact that any discussions about reality are relative. Even the deterministic pattern suggested by the "man – environment" antithesis was placed in doubt. The authorial relativism in "Ward Six" is more measured: for example, as stated about, it almost doesn't touch the causal links between the characters' psychology and the effect of that same environment. In other words, Chekhov is closer to the earlier, didactic form of rationalism. This is also somewhat difficult to understand if one considers the

tale, he chose precisely this path, which is based on the mutual definition of two forms of rational interpretation of the depicted world.

The novelists of the Natural School had no other way to novelize their works. The 1840s were one of those literary periods when rational and analytical thought played a relatively distinct role in the process of artistic cognition. The aesthetic potential of the new forms created by the Natural School had not yet emerged and developed to its full extent. The new literature was demonstratively "non-poetic" and as close as possible to the forms of scientific, publicistic and utilitarian writing, having distanced itself from traditional criteria of what makes a literary work. In this situation rational thought naturally constituted the main organizing force of the typical novel of the time. Only the analytical approach (whether imposing a framework or based on a discussion of problems) could impose a unity on the heterogeneous levels of existential material, subordinating them to the framework of the art form, which limited itself to the task of generalizing on a strictly empirical basis. The actual artistic links could evidently arise here only as a sort of surplus that exceeded the requirements of the colliding analytical forms. The collision in turn was necessary in order for the surplus to be produced, since it made possible to escape from the dictatorship of any one of the forms and all of them at once.

In the case of the young Herzen (or the young Goncharov) such structures were the most appropriate ones and for some time even excluded any serious alternatives; Chekhov's situation was however entirely different. He had at his disposal the experience of the literature of "large" forms of the second half of the nineteenth century and had endured along with his generation the crisis of philosophical and artistic positivism. This meant that he could use more up to date, productive and, most importantly, more artistic techniques for creating a dynamically open "novelistic" discourse.[18] Moreover, by the time he was writing "Ward Six," Chekhov had already mastered these techniques, as Alex-

---

general increase in skepticism as a characteristic feature of the intellectual atmosphere of the 1890s.

[18] The importance of the question of the artistic nature of Chekhov's prose is convincingly argued by Tiupa. See his *Khudozhestvennost' chekhovskogo rasskaza*; and *Khudozhestvennyi diskurs (Vvedenie v teorii literatury)*.

ander Chudakov and Vladimir Kataev have demonstrated.[19] Why then did he eschew them here in favour of constructions and conceptions that had become "archaic"? To seek an answer to this question let us turn our attention to the presence in the tale of even more archaic constructions than those we have just examined.

The initial description of ward six (in chapter one) gives rise to certain mythological associations. The building in which the insane are kept is apparently located on the edge of the town (next to it is a field). Since in Chekhov's tale the city is a sort of microcosm of the world, we can say that we are on the edge of the "ecumen." On one side the building is cut off by a fence with nails (i.e., an impenetrable defence), and on the other "by a whole forest of burdock, nettles and wild hemp" (S 8: 72). Then there is another defence hindering access to the ward: "Opening the first door we enter the hallway. Here whole mountains of hospital junk are piled against the wall and around the stove. Mattresses, old torn dressing gowns, trousers, shirts with blue stripes, useless worn-out shoes—all this garbage was piled into heaps, squashed, mixed up, rotting, and gave off an oppressive smell" (ibid.). This accumulation of "junk" (i.e., the corpses of things), and the atmosphere of rot and putrefaction, add signs of mortality to those sensations of being on the periphery. The building is described as if it were a world existing in complete isolation from the usual life of people. One might even get the impression that the denizens of the building (Gromov, for example) do not even know what season it is outside (S 8: 100). All this is reminiscent of features typical of peripheral spaces in horizontal cosmic models of ancient mythologies. Even the vegetation surrounding the building serves as a metaphor for the forest, a reference to magical folk tales in which the forest frequently demarcates the boundary between "this" world and "the other." The mythological parallels become even more apparent when the guardian Nikita appears. His resemblance to a steppe sheepdog is evocative of the mythical hound Cerberus who guarded the entrance to the realm of the dead. This is followed by another association of a similar type, for Nikita, who regularly deprives Moiseika of his pitiful gains, is associated with Charon, the ferryman who exacted a tribute from the dead and deprived them of their belongings while ferrying them across to Hades. In the middle of chapter one the parallels linking

---

[19] See Chudakov, *Poetika...*; and Kataev, *Proza Chekhova*.

ward six with Hades are already clear enough for any reader to recognize. Moreover, the discussion in the ward about the "final questions" creates another parallel of a literary nature, but also laden with mythological allusions, namely the resemblance of the argument to the ancient plot situation "conversations in the realm of the dead," the best example of which being the book of that name by Lucian of Samosata. On the formal level texts of this kind can be reduced simply to a dialogue and nothing more. However, the abundance in such "conversations" of everyday allusions and images of public figures or events of the day can be viewed as a sort of background against which the discussion takes place. Quite simply, two elements that later were separated at this time still constituted a syncretic unity.

Lucian is not mentioned in "Ward Six," but there are three references to Diogenes, the positive hero in Lucian's works and main character in "Conversations in the realm of the dead." Diogenes is twice mentioned by name and once is referred to anonymously, when Gromov recalls that "one of the Stoics sold himself into slavery" (S 8: 102). It was precisely Diogenes who made this step, and Lucian who described it in his satirical dialogue "The Sale of Lives," from which Chekhov may have borrowed the entire situation. In this case, however, it was not Lucian himself who was so important, but that plot situation — or rather that genre — of which Lucian was the classical example and which many centuries later Chekhov used in his own way.

In "Ward Six" (more precisely in the plot structure of the tale) the features of the so-called menippea are self-evident. The first of these is the combination of a philosophical dialogue with a brutal existential and physiological reality: in Ward Six" the latter function is assumed by the shocking disorder reigning in the hospital. As in the menippea the conditions are created here for a test of universal philosophical ideas. It turns out that the ideas of the Stoics and the Cynics, along with Tolstoy's idea of the non-resistance to evil, can be used to justify the conformism and laziness of a provincial doctor who receives a state salary with all the privileges that entails, but still does not want to do anything. The extreme provocativeness of such an estranged view of the concept of authority is almost without precedent.

It is further worth noting the presence in "Ward Six" of another menippean feature: the fact that the psychological abnormality of one of the characters in the tale plays an important role in the testing of the philosophical ideas. The role is a liberating one: Gromov's insanity is an example of the destructive experiences that, in the words of Mikhail Bakhtin, "bring the individual beyond the limits of his fate and his character and reveal the latent possibility in him or her of another person and another life."[20]

There is also in "Ward Six" a typically menippean play with sharply alternating situations or oxymoronic combinations of character traits (such as "the wise fool," etc.). There is a traditional menippean combination of a universal set of problems with motifs of everyday frequency. In short, this profoundly archaic genre provides one of the "integral" constructions on which the tale is based, although it seems to be inserted in a totally different historico-cultural context.

The combination of two traditions that are genetically very far apart—that of the rationally didactic (in the sense of "critical realism") and that of the carnivalesque and playful (oriented towards a dialogic form of literary prose)—was not an isolated phenomenon in the literature of Chekhov's time. Russian literary consciousness still retained a link with the experience of Dostoevsky, in whose novels such a combination was something like a generic canon.[21] But for Chekhov such a link was not characteristic. Even in the 1880s (for example in "An Enigmatic Nature" or "The Swedish Match") he made fun of the author of *Crime and Punishment*, considering his conceptions to be clearly out of date. Given this, the close resemblance of the two writers in this tale seems rather strange. This is especially true since the link between the two types of archaic writing in Chekhov is much more fundamental than those links present in more frequent types of intertextuality of the time. In the tale we have to do with neither reminiscences that imbue the text with certain additional meanings, nor with parody, nor with a polemic with preceding texts, nor with a creative, mutually enriching interaction with such texts. In "Ward Six" the archaic constructions are reproduced in their entirety, carry the entire burden of the tale and are the main elements in the creation of meaning. This historico-literary "inversion"

---

[20] Bakhtin, *Problemy poetiki Dostoevskogo*: 156.
[21] In Dostoevskii's novels the combination of two conflicts was always made more complex by the "polyphonic" nature of the narrative forms. But the initial two-component pattern discussed here was retained and adapted itself easily to the renewal of the narrative structure.

needs explanation and is at the same time puzzling in its strangeness. Such an explanation entails a broad-based special investigation of the text and its context, and is beyond the limits of this article. One can only enunciate here certain hypotheses of a preliminary character.

The simplest of these has to do with the fact that Chekhov sought to express the transhistorical content of contemporary disagreements. The intention was probably to make the reader understand that contemporary issues could easily be examined using artistic principles conceived at periods remote not only from contemporary society, but also from each other. The reader was evidently to feel how what happened thousands of years ago and about which people have thought, argued and written thousands of times, is happening today. Depending on his or her own point of view, this might provoke different reactions—from tragic inspiration to despondency. But in any case a sense of the importance of what was being portrayed ought to be evoked (in other words, a sense of the significance of the "problems of the here and now").

The strangeness of "Ward Six" can be viewed as the product of an experimental improvisation undertaken without any definite goal. Alexander Chudakov has pointed out the experimental nature of the tale, while at the same time making certain reservations.[22] One must evidently concur with his thesis as one of a number of possible solutions.

Finally, one can attribute another meaning to this same "inversion." Despite all the differences between the ancient menippea and the novels of the Natural School, they resembled each other in the way they both established a particular kind of relationship between literature and reality. In both cases the object depicted was placed in immediate contact with reality. Or at least, both genres had as their objective such a contact and at the time of their appearance it was felt that they had achieved it. However, in the beginning of the 1890s Chekhov's prose writings had already shown both authors and readers another way of achieving this type of goal. The sense of contact with reality was now achieved primarily through the "personal narrative situation" (F. Shtantsel's term), by a transposition of the entire depicted world into the perspective of the main character, by the integration of the narrator's voice into the objective narration, and by the identification of the reader with the main character and consequently the initiation of the reader into the depicted

---

[22] Chudakov, *Poetika…*: 77.

world and his involuntary "co-authorship." Seen against the background of such a system of devices, the former techniques for achieving the illusion of reality no longer had the same effect on the reader. What was formerly seen as a literary breakthrough now, when contrasted with the new forms of creating the illusion of reality, seemed simply another type of literary convention. Moreover, since in "Ward Six" the boundaries between the various discourses are not marked out, sooner or later in the reader's consciousness the thought could arise that even the new illusion of reality (that had struck the reading public like a thunderbolt) was nothing more than the latest literary convention that had not yet had time to become the norm. By introducing clearly archaic elements into his artistic system Chekhov evidently was reminding the reader that he had to do not with reality nor with its analogue, but with literature, which by its very nature is always different from reality.

This offered a solution to the question of the reader's freedom, by permitting him to translate his illusions into a "higher state" (to use Gadamer's well-known expression). By realizing the presence of an illusion, the reader was empowered to recognize the virtual nature of its content and distance himself from its hypnotic effect. By the same stroke the issue of the author's freedom was also solved, since by reverting to "archaic" forms and turning them into the basis of his poetics, the author escaped from the necessity of the permanent forward movement of literature. In other words, the author affirmed his right to move in any direction, independently of the requirements of the situation and the somewhat powerful cult of novelty, and independent even of the already fixed logic of his own evolution. These special, uniquely Chekhovian forms of freedom evidently need to be a prime target for further investigation.

Translated from the Russian by J. Douglas Clayton.

WORKS CITED

Aseev, Nikolai. "Kliuch siuzheta," *Pechat' i revoliutsiia* 1925, Kn.7.
Bakhtin, Mikhail. *Problemy poetiki Dostoevskogo*. 2nd ed. M.: Sovietskii pisatel', 1963.
Chudakov, Alexander. *Poetika Chekhova*. M.: Nauka, 1971.

Derman, Abram. *Tvorcheskii portret Chekhov*. M.: MIR, 1929.

Fisher, V. "Povest' i roman u Turgeneva." In: *Tvorchestvo Turgeneva: Sbornik statei.* M.: Zadruga, 1920.

Kataev, Vladimir. *Proza Chekhova: Problemy interpretatsii*. M.: Izd-vo Moskovskogo universiteta, 1979.

Lopushin, R. *Ne postigaemoe bytie…: Opyt prochteniia Chekhova.* Minsk: Propilei, 1998.

Lotman, Iuri. *Struktura khudozhestvennogo teksta.* M.: Iskusstvo, 1970.

Lukian. *Izbrannye razgovory bogov i Razgovory v tsarstve mertvykh.* 3rd. ed. M., 1890.

————. *Sochineniia.* Vyp. 1–3. SPb., 1889–91.

Stepanov, Andrei. *Problemy kommunikatsii u Chekhova.* M.: Iazyki slavianskoi kul'tury, 2005.

Tiupa, Valeri. *Khudozhestvennost' chekhovskogo rasskaza.* M.: "Vysshaia shkola," 1989.

————. *Khudozhestvennyi diskurs (Vvedenie v teoriiu literatury).* Tver': Tverskoi gosudarstvennyi universitet, 2002.

Tsilevich, Leonid. *Siuzhet chekhovskogo rasskaza.* Riga: "Zvaigzne," 1976.

"Ward Six"—the Protagonist and His Idea

ANATOLY SOBENNIKOV
Irkutsk State University

Much has been written about the depiction of ideas in Chekhov. As Alexander Chudakov wrote: "...it is a fundamental principle that an idea does not exhibit all its possibilities and is not explored to the end; neither is its inception identified, nor is its movement traced. [...] The historical and philosophical framework of the idea is minimal. [...] In Chekhov an idea, from the point of view of logic, has no clear authorship, nor is it an exhaustively worked out dogma."[1] Vladimir Kataev has pointed out the principle of "equality of perspective" and of relativity of opinion, its "dependence on circumstances."[2] Igor Sukhikh suggests that "the examination of some 'general idea' or other is conducted in a similar way. It is not challenged by direct logic (which justifies speaking of Chekhov's 'gnoseological approach'). The existential position of the protagonist is subjected to doubt, but in that way the limitation and incompleteness of the idea itself is recognized."[3] On the specifics of ideological disputes Andrei Stepanov writes: "Chekhov's hero is incapable of maintaining the intentional unity of his discourse. The affective, expressive and poetic functions usually overwhelm the informational function, and no truth (a coherent conceptualization of reality) can emerge from such an argument."[4]

The textbook reading of "Ward Six" boils down to the argument between Dr Ragin and his patient Gromov, and to the testing of Ragin's world-view against reality. However, contemporaries of Chekhov already perceived that the very way Chekhov depicts the idea is crucial, and the author's stance vis-à-vis his ideological protagonists is far from unequivocal. Alexander Skabichevsky commented: "Mr Chekhov never

---

[1] Chudakov, Mir Chekhova: Vozniknovenie i utverzhdenie: 315, 317.
[2] Kataev, Proza Chekhova: Problemy interpretatsii: 146.
[3] Sukhikh, Problemy poetiki A.P. Chekhova: 157.
[4] Stepanov, Problemy kommunikatsii u Chekhova: 127.

formulates his ideals in a theoretical manner [...] he is too objective, never once letting on what is the basic thought of the story..."[5] M. Nevedomsky was justified in thinking that "both ideologies lead to one and the same dismal end: ward six." He noted the "atheoretical" stance of the author, and his "alienation from all kinds of social theories in the first place, and in the second, his general distrust of any theory or idea, his skepticism with regard to them."[6]

A reading of the tale leaves a feeling of secrecy, mystery, inexhaustiveness of meaning, and a refusal to explain everything. This feeling itself bears witness to the truly artistic nature of the work, for inexhaustiveness of meaning is a condition of an artistic text. The creative function of a text lies in "the development of a thought, not the communication of a ready made thought."[7] By what mechanisms does the thought develop in the tale? Why does the author need to maintain equal distance and equality of perspective? Why is the philosophical apparatus of the idea reduced to a minimum? Who is Chekhov: a gnoseologist, a natural scientist, an agnostic, a Christian, an ironist, or a stylist? The answer to any of these questions is destined to be limited and incomplete.

In the plot structure of the tale there are two centres: the image of ward six, and the main characters as representatives of specific ideologies. The tale begins and ends with a description of the ward. Both descriptions include the fence with the nails on top, the comparison of the hospital building to a prison, and the motif of the transitory nature of all material things: "Its roof is rusty, half the chimney has fallen down, the steps up to the porch and the porch itself are rotten and overgrown with weeds, and only traces remain of the stucco" (S 8: 72). At the end of the tale the "flame in the bonemeal factory" bears witness to the transitory nature of organic material. Moreover, in the first description it is daytime, and ward six is described in a sociological and existential fashion — both space and time are temporal in nature. In the second description it is night; the protagonist's anxiety, the moon, the "flame in the bonemeal factory" give the chronotope an infernal tinge.

The motif of the transitory nature of everything material links the beginning and end of tale with the dominant theme of the speeches of

---

[5] Skabichevskii,"Est' li u g-na Chekhova idealy? 'Palata No 6'": 145, 147.

[6] Nevedomskii, "Bez kryl'ev," *A.P. Chekhov: Pro et contra*: 813.

[7] Tiupa, *Analitika khudozhestvennogo: Vvedenie v literaturovedcheskii analiz*: 28.

the main characters, namely immortality. Gromov believes in immortality, whereas Dr Ragin does not, although logically it should be the other
way around: Ragin's position on the ideological plane is that of someone
who intended to become a priest ("he had been very pious"), and as an
admirer of Marcus Aurelius ("Marcus Aurelius said..."). Marcus Aurelius did not believe in personal immortality, but rather immortality of
everything: "As a part, you inhere in the Whole. You will vanish into
that which gave you birth; or rather, you will be transmuted once more
into the creative Reason of the universe."[8] Chekhov himself did not accept this kind of immortality ("a la Kant"), and neither does his hero:
"The transubstantiation of matter! How cowardly to console oneself with
this surrogate for immortality!" (S 8: 91). Gromov's stance is that of the
natural scientist and exposer of social evil, but he knows that "God made
[him] out of warm blood and nerves," and as support for his arguments
he refers to Christ, i.e., he has in mind personal immortality.

This is not fortuitous. Chekhov's characters do not possess a well-
thought-out, logical ideology. Both Gromov and Ragin, in the words of
the narrator, repeat "a pot-pourri of old, but not yet exhausted songs."
Chekhov's character description focusses not on the ideas of the stoics,
tolstoyans, positivists or Christians, but their reflection in the characters'
consciousness. The idea manifests itself, becomes a fact of social consciousness, and hence a myth. In "Lights" ("*Ogni*") the "vanity of vanities" referred to Ecclesiastes ("Solomon's 'vanity of vanities'") and is surrounded with an aura of authority. In "Ward Six" "vanity of vanities" is
juxtaposed with "rubbish" ("everything in this world is rubbish and
'vanity of vanities'"). In the text only one small fragment takes the form
of a quotation: "Marcus Aurelius said: 'Pain is the existential idea of
pain: you only have to make an effort of the will to change the idea,
throw it out, cease to complain, and the pain will disappear'" (S 8: 100).[9]
Chekhov's characters are interpreters, using "someone else's words,"
they make them their own; they have not tested the idea through their
own suffering, unlike the characters of Dostoevsky or Tolstoy. Hence the
author through the comment of the narrator labels the characters' ideol-

---

[8] Aurelius, *Meditations*: 66.

[9] Quote checked by A.G. Golovacheva against the copy in the A.P. Chekhov Mu-
seum-House in Yalta (*Razmyshleniia imperatora Marka Avreliia Antonina o tom, chto
vazhno dlia samogo sebia*. [Tula: Tip. Gub. pravl., 1882]: 35–36).

ogy a "pot-pourri."

In the artistic space of the text it is not their opposition that is important, but rather their similarity: both characters are alone, both love to read, both believe in the force of intellect, both are sick, both end up in ward six, and so on. They may be contrasted in the area of their consciousness, but they become equated in life, where health and sickness turn out to be ambivalent, and the ideology of resisting evil is as impotent as is the "philosophy of indifference." Real existence is represented in the tale by the symbolic image of ward six and the generalized, token-like image of the provincial town. Ward six is part of the town, the town—a part of the world. This very formula may be derived from Marcus Aurelius ("My own nature is a rational and civic one; I have a city, and I have a country; as Marcus I have Rome, and as a human being I have the universe...").[10] From a philosophical perspective the image of ward six is not so much a limitation of personal freedom as an inevitability. "Man finds an inevitability in the world; the experience of his impotence teaches him to be a fatalist," comments Alexei Losev on Marcus Aurelius.[11] Chekhov viewed the stoics quite seriously. It has already been pointed out more than once that the idea Chekhov's characters have of the world as a unified whole ("The Student," "On Official Duty," etc.) is derived from *The Meditations*. The plot motif of a withdrawal from the world ("A Teacher of Literature," "At Home," *Three Sisters,* "My Life," etc.) also has a parallel in the position of the Roman stoic: "Whether a man's lot be cast in this place or in that matters nothing, provided that in all places he views the world as a city and himself its citizen."[12] The conclusion of "The Archbishop" refers back to the assertion: "How fleeting are the lives of him alike who praises and him who is praised; of the rememberer and the remembered...."[13] The "tiresome whirl of life" is usually linked with Ecclesiastes, but Marcus Aurelius postulated: "Reflect often how all the life of today is a repetition of the past; and observe that it also presages what is to come [...] The performance is always the same; it is only the actors who change."[14]

---

[10] Aurelius: 101.

[11] *Rimskie stoiki: Seneka, Epiktet, Mark Avrelii*: 358.

[12] Aurelius: 157.

[13] Ibid.: 125.

[14] Aurelius, op. cit.: 159.

The author's "serious" attitude towards Marcus Aurelius obliges us to scrutinize Dr Ragin's "mistakes."[15] In Marcus Aurelius "the achievement of inner harmony, inner order and peace is seen to be the basic and sole objective of philosophy."[16] The path to this objective is difficult, one of the conditions of acquiring inner harmony being tolerance of others. "The chief good of a rational being is fellowship with his neighbours";[17] "[...] a concern for every man is proper to humanity";[18] "Human beings [...] have reason; so treat them in a spirit of fellowship."[19]

In Chekhov the scenes where a character communicates with others are couched in an ironic narrative style. In answer to all Ragin's ruminations on reason Mikhail Averyanovich replies: "Absolutely right," while Daryushka listens to the doctor with an expression of "vacant sorrow." Ragin has neither been able, nor wanted, to "take care of all people." His attitude towards the inhabitants of the town was that of intellectual superiority. One of the most important philosophical motifs in the tale is the absence of communication. There is a tragic paradox in the fact that the only clever person in the town is a madman. At the end of the eleventh chapter Ragin says to Gromov: "If only you knew, my friend, how sick I am of the general folly, lack of talent, stupidity, and what a joy it is each time for me to chat with you! You are an intelligent man, and I delight in you." However, in this passage the narrator directs the reader's attention to Gromov's behaviour: "The madman grimaced, shuddered, and wrapped himself convulsively in his dressing-gown..." (S 8: 105).

The key words or concepts in Gromov's speeches ("dawn of a new life," "truth," "forward") are also couched in the ironic narrative style. The character's pose as he pronounces his speech is overtly theatrical: "Ivan Dmitrich rose up with gleaming eyes and, stretching out his arms towards the window, continued with excitement in his voice: 'My blessing upon you from behind these iron bars! Long live the truth! I am filled

---

[15] These errors have been pointed out by critics. See: Skaftymov, "O povestiakh Chekhova 'Palata No. 6'...": 381–404; Dolzhenkov, *Chekhov i pozitivizm*: 81.
[16] Losev, op. cit.: 455.
[17] Aurelius, op. cit.: 85.
[18] Aurelius, op. cit: 56.
[19] Ibid.: 96.

with joy!'"(S 8: 96). The doctor's main counter-argument is "the coffin" and "the pit" ("No matter what magnificent dawn lights up your life, after all is said and done you will be nailed into a coffin and thrown into a pit" (S 8: 97). It is precisely this argument that is dominant in the tale; against it any ideology or logic is powerless. Gromov states: "... when you are dead workmen will come and drag you by the arms and legs into the basement" (S 8: 121). And indeed, when Ragin dies, "workmen came, took him by the arms and legs and carried him off into the chapel" (S 8: 126).

In Ragin's musings the image of an earth grown cold in "a million years' time" occurs several times. The theme of death leads to the theme of the meaning of human life and the characters' search, not for a "general idea" (which is what they articulate), but the meaning of their personal existence. The artistic and philosophical dominant in the tale is the process of living one's life ("life in general"). After Sakhalin, Chekhov became interested in liminal situations: life and death, health and sickness, the norm and departure from it—namely, crime. The Sakhalin text embodied in "Ward Six" is the search for a model of existence, in which life is truncated and the existential intentions of the personality are reduced. "The violence of the world" that the sick Gromov so fears, and which is personified in the guard Nikita's fists, finally overtakes Ragin as well. However, this does not mean that in Chekhov evil is incarnated in evil people; it lies in ontology, not anthropology. Mikhail Averyanych is "kind and sensitive," while Sergei Sergeich is "religious and loves splendour," and the guard Nikita is one of those "simple-hearted, positive, helpful people"; when he brings Ragin his dressing-gown, he says "quietly": "Here's your cot, please come over here" (S 7: 120). Nikita beats the patients not because he is a sadist, but because he "likes order." And Dr Khobotov is not a villain, he "considered it his duty to occasionally visit his sick colleague" (S 8: 115).

The image of ward six in the tale emerges from the intersection of two cultural codes. On the sociological and existential plane, which is the one corresponding most closely to the "denunciatory" tendency in Russian realism, it can be read as a sketch about the "specialized" situation of medicine in the style of Gleb Uspensky. This group of specialized problems focuses on the staff timetable in the hospital, the conditions in which patients are held, the availability of medicines, issues concerning the repair and maintenance of the hospital, and statistics. We learn that the staff consists of one doctor and an orderly, "until the local council had a fit of generosity and decreed an additional yearly disbursement of three hundred roubles," whereupon one more doctor was engaged. The doctor saw thirty to forty patients a day, and in a year some twelve thousand patients came; conditions in the wards were terrible ("stench," dirt, "soup made of stinking cabbage"); in the surgical department there were "only two scalpels and not one thermometer," and so on.

On the mythological level we find the Christian myths of heaven ("the dawn of a new life") and hell (ward six), a heavenly Jerusalem ("the truth will triumph") and "the unrighteous city." In this context the figure "6" acquires special significance (being the number of the animal of the apocalypse) as well as Christological allusions (Gromov's age). In the town Gromov is regarded as a holy fool ("despite the sharpness of his opinions and his nervousness, they liked him and behind his back gave him the affectionate nickname of Vanya"; S 8: 76). In the attestation scene the doctor describes him as a "prophet." On the level of Christian mythology Ragin receives a saintly role. The narrator emphasizes his poverty; he has no practice, and always wore the same frock-coat; "but this was not out of avarice but rather total indifference as to his appearance" (S 8: 83). In the attestation scene the military head calls Ragin "a monk" ("you don't play cards, you're not partial to women"). Ragin makes Gromov's acquaintance at the end of March ("fully spring"), i.e., during the Easter season. It is precisely this meeting that changes his consciousness and lifestyle. The plot motif of the resurrection of a "dead soul" recalls in the reader's mind the genre of the Easter story. Thus, the code of Russian orthodoxy reveals in the characters the theme of sanctity, otherworldliness and attainment of secret knowledge (both Gromov and Ragin are alien for the inhabitants of the town from the point of view of their values). In the mythological plot the narrator plays the role of mediator or guide into another world ("Opening the first door, we enter the hallway" [S 8: 72]).

The semantics of the "literary city" is even richer. Scholars have revealed in this plane of Chekhov's writing echoes of Dostoevsky, Dante, Gogol, Griboedov and other writers.[20] In our view Gogol is particularly important here. The literary genealogy of the image of a provincial town

---

[20] See: Kapustin, *Chuzhoe slovo...*, 222–228; Durkin, "Chekhov's Response to Dostoevskii..."; Kh. Manolakev, "Palata No. 6 i konets geroia," et al.

(not only in "Ward Six," but also in "My Life," *Three Sisters*, "Ionych," "The Lady with the Little Dog," and "The Bride") goes back to Gogol's *The Government Inspector*. In Gogol the town is run by semi-literate bureaucrats who neglect their direct responsibilities. The doctor's patients die like flies, the judge takes bribes in the form of borzoi puppies, the postmaster opens and reads other people's letters. In the description of day-to-day society and social psychology Gogol doubtless exaggerated. But the hyperbole and symbolism were necessary for him to evoke the "heavenly city" in the reader's mind.[21] Chekhov adopted a similar tack. In his description of the "animal house" and in the comparison of Nikita to a "steppe sheepdog" we sense the features of Gogol's zoomorphism. Just as in Gogol, the city is governed by "semi-literate members of the middle class." In Chekhov the official town departments are the same as in Gogol: the law court (Gromov had served as court bailiff); the post office; the hospital; the town council; and everywhere the rules are broken. The medical service cannot be placed in the hands of the council, for the funds would be embezzled. In the post office Mikhail Averyanovich yells at the customers; in the hospital "the supervisor, the head of housekeeping and the orderly robbed the patients" (S 8: 83). Dr Ragin is sick, of course, but only in a mild way, so that the way he is treated is another example of high-handedness on the part of the authorities.[22]

In the life of his characters the author emphasizes two Gogolian principles: consistency and alogicality. Gromov is *"always* excited," *"always* pale"; in the mornings his mood is *"as always"* gloomy; "he *always* read lying down," etc. Dr Ragin *"usually* […] gets up at about eight"; he *"always* reads with great pleasure"; "next to his book there *always* stood a carafe of vodka"; "in the evening the post master *usually* came over"; and so on. Moreover, this principle extends to ward six and to the life of the provincial town as a whole. "On top of the rubbish the guard Nikita *al-*

---

[21] On Gogol's city as parable, see: Mann, *Poetika Gogolia*, 391–401; Virolainen, *Rech' i molchanie*, 360–373.

[22] V. S. Sobennikov, a doctor of medicine and Irkutsk psychiatrist, made the following diagnosis of Ragin, based on the facts in the text: "A psychotic depressive disorder with elements of 'depressive pseudodementia' and slight cognitive disorder provoked by damage to the blood vessels of the brain, possibly the result of a tumour." In the opinion of this psychiatrist, in the light of this diagnosis the patient had no business being in a ward for schizophrenics (from an unpublished article).

ways lay with a pipe between his teeth"; "little Moisey *every day* goes about the town and begs for alms." In chapter six the description of one day in the life of the inhabitants of ward six is preceded by a commentary by the narrator: "Probably life in no other place was as monotonous as in this wing of the hospital" (S 8: 81).

The principle of alogicality is best expressed in Gogol's phrase: "All is not what it seems." "Being tall and broad-shouldered Ragin's arms and legs were huge [...] but his gait was quiet"; he speaks "not in a bass, as one would expect, but in a thin, soft tenor" (S 8: 82). The orderly Sergey Sergeich was "more like a senator than an orderly" (S 8: 86). Gromov "was attracted to people," but "had no friends," he talked "about women and love passionately, with rapture, but had never once been in love" (S 8: 76). Ragin "was preparing for a career in the clergy," but became a doctor. He "loves wit and honesty, but does not have the character and belief in himself necessary to organize his life in an intelligent and honest way. [...] he feels guilty, but still signs the accounts" (S 8: 84). Syntactical constructions with the contrastive conjunction "but" convey the gap between the character's inner "I" and his social role, the disconnect between the man and his life.

In Chekhov the illogicality of reality is complemented by the illogicality in the consciousness of the characters. Dr Ragin is pursued by an eschatological vision of the cooling earth a million years hence, and "he threw up his hands and stopped going to the hospital every day" (S 8: 85). It does not enter his head that in a million years he will not be alive, that one should live "here" and "now." Gromov, on the other hand, who will now never leave the hospital ward, "greets the dawn of a new life." The boundary between ward six and the rest of the world turns out to be illusory. The fifth denizen of the wing has an "intelligent, peaceful gaze"; he "keeps his own counsel and conceals some very important and pleasant secret" (S 8: 81). This secret consists in the fact that the former letter sorter "had been recommended for the order of Stanislas second class with star." But how is this different from the orderly, who "resembles a senator"? It would seem that in the system of characters Ragin and Khobotov are represented as antitheses, but with one detail the author makes them equal: of all the medical journals, Dr Ragin has a subscription "*only to The Doctor*," while Khobotov "has *only* one book: *The Latest Prescriptions of the Viennese Clinic for 1881.*" Ragin is indignant that from the capital ("where there is no intellectual stagnation, where there is progress") they have sent Dr Khobotov ("for some reason they always send us such people as are horrible to behold" (S 8: 98). But then again, Ragin himself was also "sent," so that this evaluation applies to him as well.

"Ward Six" is also unusual from the point of view of the quantity of numbers it contains, and the variety of the numerical symbolism. The figure six of the title breaks down into the following natural figures: 1, 2, 3, 4, 5, 6. It is curious that these figures accompany Ragin both in life and in the spiritual and ideological sphere. Ragin had lunch at three, drank beer after four, put out his lamp at three at night. The house of Mrs Belov, his middle-class landlady, where he lives, has three rooms. When he takes his trip with Mikhail Averyanovich they travel two hundred versts in two days, and spent two nights on the road. Two years ago "the local council had a fit of generosity" and assigned three hundred roubles.

In Ragin's ruminations attention must be paid to the figure one, expressed in various forms based on the Russian *odin* ("one"). For this character it has the meaning of the realization of the self: "How pleasant to lie motionless on the divan and feel one is the only one in the room! True happiness is impossible if you are not one *alone*. The fallen angel probably betrayed God because he wanted to be *alone*, something that the angels do not experience" (S 8: 111). Paradoxically, Dr Ragin is added to the five patients in the ward (5+1=6). It was precisely Ragin who was needed to complete the contingent in the ward, where it is totally impossible to be *alone*. Only death will bring him the desired isolation (*odinochestvo*): "There he lay on the table with open eyes, and at night the moon lit him up" (S 8: 126).[23]

The figure "one" also occurs in the number 1,000,000, which is the sign of the protagonist's eschatological expectations. This figure is mentioned three times in the tale. The first time it occurs in the high-flown language of a lyrical, pathos-filled internal monologue: "'Oh, why is man not immortal?' he thinks, 'Why do we have brain centres and convolutions, sight, speech, a sense of self, genius, if all this is destined to disappear into the earth and ultimately grow cold along with the earth's crust,

---

[23] This Chekhovian detail testifies to the existential loneliness of the character. Despite the fact that he is in a Christian country, no one cared to close the eyes of the deceased. It was only on the following day that the orderly Sergei Sergeich thought to do so.

and then with neither rhyme nor reason circle around the sun for a million years along with the earth?'" (S 8: 90). The second and third times are stylistically different: "If we imagine that in a million years some sprite will fly past the earth, all he will see is clay and bare rocks. Everything — culture and moral law — will have disappeared and will not even be grown over with burdock. [...] But such considerations were no longer helpful. Hardly had he imagined to himself the earth's sphere in a million years, than from the bare rock Khobotov appeared in high boots or a tensely laughing Mikhail Averyanovich..." (S 8: 116). Khobotov and Mikhail Averyanovich (1+1=2) remind the hero about the "here" and "now," from which one can hide neither in the house of the bourgeois Belova, nor in Ward Six.

The figure "6" is one of those numbers that determine the fate of the hero. Ragin had graduated from high school in 1863, at a "sacred," in the hero's words, time. But Ragin was a man of the sixties only in the literal sense, not in spirit. He had only 86 rubles left when he returned from his trip to Warsaw. The monetary figures are most probably fortuitous, but their abundance, of course, is not. When Gromov was studying in St Petersburg he received 60–70 rubles from his father. Apart from issues of heredity (his brother died of consumption, and he himself "was subject to colds" and "slept badly") his lack of a social position played a considerable role in his illness. After his father's death his accustomed pattern of life was interrupted, and Gromov found himself without money. The author has Doctor Ragin follow the same path as Gromov. Upon retirement he too found himself without money (he had saved 1000 rubles, loaned 500 to Mikhail Averyanovich, spent 414 on his trip, and all that remained was 86 rubles, less 32 to pay off the beer debt). Day-to-day existence consists of humdrum details, including the daily settling of accounts, and day-to-day responsibilities. Chekhov's artistic conception confirms the ambivalence of day-to-day existence and humdrum details, and any ideology sooner or later turns out to be just "opinion," i.e., a subjective view of things.

Thus in "Ward Six" it is not ideology, but the consciousness of the characters that is depicted. The narrator's task is to demythologize this consciousness, and his irony is his way of distancing himself both from Ragin's "philosophy of indifference," and Gromov's social activism. We have to do here with "the readiness or unreadiness of an individual for a creative, responsible existence in this world."[24] At the same time, the ethical idea of "responsibility" does not save the individual from existential isolation, and from the world of ward six.

Translated from the Russian by J. Douglas Clayton.

WORKS CITED

Aurelius, Marcus. *Meditations.* Translation by Maxwell Staniforth. Middlesex, England: Penguin Books Ltd., 1975.

Chudakov, A.P. *Mir Chekhova: Vozniknovenie i utverzhdenie.* M.: Sovetskii Pisatel', 1986.

Dolzhenkov, P. *Chekhov i pozitivizm,* 2nd ed. M.: "Skorpion," 2003.

Durkin, Andrew. "Chekhov's Response to Dostoevskii: The Case of 'Ward Six'." *Slavic Review,* 40 (1981): 49–59.

Kapustin, N.V. *Chuzhoe slovo v proze A.P. Chekhova: zhanrovye transformatsii.* Ivanovo: Ivanovskii gosudarstvennyi universitet, 2003.

Kataev, V.B. *Proza Chekhova: Problemy interpretatsii.* M.: Izd-vo Moskovskogo universiteta, 1979.

Losev, A.F. *Rimskie stoiki: Seneka, Epiktet, Mark Avrelii.* M.: Terra-knizhnyi klub, 1998.

Manolakev, Kh. "Palata No. 6 i konets geroia," in: *Dialozi s Chekhov: 100 godini pok'sno* (Sofia, 2004): 114–122.

Mann, Iu.V. *Poetika Gogolia: variatsii k teme.* M.: Coda, 1996.

Nevedomskii, M. "Bez kryl'ev," in *A.P. Chekhov: Pro et contra.* SPb.: Izd-vo Russkogo khristianskogo gumanitarnogo instituta, 2002.

Razumova, Nina. *Tvorchestvo A.P. Chekhova v aspekte prostranstva.* Tomsk: Tomskii gos. universitet, 2001.

Virolainen, M. *Rech' i molchanie: siuzhety i mify russkoi slovesnosti.* SPb.: Amfora, 2003.

Skabichevskii, Aleksandr. "Est' li u g-na Chekhova idealy? 'Palata No 6,' 'Rasskaz neizvestnogo cheloveka',"*A.P. Chekhov: Pro et contra.* SPb.: Izd-vo Russkogo khristianskogo gumanitarnogo institute, 2002.

Skaftymov, Aleksandr. "O povestiakh Chekhova 'Palata No. 6' i 'Moia zhizn',"*Nravstvennye iskaniia russkikh pisatelei.* M.: "Khudozhestvennaia literatura," 1972.

Stepanov, Andrei. *Problemy kommunikatsii u Chekhov.* M.: Iazyki slavianskoi kul'tury, 2005.

---

[24] Razumova, *Tvorchestvo A .P. Chekhova:* 293.

Sukhikh, Igor. *Problemy poetiki A.P. Chekhova*. L.: Izd-vo Leningradskogo universiteta, 1987.

Tiupa, Valerii. *Analitika khudozhestvennogo: Vvedenie v literaturovedcheskii analiz*. M.: Labirint, RGGU, 2001.

Restor(y)ing Health: Case History of "A Nervous Breakdown"

CATHY POPKIN
Columbia University

This paper is predicated on Chekhov's interest in both how we account for things and how we frame our accounts. While Chekhov's wariness of ready-made paradigms is well established,[1] there is no form of inquiry without form. Chekhov's writing might usefully be looked at as an exploration of the possibilities and pitfalls of form-giving as a means of understanding: as a writer's exploration of the exegetic capacity of diverse genres; as an artist's consideration of the expository potential of different media; and as an artist-doctor's examination of the diagnostic procedures brought to bear by different disciplines.

"A Nervous Breakdown" ("*Pripadok*," 1888; S 7:199–221) gives us all of the above: a proliferation of professional points of view (featuring a medical student, an art student, a law student with an additional degree in the natural sciences, and a practicing psychiatrist); it gives us operatic and dramatic performance vying with the narrative prose; and it supplies an account that is simultaneously short story and case history. The object of these diverse interpretive practices is the most elusive one: somebody else's pain. We watch the hero's adventures in sense-making as he attempts to establish *"kakuyu formu pridat voprosu"* (how to formulate the question; 207) when confronted with *chuzhaia bol'*, that consummate challenge to cognitive mastery. Chekhov foregrounds the dilemma of the inquiring subject by *framing* Vasiliev's inquiry into the anguishing problem of prostitution in several ways—firstly, and strikingly, by encoding it in the same symbolic register he uses to describe his own research trip to Sakhalin Island, figuring the pursuit of knowledge as an epic journey to uncharted terrain, and imagining the brothels as the bleak mysterious shores of a dark continent. Consider the aria (from

---

[1] Most elegantly by Vladimir B. Kataev, in his *Proza Chekhova: Problemy interpretatsii.*

Dargomyshky's *Rusalka)*—"Against my will to these sad shores ..." —that Vasiliev and his two friends intone compulsively en route to the infamous S. *pereulok* [S. Street; 202–205].

There is a literal frame to "A Nervous Breakdown" that gives it an institutional "framework." The story begins with the appellation "student" and ends by naming the destination "university"; note how it introduces its principals in the first paragraph:

> Medical student Mayer and student of the Moscow School of Painting, Sculpture and Architecture Rybnikov dropped in one evening on their friend, law student Vasiliev and invited him to go with them to S. *pereulok*. For a long time he could not be persuaded, but in the end he put on his coat and set off with them. (S 7: 199).

First and foremost we are accosted by their academic status and field; their names take third billing to their university credentials and institutional affiliation. The degree of specification here is extraordinary, especially given the long name of the institute.

Whether the point of this is the juxtaposition of disciplines, or whether the thrust of this barrage of academies is to contrast the institutional with the personal experience of knowledge, the text is surely crafted as a descent from an ivory tower to a personal, epistemological hell, and back to the university at the end. Vasiliev leaves the halls of academe for extramural research; his collapse during his field work conducted far away from his institute might be read as a function of the unaccommodated position from which he attempts to know his object.

On the other hand, he's hardly unaccommodated. Consider the second paragraph—this establishes the discursive frame, detailing what Vasiliev already knows about the object of his impending investigation:

> He knew fallen women only by hearsay and from books and had never in his life been in those "houses" where they lived. He knew that there were such immoral women who were forced by fateful circumstances—their environment, poor education, poverty, and the like—to sell their honour. They never know pure love, never have children, have no civil rights; their mothers and sisters mourn them as if they were dead, science treats them as an evil, men address them familiarly. But in spite of all that, they do not lose the image and likeness of God. They all recognize their sin and hope

for salvation. There are any number of means to salvation they can avail themselves of to the broadest extent. It is true that society does not forgive people for their past, but to God, St. Mary of Egypt is no less sanctified than the other saints. Whenever Vasiliev happened to recognize a fallen woman on the street by her outfit or her mannerisms or see a picture of one in a comic journal, he would always recall the same story he had read somewhere at sometime or another: a pure and selfless young man fell in love with a fallen woman and proposed to her, but she considered herself so unworthy of such happiness that she poisoned herself. (S 7: 199)

This frame is essentially a catalogue of clichés on the subject of prostitution garnered from rumour, sentimental fiction, popular culture, the rhetoric of social determinism, legal jargon, and Christian writ. If paragraph one establishes university disciplines, paragraph two gives us public discourses more broadly—all the stuff "he had read somewhere at sometime or another." Indeed, Vasiliev's competence in the matter of prostitution consists of a veritable cacophony of discourses ultimately not unlike the *"zvukovaia putanitsa,"* the chaotic tangle of music, of S. *pereulok*—"sounds that came flying out of all the doors and combined in a strange muddle that sounded as if, somewhere in the dark above the roofs, an invisible orchestra were tuning up" (S 7: 202–3). Without form, there is only confusion. The aria the students are singing "out of synch with one another" (*"ne v takt drug drugu"*; S 7: 202) only completes the discordant symphony of discourses.

What closes this "discursive" frame on the other side of the story is the episode with the psychiatrist, who plies his own research practices and diagnostic discourses, equally muddled and equally out of rhythm with his object.

All three frames address the problem of form-giving as sense-making, foregrounding the paradigms we bring to bear in our attempts to make sense of things, and understanding is definitely the issue. Vasiliev and his friends visit several brothels and, for all the voyeuristic potential of a sequence like this, Chekhov presents us chiefly with the spectacle of Vasiliev trying to figure out prostitution and understand prostitutes: "It's essential to understand them; yes, I must try to understand" becomes some kind of mantra for him. Eros, in short, is supplanted by his "burning desire to find out" (*"silnoe zhelanie uznat"*; S 7:

205–207).

Interestingly, Vasiliev's research agenda has a significant dia-chronic component, and not only because he looks forward for a solu-tion, a *razviazka*. "*Zadacha*," he stipulates repeatedly: "*Kak oni popali siuda?*" ("The problem to solve: how did they wind up here?" [S 7: 207–209]). How did innocent girls come to be prostitutes? What is the connec-tion between the present and what preceded it? How was "then" trans-formed into "now"? What is the story?

The *form* the question takes, then, is not just the "*kuda?*" (where to?) of where do we go from here, but an almost obsessive "*otkuda?*" (from where); and "*otchego?*" (as a result of what?) and "*kak?*" (how); and "*radi chego?*" (for the sake of what?); and "*zachem?*" (to what purpose?). We are used to the "*kak?*" that gives us the open ending of "Lady with the Little Dog," but this story emphasizes that which points backward to what precipitated the action: "*Kak oni popali siuda?*"—how did they wind up here? Our determined investigator inquires about motivation ("For the sake of what do they sin?"; "What do you come here for?"); he craves explanations ("why is it that they're not ashamed?"); he tries to account for process ("Where was he before and what did he do?"); he wonders about origins ("By means of what treachery was the fallen woman felled?"). Vasiliev's indefatigable "*otkuda*" (where from?) reaches back into the very preconditions of prostitution: if only he could find a way to "save" the men who frequent brothels, there would be no more call for prostitutes and S. *pereulok* would spontaneously cease to be. Vasiliev subscribes wholeheartedly to the laws of cause and effect (If you run down the stairs, *ottogo* [as a result] your legs will feel tired; if you drink tonight, *ottogo* your head will hurt in the morning). There has got to be some logic to what people do. The prostitutes ask customers to buy them drinks, he learns, expressly because they're instructed to do so by the proprietor, who stands to profit from the sale. "Why in the world don't you leave here?" he wants to know.

The questions are easier asked than answered, however. Further-more, despite Vasiliev's well-documented proficiency in scientific rea-soning (S 7: 215), Chekhov emphasizes the debilitating difficulty of the hero's cognitive enterprise by showing us vividly the mental, emotional, even physical prostration that results from his efforts to account for the how, whence, and wherefore of prostitution: cognition, or attempted cognition, is followed by collapse. The added fact that his hysteria is chronic not only suggests that there *are* no ready solutions to the problems he seeks to redress, but also emphasizes that the problem here resides in S, the knowing subject, rather than in this or that particular object of knowledge "p."[2] So what is his problem?

Most apparent is the complete dissociation of this "S" from his "p." All those symbolic terms in which Vasiliev envisions his research (the sad shores of a dark continent), the professional affiliations of which he boasts, and the cultural discursive arenas in which he is adept) seem to sever intellectual proficiency from direct, personal knowledge. There is no epistemological connection between the subject Vasiliev and the object of his inquiry, only a profound disconnect. He can whistle all the Dargomyzhsky, amass as many advanced degrees, and recall as many brothel narratives as he wants, but the fact remains, as he sings his way to S. *pereulok*, that he has no personal knowledge of prostitutes.

However, once he gets there he does have a response—a visceral one, the physical symptoms of his emotional distress. Perhaps Vasiliev, who is profoundly sentient, is being offered up as a challenge to the late nineteenth-century cult of objectivity, the faith in empirical observation, documentation—all the impulses visible in experimental science and other data-gathering disciplines that might be brought to bear in a concerted effort to "understand" and "figure out.'" Against his era's fetishization of objectivity, Chekhov gives us Vasiliev, whose chief "talent" is precisely subjectivity. As the famous passage at the end of the story puts it:

> One of Vasiliev's friends once said that he is a talented person. Talent comes in many forms—literary, dramatic, and artistic—but his talent is of a very special sort: a "humane" talent. He possesses a fantastically keen sensitivity to pain in general. As a good actor reflects in himself the movements and voices of others, Vasiliev is able to reflect in his own soul another person's pain (*chuzhuiu bol'*). Seeing someone's tears, he cries; if he's around a sick person, he himself becomes ill and groans; if he sees violence, it seems to him that the violence is being inflicted on him; he gets scared and runs for help. Someone else's pain irritates him, arouses him, and produces in him a state of ecstasy, and so on. (S 7: 217)

---

[2] I refer to the proposition "S knows that p," analytic philosophy's formulation of epistemological possibility.

The narrator goes on to say "Whether that friend was right I don't know." Certainly he is correct in that Vasiliev assumes other people's pain. The narrator's description of Vasiliev's propensity accords perfectly with what we've just witnessed ourselves. When a woman in the brothel is slapped around, Vasiliev becomes upset because he is certain that people are trying to beat him. When he is knocking his head against the wall over the solution to prostitution, it is because he has imagined that he is first the brother of a fallen woman and then the father, and then that he is the fallen woman herself—which makes the problem he sets out to solve "not someone else's, but his very own" ("*ne chuzhoi, a ego sobstvennyi*"). So much for making sense of *chuzhaia bol'*.

Where the friend mentioned above might not be so right, in other words, is in asserting that Vasiliev's prowess is such a talent. The upshot of his spurious identification with the victim is that he cracks up. This is pathology, not prescription and, moreover, for all of Vasiliev's much vaunted "feeling" (*chuvstvo*) there is not a shred of empathy. Vasiliev is only disgusted by the fallen women: he has all kinds of feelings about them, but his procedure is pure objectification; he cannot conduct a conversation with one, cannot elicit a single story of "*kak ona popala siuda.*" Not only does he not solve the problem of prostitution he so grandiosely undertakes to address—he does not understand the experience of a single prostitute. Rather, he usurps their subjectivity, makes their pain his own, and renders them speechless, affectless, and story-less. The prostitutes cannot be grammatical, emotional, or anatomical subjects any more than they are legal ones—which makes Vasiliev ultimately as guilty of "killing" prostitutes as are his sexually active friends.

This, I think, is another part of the key to Vasiliev's epistemological failure—the obliteration of the subjectivity of the object of knowledge. While affect may be a step in the right direction, Vasiliev's radical subjectivity objectifies as much or more than the medical student's objectivity does. It is a kind of solipsism, a confirmation that the self can know only the self. Indiscriminate conflation is no better than dissociation; if dissociation severs connections, subsuming the other precludes them. Understanding is a matter of connecting dots, not erasing them.

So where does this leave us? If the story is just about the failure of inquiry, why does Chekhov go to so much trouble to slog through Vasiliev's mental constructs, his physical sensations, his objectivity, subjectivity, and even his potentially valuable line of questioning if they all come up empty? For this we have to go back to interrogate the original sequence I set up—cognition and attendant collapse—which describes the basic shape of the story. What makes Chekhov's story infinitely more interesting and much less defeatist is that, along with cognition and collapse, it is also about collapse and cognition, that is, collapse and self-cognition. It is charged with understanding collapse, with making collapse meaningful, with determining where *it* came from (and *otchego*), how it took shape, and what kind of form of account might adequately account for it. The attack proper comes late in the game and the consideration of prostitution takes up a lot of textual space. Yet the title, "the nervous breakdown," hovers over us the whole time and forces readers to consider its origins and development as they go along. The breakdown is coming into being as the title is coming gradually into its own.

The object of desired knowledge, in other words, is not just prostitution, but also hysteria, not just *padshikh* (fallen women), but also *pripadochnykh* (hysterics); the story gives us both Vasiliev's attempt to understand and an attempt to understand Vasiliev. There are two pathologies to investigate here, two forms of *chuzhaia bol'*, the ultimate test of comprehension. The position for S, then, is not necessarily the one on S. *pereulok*, and prostitution is not the only p. We have seen the way Vasiliev's mental constructs and emotional urges fail to account for, describe, save, or even know prostitutes. The story evinces an equally pressing need to invent an effective mode of discourse: a form in which to account for and describe, perhaps cure, the *chuzhaia bol'* of emotional disturbance; to find a way, narratively, even clinically, of reassembling pieces of mind.

Thus, I think that among other things Chekhov's story has to be seen as a response to prevailing psychiatric practice and as a kind of corrective to the genre—the poetics, as it were—of the psychiatric case history. Chekhov read such histories avidly in the newly minted medical and psychiatric press in the 1880s, especially those that appeared in *Vrach* (*The Physician*), with particular attention to case studies of hysterics, and notably the growing number of accounts of male hysterics.

The end of the nineteenth century was a moment of transition in the study of hysteria, a paradigm shift from the neurological understanding of the disease as brain and nerve dysfunction to a psychological paradigm that attributed hysterical symptoms to emotional disturbance rather than physiological causes. The Russian psychiatric arena still leaned heavily toward the neurological model, although Russian psychiatrists were beginning to gesture toward a kind of "semiotics of suffering" that would recognize the etiologic force of emotional trauma and its translation into physical pain. I. R. Pasternatsky, the leading Russian theoretician of hysteria at the time, defined the disease as *"vyrazhenie stradaniua vsei nervnoi sistemy."*[3] Hysterical fits were "expressions", or signs, of suffering (albeit of a nervous system rather than of a self). Significant for us, and for Chekhov, is how the clinicians read those expressions and how they chose to write them.

First, the Russian case studies place an inordinately high premium on objectivity. They are also formulaic. After a brief introduction comes the account of the case itself, set in closer type, as if to suggest that this is now pure data, untainted by any unseemly subjectivity on the part of the observer. The small print itself is divided into three parts: first, the *anamnesis* (literally, an act of remembering; the medical history of the patient [the *otkuda*—whence]); second, the *status praesens*, which enumerates the patient's (primarily physical) symptoms and records in detail the results of the initial examination (reflexes, measurement of skull, quantity of urine passed, sensitivity of skin, and so forth (the *chto*—what); and third, we get, the *decursus morbi*, which chronicles the progress of the treatment (the *kuda*—whither).

As for the *anamnesis*, "acts of remembering" notwithstanding, there is very little reminiscing or recovery of a personal past discernible in most of these patients' medical "histories." *Anamnesis*, it turns out, is important principally in establishing *nasledstvennost'* (heredity): what in the patient's past—or rather who—can be used to document a genetic proclivity toward nervous disorders (the psychiatrists loved to turn up an epileptic sibling or a parent who was prone to fainting). Organic explanations take clear precedence over emotional ones, neurology continues to edge out psychology, and, as a result, narrative content is at a minimum. Indeed, connections (other than family ones) are seldom mentioned in the *anamnesis*. The section is "diachronic" insofar as it proceeds in chronological order, but it makes little effort to discern progressions from one state to another, to craft connections between "episodes," or to link "then" and "now," to establish how the patient got "here" from "there"—*otkuda i otchego*. Above all, there are no correlations drawn be-

---

[3] Pasternatskii, "Istero-epilepsiia": 49.

tween the emotional "suffering" (then) of these patients and their regrettable "symptoms" (now), Pasternatsky's eloquence about the "expressiveness" of hysteria notwithstanding. Never do the voices of the patients themselves sound, and rarely do we hear what counts to the self. The hysterical self is thus doubly effaced and silenced: first by the disease and its fits and aphasias, second, by the discourses that diagnose it. (It is a far cry from Freud's "talking cure.")

Part two, the *status praesens* (or, the clinical report of the patient's symptoms), is not a record of "what ails you?" any more than the *anamnesis* answers the question "how did this come about?" What drives the *status praesens* is hysteria, not the hysterical patient. The protocol for the examination is set not by what the individual exhibits but what the disease stipulates, and what is recorded is rather the presence or absence of each classic symptom in the given case. "Present status" thus refers less to how well a patient is than to how well he or she fits the bill: is the patient a bona fide hysteric, or not?

The examination thus really is an "objective investigation" for the *status praesens* admits no suffering subject. The patient is scanned, placed on a grid, and his or her disease is charted to see whether it qualifies as hysteria. Connections are fully severed here not only between symptoms and story but also between symptoms and self.

Like their predecessor Charcot, Russian psychiatrists focus on those visible, clinical signs that make knowledge about the patient a matter of seeing from the outside at a particular moment and snapping a clinical picture. The alternative, a more "narratological" procedure, would elicit in words what has befallen the patient over a period of time, overcome the dissociation between then and now, and reconstitute a clinical story.[4] The narratological method, which privileges plot over image, views the patient as a bona fide subjectivity with a coherent story to tell and demands knowledge of that individual, not just a classificatory grid.

As for the *decursus morbi* (the course of treatment), the less said

---

[4] If pain has a history, so does the juxtaposition of narrative and pictorial treatments of pain. See, most famously, Lessing's comparison of the verbal and visual depictions (in epic poetry and classical sculpture, respectively) of the terrible destruction of the Trojan Laocoon and his children. "Laokoon oder über die Grenzen der Malerei und Poesie": 165–326.

about the jets of cold water aimed at this or that part of the body, the better. Suffice it to say that the prescriptions recorded in this section bear little relationship to the patient's symptoms, let alone to the suffering that produced them: the dissociation is absolute. Nor is there much narrative in the chronicle of successive days of treatment, since significant improvement was rare and progress was scarce.[5]

These psychiatric case histories are lampooned quite explicitly in Chekhov's concluding chapter, set up as interview (*anamnesis*), examination (*status praesens*), and treatment (*decursus morbi*) in the psychiatrist's office. The psychiatrist sets the tone by welcoming Vasiliev. With "Come in, I've heard so much about—your disease." In good classificatory form, he has focused on the syndrome, not the sufferer. The taking of the medical history (explicitly called *anamnesis*) is a caricatured witch hunt for neurasthenic relatives (which even the patient lays bare). And although the doctor *is* posing questions, they are uniformly useless ones; also, he directs them to Vasiliev's friend rather than to Vasiliev. Altogether, he learns nothing, but writes down a lot.

The physical exam he then conducts comes right out of the standard *status praesens*; he is fixated on the reflexes in Vasiliev's knees, the *chuvstvitelnost'* of his skin, "*i prochee*," a concise way of invoking the whole standard checklist of symptoms. As it turns out, the only classic symptoms that are present are facial asymmetry and motor abnormality, and these are attributed to the psychiatrist, not to Vasiliev: the doctor smiles with only one side of his face. In an inspired parody of empathy, Chekhov afflicts his psychiatrist with the symptoms the latter seeks in his patient—a nice twist on Vasiliev's compulsive usurpation of *chuzhaia bol'*.

The psychiatrist is, however, an easy target, and the coda in his office is only the coup de grace. From the very beginning the story presents a case history that achieves what the ones in *Vrach* do not, for although the authors of the case histories Chekhov read asserted the expressiveness of hysterical symptoms (seeing them as "signs" of emotional trauma), they had not for the most part been able to put that insight to constructive use by reconstructing and telling patients' stories. But narrative, belletristic or otherwise, is the only way to address the question Va-

---

[5] For a fuller discussion of specific cases, see my "Hysterical Episodes: Case Histories and Silent Subjects":189–216.

siliev had formulated as his own *zadacha* (problem to solve): "*Kak oni popali siuda?*"—how did they wind up here?

Vasiliev himself admits that he is a failure at eliciting the stories of his fallen interlocutors. The best *anamnesis* he can put together is a chronology of breakfast, lunch, and dinner at the brothel and the only point of origin he can adduce is geographic, not emotional. The authors of the case histories exhibit the same failing in their determined severing of present symptoms from past suffering, even though the former ostensibly "express" the latter. We do not see how a single breakdown came about. The elision of the question "*kak oni popali siuda*" is what makes the case studies troubling (and not much of a conduit to understanding).

This failing in the psychiatric case study is, I believe, what Chekhov attempts to rectify by harnessing narrative himself. Not that narrative per se is sufficient—I think of Katherine Mansfield's appropriation of "Sleepy" that eliminates the flashback that helps account for the conversion of a young girl into a baby murderer.[6] Nor is Chekhov writing case history per se. That is, however, the discursive register he begins with—his frame—and he *is* improving on it. Moreover, he actually conceives of his fictional accounts as individual "cases" (*sluchai*). Chekhov offers his story as a form of inquiry, analysis, and diagnosis of how "that" became "this"—an attempt to understand and convey *kak Vasiliev popal*—how and and why he had a great fall and what it felt like to him, rather than just what it looked like from the outside once it was at its most intense.

Chekhov manages this by starting well before the attack itself (which doesn't materialize until the penultimate chapter) and allowing the self to unfold—or degenerate—before our eyes. He describes a true anamnesis. We hear Vasiliev's voice, we feel his pain; in short, Chekhov makes the symptoms "expressive" and the attack intelligible by returning to the victim his own subjectivity. He thus succeeds where Vasiliev had failed with his fallen women, where the psychiatrist had failed with Vasiliev, and where the case histories founder with hysteria at large, in reading and describing *chuzhaia bol'*. As revisionary case history, the story actually attempts to counteract a number of the forms of dissociation fostered by the discourses it draws upon: the severing of past and

---

[6] See Katherine Mansfield's story "The Child-Who-Was-Tired." I am grateful to Carol Flath for this connection.

present; the classic dissociation of mind and body; the separation of visually observable symptom from story of origins; and the rivalry of divergent but wholly compatible discourses like the narrative and the clinical, the belletristic and the scientific. Also, as successful case history, it establishes a viable epistemological connection between the inquiring subject and the suffering object by making sense of the latter's pain without appropriating it wholesale.

This story, which is both a critique of the way accounts of suffering are framed and an attempt to frame such an account itself, is richly suggestive for Chekhov's poetics and hermeneutics in several ways. The first is in its proposition that giving form to pain (whether one's own or someone else's) is the only hope not only of connection and communication, but also of diagnosis and treatment, that narration and representation are not alternatives to medical science but essential to it. Secondly, it scrutinizes a particular kind of form, one that plays out in time—namely narrative—and it is committed to a kind of temporality that is not just chronological, but logical, composed not only of sequences but of consequences: the formal representation of *kak* this, that, or the other, *popalo siuda*, how that got to be this—*otkuda* (from where), in other words, and *otchego* (as a result of what)? The third example is in the story's predication precisely on connection—between, for instance, past and present, between self and other (cast as the confrontation with somebody else's pain, whether as doctor and patient or storyteller and audience). We are reminded of "The Student" (1894), where someone else's pain becomes comprehensible expressly through the linkage of present and past. Importantly, though, Chekhov insists not on the *identity* of then and now, the repetition of the past in the present, but on development, evolution, how we got here *from* there.

Wolf Schmid suggests that Ivan Velikopolsky's radiant conclusion—that Vasilisa cried because "Peter is close to her," that the present is connected to the past in an unbroken chain—is *erroneous* precisely because it mistakes equivalence for contiguity: Vasilisa's betrayal of her daughter is essentially a repetition of Peter's disavowal of Christ, rather than any evidence of proximity and connection between woman and apostle, and her tears pertain to her own situation rather to than Peter's anguish.[7] Vasilisa's distress is not entirely unrelated to Vasiliev's pro-

---

[7] See Schmid's extremely suggestive reading of Chekhov's story in his "Modi des

pensity to make *chuzhaia bol'* his own. Authentic connections are forged, rather, in the *transformation* of past to present, the transition from health to pathology and, with any luck, back again. Therapeutic value (not to mention narrative worthiness) seems contingent on the working out of a plot, a syntax, the apposite conjunctions and connections—not just the tipping of paradigmatic equivalents onto a syntagmatic axis.

This is what is wrong with the kind of typology harnessed by the *status praesens*: it is substitutional rather than developmental. It just plugs in a different subject rather than drafting a diachronic account. It is what is wrong with heredity as etiology for hysteria (in terms of repetition and eternal return, not derivation): Mother was, hence I am. This is also what is wrong with appropriating someone else's pain, which is Vasiliev's ostensible "talent." If you appropriate someone else's pain, it is without foundation, without a development, without syntax. It is ready-made, full-blown; it *popala niotkuda* (landed here from nowhere). Dissociation of this sort even pinpoints what is wrong with replacing one pain with another, as Vasiliev does when he contemplates suicide to take his mind off his current distress. Another example would be serially replacing one man with another, as Chekhov's "Darling" does, compulsively repeating what she does not understand and attempting to still a pain whose origin she cannot divine.[8]

Chekhov's penchant for narrative continuity, development, and progression in the face of iteration is what makes the psychiatric case study as crafted by Chekhov's contemporaries a logical target for a critique of both how suffering is read and how accounts of it are written. It is also what authorizes psychoanalytic readings of *both* psychopathology and prose fiction. Such interpretations represent hermeneutic efforts to articulate ("tactfully," as Shoshana Feldman would say, rather than vulgarly,[9] and "in synch" as Chekhov might put it, rather than as "confu-

---

Erkennens in Čechovs narrativer Welt": 534–536.

[8] I have suggested elsewhere that Olen'ka's successive attachments and bereavements might be read as a repetition compulsion born of a repressed sense of loss connected with one or both parents. "Chekhov's Corpus: Bodies of Knowledge": 60–64.

[9] In Feldman's discussion, "vulgar" means not "indecent" or "unrefined," but "literal" and vulgarity consists of the reduction of ambiguity and the elimination of the indecision that inhabits meaning. "Turning the Screw of Interpretation": 106–10.

sion") the connections repressed or muddled by the text (and/or its troubled characters), to put together what's not said, reconstructing a coherent and compelling *anamnesis*, making logical and psychological sense and restor(y)ing health.

The present has a density, like a text; and just as in Chekhov's texts the *razviazka* (conclusion, denouement) is prepared from the very beginning, as is the present moment the coagulation of everything that came before. The failure to retain one's personal history is crystallized in the colossal failure of memory of Yakov ("Rothschild's Fiddle," 1894), whose dissociation from his past is complete, and whose pain is sublimated into his music and manifested in his obsessive tallying of financial losses and his otherwise inexplicable and disproportionate hatred of Rothschild. Only in the recuperation of that repressed past and the reestablishment of the links between then and now, between the suffering of long ago and the pathology of today, can Yakov begin to forge any human connections in the present.

Not to privilege origins; to fetishize a "first principle" would be as misguided as to lose track of it. The Biblical stories that seem to engage Chekhov most do tend to be etiological narratives that account for why things are the way they are, but without a "creationist" insistence on an ultimate beginning; a "creation *ex nihilo*." Rather than enshrining discrete, miraculous moments, Chekhov gives us a view of the human condition as very much "subject to chance and time"[10]—*evolutionary*, developmental, continuous, cumulative.[11] Admittedly, this is a peculiar claim, given that Chekhov explicitly does not write *Bildungsromane*, and we have come to think of him precisely as the master of the single moment. However, if moments are pregnant, there is a story about how they got that way.

The dissociation from the past in its most extreme form produces the amnesia of a Yakov; elsewhere it consigns one to the parodic Ouija board-like conjuring of dead ancestors practiced by Ariadne's vaporous brother, who summons up bodiless spirits from the distant past to forecast an unattainable future ("Ariadne," 1895).

---

[10] Aileen Kelly has probably been the most explicit about the Darwinist spirit of Chekhov's take on life. See her *Views from the Other Shore*: 181–88.

[11] In this respect, Chekhov's (good) news takes the form of the historical and ethical *becoming* of Luke's Gospel rather than the eternal *being* of John's.

The fact is, we do have bodies, and these are perhaps the most indelible reminders that we are creatures in and of time. How much more poignant for someone whose bodily "conclusion" is being accelerated by the ravages of a disease that is irreversible, whose anamnesis can have only one denouement. But all life consists of one-way traffic, and any single moment, full as it may be, is already yielding to the next. Chekhov knew that, and he kept not one, but two calendars. The first is the kind that shows today's date only, yesterday's page having already been torn off and tomorrow's as yet obscured by today's; the second calendar, in monthly format, counteracts that dissociation of today from the days that precede it, embedding any individual "today" in continuous sequence with the days already experienced and those soon to come.[12] Chekhov's conviction about the complementarity of synchrony and diachrony is perhaps most conspicuous there in his bedroom in Yalta, where time is inscribed in more than one form, where *"present status"* is framed by bona fide *anamnesis* and potential *decursus morbi*. When life stories are ongoing and individual episodes are connected, psychiatry has a leg to stand on, and our *byloe i dumy* (past and thoughts) take on narrative form.

Interestingly, in a recent essay in the *Times Literary Supplement*, Galen Strawson argues forcefully and persuasively against the commonly held view that "human beings experience their lives as a narrative or story of some sort...this is how we are, it says, this is our nature." Moreover, according to this widespread assumption, "a richly Narrative outlook on one's life is essential to living well, to true or full personhood." Strawson makes no bones about his feelings on this score: "It is not true that there is only one way in which human beings experience their being in time. There are deeply non-Narrative people and there are good ways to live that are deeply non-Narrative": the proclivity to narrativize is neither natural nor inherently "good. "[13]

The crux of Strawson's argument is that even in remembering past experiences, not everyone perceives them as having been experienced by the same self who perceives in the present; there is no continuous con-

---

[12] Michael Finke is the one who has taken note of the double system of calendars Chekhov maintained. See his comments in the Conclusion to *Seeing Chekhov*: 187–88, 230.

[13] Strawson, "A fallacy of our age: Not every life is a narrative": 13.

sciousness that links then and now. It is an age-old riddle: can the adult be construed as the same person as the child learning to walk? Think of all those Thebans stymied by the Sphinx's demand that they name a creature that walks on four feet in the morning, two feet in the afternoon, and three feet in the evening. Is the self always and forever the same self? What is the significance of change?

"A Nervous Breakdown" is built around this tension between the same and not the same, continuity and discontinuity. Can you reform prostitutes? Invariably, we hear, they forsake the sewing machines of their magnanimous reformers and return to the comfortable routine of the brothel (once a prostitute, always a prostitute). Chekhov reminds us, however, that they have not always been prostitutes; they fell here from somewhere else. Moreover, the index of success of the one example of real reform is that in the angelic wife and mother she becomes, there remains no recognizable trace of the "fallen" being she was before.

Indeed, "A Nervous Breakdown" is a story (and a case study) because Vasiliev is "not himself": illness (pathology) is constitutive of narrative precisely because it represents something abnormal, different, and eventful, as opposed to the continuation or repetition of the same old thing. Falling ill, as a patient does, or falling from virtue, as a prostitute has, is an apt metaphor for the narrative event, something significant happening—just as The Fall (with a capital F) expelled Adam and Eve from the never-never land of Eden into the vicissitudes of history. Understanding a story is tantamount to diagnosing the hero's ailment, figuring out both what makes and breaks connections, what makes him discontinuous with himself.

"Ariadne," as a framed story, plays explicitly on the relationship between the present moment (Shamokhin on board ship telling his tale) and the events that precede it (his account of *"kak on popal siuda"*). For although the story may be about the wily title character, it is more of a case study of the first-person narrator and how he came to be the raving misogynist who tells the tale. There is a glaring disconnect between the innocent young man of the internal tale and its pontificating narrator. In a story that claims to be about the difference between men and women (*"Zhenshchina est' zhenshchina, a muzhchina est' muzhchina"* ["A woman is a woman, whereas a man is a man"; S 9:117]), much more interesting than the contrast is the identity claim, the assertion that a=a. "A man is a man" is problematic, not only because the naive Shamokhin is so different from his cynical rival, but because he is so different from himself: Shamokhin does not equal Shamokhin.

If Strawson is right in hypothesizing that there are two kinds of people (Diachronics and Episodics) and two types of personalities (Narrative and non-Narrative), surely Chekhov belongs to the first in each pair. Despite the fact that he tells aspiring writers to throw away their expositions, Chekhov's prose traces pathways *ottuda-siuda* (from there to here)—narrative ones, neurological ones, emotional ones, and physical trajectories; and, while the image is spatial, the movement is across time, from then to now, as a precondition to where we can possibly go from here. No matter how graphic and well developed the snapshot of the *status praesens*, there can be no *decursus morbi*, no treatment, no intelligible denouement, without a viable *anamnesis*. Without narrative, "you can't get there from here." It is the synaptic structure that enables the synoptic move of diagnosis and treatment, comprehension and interpretation—all of which makes "A Nervous Breakdown" the consummate "*Sluchai iz praktiki*" ("Case From the Practice," 1898), a richly elaborated case study for a number of interpretive practices, including our own.

WORKS CITED

Feldman, Shoshana. "Turning the Screw of Interpretation," in *Literature and Psychoanalysis: The Question of Reading: Otherwise*, ed., Shoshana Feldman. Baltimore: Johns Hopkins University Press, 1977: 94–207.

Finke, Michael. *Seeing Chekhov*. Ithaca: Cornell University Press, 2005.

Kataev, Vladimir. *Prosa Chekhova: Problemy interpretatsii*. M.: Izdatel'stvo Moskovskogo universiteta, 1979.

Kelly, Aileen. *Views from the Other Shore: Essays on Herzen, Chekhov, and Bakhtin*. New Haven: Yale University Press, 1999.

Lessing, Gotthold Ephraim. "Laokoon oder über die Grenzen der Malerei und Poesie," *Lessings Werke in fünf Bänden*. Berlin: Aufbau-Verlag, 1975.

Pasternatskii, Dr. I. "Istero-epilepsiia," *Vrach*, 1881, no. 3.

Popkin, Cathy. "Chekhov's Corpus: Bodies of Knowledge," *Essays in Poetics* 18, September 1993: 44–72.

————. "Hysterical Episodes: Case Histories and Silent Subjects," in *Self and Story in Russian History*, eds. Laura Engelstein and Stephanie Sandler. Ithaca: Cornell University Press, 2000: 189–216.

Schmid, Wolf. "Modi des Erkennens in Čechovs narrativer Welt," in *Anton P. Čechov—Philosophische und religiöse Dimensionen im Leben und im Werk*, eds. V.

Kataev, R.D. Kluge, and Regine Nohejl. München: Verlag Otto Sagner, 1997: 529–536.

Strawson, Galen. "A fallacy of our age: Not every life is a narrative," *Times Literary Supplement*. October 15, 2004.

Ionych the Decadent

YURY DOMANSKY
Tver State University

T he story "Ionych" (1898) is one of the most anthologized of Chekhov's works. Consequently, the study of this text in schools has produced a tendency to interpret in a one-sided way both the story and its eponymous hero and produced a reading focusing on the ethical problems in the text. As Georgy Berdnikov put it, in "Ionych":

> Chekhov depicted "the drama of the disintegration of a man, his absorption into the prevalent social system. [...] Without noticing it, he [the main character—Y.D.] was overcome by a life that was hateful to him, and turned into one of the most repulsive, terrible, self-satisfied members of society. The story of Ionych is very striking. Never before had Chekhov shown so clearly the lethal danger of compromising with the existing system, and subordinating oneself to the reigning customs and accepted morality."[1]

However, even Berdnikov could perceive in the youthful Startsev several possibilities: "Ionych does not make his peace with the hypocritical small-town world; not only that, in the beginning he even tries to talk about progress, freedom, and the importance of work in a person's life."[2] We would like to focus here precisely on the image of Dr Startsev at the outset of his life's journey, and in the area not so much of ethical problems, but of aesthetics.

The motivation for this investigation is to be found in one of the episodes in the story, namely the cemetery scene:

> He walked for about half a verst through the open country. The cemetery could be seen in the distance in the form of a dark stripe, like a forest or a large garden. The white stone wall and the gates

---

[1] Berdnikov, *A.P. Chekhov*: 434–435.

[2] Ibid.: 435

became visible... In the moonlight one could read over the gates: "The hour will come, and in that..." Startsev went in through the wicket gate, and the first thing he saw was the white crosses and monuments on both sides of the broad alley and the black shadows formed by them and by the poplars: and all around into the distance could be seen the white and the black, and the sleepy trees bent their branches over the white shapes. It seemed brighter here than in the fields: the maple leaves, like paws, stood out sharply against the yellow sand of the alleys and on the slabs, and the inscriptions on the monuments were clear. At first Startsev was struck by the fact that he could see now for the first time in his life, and what he probably would never happen to see again, the world, not like anything else, the world, where the moonlight is so beautiful and soft, as if this were its cradle, where there is no life, no, no, but in each dark poplar, in each grave could be felt the presence of a secret that promised a quiet, beautiful, eternal life. From the slabs and withered flowers, together with the autumnal smell of the leaves, came the fragrance of forgiveness, sadness, and peace.

All around was silence: the stars looked down from the sky in deep reconciliation, and Startsev's steps rang out so sharply and inappropriately. And only when the church clock started to chime and he imagined himself dead and buried here for ever, did it seem to him that someone was looking at him, and for a moment he thought that this was not peace and quietness, but the numb melancholy of oblivion, suppressed desperation...

Gemetti's monument in the form of a chapel, with an angel on top: once in the town of S. an Italian opera had traveled through and one of its singers had died, they had buried her and erected this monument. Already no one remembered her, but the votive lamp over the entrance reflected the moonlight and seemed to be lit.

There was no one. And indeed, who would come here in the middle of the night? But Startsev waited, and, as if the moonlight was warming the passion in him, he waited passionately and imagined kisses and embraces. He sat for about half an hour by the monument, then walked along the side alleys with his hat in his hand, waiting and thinking about how many women and girls lay buried here in these graves, how they had been beautiful, charming, had loved, and had burned at night with passion as they surrendered to caresses. How bad it is in essence the way Mother Nature mocks humankind, how hurtful it is to realize this! Startsev thought this, and at the same time he wanted to shout out loud that he wanted, was waiting, for love, whatever the cost.: in front of him it was no longer chunks of marble that gleamed, but the whiteness of beautiful bodies; he could see their shapes bashfully hiding in the shadow of the trees, could feel their warmth, and this torment became hard to bear...

And as if a curtain had come down, the moon went behind a cloud, and suddenly everything went dark all around. Startsev hardly found the gates—it was already as dark as on an autumnal night— then he wandered around for an hour and a half, looking for the lane where he had left his horses.

This scene has more than once been the object of analysis, beginning with the work of Dmitry Ovsyaniko-Kulikovsky:

Chapters one and two are written in such a way that the reader can already sense the vulgarity, emptiness, routine and prose of these people, their life, even the love of Startsev himself; but all this is as it were covered with a light covering of poetry,—you can feel its feeble influence colouring the joyless prose of this life; you can follow this influence and observe how it strengthens and grows and finally in the scene in the cemetery [...] reaches a peak. This is where the "poetry" ends, and from chapter three on to the end there is only solid "prose," the unvarnished, undisguised, cruel prose of life, depicting for us the growing staleness of the soul of the young doctor [...]. The basic idea, which I have tried to elucidate in this article, emerges clearly and powerfully in the consciousness of the reader, because he receives it not just intellectually, but as a feeling. This feeling is complex and peculiar. It is the particular *mood* of a soul evoked by the masterly depiction of the fragile and timid substance of "poetry" as it languishes in a dry and prosaic soul, and as it were its swan-song at the cemetery, juxtaposed with the all-powerful, all absorbing, triumphant "prose" of life.[3]

In the 1950s Maria Sosnitskaya, taking up the same refrain as Ovsyaniko-Kulikovsky, applied the epithet "poetic" to the description

---

[3] Ovsianniko-Kulikovskii, "Etiudy o tvorchestve...": 480–481.

of the cemetery scene:

> "Startsev at the cemetery" is one of the most poetic pages in Chek-
> hov's works and the most poetic moment in Startsev's life [...]. This
> exquisite example of the fusion of man with nature in all the full-
> ness of interpenetration is not simply the personification, but the
> "humanization" of nature, a feature characteristic of Chekhov's
> landscapes, when nature is included in the action and begins to live
> jointly with the protagonist [...]. The illusion ends, the most in-
> spired page in Startsev's life is closed, and reality claims its rights.[4]

As we can see, the unusual nature of this scene in the context of
the entire story and particularly the image of Ionych was noted early
on. The divergence of perspective between Startsev-Ionych[5] in the
cemetery scene (and in this scene, as Vladimir Markovich notes, "the
point of view of the protagonist is most sharply perceived precisely as a
point of view"[6]) and the generally accepted meaning of the image of
Ionych in the tale is most striking.

Here are some other scholarly opinions concerning the divergence of perspective:

> The three hours spent by Startsev in the cemetery are the most in-
> tense, most alive period in his life: his senses of vision, smell and
> hearing pick up the slightest details of his surroundings [...]; his
> thoughts, feelings and imagination work intensely, transforming
> what is dead into what is alive, cold into warm, extinguished into
> flame, resurrecting the past and racing towards the future. His
> range of emotions is broad: the mood of sadness and peace, alter-
> nating "by the minute" with a feeling of numb melancholy of non-
> existence, is driven out and conquered by passionate expectation
> and a thirst for love [...]; the mystical idea of a secret promising "a
> quiet, beautiful, eternal life" — an unearthly, other worldly one —
> alternates with a feeling of the beauty and eternity of life — earthly,
> fleshly, hurly-burly existence...[7]

---

[4] Sosnitskaia, "Ionych" i "Vishnevyi sad"...: 10–11.

[5] We should remember that we learn the name of the hero "Ionych" only in the
final part of the story.

[6] Markovich, "Pushkin, Chekhov...": 30.

[7] Tsilevich, *Siuzhet chekhovskogo rasskaza*: 223.

...everything in the scene in the cemetery that is associated with the overcoming of death and oblivion is marked by the spiritual presence of the observer, his ability to "make human" what had become impersonal, and to resurrect the forgotten.[8]

When a gnawing love is born in the soul of Dmitry Ionych Startsev, the alien secret of personal existence becomes open to him: in the cemetery he sees for the first time in his life a special world where "in each grave can be felt the presence of a secret."[9]

The frivolous girlish joke—to set a rendez-vous in the cemetery—gave him the possibility of seeing for the one and only time in his life "a world like no other, a world in which the moonlight is so beautiful and gentle," and touch a secret "promising a quiet, beautiful, eternal life." The magical night in the old cemetery is the only thing in the story that does not bear the stamp of the everyday, of routine. It alone remains disturbing and unrepeatable in the hero's life.[10]

---

[8] Lapushin, Ne postigaemoe bytie...: 43. It is interesting how Lapushin analyzes "the Gemetti monument": "Here everything is significant: the fact that the opera was Italian, that it had just been traveling through this remote town of S at 'some time,' and that no one remembered the actress who had died there. Are these, so to speak, final, incontestable truths? It turns out not. It takes moonlight. It takes a person. It takes the two of them to come together. And then the 'votive lamp' over the entrance 'lights up,'the oblivion is no longer valid. [...] Death and immortality do not simply coexist. Death and oblivion exist on the map of the world from the very beginning. Immortality, memory needs still to be acquired. But even what is acquired does not have an absolute character. It is knowledge that one cannot pass on—not only to the following generation, but even to the following moment of one's life. This is the question to which in Chekhov no one succeeds in obtaining a final answer. Perhaps it is precisely in the face of the insolvability of this question that so many heroes capitulate without question, rushing to cast off this unbearable burden? And it is with the same unquestionably that the melody of inextinguishable humanity passes from one protagonist to another, a humanity understood as the will to instill a spirit in the surrounding world" (op. cit.: 43–44).

[9] Tiupa, Khudozhestvennost'...: 55.

[10] Kataev, "Startsev i Ionych": 13. Cf. the remark from an earlier work of Kataev's analyzing the thoughts of Gurov (in "The Lady with the Little Dog") on "the

In the cemetery Startsev "lives through minutes of a certain vision, of discovery of something formerly unknown and the need to somehow change one's life"; "Being at the cemetery is like an examination for the hero. Startsev is offered the choice of love and beauty or—on the other hand—existential pragmatism; a spiritual world opens up to him, but Startsev runs away from it..."[11]

The self-evident unusualness of the scene at the cemetery, the "aesthetic subtext" it contains, has led some scholars to seek possible links between this scene and preceding developments in art. Nikolai Kapustin convincingly argues that the scene in the cemetery should be related to the "churchyard" elegy, which leads him to an extremely interesting interpretation:

> The hero of the "churchyard elegy," which for a little while Startsev becomes, is transformed into a lover whose carnal drive compares favourably with that of Pushkin's or Batiushkov's lyrical heroes: "Pressing lips to burning lips, / Embracing lovers then to die" [Aleksandr Pushkin: "Liubov odna—vesele zhizni khladnoi..."] or "O ecstatic flame! O passion's intoxication! / O voluptuousness... oblivion of self, of all!" [Konstantin Batiushkov, "Revenge: From Parny"]. "The beautiful bodies," chaste forms hiding in the shadows of the trees, which appear to Startsev's inflamed imagination, can be fully related to the lyrics of the anthology: "The virginal goddess's round form. / In all the greatness of its gleaming nakedness, / I saw between the trees above the waters clear" [Afanasy Fet, "Diana"]. Another parallel is possible which perhaps even more precisely reveals the feeling that seizes Chekhov's hero: "The burning attire slipped down ever lower, / and the young breast was more and more revealed, / and the passionate eyes, drunk with tears, / moved slowly, filled with desire" [Afanasy Fet, "Vakkhanka"].

---

lofty goals of existence": "Almost the same feelings that Gurov experiences 'in view of this fairy-tale surrounding—sea, mountains, clouds, broad sky,' are felt by another of Chekhov's heroes, Dmitrii Startsev, in the only moonlit night in his life in the cemetery in the town of S. At a given moment Laevskii, Ionych, and Gurov each experiences lofty thoughts and thinks about the eternal..." (Kataev, *Proza Chekhova*: 265).

[11] Zorkaia, "Motiv 'smirennogo kladbishcha'...": 172, 173.

Kapustin continues: "The erotic impulse experienced by Startsev in the cemetery is not clinically pathological. The movement of his experiences [...] first and foremost bears witness to his 'breadth' [...], his tenuous balance, confusion, contradictoriness, and the rapid transitions in his world-view."[12] A somewhat different genesis for the scene in the cemetery is offered by N.F. Ivanova, who examines the romance "Night" ("Your voice for me is languorous and tender") which is featured in "Ionych": "Beyond the 'frame' of the story the romance begins to be heard, creating a second, lyrical plane, a poetic background against which the events of the epic work develop." As a result Chekhov, "through his use of the romance 'Night' imbues the most poetic, 'pivotal' scene in the story with the flavour of a romance." The scene in question is that in the cemetery. Finally, "... in Chekhov's narrative itself there is a constant switching between two planes, as if two principles were in collision—the fragile, poetic, exalted, and spiritual, and the prosaic, soberly calculating, crude element, which in the end wins out."[13]

Alexander Smirnov goes even further in his analysis of the *poetic* through its cultural genesis when he examines the cemetery scene. Like Ivanova, he turns his attention to the romances in "Ionych"—"Night," to verses by Pushkin, already discussed, and "When, o soul, you sought..." to verses by Delvig. This scholar comes to the following conclusion: "The feeling of beauty and peace that enters him [Startsev—Y.D.] at the cemetery turns out to be the most inspired pages in his life, and for a moment he becomes a poet; this is the peak of his happiness. It is not by chance that the next day he is still in that state of 'intoxica-

---

[12] Kapustin, "O metamorfozakh malykh zhanrov...": 112, 114. Cf. another comment by the same scholar: "The story 'Ionych' uses the same traditions of the 'churchyard' elegy, whose sources in Russian literature go back to Zhukovskii's translation of Grey's 'Elegy in a Country Churchyard.' In this thesis there is an analysis of the episode where the hero finds himself in a cemetery. The doctorant identifies the features of the 'churchyard' elegy (motifs, images, stylistics) in the given episode, and at the same time stresses its rapid disappearance from the hero's consciousness, explaining this by the Chekhovian concept of the 'mediocre' individual who is inconstant and shaky in his ideas about life" (Kapustin, "*Chuzhoe slovo*"...: 35–36).

[13] Ivanova, N., "K poetike chekhovskoi prozy...": 110, 111.

tion' that is the dream of poets"; "Startsev for a moment becomes a poet; everything that surrounds him in the cemetery presents itself to him in an aesthetic light [...]. For a moment he had touched the secrets of human existence, about which the romantics spoke so much."[14]

Let us accept the proposition that in the scene in the cemetery Startsev becomes a poet. Already on the basis of this we can deduce that the story "Ionych" enshrines not only the ethical, but also the aesthetic views of the author. But *what kind of poet* does Startsev become? Alexander Smirnov suggests that he becomes a romantic poet. Can one however limit oneself to that sole "diagnosis"? Let us examine one micro-episode in the cemetery scene:

> He sat for about half an hour by the monument, then walked along the side alleys with his hat in his hand, waiting and thinking about how many women and girls lay buried here in these graves, how they had been beautiful, charming, had loved, and burned at night with passion as they surrendered to caresses. How bad it is in essence the way Mother Nature mocks humankind, how hurtful it is to realize this! Startsev thought this, and at the same time he wanted to shout out loud that he wanted, was waiting for love, whatever the cost: in front of him it was no longer chunks of marble that gleamed, but the whiteness of beautiful bodies; he could see their shapes bashfully hiding in the shadow of the trees, could feel their warmth, and this torment became hard to bear...

Two elements in this micro-episode are linked to Charles Baudelaire's *Les Fleurs du mal*, in particular his famous poem "Une charogne." Let us compare these elements with the translation of the poem (entitled "Padal") by Petr Yakubovich-Melshin, made in 1880:

Chekhov:
> "...thinking about how many women and girls lay buried here in these graves, how they had been beautiful, charming, had loved, and burned at night with passion as they surrendered to caresses. How bad it is in essence the way mother nature mocks humankind, how hurtful it is to realize this!"

Baudelaire:

---

[14] Smirnov, "Romantika Pushkina...": 98, 99.

И, однако, и вам этот жребий грозит –
Быть таким же гнилым отвратительным сором,
Вам, мой ангел, с горячим румянцем ланит,
     С вашим кротко мерцающим взором!
Да, любовь моя, да, мое солнце! Увы,
Тем же будете вы… В виде столь же позорном,
После таинств последних уляжетесь вы
     Средь костей, под цветами и дерном.[15]

Chekhov:

"…in front of him it was no longer chunks of marble that gleamed, but the whiteness of beautiful bodies; he could see their shapes bashfully hiding in the shadow of the trees, could feel their warmth, and this torment became hard to bear…"

Baudelaire:

И неслась над ней музыка странная. Так
Зёрна хлеба шумят, когда ветра стремлением
Их несет по гумну; так сбегает в овраг
     Говорливый ручей по каменьям.
Формы тела давно уже были мечтой,
Походя на эскиз, торопливо и бледно
На бумагу набросанный чьей-то рукой
     И закинутый в угол бесследно.[16]

True, this translation of "Une charogne" was not included in the edition of *Les Fleurs du mal* published in 1895 with an introduction by Konstantin Balmont and no mention of the name of the translator.[17] Only in the edition of 1909 prepared by Yakubovich himself was "Une charogne" included. In his introduction to the 1909 edition the translator noted: "My first translations of Baudelaire began to be published in 1879 (in the magazine *Slovo*), but I completed the main work significantly later (1885–1893) in the fortress of SS Peter and Paul, in Kara and Akauta."[18]

    To be sure, we have not managed to discover "Une charogne"

---

[15] Bodler, *Tvety zla*: 95.

[16] Ibid.: 94.

[17] See Bodler, *Stikhotvoreniia*…

[18] Iakubovich-Mel'shin, "Ot perevodchika": 2.

among the translations of Baudelaire published in *Slovo*.[19] However, Chekhov could have been acquainted with some of the other translations of *Les Fleurs du mal*, for in the 1880s and 1890s Baudelaire was extremely popular in Russia. That is to say, it seems improbable that Chekhov could have missed *Les Fleurs du mal*. At the same time, searches on the topic of "Chekhov and Baudelaire" have yielded practically no results. Thus, in the Academic edition of Chekhov's complete works and letters only two mentions of Baudelaire are to be found, both in the commentaries: the commentary to the story "A Woman's Kingdom" contains excerpts from a review by Ivan Ivanov in which, among other things, it is stated that Lysevich (a character in the story) "literally repeats the same thing that Baudelaire and his disciples lauded in their verse," but that "the figure of Lysevich is filled with existential truth, it remains in reader's memory down to the finest details, and something greater remains than the features corresponding to Baudelairism" (S 8: 500); and in the commentary to a letter to Leonid Sredin of January 20, 1904, there is an excerpt from the memoirs of Skitalets concerning the premiere of *The Cherry Orchard* at the MAT on January 17, 1904,[20] in which the celebration of the author after the third act is described: "Chekhov was a touching and at the same time pitiful figure as he stood onstage [...] surrounded in a semicircle by the crowd of actors; at this moment he looked like Don Quixote in front of Aldonsa, or Baudelaire's albatros" (P 12: 258). It is also interesting to note that in the volume of *Chekhoviana* entitled *Chekhov and France* there is not a single mention of the name of Baudelaire.

Does this absence mean that Chekhov was indifferent to Baudelaire? I would suggest not. At the very least, he must have been aware of Baudelaire's reputation. An oblique confirmation of this is to be found in the opinion of Andrew Wachtel, who reads Chekhov's *Seagull* as an "antisymbolist play," and as "a symbolic play about the danger of

---

[19] Under the initials P.Ia. in the September number of *Slovo* for 1879 we find "Portret" "Vampir" ("Le vampire") and "Golos"; in the December number of the same year, "Beatriche" ("La Béatrice") and "Razrushitel'"; in the February-March 1880 edition "Gimn krasote," "Duma," "S otradoiu gliadish', kak solntse po utram..." and "Smert' bednykh"; in the September 1880 edition "Stremlenie k nebu" and "Splin."

[20] Skitalets, *Izbrannye proizvedeniia*: 556–558.

believing in symbolism." Among the sources for the "image of the seagull" Wachtel mentions Baudelaire's "L'albatros" —a poem that "without a doubt had been seen" by Treplev.[21]

What then could Chekhov have known about Baudelaire? Let us
examine some testimonies regarding the reputation of Baudelaire and
Les Fleurs du mal in Russia in the 1890s. For example, Zinaida Ven-
gerova writes about the aesthetics of the French poet in the Brockhaus
and Efron Dictionary: "… love is not the healthy feeling of a young
soul, but the morbid curiosity of a sated imagination [...]. The frustrated thirst for an ideal drives Baudelaire to seek artificial pleasures
and oblivion in unnatural sensations."[22] Here too is the opinion of an
American Slavist about the "Russian Baudelaire" of the nineteenth century:

> … the greater part of Russian critics of the 1890s took a negative at-
> titude to modernism and saw in Baudelaire a doubtful "archdeca-
> dent" figure. A considerable role in this was played by the antide-
> cadent book by Max Nordau *Die Entartung*, which appeared in
> Russian translation in 1894. [...] The impact of Baudelaire was es-
> pecially strongly felt by the first, "decadent" generation of Russian
> modernism, which was fascinated by the unusual, "scandalous"
> sides of Baudelaire's poetry. The flight from vulgarity into an "arti-
> ficial paradise" of exotic and beautiful worlds, elite individualism,
> eroticism and the "cult of evil" seemed at that time to certain au-
> thors who were looking for new paths in Russian literature, to be
> the most attractive features of the French poet's work.[23]

It turns out that Baudelaire was viewed in the 1890s as a modern-
ist, a symbolist and a decadent (all of which terms were frequently used
interchangeably). Analyzing Russian mass media of the 1890s, Anatoly
Sobennikov came to the following conclusion: "On the one hand, the
Russian periodical press at the beginning of the 1890s clearly showed a
tendency to accept and promote the achievements of the French sym-
bolists; on the other hand, there was another tendency, to view critically
and reject those tenets of symbolist theory and practice that contra-

[21] Vakhtel, "Parodiinost' 'Chaiki'…": 72–90.
[22] V[engerova], "Bodler": 214.
[23] Vanner, "Bodler v russkoi kul'ture…": 25–26, 27.

dicted the traditions of Russian classical realism." And although "Chekhov did not participate in the polemics around symbolism and the symbolist conception of the symbol, nevertheless he was undoubtedly acquainted with their development."[24] Moreover, in the opinion of Gaints Zettser, "at the turn of the century no scholarly terminology yet existed for the cluster of words reflecting the concept of 'decadence,' but there was a hazy common conception. As we know, Chekhov, as a sensitive observer and chronicler of his time, did describe in his works the phenomenon of decadence: his characters use the concept and are projected into its context, and in Chekhov's correspondence one may find many references to decadence."[25]

It was precisely Baudelaire that could be the most typical decadent for Chekhov. In this connection we find an interesting comment in the work of Elena Tolstaya. Here is what she writes about Merezhkovsky's play "The Storm is Over," one of the characters of which—Visconti—is ecstatic about the true artist and greatest pessimist Palitsyn, who has formed a group around the concept of "death": "The Visconti family contains an allusion to the princely title of the advocate Alexander Ivanovich Urusov, the aesthete and connoisseur of contemporary art, who recommended that poets study Baudelaire, and prose writers Flaubert, and whom Chekhov depicted in the form of the lawyer Lysevich in 'A Woman's Kingdom'"[26] (see above the comment of I. Ivanov on this story). It was Prince A. Urusov (1843–1900) who, together with Mallarmé published in 1896 the collection *Le Tombeau de Charles Baudelaire*. Urusov's article *L'architecture secrète des Fleurs du mal* was the first serious textological study of *Les Fleurs du mal*.[27] Moreover, in that same play by Merezhkovsky we find a character linked with Chekhov: "...among the list of secondary characters there is one more— Startsev, 'a novelist of about thirty, seemingly withdrawn, cunning, and self-interested.' Startsev thinks only about money." He is the author of a tale entitled "Young Shoots," "which with its somewhat vulgar title

---

[24] Sobennikov, *Khudozhestvennyi simvol...*: 10, 36.

[25] Zettser, "Chekhov, dekadans i Maks Nordau": 182. On the subject there is another extremely questionable work that tends to muddy the waters: Dolgenko, "Chekhov i dekadenty": 182–184.

[26] Tolstaia, *Poetika razdrazheniia*: 233.

[27] Vanner, op. cit.: 27.

suspiciously resembles 'Belated Flowers.' The greedy Startsev is a caricature of Chekhov, whose absence of 'idealism' and premature old age
were everyday themes in literary circles in St Petersburg [...]. It is
hardly by chance that Chekhov appropriated the name 'Startsev' for the
story 'Ionych,' which developed the same set of issues: premature old
age, love of money, and growing apathy."[28] And although "the name
'Ionych' with its backwoods aura and habits was the pseudonym of the
ethnographer and feature-writer Filipp Diomidovich Nefedov, a col-
laborator on the magazine [*Severnyi vestnik*—Y.D.] who wrote articles
with titles like 'On the life and customs of the forest region,'"[29] Chekhov
could indeed have simultaneously borne in mind several layers when
creating the image of Startsev: the grasping Startsev from
Merezhkovsky's play (which suggests that the character Ionych contains elements of a self-portrait), the "provincial" Ionych from *Severnyi
vestnik*, and some "typical decadent"—for after all the title "Young
Shoots" clearly referred the reader of the 1890s not only to Chekhov's
"Belated Flowers" but also to *Les Fleurs du mal*. This is of course far
from enough to link Baudelaire's aesthetics with Startsev's "aesthetics"
in the cemetery scene. The lack of factual evidence permits one only to
speak of a typological similarity. However, it is to be hoped that future
scholars will take up the question of "Baudelaire and Chekhov."

The search for Baudelairean traits in Chekhov leads inevitably to
another figure that is much more legitimately related to the possible
genesis of the image of Dr Startsev. We recall that the introduction to
the collection of Baudelaire's poetry translated by Yakubovich (1895)
was written by Konstantin Balmont. It was Balmont, largely despite the
logic of Yakubovich's translations, who declared Baudelaire to be a
decadent. Here is a fragment from Balmont's introductory sketch:
"From time immemorial love has drawn from the breasts of poets the
most tender of sounds, but here it goes hand in hand with hatred, is
linked with crime, horror and madness. On the banks of Yedem hang
huge coffins in which there is more black melancholy than beauty. The
lacklustre sky is devoid of pure stars; in it a dead, cold moon glimmers.
This sad luminary that had once been the genie of nocturnal trysts now

---

[28] Tolstaia, op. cit.: 233, 234.
[29] Ibid.: 58.

only illuminates ruins in its realm of faded joy."[30] Here too are two lines from a poem Balmont himself published about Baudelaire—a sort of decadent quintessence of baudelairism:

> ...он в грязной тине преступления
> Искал сиянья красоты[31]

[... in the dirty effluvia of crime he sought the brilliance of beauty.]

Thus, the moon and the aestheticization of death are at least two elements characteristic of the scene in the cemetery. They are equally typical of Balmont's own work—and not only Balmont's.

There is no need to go into detail on the subject of "Chekhov and Balmont"—this already has a rich scholarly tradition. Nevertheless, one aspect needs to be stressed. As early as 1980 Alexander Ninov linked Balmont with the character of Treplev in *The Seagull*. Here is some of what Ninov has to say:

> [in Treplev] the public immediately recognized the precise psychological outline of newly born Russian decadence. The figure of Treplev in *The Seagull* evokes a whole series of literary associations, among which Balmont and his poetry occupy a very special place[32]; his [Treplev's—Y.D.] psychology, aesthetics and creative programme, his way of speaking and his mannerisms, and lastly his biography and fate comprise a synthesis of much of what Chekhov knew and thought about the young adherents of the "new art." As a literary image Treplev is without a doubt one of the most faithful artistic types of the Russian modernist of the time; Treplev formulates his aesthetic credo in the spirit that life should be depicted "not as it is, and not as it should be, but as we see it in our dreams." At the time when Balmont's first collections of poetry "Beneath a northern sky" and "In a limitless world" appeared, he could have subscribed to this formula of Treplev's in *The Seagull* without any significant reservations.[33]

---

[30] Bodler, *Stikhotvoreniia Bodlera*: 4.

[31] Ibid.: 8.

[32] Ninov, "Chekhov and Bal'mont": 100.

[33] Ibid.: 103, 104.

Ninov additionally notes that Balmont played in turn the roles of "'demonic superman,' and Don Juan, and Russian Baudelaire."[34]

Following Ninov we can point out one other fact: "There is reason to believe that after making Balmont's acquaintance and meeting him a first few times in Moscow in 1895–1896, Chekhov got to know the poet better abroad while in France in 1897–1898 [...] The well-known Moscow lawyer and writer Urusov was their common friend; Urusov knew Balmont from the time when he was a hungry and unemployed youth, and could tell more about him than anyone else."[35] This is indeed the same Urusov who was the prototype for Visconti in Merezhkovsky's play and the investigator of Baudelaire's poetry.

As we can see, a sort of aesthetic system emerges: Baudelaire–Balmont–Urusov–Treplev–Chekhov (not necessarily in this precise order—this is not a chain, but a system). The Balmont–Treplev topic has been well researched in recent years. Elena Tolstaya noted that in Balmont's poetic world "'the death of the soul' seemed fearful, while real death, on the other hand, seemed 'eternal, peaceful'; earthly existence seemed destructive for the soul and therefore not at all desirable. It seems, however, that Balmont's poem 'Fantasia' (1893)—evidently the main source for the motif of the 'wandering lights' in Treplev's little play—had been read by Chekhov not at all in the way the author had intended."[36] Tolstaya is the source of an even greater generalization on the sources of Treplev's play and in general on the decadents: "In *The Seagull* and not only there, the source of his [Chekhov's—Y.D.] 'image of the decadent' was the collective filter of bourgeois intellectual opinion."[37] To this can be added the extremely important observations by Viktor Gulchenko: "In Treplev's very behaviour the element of decadence was no less detectable and significant than in the products of his artistic activity"; "If we take the age depicted in *The Seagull* to have actually happened, then we have to recognize Treplev as one of the personalities of that age—as a personality traditionally opposed to the dominant trend in art and the dominant mode of existence."[38]

---

[34] Ninov, op. cit.: 105.

[35] Ibid.

[36] Tolstaia, op. cit.: 250.

[37] Ibid.: 255.

[38] Gul'chenko, "Treplev-dekadent": 182, 191.

Perhaps the most penetrating study of decadence in *The Seagull* in connection with the figure of Balmont belongs to Alla Golovacheva, who discovered the textual echoes in Treplev's play of Balmont's poetry (the book *Pod severnym nebom* [*Beneath a northern sky*], a copy of which was presented to Chekhov by the author in 1895). In particular, Golovacheva points to the motif of the moon, which is extremely frequent in the early Balmont and plays an important role in Treplev's play: "Treplev's play is itself is a typical example of the vision of chaos illuminated by a pale moon."[39] Golovacheva's general conclusions are also important for us here: "Contemporaries immediately determined that Treplev's play belonged to the new direction in art. And indeed in *The Seagull* itself his work is called 'decadent nonsense,' and its author a 'decadent.' And it was precisely in this way that the public perceived Chekhov's protagonist"; "...in the image of Treplev he [Chekhov— Y.D.] reflected in part that of Balmont, whose talent he liked. Nevertheless, the main task of the author of *The Seagull* was to portray his hero as a sort of objective phenomenon of Russian life of the period."[40] All the more, since "the very concept of 'decadent' had first and foremost an ethical, and only then an aesthetic meaning."[41]

Thus we can say with certainty that in *The Seagull* (1893) the play within the play reflects the author's view of decadence, of which Balmont was a striking and typical example—both as a poet and as a person. If we are to believe Ninov, then Chekhov's acquaintance with Balmont took place after the creation of *The Seagull*, in 1895, and for the following three years the two writers communicated fairly frequently— in 1895–1896 in Moscow, and in 1897–1898 in France. "Ionych" was written in 1898; whereas Balmont presented him with the book *Pod severnym nebom* in 1895 (this book is listed in the description of Chekhov's library carried out in 1904). I believe it makes sense to view this book from the position of the possible realization of motifs from it in the cemetery scene. Let us examine a few fragments from Balmont's book that bear comparison with the point of view of Ionych in the cemetery and linked with the system of motifs of the Moon, Death and Beauty:

---

[39] Golovacheva, "'Dekadent' Treplev i blednaia luna": 193.
[40] Ibid.: 186, 189.
[41] Gul'chenko, op. cit.: 181.

Не верь тому, кто говорит тебе,
Что смерть есть смерть: она—начало жизни,
Того существованья неземного,
Перед которым наша жизнь темна,
Как миг тоски—пред радостью беспечной,
Как чёрный грех—пред детской чистотой.
Нам не дано понять всю прелесть смерти,
Мы можем лишь предчувствовать её
[...]
(«Смерть»)

[Do not believe the one who says that death is death: it is the beginning of life, of that unearthly existence, next to which our life is as dark as a moment of melancholy next to carefree joy, as black sin next to childlike purity. It is not given to us to understand all the charm of death; we can only have a foretaste of it [...]
(Death)]

Как живые изваянья, в искрах лунного сиянья,
Чуть трепещут очертанья сосен, елей и берез;
Вещий лес спокойно дремлет, яркий блеск
Луны приемлет
И роптанью ветра внемлет, весь исполнен тайных грез.
[...]
Чьи-то вздохи, чьё-то пенье, чьё-то скорбное моленье,
И тоска, и упоенье,—точно искрится звезда,
Точно светлый дождь струится,—и деревьям что-то мнится,
То, что людям не приснится, никому и никогда.
[...]
А Луна все льёт сиянье, и без муки, без страданья,
Чуть трепещут очертанья вещих сказочных стволов;
Все они так сладко дремлют, безучастно стонам внемлю,
И с спокойствием приемлют чары ясных светлых снов.
(«Фантазия»)

[Like living sculptures, in the sparks of the moon's gleam, the shapes of the pines, firs and birches barely tremble; the wise forest dozes peacefully, receives the bright glitter of the moon and harkens to the grumble of the wind, all filled with secret dreams. [...] Someone's sighs, someone's song, someone's grieving prayer, and melancholy, and intoxication, the star sparkles, the bright rain pours, and the trees imagine something that people do not dream of, no one, never. [...] And the moon keeps pouring down its glow, and without pain or suffering the shapes of the wise folktale trunks barely tremble, listening indifferently to the groans, and receive the charms of clear bright dreams calmly.

("Fantasia")]

Когда Луна сверкнёт во мгле ночной
Своим серпом, блистательным и нежным,
Моя душа стремится в мир иной,
Пленяясь всем далёким, всем безбрежным.

К лесам, к горам, к вершинам белоснежным
Я мчусь в мечтах, как будто дух больной,
Я бодрствую над миром безмятежным,
И сладко плачу, и дышу—Луной.

Впиваю это бледное сиянье,
Как эльф, качаюсь в сетке из лучей,
Я слушаю, как говорит молчанье.

Людей родных мне далеко страданье,
Чужда мне вся земля с борьбой своей,
Я—облачко, я—ветерка дыханье.
(«Лунный свет»)

[When the moon shines in the nocturnal gloom with its shiny, gentle sickle, my soul seeks a different world, captivated by all that is distant and limitless. In my dreams I hasten towards the forests, the mountains, the snowy-white heights as if I were a sick spirit. I watch over a passive world, and cry sweetly, and breathe the Moon. I suck up its pale gleam, like an elf, I swing in a net of rays; I listen to the talk of the silence. The suffering of my relatives is remote from me; all the earth with its struggles is foreign to me; I am a cloudlet; I am the breath of the wind.

("Moonlight")]

[...]
Как отрадно в глубокий полуночный час
На мгновенье все скорби по-детски забыть,
И, забыв, что любовь невозможна для нас,
Как отрадно мечтать и любить,

Без улыбки, без слов,
Средь ночной тишины,
В царстве вечных снегов,
В царстве бледной Луны.
(«Без улыбки, без снов»)

[How joyful it is in the deep midnight hour like a child to forget for a moment all the grief, and, having forgotten that love is impossible for us, how joyful it is to dream and love, without a smile, without words, amidst the hush of night, in the realm of eternal snows, in the realm of the pale moon.

("Without a smile, without dreams")]

Когда между тучек туманных
Полночной порой загорится Луна,
Душа непонятной печали полна,
Исполнена дум несказанных,
Тех чувств, для которых названия нет,
И той Красоты бесконечной,
Что, вспыхнув, зарницею вечной,
Сияет потом в чёрном сумраке лет.
(«Когда между тучек туманных...»)

[When between the foggy clouds the moon begins to shine at the midnight hour, the soul is filled with incomprehensible sadness, filled with unspoken thoughts, those feelings for which there is no name, and that endless Beauty that, flaring up like eternal lightning, then shines in the dark gloaming of the years.

("When between the foggy clouds...")]

Есть красота в постоянстве страдания
И в неизменности скорбной мечты.
Знойного яркого Солнца сияние,
Пышной Весны молодые черты
В сердце не так вызывают сознание
Ласки больной, неземной красоты,
Как замка седые руины, печальной Луны трепетание,
Застенчивых сумерек скорбь, или осени грустной листы.
(«Есть красота в постоянстве страдания...»)

[There is a beauty in the constancy of suffering and in the immutability of the grief-filled dream. The shining of the hot bright sun, the youthful features of the voluptuous spring do not evoke so much in the heart the consciousness of the caress of morbid, unearthly beauty, as do grey ruins of a castle, the trembling of the sad Moon, the grief of bashful twilight, or the leaves of sad autumn. ("There is a beauty in the constancy of suffering")][42]

Let us add one more poem also written in 1894, "Nadgrobnye tsvety ("Flowers on the tomb"):

Среди могил неясный шёпот,
Неясный шёпот ветерка.
Печальный вздох, тоскливый ропот,
Тоскливый ропот ивняка.

Среди могил блуждают тени
Усопших дедов и отцов,
И на церковные ступени
Восходят тени мертвецов.

И в дверь церковную стучатся,
Они стучатся до зари,
Пока вдали не загорятся
На бледном небе янтари.

Тогда, поняв, что жизнь минутна,
Что безуспешна их борьба,
Рыдая горестно и смутно,
Они идут в свои гроба.

Вот почему наутро блещут
Цветы над тёмною плитой:
В них слёзы горькие трепещут
О жизни—жизни прожитой.

[Amongst the tombs there is a vague whisper, the unclear whisper of the wind. A sad sigh, a melancholic grumble, the melancholic grumble of the willow. Amidst the tombs wander shades of departed grandfathers and fathers, and the shades of the dead climb the church steps. And they knock on the door of the church; they knock till dawn, until in the distance the ambers glow in the pale

---

[42] Quoted from Bal'mont, *Sobranie sochinenii*, vol. I.

sky. Then, understanding that life is but a minute, that their struggle is futile, sobbing grievously and quietly, they go to their coffins.
This is why the flowers shine in the morning on the dark slab: in
them tremble bitter tears for life, for life lived.][43]

As we can see, the motifs of moon, beauty and death occur frequently
in Balmont and in the book of poetry *Pod severnym nebom* (*Beneath a
northern sky*) form a system. This system incorporates the semantics of
the aestheticization of death and its beauty, so visible beneath the pale
moon. We encounter a similar system in the cemetery scene in "Ionych." Suffice it to say that the word combination *lunnyi svet*
("moonlight") is repeated four times in a relatively short episode. It is
under the influence of the moonlight that Startsev becomes a poet:
"…as if the moonlight was warming the passion in him, he waited passionately and imagined kisses and embraces." Beneath the moon Startsev, like a true poet, empathizes with a humanity doomed to an unavoidable death, and mainly sees physical beauty in a place where it
would seem to be most difficult to find: in the tombstones. This is the
peak of Ionych's career as a poet. Furthermore, I would suggest that it is
precisely at that moment that the key is revealed to the aesthetics of
Startsev the poet: he is a decadent, capable of perceiving the beauty of
death in the light of the moon, capable of aestheticizing the most terrible thing—the destruction of man. But the hero becomes a decadent
poet only for one moment: as soon as the moonlight disappears, the
poet immediately turns back into an ordinary person ("And as if a curtain had come down, the moon went behind a cloud, and suddenly everything went dark all around. Startsev hardly found the gates—it was
already as dark as on an autumnal night—then he wandered around for
an hour and a half, looking for the lane where he had left his horses.")

Having related Ionych in the cemetery scene to the specifics of the
artistic world of Balmont and, more broadly, the entire aesthetic of that
movement (which in Russia was frequently called decadence and for
which the benchmark in Russian culture was for a long time Charles
Baudelaire), we must next ask the question: what does this information
add to our interpretation of the story? I would argue that it permits us
to see at least two things: the clear outlines of the image of Startsev, and

---

[43] Quoted from Bal'mont, *Stikhotvoreniia*.

the author's perception of the art of his time. These two are interlinked; each affects the other.

Ionych for a moment becomes a poet. But does this imply the presence in Startsev of the potential to perceive the world aesthetically, the possibility of a different path other than the path along which he goes? I would suggest that the position of the author obliges us to answer this question in the negative. The aesthetic conception of Startsev the poet is decadence, and because of the influence of Nordau's *Die Entartung* "many critical works begin to characterize the 'decadents' as 'degenerates'."[44] That is to say, Startsev's aesthetics in the cemetery scene signifies his degeneration—that same degeneration that subsequently occurs on the ethical level in the story: the degeneration of Startsev into Ionych. Such an understanding of the aesthetic level of the story helps us to understand more deeply the image of Startsev, to whom the author allows no chance of renewal even in his poetical dreams. At the same time it convinces us that Chekhov's view of decadence had changed since 1893, the year he wrote *The Seagull*, despite his acquaintance and even friendship with Balmont, and that he had become less accepting of decadent aesthetics. Moreover, if Treplev the decadent, despite all the contradictions in his art, had nevertheless evoked sympathy in the reader and in audiences,[45] Ionych the decadent in the end evokes only antipathy. Thus, based on the comparison of the images of Treplev and Startsev, one can speak of an evolution in Chekhov's attitude towards decadent art in the period 1893–1898. However, not all this is directly expressed in Chekhov's story, for his "style of stylization is the style of a secret dialogue with alien positions, alien plot elements and images," in which "the fundamental position is occupied by a form of subdued stylization, in which the base voice in the dialogue is hidden and requires an creative contribution on the part of the reader."[46]

---

[44] Sobennikov, op. cit.: 29.

[45] "In Chekhov's attitude to Treplev there are two sides: he sees in Treplev's searchings genuine creative impulses, and therefore in part is sympathetic to him. Alongside the successful professional Trigorin the young experimenter lacks not so much talent as the existential force to express the new feelings he has inside. The shoots of his new art turn out to be too weak to turn into anything significant" (Ivanova, E.V., "Chekhov i simvolisty...": 33).

[46] Kubasov, *Proza A.P. Chekhova*: 381, 382.

What conclusions can we draw from all this? As in *The Seagull*, where Chekhov introduced the opposite type of art in the figure of Trigorin, in "Ionych" the aesthetic player is not limited to the scene in the cemetery. The role of aesthetic antagonist can be discerned, for example, in the figure of Vera Yosifovna, who writes novels "about things that never happen in life." It turns out that popular writing for a mass audience is also a sign of degeneration. Why are both decadence and popular writing doomed in the author's view? Quite simply, I would argue, the author avoids extremes: for him decadence on the one hand and popular fiction on the other were extremes. From an aesthetic standpoint these phenomena were opposed, but as regards their future development Chekhov believed both were equally doomed. As Startsev is doomed to degenerate, so is Vera Yosifovna doomed to a boring monotony that drags on from year to year.

What then is the story "Ionych" about? Of course it is a love story, and to an equal extent a story of moral degradation. However, it is a story about many other things as well. In particular it is a story about art, a story that allows us to see the clear outlines of the author's views on art—not only the ethical, but also the aesthetic position of its author.

Translated from the Russian by J. Douglas Clayton.

WORKS CITED

Bal'mont, Konstantin. *Sobranie sochinenii*. 2 vols. M.: Mozhaisk-Terra 1994.

———. *Stikhotvoreniia*. 2nd ed. L.: Biblioteka poeta, bol'shaia seriia, 1969.

Berdnikov, Georgii. *A.P. Chekhov: Ideinye i tvorcheskie iskaniia*. M.-L.: Goslitizdat, 1961.

Bodler (Baudelaire). *Stikhotvoreniia Bodlera*. M.: Izd. Petrovskoi biblioteki v Moskve, 1895.

———. *Tsvety zla*. Trans. P. Iakubvich-Mel'shin. SPb.: Obshestvennaya Pol'za, 1909.

Dolgenko, Aleksandr. "Chekhov i dekadenty," *Dialozi s Chekhov: 100 godini po-k"sno*. Sofiia:, Fakel, 2004: 182–184.

Golovacheva, Alla. "'Dekadent' Treplev i blednaia luna," *Chekhoviana: Chekhov i "serebrianyi vek"*. M.: Nauka, 1996: 186–194.

Gul'chenko, Viktor. "Treplev-dekadent," *Chekhoviana: Polet "Chaiki"*. M.: Nauka,

2001: 178–195.

Iakubovich-Mel'shin, Petr. "Ot Perevodchika," in Bodler (Baudelaire), *Tsvety zla*. SPb: Obshchestvennaia pol'za, 1909: 2–4.

Ivanova, E. "Chekhov i simvolisty:neproiasnennye aspekty problemy," *Chekhoviana: Chekhov i "serebrianyi vek."* M.: Nauka, 1996: 30–34.

Ivanova, N. "K poetike chekhovskoi prozy (Tri romansa na stikhi A.S. Pushkina," *Chekhoviana: Chekhov i Pushkin.* M.: Nauka, 1998: 106–112.

Kapustin, Nikolai. "'Chuzhoe slovo' v proze A.P. Chekhova: Zhanrovye transformatsii. Avtoreferat diss. Dokt. Fil. Nauk. Ivanovo, 2003.

————. "O metamorfozakh malykh zhanrov v rasskaze A.P. Chekhova 'Ionych'," *Potaennaia literatura: Issledovaniia i materialy*, vyp. 3. Ivanovo: Ivanovskii gosudarstvenii universitet, 2002: 110–115.

Kataev, Vladimir. *Proza Chekhova: problemy interpretatsii.* M.: Izd-vo Moskovskogo universiteta, 1979.

————. "Startsev i Ionych," *Russkaia slovesnost'*, 1998, No. 1: 11–16.

Kubasov, Aleksandr. *Proza A.P. Chekhova: iskusstvo stilizatsii.* Ekaterinburg: Ural'skii gosudarstvennyi pedagogicheskii universitet, 1998.

Lapushin, Radislav. *Ne postigaemoe bytie...: Opyt prochteniia A.P. Chekhova.* Minsk: Propilei, 1998.

Markovich, Vladimir. "Pushkin, Chekhov i sud'ba 'lelejushchei dushu gumannosti'," *Chekhoviana: Chekhov i Pushkin.* M.: Nauka, 1998: 19–34.

Ninov, Aleksandr. "Chekhov i Bal'mont," *Voprosy literatury*, 1980, No. 1: 98–130.

Ovsianniko-Kulikovskii, Dmitrii. "Etiudy o tvorchestve A.P. Chekhova. Ionych," Literaturno-kriticheskie raboty. 2 vols. M.: Khudozhestvennaya literatura, 1989., vol. 1: 459–519.

Skitalets, *Izbrannye proizvedeniia.* M.: Goslitizdat, 1955.

Smirnov, Aleksandr. "Romantika Pushkina—antiromantizm Chekhova (elegicheskaia kontseptsiia romantikov v sisteme novelly Chekhova Chekhova 'Ionych'," *Chekhoviana: Chekhov i Pushkin.* M.: Nauka, 1998.

Sobennikov, Anatolii. *Khudozhestvennyi simvol v dramaturgii A.P. Chekhova.* Irkutsk: Izd-vo Irkutskogo universiteta, 1989.

Sosnitskaia, Maria. *"Ionych" i "Vishnevyi sad" A.P. Chekhova.* M.: Uchpedgiz, 1958.

Tiupa, Valery. *Khudozhestvennost' chekhovskogo rasskaza.* M.: Vish Shk, 1989.

Tolstaia, Elena. *Poetika razdrazheniia: Chekhov v kontse 1880–nachale 1890-kh godov.* M.: Rossiiskii gos. gumanitarnyi universitet, 2002.

Tsilevich, Leonid. *Siuzhet chekhovskogo rasskaza.* Riga: "Zvaigzne," 1976.

Vakhtel, Andrew. (Wachtel, A.) "Parodiinost' 'Chaiki': simvoly i ozhidaniia," *Vestnik moskovskogo universiteta*, ser. 9 (Filologiia) 2002, No. 1.

Vanner, Adrian. "Bodler v russkoi kul'ture kontsa XIX–nachala XX veka," *Russkaia literatura xx veka: Issledovaniia amerikanskikh uchenykh.* Sankt-Peterbourg: Sankt-Peterburgskii gos. universitet, 1993.

V[engerova], Zinaida. "Bodler," *Entsiklopedicheskii slovar'*, vol. 4 (7) SPb.: Brokgauz i Efron, 1891: 214.

Zettser, Gaints. "Chekhov, dekadans i Maks Nordau," *Chekhov i Germaniia*. M.: Moskovskii gosudarstvennyi universitet, 1996.

Zorkaia, Neia. "Motiv 'smirennogo kladbishcha' v proizvedeniiakh Pushkina in Chekhova," *Chekhoviana: Chekhov i Pushkin*. M.: Nauka, 1998.

Variations on the Man in a Case in Chekhov's "Man in a Case" and "On the Harmfulness of Tobacco"

HERTA SCHMID
Potsdam University

The theme of the "Man in a Case" may be considered one of the most important in Chekhov's oeuvre. As Vladimir Kataev demonstrates, in the so-called "little trilogy" comprising the stories "The Man in a Case," "Gooseberries," and "About Love," the concept of "being encased" (*futliarnost*) is illustrated three times through the example of a life led according to a pattern that in different ways leads to failure.[1] However, the theme recurs not only in these three stories, but also in Chekhov's dramaturgy, and with especial clarity in the last version of the one-act play "On the Harmfulness of Tobacco." An examination of the incarnation of the man in the case in the dramatic genre reveals that in working with this central theme Chekhov was also pursuing a formal issue, namely the search for a link between different art forms.

The link between Chekhov's writing and music has frequently been a topic for research; the link with painting has been less frequently examined. Yet the motif of a painted portrait is especially important in the first story of the "little trilogy," "The Man in a Case," and elements of this picture return in the one-acter "On the Harmfulness of Tobacco." For this reason we shall examine here not the entire trilogy, but only the ini-

---

[1] Kataev also notes that the technique of the framed narrative, which will be the point of departure for the following analysis, permits the creation of numerous evaluative perspectives concerning the life being narrated. However, he ignores the ecphrastic vision, which will be the focus of this study. It is precisely this that affords a further evaluative perspective close to that of the main narrator. Instead, Kataev's reference point is the norm of real life that the author has in view, but the characters less so. However, norms can easily become rigid and lend themselves to "encasement," so that the choice of term seems unfortunate. See Kataev, *Proza Chekhova*: 238.

tial story and the one-acter. By the same token, the term "variations" in the title of this study refers not to variations in the social type of the "man in the case" in the sense of a typology, but variations in the thematics of the man in a case in the dramatic and narrative genres, and painting in both genres. An additional reason for the choice of these two works is the date of their creation: "The Man in a Case" was written in 1898, and the last version of "On the Harmfulness of Tobacco" in 1902 (and published in 1903). Chekhov insisted that this final version be regarded as a completely new work and that practically the only thing that it and the previous versions had in common was the title.[2] And indeed it is what it has in common with the last version of "Man in a Case" that makes it different from the earlier versions. In taking up again the old one-acter, Chekhov seems to have brought into play the problematics of the man in a case, and to have incorporated an intertextual link to "The Man in a Case" by the references to certain imagery contained in it.

Chekhov's biography is marked by some links with painting. First, his brother Nikolai Pavlovich was a painter, and in his early years Anton Pavlovich, along with Nikolai, composed some "Drawings with Captions" (risunki s podpisiu) for newpapers containing illustrated short scenes of everyday life in dialogue.[3] Aleksandr Chudakov is of the opinion that the technique Chekhov developed here of presenting an individual in a concrete place (gde) surrounded by concrete things (chto) that define the individual even before he has defined himself (kto), what Chudakov calls the genre of the "short story/little scene," was to influence Chekhov's later narrative technique, especially the "in medias res" beginning (s serediny) and the null (nichem) ending. Also important for the "man in the case" theme is Chudakov's remark that the figures in the "little narrative scenes" are unable to liberate themselves from the where and what of the objects that surround them, for in a painting of a scene of every-day life the individual is conceived of and defined as a correlative of his spatial and material surroundings. In this context the genre of the "monologue scene" is particularly important for the play under discussion "On the Harmfulness of Tobacco." An echo of the "scene" genre even creeps into Burkin's tale of the "man in a case" Belikov in the story "The Man in a Case." When Burkin describes the relationship between

---

[2] Cf. Skaftymov, "Primechaniia": 700.

[3] See Chudakov, Anton Pavlovich Chekhov: 68, 73–74.

Varvara, Belikov's intended, and her brother Kovalenko, he begins to recount a characteristic episode with the words "Here's a scene for you," and there follows a description of how brother and sister cross the street each laden with books and argue about whether Kovalenko has actually read a certain book.[4] The description of the two figures and the brief argument evoke the genre of the "drawing with caption," with which the two Chekhov brothers had earned their first money in their youth.

Secondly, a link with painting can be found in a special system of motifs in Chekhov's narrative poetics. Chudakov emphasizes the years 1886–87 as a phase in the evolution of the poetics of the Chekhov's landscape description.[5] This was when he abandoned the early parodies of hackneyed landscape descriptions found in popular literature (as for example in "A Disgusting Story," 1882) and attained an objective method of landscape depiction that described only what was visible to the protagonist. Finally, in "The Steppe" (1888) he overcame this technique, so that now the landscape was also described and experienced emotionally from the standpoint of the narrator.[6] There thus appear two subjective points of view, that of the protagonist and that of the narrator standing behind him, both orientated towards the same object, but not necessarily perceiving it in the same way. We will encounter this technique of the double perspective in landscape description again in "The Man in a Case." However, in the case of this story a third point derived from Chekhov's biography also appears relevant.

Chekhov was a friend of the landscape painter Isaak Levitan (1861–1900). In a letter of 2 January, 1900 to Olga Knipper Chekhov dis-

---

[4] We do indeed have to do here with a "scene-dialogue." Several such scenes can be found in "The Man in a Case," for example the scene of the bicycle-riding Kovalenko brother and sister on the day of the teachers' excursion (this recurs in *The Three Sisters* without the bicycles) and the entire scene of Belikov falling down the stairs. (This recurs in *The Cherry Orchard* with regard to Petia Trofimov, also an admirer of galoshes.) The speech elements are integrated in different ways. A plot analysis of "The Man in a Case" with regard to Belikov would show that the "scenes," together with the caricatural portraits which we shall examine further on, form a subplot that brings the central plot out of its track and from Belikov's perspective has to do precisely with the "scenes."

[5] "The poetics of the Chekhovian landscape" (Chudakhov, *Anton Pavlovich Chekhov*: 107).

[6] Ibid.: 109–110.

cusses a painting that Levitan had painted for him and which now hung over his fireplace: "On my fireplace he depicted a moonlit night during the haymaking. Meadow, haystacks, in the distance forest, and over everything rules the moon" (P 9: 8). In an earlier letter to Suvorin (19 January 1895) he criticizes Levitan after visiting his studio. He considered the painter "the best Russian landscape artist," but he had wasted his youth on women and was now painting not "in a young way" but "with bravado." However, a landscape cannot be painted "without passion and enthusiasm" (P 6: 15). Levitan has gone down in the history of Russian painting as one of the most significant landscape painters of the nineteenth century, whose plein-air paintings often have an elegiac tone.[7] He is also recognized as having "philosophical depth."[8] The expectation of passion and enthusiasm in landscape painting is perhaps fulfilled in one painting described in Chekhov's tale "Three Years " (1895). There at a painting exhibition the female protagonist Yuliya Sergeyevna contemplates with initial indifference a rather small painting that the narrator describes ecphrastically: in the foreground is a river with a wooden bridge over it, on the other bank a path that disappears into the dark grass, a field, and then to the right a bit of forest, next to that a sort of wooden shack, and in the distance the red glow of the sunset (S 9: 65–66). Next to her husband Laptev, who had the reputation of being a connoisseur, Yuliya had previously considered herself an ignoramus as far as painting was concerned, but suddenly she experiences the effect of the painting, an effect comparable to that described by Vasily Kandinsky as the only appropriate attitude. Kandinsky wanted the viewer to be drawn by the painting into a world previously unknown to him or her, to step into the painting.[9] This is precisely what happens with Yuliya: she imag-

---

[7] This evaluation is to be found in *Encyclopedie* ...: 337–338. In the same place it is noted that Chekhov valued Levitan's art higher than that of the French Impressionists. In the encyclopedia there is a reproduction of a painting entitled "Eternal Peace" which, with its religious-metaphysical object symbolism (there is a chapel in the foreground) and the depth perspective of the water reaching away to the sky, is reminiscent of the metaphysical paintings of German Romantic Caspar David Friedrich.

[8] In *Peredvishniki* (no pagination).

[9] See Kandinsky, *Essays*: 246. With regard to the desired effect on the beholder of the picture Kandinsky makes no distinction between objective and abstract (he calls it "concrete") art. For Kandinsky represented objects are "literary," "speak-

ines that she is walking along the path in the direction of the sunset "where [...] there lay the reflection of something unearthly, eternal" (S 9: 66). This encounter with the world of the painting changes Yuliya permanently. Even though the work described in "Three Years" was not by Levitan,[10] it nevertheless corresponds in its cosmic dimension to Kandinsky's artistic theory and no doubt also to Chekhov's conception of art.[11]

Before we begin the analysis of the two works "The Man in a Case" and "On the Harmfulness of Tobacco," a common feature of their structure should be mentioned, namely the fact that both are framed. "The Man in a Case" is a so-called framed narrative, in which a person introduced by an anonymous third-person narrator (henceforth called the

---

ing" objects that can distract from the actual effect created by patches of colour, their forms and proportions.

[10] The painter named in "Three Years" is Ivan Shishkin (1832–1898), whose paintings Laptev evaluates authoritatively, while he can muster no enthusiasm for the piece by the unknown painter preferred by Iuliia (we later learn that he nevertheless bought it for her, and that it hangs in her room). Like Levitan, Shishkin belonged to the Russian movement known as *Peredvizhniki* (travelling exhibiters), which had turned away from academic painting and chose to paint landscapes and scenes from the life of the poorer people, which they made accessible to these classes in their exhibitions. Instead of the metaphysical dimension of many of Levitan's paintings, Shishkin's canvasses are marked by an attention to the material aspect of objects (often trees or the forest floor). This explains the divergence between Iuliia and Laptev with regard to the exhibition they visit, and also the different development of both in the course of their marriage: Iuliia, who has married without love, finds her way to love, conceivably through the experience of the landscape painting, while her husband, who had married her for love, falls out of love, but remains in the shell of the marriage out of habit. The information about Shishkin is from *Peredvishniki*, 1982.

[11] In a letter to Suvorin of 3 November 1888 (P 3: 53–56) Chekhov discusses the laws that all forms of art have in common. These constitute the immortal aspect of the work. It is the task of the philosophy of artistic creation to identify these laws. Chekhov evidently had an inkling of what Oskar Walzel pursued in his project of the "mutual illumination of the arts" from a theoretical perspective. See Walzel, *Gehalt und Gestalt*. Walzel is guided by the theory of inner form of Greek antiquity. Wilhelm von Humboldt also uses this term (with regard to language) and it recurs in the theory of Karl Bühler used in this study. In addition to language theory Bühler also touches on the inner form of literary genres, and in part of painting.

"principal narrator") recounts the story of an absent third person to his listener. Such a frame is well adapted for narrative cycles and indeed the framed narrative recurs in all three stories of the "little trilogy," in which different persons take over the role of the narrator of the framed story. Such forms are familiar from *A Thousand and One Nights* or Boccaccio's *Decamarone*. In "On the Harmfulness of Tobacco," the framing corresponds to the rhetorical situation of the single dramatis persona of this monodrama, who is supposed to give a speech about tobacco, but then abandons the initial frame topic in order to give the story of his marriage, which is analogous to the first-person narrative.

Following Karl Bühler we can trace the difference between frame and framed narratives back to the concepts of "speech action" and "speech product." By the former is meant the utterance of a speaker in an actual situation, whereas the latter refers to the spoken structure as a linguistic object viewed in isolation from the speaker and situation.[12] Within the initial framing situation the speech of the person depicted represents his speech action, i.e., a speech activity inserted in a communicative situation with intentions directed at the situation and the speech partner as listener. Within the framed action this speech represents a speech product created by the speaker. The centre of gravity is the story of the third person. Using Bühler's concepts we can further link two different aspects that will bridge the gap with painting. Bühler distinguishes between *demonstratio ad oculos* and *deixis am phantasma*. The former uses the demonstrative field immanent in the language, formed out of personal pronouns and markers of time and place, in order to create for the values of the symbolic field, formed from the semantics of the non-deixic parts of speech (nouns, verbs, adjectives, adverbs) a locational system analogous to a cartographical work or a page of notes. The *demonstratio ad oculos* can then be linked with the framing situation and the narrative speech action insofar as a specific situation is located in a determined here and now,

---

[12] To distinguish the frame situation and the framed story or stories Eberhard Lämmert uses the terms "speech act" (Redeakt) and "speech utterance" (Redeaussage). These originate in Bühler's doctrine of the three functions of the speech model: expression, appeal, and representation. In the frame situation the speaker and listener orientated functions of expression and appeal dominate, whereas the framed story grows out of the function of representation. See Lämmert, *Bauformen des Erzählens*: 208.

wherein speaker and listener occupy the local fields of "I" and "you" that mark their position relative to each other and to the spatial surrounding. The *deixis am phantasma* pertains to the framed story of a third, absent person, located in his/her own deictic field (a there and then). The nature of the links between field presented *ad oculos* and that represented as *phantasma* is significant. Bühler names two kinds of link, "extension" and "displacement." By extension is meant the continuity of the spatial and temporal axes in the sense that the temporal axis of the field presented *ad oculos* is in a linear correlation with the time of the fantasmatic field, and the same is true of the spatial axis; the "now" and the "then," the "here" and the "there" thus belong in a single, unified, extended time and space. The personal pronoun can also be related to the process of extension if the narrator is identical to the object of narration as far as first-person narration is concerned, or if the narrator is in an inclusive first-person plural ("we") relationship. As we shall see, in "Man in a Case" it is not the first-person narrator Burkin but his speech partner Ivan Ivanych that brings about this personal extension. Displacement, on the other hand, comes into play when the spatial and temporal relationship is not continuous and a rupture takes place. It can then happen that the speaker (and the listener) abandon the demonstrative field of the *demonstratio ad oculos* and insert themselves in the demonstrative field of the story being narrated. In an extreme case he can also forget the field demonstrated *ad oculos*. In drama, on the other hand, Bühler asserts that one observes a fundamentally different relationship: the *deixis am phantasma* invades the temporal zone of the field being demonstrated *ad oculos* and overlays it.[13] Bühler concedes the possibility that an epic work can function with both extension and displacement simultaneously, so that an oscillation takes place between the *demonstratio ad oculos* and the *deixis am phantasma*. In drama on the other hand it is the overlaying of the two fields that is in principle dominant.[14] We shall show, however, that in his monodrama Chekhov experiments with displacement.

---

[13] For epic displacement Bühler uses the memorable formula "Mohammed goes to the mountain," and for dramatic superposition of the two demonstrative fields the formula "the mountain comes to Mohammed." See Bühler, *Sprachtheorie*: 134–135.

[14] This has to do with the sign structure of the stage and all its components, which are signs in the sense of *aliquid stat pro aliquo*. In the one-acter "On the

Bühler's concept of the demonstrative field and his two variants of the relationship between *demonstratio ad oculos* and *deixis am phantasma* are helpful not only for literary framing structures, but also for the investigation of painterly depiction in literature. All forms of art have their particular field systems, but at the same time one must be alert for analogies. In the two works under investigation Chekhov seems to have questioned both the laws peculiar to literature and painting, and also their possible links. Since in "The Man in a Case" a painted depiction is inserted perfectly in the text through the demonstrative use of the device of ecphrasis, our analysis will begin with this chronologically earlier narrative work.

I. Framed Narrative and Ecphrasis in "The Man In A Case"

By ecphrasis is meant the verbal description of a real or invented painted or general type of picture. The description can (if there is an original) serve informative purposes, but it can also be inserted for artistic reasons, for example, when a poem refers to a painting to such an extent that it turns into a so-called picture poem.[15] A description made for practical purposes usually encompasses the dimensions, the compositional structure, the illumination, the colour values and their distribution, as well as the objects depicted, the painterly style, and conceivably the interpretative meaning; in a picture poem, on the other hand, the description is much freer from such precise tasks. In poetic ecphrasis the decision as to what aspects of the painting are captured and whether and

---

Harmfulness of Tobacco" this basic structure is offset, since the dramatis persona Niukhin (the signified to the actor's signifier) appears in the role of a lecturer before an invited public. Structurally this corresponds to the offset sign system of the epic narrative situation in which a main narrator allows a person described by him to become in turn the narrator, as in "The Man in a Case."

[15] On the theory and history of the picture poem see Gisbert Kranz, *Das Bildgedicht in Europa*. Kranz gives rich material from many European literatures. Kranz distinguishes between the picture poem proper, containing a true ecphrastic reference to a painted original and simple transposition of painterly means of expression into linguistic ones. Chizhevsky's relating of Chekhov to Impressionist painting should be considered a transposition. However, crossovers between true ecphrasis and simple structural transposition are numerous and seamless. See Chizhevsky, "Chekhov in the Development of Russian Literature": 49–61.

how they will be interpreted is subjugated to the overall objectives of the poem. Ecphrasis is thus poetically determined, and it is precisely this that makes it not always easily recognizable.

In "The Man in a Case" ecphrasis occurs in an easily recognizable form, and also in one that is more difficult to recognize. One is present on one level of the frame narrative, and the other on the other level. In the *ad oculos* frame situation the characters Ivan Ivanych Chimsha-Gimalaisky, an old veterinarian, and the high-school teacher Burkin find themselves in a barn belonging to the village elder after a hunting trip. Before sleeping they pass the time in conversation. It is on this level that the ecphrasis occurs which is more difficult to recognize, and which we will examine later. The easily recognizable ecphrasis is to be found in Burkin's tale about the third character, the Greek teacher Belikov; that is to say, on the level of the *deixis am phantasma*. Burkin gives it special emphasis in the flow of his speech action through a phatic comment to his interlocutor Ivan Ivanych, so that the reader's attention is drawn to the coming description of a picture: "Now listen what comes next. Some joker drew a caricature of Belikov in galoshes, his trousers tucked up, under an umbrella, and hand in hand with Varenka; underneath was the inscription: ‚Enamoured Anthropos.' You know, the likeness of the expression was astonishing. […] The caricature made a most disturbing impression on him [Belikov]." (S 10: 49). Before the description itself Burkin defines the genre of the picture as a caricature, and then defines the main figure, Belikov, through a verb of motion (*idet*) and three attributives ("in galoshes"; "his trousers tucked up"; "under an umbrella"). The phrase "and hand in hand with Varenka" comprises a secondary figure loosely associated with the main figure Belikov through the copula "and." Burkin gives the objective description a generalized, subjective evaluation ("the likeness of the expression was astonishing") and information about the effect of the picture on Belikov himself ("a most disturbing impression"). As a rule, a painterly caricature limits itself to representing significant visual features of the caricatured object through exaggeration and distortion, while at the same time other features of the object are ignored. In the case of Belikov the significant features are thus the fact of his walking, as well as the three attributes of clothing and accessories, while it is precisely the form of the body and his visual expression, which in a caricature are usually decisive, that are ignored. Belikov's "expression" is thus conveyed not by his face, but rather by the external attributes of clothing on the walking body, so that we have to do with metonymy (the shift from the face to the external accoutrements). In his ecphrasis Burkin does not say exactly what evokes the "most disturbing impression" in Belikov, but the reader can conclude that it is precisely this dehumanizing metonomy. It is also conceivable that Belikov has recognized in the picture the loose nature of his association of his person with Varvara, which can also logically suggest dissociation. By association and dissociation is meant the plan that the teachers have pursued towards their colleague Belikov and which comprises the entire plot structure (in the sense of the term *fabula* as defined by the Russian formalists): Belikov, the aging bachelor, is to be married off to the thirty-year old Varvara, who has newly arrived in the provincial town (association), but the plan founders on their mutual incompatibility (dissociation), and instead of marriage Belikov ultimately ends up in the coffin and grave.

Using Bühler's concepts we can now analyze the ecphrasis of the caricature in the following way: in the frame situation concerning the two hunting companions Ivan Ivanych and Burkin the latter assumes the role of the first-person narrator, whereby he narrates the story of an absent third person Belikov in such a way that a description of a picture is inserted into the *deixis am phantasma*. This requires a corresponding displacement of the viewer of the image (Kandinsky's "enticement" into the world of the image). Such an act of displacement seems to have occurred with Belikov, what Burkin describes appropriately as a "most disturbing impression"—appropriately since the persona caricatured, when placed in the world of the picture, feels as if he is in a chamber of horrors. The horror and anxiety created by the caricature is invoked a second time in another place: when Belikov, according to Burkin's account, seeks out Varvara's brother Kovalenko because of the stress caused him by the many copies of the caricature being circulated among the teachers and in view of another anxiety-causing experience[16]; his attempt to excuse himself because of the caricature and instill in Kovalenko the rules of behaviour of an ideal teacher leads to an argument between them when Kovalenko rejects Belikov's precepts. He even throws him down the stairs. Varvara witnesses Belikov's humiliation and bursts out laughing. Belikov is seized with anxiety at the thought that this scene could lead to a new

---

[16] This has to do with Varvara and Kovalenko's bicycle tour. See above Note 4.

caricature and as a further consequence cause him to retire prematurely, given his concern for his public harassment. This means that he is afraid of a new scandal, and in this context it is important to note that Burkin had characterized the business of the caricature entitled "Enamoured Anthropos" using the term a "colossal scandal" (S. 10: 48). One might say that Belikov had become so absorbed into the world of the caricature that his imagination had made him into his own caricaturist. His dread drives him to illness, sickbed, and coffin. Describing Belikov's facial expression, Burkin comments ironically on the panic victim's last resting place in the coffin: "Now, lying in the coffin, his expression was gentle, pleasant, even light-hearted, as if he was happy that finally he had been placed in a case which he would never leave. Yes, he had reached his goal!" (S 10: 52). The description of the human face, omitted in the ecphrasis of the caricature, is now completed by Belikov's expression in death.

The ecphrasist Burkin's reaction to the caricature stands in opposition to that of Belikov. He does not become displaced into the depicted space, does not identify himself with the object of the caricature, but rather remains outside it as a cool observer. This stance of the distanced observer corresponds to the description of the ecphrasis as a "colossal scandal," an expression that by its very semantics expresses an external perspective. This conceptual distance is typical for the entire story of Belikov and is thus characteristic of Burkin's entire speech product. However, when reconstructing the distancing concepts in Burkin's speech product one must be aware that Chekhov's story incorporates not one, but two framed stories. Before Burkin begins his story, the two hunting companions talk about Mavra, the wife of the village elder in whose barn they are going to spend the night. We learn that, for ten years already, Mavra has developed the habit of spending her days sitting by the stove and wandering the village street by night. It is not clear which of the two interlocutors has told this story, but Burkin's reaction is the one that is emphasized. He sees in Mavra an example of the type of person that is "solitary by nature" (S 10: 42), comparing her to such animals as the hermit crab or the snail with its house, and attributes it to an atavistic effect. He offers the story of Belikov as a further example of atavism. This conceptual chain is completed in the course of the story by the terms "man in a case" (S 10: 45) and finally in the plural "people in cases" (S 10: 53).

Ivan Ivanych, the listener, reacts both to the story of Belikov and also to the formal, generalizing terms that Burkin uses, that is to say to

the entire speech product. When Burkin gets to the plan to marry off Belikov, Ivan Ivanych first takes it as a joke ("you're joking"; (S 10: 45), no
doubt because the mere idea of a "man in a case" being coupled in marriage strikes him as impossible. Consequently he suggests a condition for
the marriage: "Then he would have to give up his galoshes and his umbrella" (S 10: 48) that Belikov clearly could not fulfil. His reactions to the
conceptual generalizations are particularly instructive. Burkin describes
the impact of "people like Belikov" (S 10: 44) on the inhabitants of the
town over the last ten to fifteen years: the intelligentsia, including Burkin,
had subjugated itself to the interdictions resulting from the anxieties of
the "man in the case" because it was itself anxiety-ridden; at this Ivan
Ivanych declares "Yes. Decent thinking people read Shchedrin and Turgenev and writers like Buckle and so on, and yet they knuckle under pa-
tiently… That's the way it is" (S 10: 44). He repeats his conclusion word
for word—"that's the way it is"—when, at the end of the story about Belikov, Burkin once again touches on the fact that the general phenomenon
of the "man in a case" is still present even after Belikov's death, and will
be there in the future. However, the matter does not rest with the simple
confirmation of the fact of a class of people in cases. At the end of the entire tale Ivan Ivanych utters a long monologue about the toleration of lies,
insults, and the humiliation of those that "stand on the side of honest,
free people" (S 10: 54), and comes to a quite new conclusion that points to
the shattering of social encasements: "[…] no, it can't go on any longer!"
(ibid.).

Based on the ecphrasis phenomenon one can discern a three-fold
gradation of recipients: Belikov the beholder of the caricature is absorbed
empathetically into its pictorial world and identifies himself with the
main object represented there; Burkin in turn views him from the perspective of the generalizing conceptions that characterize his speech
product as the type of an atavistic "man in a case"; and Ivan Ivanych observes and compares the concepts used by Burkin with the caricature and
the plot situation of the marriage of the "man in a case," but also with the
instigators of the marriage plan, and articulates his revolutionary conclusion concerning a universal class of people in cases.[17]

---

[17] On this subject cf. Kataev, *Proza Chekhova*: 242. However, Kataev points out that
in the entire trilogy Ivan Ivanych's revolutionary vision is downplayed, whereas
Burkin also comes close to feeling his way into the metaphysical landscape (in

Regarding both Burkin and Ivan Ivanych we can now decide the question arising from Karl Bühler's theory as to whether the relation between the framing situation as *demonstratio ad oculos* and the framed story as *deixis am phantasma* is one of extension or displacement, that is to say, one of continuity of the spatial and temporal axes, or rupture of continuity. In the case of Burkin there are clear indications of continuity. These comprise the information given at the very beginning of the story concerning Belikov to the effect that "about two months ago in our town there died a teacher of Greek by the name of Belikov, my colleague" (S 10: 42–43). Lines can be drawn from the "here" and "now" of the narrative situation (the barn, the evening after a day's hunting) defined as the origin of the spatial and temporal axes because of the first-person pronoun (expressed in the possessive "my") to the nearby provincial town on the spatial axis and the recent past on the temporal one. Regarding Ivan Ivanych, there is again an indication of the continuity through the treatment of the personal pronouns. At the end of Burkin's story Ivan Ivanych gives his only lengthy speech. In it he relates the concept of the case to the life-style of the intellectuals, among which he includes himself through use of the first person plural: "Isn't the fact that we live in the stuffiness and crowded conditions of the city, write useless papers, play whist—is that not like a case?" (S 10: 53). However, his interlocutor Burkin objects to such an inclusion in the concept of the class of humanity in a case, breaking off the conversation and suggesting to Ivan Ivanych that they go to sleep. In this way Belikov remains a third person (he) for Burkin; to be sure, the latter does localise him in his own deictic field and interprets him conceptually, but at the same time he keeps his distance from him, while Ivan Ivanych uses first and third-person singular pronouns (I and he), but also Burkin's second person singular (you) as a representative of the social class of intellectuals to create an all-embracing first-person plural, thus universalizing the concept of the man in the case.

Let us now turn to the already mentioned hidden ecphrasis, which belongs to the *demonstratio ad oculos* of the framing situation. In this case the pictorial element comprises the entire spatial situation, which typo-

---

"Gooseberries"). There is thus no sharp contrast between the two figures, but rather a relationship of gradually shaded approach to what Kataev calls the norm of everyday life.

logically corresponds to the landscape painting; it is difficult to recognize because unlike the ecphrasis of the caricature, the painting type or title is not mentioned, but more than anything because the construction and elements of the picture are not given at once, but divided between the beginning and the end of the text, that is to say through the device of completion over a large textual distance. The first sentence of the entire story determines the "where" and the number of the "who": "Once, on the very edge of the village of Mironositskoe, in the barn of the village elder Prokofii, belated huntsmen settled down for the night. There was only two of them" (S 10: 42). Shortly thereafter one of the two characters (Burkin) is separated out of the visual field (the principal narrator tells us that he is lying in the barn invisible: "He was not visible in the gloom": ibid.). In this way the spatial position and perspective of the principal narrator is defined: he is located outside in front of the barn. Only Ivan Ivanych, the figure sitting in front of the barn, is visible to him in the light of the moon ("he was lit by the moon": ibid.). The mention of the moonlight making objects in the space visible, reveals the first orientation towards a painterly vision, although it is not yet enough to allow us to speak of the ecphrasis of a landscape painting.[18] It must however be kept in mind that given the visual field illuminated from above and the fact that Burkin is hidden in the barn, his narrating speech action is for the listener Ivan Ivanych, and for the reader, a purely acoustic phenomenon: one can only hear Burkin's voice, but cannot see him in the field of the *demonstratio ad oculos*.

   Throughout Burkin's entire narrative speech action the visual field

---

[18] Discussing Leonardo da Vinci, Bühler remarks: "[...] in his painting the master of the brush wilfully puts light, shade and all other effects exactly where he wants them. [...] Thus the fact that the painter has to consider the means of creating a pictorial space and illuminating it in a particular way simultaneously liberates him from the *co-physical* surroundings [...]" Bühler, op.cit: 371, Bühler's emphasis. The co-physical surroundings refer to the real surrounding space in which the painting as a physical object is located. Chekhov's mention of the moonlight that in the construction of the landscape painting recurs at the very end of the story can thus be understood as the beginning of the construction of a co-physically liberated pictorial space. All the objects in it receive a new, systematic distribution in the deictic and symbolic field of the painting. This overlies the *demonstratio ad oculos* of the frame situation and its symbolic values.

with Ivan Ivanych in it is only indirectly evoked through mentions of his bodily actions (he smokes his pipe and looks at the moon [S 10: 44]; he turns quickly and looks into the barn [S 10: 45]; he smokes his pipe [S 10: 53]). These few mentions are however enough to remind the reader that the visual field of the *demonstratio ad oculos* is continuously present.

When Burkin has finished his narration, he steps out of the barn and into the visual field. Now the initial description of the body of Ivan Ivanych is complemented by that of Burkin's appearance and the two hunting dogs accompanying him. Now for the first time the principal narrator provides a landscape description: in the midnight moonlight, that is to say, when the moon is at its highest, the village can be seen to right as well as a five-verst long street, and on the left at the edge of the village begins a field that extends to the distant horizon, it also completely lit up by the moon. The arrangement of the objects to the right and left with the road probably going off at an angle (otherwise the "five versts" would hardly be visible) contains, apart from the title of the picture, all the elements of a landscape painting with two human figures on the edge and two dogs. An additional element in the principal narrator's speech leads one to believe that the prototype for the scene may have been the type of the metaphysical landscape in the style of Levitan: "When on a moonlight night you see a broad village street with its huts, hayricks, and sleeping willows, then a quiet feeling comes over one's soul; in that peacefulness, sheltered by the night-time shadows from labours, cares and sorrow, it feels meek, saddened, beautiful, and it seems that even the stars are watching it fondly and with tenderness and that there is no longer any evil in the world and all is well" (S 10: 53).[19]

This entire passage of landscape description commences with Burkin's recognition of the moon: "'The moon, the moon!' he said, looking up" (ibid.). This might be a technical reminder to the reader to imagine the moon as the light source of the picture, but it is also conceivable that the communion of souls between the "stars" and the principal narrator as beholder of the picture is also shared by Burkin, as well as by Ivan Ivanych, who is constantly located on the edge of the picture. Burkin,

---

[19] Such a harmonious landscape description recurs in "Gooseberries," except that there Burkin too opens himself to the effect of the landscape, something that does not happen in "Man in a Case." See also note 17 above.

however, does not yield to the effect of the scene for long. He suggests to Ivan Ivanych that they go to sleep and goes into the barn with him.

From the perspective of the two figures, who are almost asleep already, the principal narrator evokes a sound image that, inversely to that of Burkin's narrative, is directed from outside inwards into the barn. The sound image is of human steps that approach the barn, stop, and "after a minute" can be heard again. In all this sound image, given the one-minute pause, comprises a sort of "sound poem" with no verbal semantics: "[...] suddenly light footsteps could be heard: tup, tup... The dogs started to growl" (S 10: 54). This "sound poem" could thus be taken to contain two stanza-like lines composed of rhythmical tones and pauses, with between them a one-minute pause delimiting the boundary between the stanzas, with the barking of the hunting dogs representing the conclusion from without, through an opposing sound. The dogs, which were previously linked only with Burkin, and not Ivan Ivanych, can be viewed as further attributes of Burkin's "case," which had already been represented by the barn. (We should recall here that Burkin also, as one of the teachers, had come to Belikov's funeral with umbrella and wearing galoshes, the most important identifiers of the "man in a case." In his description of Belikov's life Burkin had designated the former's apartment and bed as additional cases. The fact that Burkin conceals himself from view in the barn can also be read as an architectural sign of his "encasement," especially through the contrast with Ivan Ivanych, who had sat in the open in front of the barn door to listen to the story of Belikov.) The growling of the dogs with its syncopic function with regard to the rhythmical sound of the steps can thus be read as the expression of the dogs protecting their master Burkin from the steps and their underlying semantics. These semantics also are evidenced in Burkin's commentary: "That's Mavra walking" (ibid.).[20] This remark is followed by the comment of the principal narrator: "The steps fell silent" (ibid.).

---

[20] An almost identical sentence recurs with another subject in *The Cherry Orchard* from the mouths of Liubov' Andreevna and Ania: "Liubov' Andreevna (*thoughtfully*). Epikhodov is walking....Ania (*thoughtfully*). Epikhodov is walking..." This is immediately followed by Gaev's metaphysical address to Mother Nature ("O nature [...]" (S 12: 224). Gaev's pathos-filled rhetoric leads to a caricatural effect that the other characters protect themselves from. This could be read as a self-

The acoustic phenomenon of the steps is therefore primarily oriented towards Burkin, the narrator of the story of the "man in the case,"
who however himself falls into this category without recognizing it. The
story of Mavra as initially related henceforth receives a quite different
meaning from the one given by Burkin, who links the atavistic lonely
walker with the "person in the case." Mavra's wandering in the night
along a long, moonlit road in the space of cosmic communion between
the stars and the human soul corresponds much more to the way Yuliya
Sergeyevna is enticed into the landscape painting in the story "Three
Years." Burkin resists such communion, supported by the growling dogs,
just as he had resisted empathy with the caricatured figure of Belikov and
Ivan Ivanych's extension of the concept of the man in a case.

The closeness of the concealed device of ecphrasis to Levitan's
landscape paintings is suggested not only through the evident cosmic
dimension, but also the combination of a moonlit landscape with the
"sound poem" of the steps. Specialists consider Levitan not just a "philosophical" but also a "lyrical" landscape painter.[21] It is conceivable that
it was precisely this characteristic of his painting that had inspired Chekhov to combine "sound poem" and landscape painting.

Stepping back to view the entire construction of "The Man in a
Case," we can now come to the following conclusion: the technique of the
framed story permits Chekhov to construct two deictic fields, the *demonstratio ad oculos* of the narrative situation with the interlocutors Burkin
and Ivan Ivanych, and the *deixis am phantasma* centred around Belikov.
The first field is overlaid with an ecphrastic landscape painting, the prototype of which could be a painting by Levitan or that type of painting. In
the second field the ecphrastic insertion is a caricature of Belikov containing the typical attributes of the "man in a case," causing one to doubt
whether the plot-forming motif of Belikov's marriage with the likewise
depicted Varvara can succeed, and the course of the plot shows its deadly
failure.

The figures in the frame situation are coordinated with the two
kinds of ecphrasis in different ways. Burkin, in the role of the narrator,

---

parody by Chekhov of his frequent landscape descriptions, which the tale "The
Steppe" had highlighted.

[21] See, for example, *Peredvishniki*. There the expression is, to be sure, meant not in
the sense of a literary term, but to denote a mood.

observes the anxiety Belikov feels as he empathetically identifies himself with the caricatural depiction, and on the level of his narratorial speech product the generalizing concepts focussing on the type of the man in a case correspond to his stance of a distant, remote observer; to these concepts Belikov and also Mavra, the heroine of the likewise mentioned "story in a story," are subsumed as visible examples. His listener Ivan Ivanych in turn becomes the observer of the observer Burkin with a special eye for the key concept in Burkin's speech product of the man in a case. From this standpoint Ivan Ivanych extends the concept in such a way that not only he himself, but also Burkin falls into it, although Burkin vehemently resists.

The ecphrasis of the landscape is provided by the principal narrator. It appears in combination with a sort of "sound poem" that represents the heroine Mavra visibly as a person who at least by night has thrown off her narrow case. There is a contrast in the way the two interlocutors relate to the "landscape with sound poem": while Burkin uses the barn and dogs to retreat into his own "case," Ivan Ivanych opens himself up to the landscape by going out again after he has listened to the "sound poem" in the barn, and spends the night at the barn door contemplating the landscape to which he was turned during Burkin's entire speech action. In his enduring borderline position with regard to the landscape with its "lyrical" and metaphysical dimensions, the reader as recipient of Chekhov's story is offered the possibility to contemplate his own position as to atavistic, but also social cases such as that of marriage into which people are driven as if by dogs, so that the peace of the coffin appears to be the only solution. Two details of the ecphrastic landscape and its two visual figures—Ivan Ivanych's pipe and Burkin's two hunting dogs—are food for thought: the pipe may be the attribute of a contemplative and reflective stance, the hunting dogs the attribute of a plot of "being driven into marriage" from which the hunted flees like an animal.[22]

---

[22] If we view the entire text as a speech product, then Burkin and Ivan Ivanych's position at the edge of the landscape is linked on this level with a model of centre and periphery. Burkin's commentary on the noise of Mavra's steps—"that's Mavra walking"—uses the verb of motion *khodit'*, which also occurs in a different form in his ecphrasis of the caricature as speech product: "Belikov is walking in galoshes." The fact that Belikov is going in a specific direction (*idti*) along with the juxtaposition with Varvara and the caption "Enamoured anthropos" suggests

II. Frame Construction and Ecphrastic Elements in "On The Harmfulness Of Tobacco"

If we examine the monodrama from the point of view of the genre of the "little scene" practiced by Chekhov in his youth and its relationship with the "drawing with caption," a proximity suggested by the definition given of a "scene-monologue" and by the subtitle-like characterisation "the husband of his wife," then it becomes apparent that here, as in "The Man in a Case," we have to do with a frame construction. Niukhin's initial situation is that of a lecturer on a podium in front of an invited public; his wife has assigned him the task of making a speech against the use of tobacco. However, the lecturer quickly abandons the assignment and instead of tobacco talks about his thirty-three year old marriage, the girls boarding school, about his wife's music school, where he has to fulfil a load of functions, and about his numerous marriageable daughters. The didactic admonitory speech thus changes both topic and genre, turning into an advertisement for the boarding school, the music school, and his daughters, but then becomes unhinged and turns into a lamentation about his wife and marriage. To this point the play could be read as a continuation of the story of Belikov in "The Man in a Case," had the teachers' attempt to drive their colleague into a marriage with the lively Varvara succeeded. The link to the story is also hinted at by the name of the street where the music school is located, "Five-Dog Street" (S 13: 193), reminding us of Burkin's hunting dogs.

The analogy of the frame situation in the story is to be found in the

---

he is going into marriage (the objective of the plot), but in actual fact he is heading into the grave (objective of the subplot). Mavra's walking without a specific direction (*khodit'*) can signify the search for a way out and a goal as far as her night-time behaviour is concerned, as opposed to her daytime activity (sitting by the oven). Both verbal expressions form the centres of the respective ecphrases and of the entire speech product of the text. The fact that they are linked means that they also create a correlation between the respective subjects, Belikov and Mavra. The pipe and hunting dogs as attributes of the two interlocutors Burkin and Ivan Ivanych are located in the part of the speech product pertaining to the main narrator. On the pictorial level of the landscape painting they serve to mark the marginal position of the respective figures, while on the level of the speech product they become symbols of their inner, contrasting attitude towards the centre.

demonstrated situation of the public lecture on tobacco. The shift of the tobacco lecture into an advertisement and then a lamentation transforms Niukhin's appearance within the framing situation into a living drawing in the style of a caricature. Niukhin is presented in the theatrical *demonstratio ad oculos* as a Belikov come alive again, complaining about the many social cases (his functions) forced on him through his marriage.

If we read the monodrama in the light of the story of the man in a case, then the additional question arises as to whether Niukhin also undertakes a flight out of this case analogous to Belikov's flight from marriage. One might further expect that the ecphrasis of the landscape painting in some form or other might recur. And indeed, on the level of the plot such an escape attempt does occur: after complaining about his wife, Niukhin attempts a kind of revolt by taking off the old frock coat in which he was married, and trampling on it. This gesture of freedom is preceded by three phantasmatic displacements, the last of which is the equivalent of a landscape painting.

The phantasmatic displacements begin with the genre of music: Niukhin sings an aria in order to spice up the "arid" theme of tobacco: "We will not blink in the heat of battle..." (S 13: 192). Then, after beginning his lamentation, he talks about the characteristic method of overcoming spatial distance and the definition of a place in the folk tale: "Here I am giving a lecture; I seem light-hearted but I actually want to scream or fly to some thrice-nine distant land" (S 13: 193). Finally he links the desire to run away with a moonlit landscape: "To run away, to chuck everything and run away and not look back ... Where? It doesn't matter where ...[...] and stop somewhere in a field far far away and stand like a tree, a column, a scarecrow, under a broad sky, and look all night long at the quiet, bright moon overhead, and forget, forget..." (S 13: 194).

If we view these three displacements into different artistic genres as a plot possibility with the rubric "Niukhin attempts a revolt against the case of his marriage," then they can be interpreted as respectively psychological self-encouragement (the aria), a bold flight into a folk-tale land, and a flight into the solitariness of a wide field in a landscape painting. The last vision however contains a decisive difference from the moonlit landscape in "The Man in a Case": Niukhin's landscape vision is completely empty and, unlike Mavra, Niukhin does not want to walk, but simply stand motionless; moreover, there is also no hint of a communion between soul and heavens. Rather, as in the case of Mavra, a partial parallel can be traced with Burkin, who, when he finally emerges from the barn, seems to see only the moon: "'The moon, the moon!' he said looking up." The comparison to a "scarecrow" is thus the equivalent of the two hunting dogs that accompany Burkin. The dogs hunt game, and the scarecrow frightens off birds and in a broader sense all living thing. Ultimately the three displacements thus represent only the caricature of a metaphysical landscape, and Niukhin's imagination is spiritually as remote from the "philosophical" and "lyrical" landscape painting in the style of Levitan as is Burkin. Niukhin, who is presented on the level of the theatrical *demonstratio ad oculos* as a caricature is, on the level of the *deixis am phantasma*, capable of generating only a caricatural picture with the potential title "Niukhin as scarecrow."

The force of attraction of the moonlit landscape with the scarecrow is so strong for Niukhin that he makes the transition from the planning stage of his flight to its first stage of realization. He tears off the frock coat from his wedding and tramples on it, so that a first case has been removed. Freed in this way, he might now begin on his legs, which are already in motion, but Niukhin needs his legs for another objective: he spins around on the spot, in order to show the public the worn-out back of his waist-coat, and compares himself to this item of apparel: "I am old, poor, pitiful, like this waistcoat with its worn-out back... (*Shows the back.*)" (S 13: 194). Shortly thereafter he puts the coat on again and returns to the topic of the speech about tobacco, ending with a rhetorical ending in Latin: "*Dixi et animam levavi!*" (ibid.). Thus the end follows right after the first phase of the plot, the flight is abandoned, and Niukhin creeps back into the shell of his clothing and the shell of the role of lecturer with the classical, archaic Latin formula; this can be seen as creating an additional intertextual link to the man in a case Belikov, who taught ancient Greek and admired dead languages. Also a typical shell noted by Ivan Ivanych occurs: Niukhin requests the public, should his wife inquire, to say that he had given the required lecture on tobacco. He thus commits a lie towards his "superior," his wife. This is reminiscent of Ivan Ivanych's final speech about the established convention of the lie in which all intellectuals participate out of fear of losing their miserable means of existence.[23]

---

[23] To be sure, the very choice of words in Ivan Ivanych's final speech also reflects the hierarchical way of thinking of the man in a case: "[...] don't dare state openly that you are on the side of honest, free people, but lie to yourself, smile,

Thus both ecphrastic pictures from "The Man in the Case" return in the one-acter in a different form. The transformation lies partly in the fact that the distribution of character and landscape picture found there is inversed (the caricature is now the *demonstratio ad oculos*, while the landscape is placed on the level of the *deixis am phantasma*), and furthermore the landscape itself is now subordinated to the caricature.

The dominance of the caricature contained in the frame situation of the speech on tobacco over the phantasmatic landscape in "On the Harmfulness of Tobacco" corresponds to a series of other features in the construction of the entire play. The first of these relates to the link in genre theory between the *demonstratio ad oculos* and the *deixis am phantasma* in drama. According to Bühler, as already discussed, a displacement link that embraces the continuity between both fields is possible in the epic, but not in drama. Consequently a "forgetting" of the field of the *demonstratio ad oculos* is impossible. Both fields overlay one another continuously, for the simple reason that *deixis am phantasma* is so closely bound with the speech action of a dramatic character that every depiction of a phantasmatic world is always also a component of its dramatic action in the situation of the here and now. Yet when Niukhin in the course of his speech action describes the field of the moonlit landscape, he attempts an action of displacement that in and of itself is contradictory: he identifies with the sole object in the landscape using the second person singular of the personal pronoun that includes the first person "stand like a tree, a

---

and all that for a piece of bread, a cosy job, *because of some petty rank or other that's not worth a ha'penny* [...]" ([S 10: 54] my emphasis—H.S.). Niukhin is also inclined to be concerned with rank. It is associated with the clothing attribute of the waistcoat. Immediately he steps onto the lecturer's stand his waistcoat and "dignified" bearing become linked: "*enters majestically, bows, and adjusts his waistcoat*" (S 13: 191). To be sure, Niukhin divests himself for a while of his marital frock coat, but not the waistcoat. Niukhin takes on his "dignified" bearing again while taking his leave. Thus, despite his lamentation concerning his marriage he is conscious of his dignity and clings to it. His verbal affirmation of his dignity, probably prompted by the worn-out state of his waistcoat, is shown thereby to be empty, rhetorical sententiousness: "But I don't want anything! I am above that, purer than that, I was once young, intelligent, studied in the university, had dreams, and considered myself a human being..." (S 13: 194). The juxtaposition of present and past tense forms of the verb in one sentence serves to underline its emptiness.

column, a scarecrow, under a broad sky, and look all night long and the quiet, bright moon overhead" (S 13: 194), thus adopting the kind of personal extension that we have already observed in the case of Ivan Ivanych, but then adds markers of forgetting that according to Bühler are possible only in epic displacement: "[...] and forget, forget... Oh, how I would like not to remember anything!" (ibid.). The conditional form ("how I would like") denotes on the level of his speech product the impossible, generically speaking, attempt at forgetting, while being also a bad omen for the immediately subsequent attempt to flee from wedding coat and marriage.[24]

Further such omens[25] are abundant in Niukhin's entire speech product. Let us single out only the most important ones. One is the term of abuse "blockhead" (*chuchelo*). It appears for the first time when Niukhin quotes his wife's speech while he is at the stage of lamenting the fact of his marriage, but has not yet conceived the idea of flight: "'There's no reason,' she says, 'to feed you, you blockhead...'" (S 13: 192). This comment is embedded in the episode of the "pancakes" in the girl's

---

[24] Bühler formulates the forgetting that arises from true displacement in this way: "[...] whoever is displaced in the phantasma *is able to forget the reason why he was displaced there*" (Bühler: 375). The conditional that is overly present in Niukhin's speech product denotes what Bühler calls the "first illusory games of a child" (53). In illusory games "what *should* happen with him and to him us only fleetingly and symbolically hinted at in the material" (ibid.; emphasis K. Bühler). Bühler contrasts illusory games with the childish "work games" occurring in a later stage of development; in these the joy at the product is predominant. Accordingly Niukhin oscillates between the stance of the illusory game player and the work player. At no point does he leave the game stance, since he keeps in view the framing conditions of the game, i.e., the lecture on tobacco he has been ordered to give. On this see also note 30 below.

[25] With regard to Chekhov's view of mankind R.L. Jackson quotes Sartre's existential verdict: "'There are no omens in the world.' This is a painful lesson that many of Chekhov's heroes experience." (Jackson, "The Seagull...": 104). However, in my estimation it remains to decide on which level of the work such omens are located and to whose perspective they belong. Someone like Niukhin, trapped in magical thought processes (witness his playing around with unlucky numbers) regards the speech product that is brought forth by his speech action as if it were composed of magical signs. From the perspective of author and reader these very same signs are conventionally constructed signals or indices.

boarding school.[26] On the verbal level however the word is also one of a series of synonyms, as can be seen from the speech quoted just previously: "'Eat these pancakes yourself, blockhead.' When she's in a bad mood, this is how she calls me: blockhead, or viper, or satan. But what kind of a satan am I?" (S 13: 192). This string of abusive terms implies Niukhin's wife's perspective regarding her husband, according to which Niukhin appears not simply as the victim of his wife, but also as the "viper in her bosom." The term of abuse "blockhead" then recurs in a further synonymous form "scarecrow," like a caption to the ecphrasis of the moonlit landscape and at the very end of the entire speech, this last time again linked with the wife's perspective and in the form of Niukhin's self-identification with the term. "If she asks, please, I beg you, tell her that there was a lecture ... that the blockhead, I mean I, conducted himself with dignity" (S 13: 194). For the reader this final instance also echoes the chain of synonyms including the terms "viper, satan" that Niukhin had defended himself against ("But what kind of a satan am I?" His omission of the term "viper" is eloquent.). The entire absence of the metaphysical, cosmic dimension in the landscape ecphrasis turns in a subtle way into a hint at the purely material nature of the marriage and the absence of the husband's love for his wife, but also for the children. The latter is demonstrated by the fact that Niukhin finds it difficult to give the precise number of his daughters. His superstitious play with unlucky numbers should probably also be seen in this context.[27] Niukhin

---

[26] This has to do with the "excessive amounts of pancakes" that Niukhin greedily gobbles down. In the earlier versions of the one-acter the enjoyment of the pancakes gave Niukhin the hiccups, one of many causes for the many digressions from the main theme of the lecture in those versions. They did not contain the attempted escape from the marital frock coat and the marriage, and the speech of praise for his wife that is only hinted at in the last version was carried out in full and Niukhin was presented as a happily married man. Thus in the last version the man who is self-satisfied in the case turns into one who is unsatisfied there. In the versions of "Gooseberries" Chekhov inverts this; on this subject cf. Rodinovaia: 538.

[27] These include the figures seven and three and their composites (daughters aged from seventeen to twenty-seven), the number thirteen for the birthday of all the daughters, the house with thirteen windows, the thirteen kopecks for brochures about the boarding school, and also the folk-tale place "somewhere beyond three times nine lands." Niukhin is locked into all this magical conjuring

is a variation of the Chekhovian complainers who blame the force of fatal, dark forces for their misfortune without asking what was the prime moving force of their lack of success.[28]

A further omen is the the actual chronological length of Niukhin's speech. It is linked with the prop of the pocket watch, which performs the function of a visible theatrical sign in the theatrical *demonstratio ad oculos*. Niukhin interrupts his rhetorical logorrhoeia three times in order to pull out the watch and check the amount of time left. Each instance is followed by an interruption in the connection with one of the topics related to the marriage: the daughters, who were all born on the thirteenth (S 13: 192), his wife who feeds him pancakes (ibid.) and finally the wife herself who—visible only to Niukhin—has appeared in the wings and is waiting for Niukhin. The entire speech process of the lecturer is thus conditioned by mechanically measured, physical time, whose ultimate source is to be found in the institution of marriage and the wife as correlative of the husband. In the field of *demonstratio ad oculos* Niukhin is bound up with a mechanical rhythm that corresponds to the genre of the caricature and stands in sharp contrast to Mavra's "lyrical" rhythm in the landscape ecphrasis in "The Man in a Case." The wife as source of the mechanical rhythm combines with the physical emotion of anxiety. Niukhin looks over his shoulder three times, because he expects the appearance of his wife in the wings, and the second time he betrays to his audience the anxiety that overtakes him: "(*Looking over his shoulder.*) Actually I don't think she has come yet, she's not here, so I can say whatever I want ... I'm afraid ... terribly afraid when she looks at me" (S 13: 193). It here becomes clear that Niukhin's wife plays the role of superior that in the case of Belikov was played by the school board. The pocket watch is only one of Belikov's many cases,[29] but for Niukhin it additionally becomes the

---

with numbers as if into a grid against which his "illusory game" in the conditional mood has no chance.

[28] To be sure, Niukhin declares his marital frock coat and marriage to be the beginning of the chain of misfortunes in his life; however, he avoids the question of why he got married at all. The reader can assume that the ultimate causes are material self-interest and the desire for promotion.

[29] Niukhin's fear of being seen by his wife may be one motif originating in Zola's novel *Thérèse Raquin*. On the possible links between this work and "On the Harmfulness of Tobacco," as well as "The Man in a Case" and other works by

indicator of the externally imposed and structured mechanical rhythm from which he flees not, like Belikov, into the grave, but in his imagination and for a precisely measured instant into a landscape resembling the lifelessness of death.

Having compared both works we can now come to some conclusions. Both ecphrastic devices encountered in "The Man in a Case" recur in inverted form in "On the Harmfulness of Tobacco." Moreover, the landscape ecphrasis in the latter is predominantly in the form of caricature, which totally deforms the nature of the landscape. On the level of the plot the sole dramatis persona in the one-acter is a married version of Belikov (also partly imbued with the properties of Burkin) who jumps out of the framework of the caricature within the epic story and onto the dramatic stage and in whom the predictable misery of marriage for Belikov is made a reality. The possibilities of flight exist only in the imagination. The dramatis persona is locked firmly into the framework of his social role as lecturer and "husband of his wife." The mechanical measuring out of time in the speech (the flowing present time—the "now"—as measured by the watch) is likewise expressive of the indissoluble bond with the "here" of the speaking role, which is only one of the functions of the role that he assumes as part and parcel of married life and which constitute the multiple encasement of Niukhin as a man in a case. The caricature of the frame situation in "On the Harmfulness of Tobacco" is reminiscent not only of the story "The Man in a Case," but also Chekhov's early technique of the "little scene" and the "drawing with caption." As Chudakov has shown, the "who"is determined by the "where" and the "what." The human figure is locked into a material environment from which it cannot escape. In "The Man in a Case" this folly was shown to be only partially present; it is precisely the framing ecphrasis of the "metaphysical" and "lyrical" landscape that make a shattering of all cases at least imaginable and thinkable. In the chronologically later one-acter the objectivizing vision of the human being in the "little scene" and the "little picture with caption," contaminated with the caricature from the story, emerges more clearly and communicates the shift of the author towards the hopelessness that lies hidden beneath the purely superficially comic figure of the hen-pecked husband. True, the hopelessness is

---

Chekhov see my article "Emile Zolas *Thérèse Raquin*: eine Inspirationsquelle für Čechov?" (in press).

also in its turn ironically disrupted: in his own childish way Niukhin is doing quite well. The only ones to come off badly are the audience that have come to actually learn something about tobacco.

Translated from the German by J. Douglas Clayton.

WORKS CITED

Bühler, Karl. *Sprachtheorie: Die Darstellungsfunktion der Sprache.* Frankfurt am Main: Ullstein Verlag, 1978.

Chizhevsky, Dmitri. "Chekhov in the Development of Russian Literature." In: *Chekhov: A Collection of Critical Essays,* edited by Robert Louis Jackson. Englewood Cliffs, N. J.: Prentice-Hall, 1967.

Chudakov, A.P. *Anton Pavlovich Chekhov: Kniga dlia uchashchikhsia.* M.: "Prosveshchenie," 1987.

Die Peredwishniki: Genossenschaft für Wanderausstellungen (1870–1923). Compiled and introduced by A. Lebedew. Translated from the Russian by Katrin Strauss. L.: Aurora-Kunstverlag, 1982.

Grossman, Leonid. "The Naturalism of Chekhov." In: *Chekhov: A Collection of Critical Essays,* edited by Robert Louis Jackson. Englewood Cliffs, N. J.: Prentice-Hall, 1967.

Jackson, Robert Louis. "The Seagull: The Empty Well, the Dry Lake, and the Cold Cave." In: *Chekhov: A Collection of Critical Essays,* edited by Robert Louis Jackson Englewood Cliffs, N. J.: Prentice-Hall, 1967: 99-111.

Kandinsky (Kandinskii, Vasilii). "Der Wert eines Werkes der konkreten Kunst," *Essays über Kunst und Künstler,* compiled and edited by Max Bill. Bern: Benteli-Verlag X, 1973.

Kataev, Vladimir B. *Proza Chekhova: problemy interpretatsii.* M.: Izdatel'stvo Moskovskogo universiteta, 1979.

Kranz, Gisbert. *Das Bildgedicht in Europa: Zur Theorie und Geschichte einer literarischen Gattung.* Paderborn, 1973.

Lämmert, Eberhard. *Bauformen des Erzählens.* Second, revised edition. Stuttgart: Metzlersche Verlagsbuchhandlung, 1967.

Mráz, Bohumír, Mrázová, Marcela. *Encyklopedie světového malířství,* Praha: Academia, 1988.

Rodinovaia, V. M. "Primechaniia." In: A. P. Chekhov, *Sobranie sochinenii,* vol. VIII, Povesti i rasskazy 1895–1903 M.: Gosudarstvennoe izdatel'stvo "Khudozhestvennoi literatury," 1962.

Schmid, Herta. "Emile Zolas *Thérèse Raquin:* eine Inspirationsquelle für Čechov?" (In press.)

Skaftymov, A. P. "Primechaniia." In: A. P. Chekhov, *Sobranie sochinenii*, vol. IX, P'esy 1880–1904. M.: Gosudarstvennoe izdatel'stvo "Khudozhestvennoi literatury," 1963.

Walzel, Oskar. *Wechselseitige Erhellung der Künste Ein Beitrag zur Würdigung kunstgeschichtlicher Begriffe; Philosophische Vorträge veröffentlicht von der Kantgesellschaft*, Berlin: Reuther und Reichard, 1917.

————."Wechselseitige Erhellung der Künste," *Gehalt und Gestalt im Kunstwerk des Dichters*, 2nd ed. Darmstadt: Wissenschaftliche Buchgesellschaft, 1957.

The Poetics of Middle Ground: Revisiting "The Lady with the Little Dog"

JULIE W. DE SHERBININ
Colby College

> "Но как мне быть с моей грудною клеткой?"

> "What am I to do with my rib cage?"
> —Boris Pasternak, *Borisu Pil'niaku* (1931)

In one of his notebooks, Chekhov famously wrote:

> Between "God exists" and "there is no God" lies a whole immense field, a field through which the true sage makes his way with great difficulty. A Russian person knows one or the other of these two extremes, but *the middle between them doesn't interest him*; and as a consequence he usually knows nothing at all, or very little. (February, 1897; S 17:224)[1]

In regard to questions of faith and ideology, Alexander Chudakov has dubbed Chekhov *chelovek polia*—"a man of the field."[2] While Chekhov does address faith in this notebook fragment, what appears to have been the most interesting to Chekhov overall was the psychology of the "field." How does an individual negotiate received codes of behavior and *a priori* cultural expectations (forms of the "extreme"), or face up to ambivalence and ambiguity, or come to terms with middle ground? Because of the propensity toward extremes in Russian intellectual culture, the "middle" was not the safe haven of a *status quo* as it has been in western bourgeois culture. It was, as Chekhov suggests, territory infre-

---

[1] Emphasis mine. Translations are mine unless otherwise noted.
[2] Chudakov, "Chelovek polia": 301–308.

quently visited, a place of potentialities alien to—even radical for—the Russian mind.

Here I revisit Chekhov's "The Lady with the Little Dog" (*"Dama s sobachkoi"*) (1899) with an eye on middling matters. This paper analyzes the motif of height that threads through the story, and demonstrates that commonplace meanings have been attached to imagery which I believe Chekhov meant to have read in very different ways. In my reading of the story I follow two crucial principles of Chekhov's poetics laid down by Savely Senderovich: first, that the importance of attention to semantic series in a text, and the relationship between semantic series, reveals the organic material of a story on which any interpretation needs to be based; and second, that seemingly incidental detail is key—if we can discover the key—to a story's meaning.[3]

"The Lady"'s famous plot paraphrases easily: a light extramarital affair in Yalta between the Muscovite Gurov and the provincial Anna Sergeyevna turns into a committed, but concealed, deeper love. The couple meets on holiday in the south; when they return to their respective homes, contrary to expectation neither can forget the other. The story appears to be a tale of conquest gone unexpectedly romantic and misogyny put right. However, it is not chiefly a story about an adulterous affair, but rather a story about transformation. We view the mini-steps toward Gurov's transformation from a cliché-ridden character controlled by strict and unimaginative narratives to a character of some substance, able to entertain ambiguity. The *result* is the satisfaction of a genuine romantic connection, but that is not the *story* itself.

A central passage for this reading occurs well into the story, when Gurov, having become obsessed by memories of Anna Sergeyevna while back in Moscow, goes to the provincial town of S. to seek her out. He finds her at a premiere in the local theatre. Here is how the meeting occurs. Upon seeing Gurov, Anna Sergeyevna "got up and quickly went to the exit, he followed her, and they both walked incoherently through the corridors and stairways, now going up, now going down [...] on a narrow, dark stairway marked 'To the Amphitheatre' she stopped" (S 10:140). That they stop in the middle of the staircase is made clear by sub-

---

[3] See Senderovich, "Poetics and Meaning in Chekhov's 'On the Road'": 135–66; "A Fragment of Semiotic Theory of Poetic Prose (The Chekhovian Type) *Chekhov s glazu na glaz*": 43–64.

sequent details: two teenagers are smoking on the landing above and looking down at them; then Anna Sergeyevna becomes agitated at Gurov's embraces when they hear someone coming up the stairs. Thus the couple's location in the middle—as they affirm this newfound love—is underscored by two pairs of framing adverbs: "above", "downward" (*povyshe, vniz*); "from below going up" (*snizu, vverkh*). Why does Chekhov go to so much trouble with these seemingly minor details?

The "middle" status on the staircase begins to resolve a set of images throughout the story that have to do with height. Physical heights, and the associated fields of prestige, sexual conquest, and lofty ideas, are attached to Gurov through a motif of masculinity. We are first clued in to the pretence of the "high up" by characteristics of Gurov's wife, who is a tall woman and whose features are distasteful to Gurov precisely because they infringe on conventionally masculine territory: she is "upright, important, substantial" and considers herself "a thinker" (S 10:128)—an incursion into the masculine realm of abstract thought within the economy of Gurov's notions. At the other end of a polarized gender framework are the women with whom Gurov engages on a physical level. He betrays his wife frequently and refers to women, memorably, as "the lower race" (S 10:128).

Gurov initially occupies the high ground—and the cerebral male ground—in relation to Anna Sergeyevna. His first sighting of "the lady with a little dog" on the Yalta embankment leads to a male fantasy involving "stories of easy conquests, trips to the mountains," (S 10:129)— i.e., to a place of height. At this first sighting, too, appears the dog that has generated so much criticism, and Chekhov's species designation for the dog presents a tricky translation question. The little dog is a *shpitz*; "Pomeranian", a fair rendering of the dog's breed, misses the emblematic association of *shpitz* with the German (and calqued Russian) word for "peak, spire, steeple."[4] The little dog has been interpreted elsewhere as a sign of sexual desire—notably in Josef Heifitz's film, where it pants suggestively as Gurov and Anna Sergeyevna scurry to her hotel room—and, indeed, the *shpitz* (which initially responds to Gurov's proffered bone)

---

[4] My thanks to Cathy Popkin for pointing out the German meaning of *shpitz* during the Ottawa Chekhov Workshop. Characteristically, Richard Pevear and Larissa Volokhonsky have handled this translation sensitively, giving us "spitz" rather than "Pomeranian." Chekhov, "The Lady with the Little Dog": 361–376.

serves as a marker of the male phallic obsession with Anna Sergeyevna. In Robert L. Jackson's analysis of the "dog-like" behavior of the pair, he notes that the *shpitz* disappears later in the story once they have moved past "an erotic adventure to the spiritual maturity of a deeper relationship."[5]

In accordance with this height-conquest motif, after their first sexual encounter, Gurov takes Anna Sergeyevna up the slopes to Oreanda. When Anna Sergeyevna leaves Yalta, Gurov senses that she has not been happy with him and that in his interactions with her "flickered a shade of light irony, the crude *lofty haughtiness* of a happy man" and he recalls that "she called him good, extraordinary, *elevated*." [Emphasis mine] (S 10:135). Gurov professes feeling guilty for misleading her, but it is clear that the classic and unoriginal man-high, woman-low paradigm is the territory in which he habitually operates.

On the other hand, motifs of a fall and lowliness consistently attend Anna Sergeyevna, not so much an ironic realization of Gurov's misogynistic words about the "lower race" as a textual sign that exposes his operating system. Upon first contact with Gurov, Anna Sergeyevna immediately lowers her eyes (*opustila glaza*). She responds to their first sexual encounter as if it is her fall (*padenie*), her facial features drop (*opustilis' cherty*), and her long hair hangs down (*viseli*). Anna Sergeyevna herself announces: "I'm a bad and lowly woman" (S 10:132). But Chekhov's intent is far from that of Dostoevsky, who raises his lowly prostitute to elevated moral heights, or Tolstoy, whose lofty Anna is subjected to a disastrous sexual fall and psychological descent. Indeed, Chekhov is really not interested in Anna Sergeyevna's self-moralizing as a matter of character depiction (Anna's character is never filled out); rather, by realizing Gurov's metaphor, the figure of Anna Sergeyevna completes the picture of the fixed height paradigm. So far, no middle ground is in sight.

However, the principle of repositioning is a key to the story. A signal of reversal in "The Lady" comes in a curious (and typically Chekhovian) sentence of the sort that could very well be labeled "random."[6]

---

[5] Jackson, "Evoliutsiia v rasskaze 'Dama s sobachkoi'": 55. See also Kataev's view of Gurov as an heir to Pushkin's Don Juan, *Literaturnye sviazi Chekhova*: 106–110.

[6] Aleksandr Chudakov, in *Chekhov's Poetics* (Ann Arbor, MI: Ardis, 1983), argues that many details in Chekhov are random, incidental, and have no bearing on the text.

When Gurov and Anna Sergeyevna go down to the pier to greet the steamship, we read: "And here two particularities of the festive Yalta crowd drew especial notice: elderly ladies were dressed like young ones, and there were a lot of generals"(S 10:131). Both these details are significant. "Generals"—men of the highest rank—belong to the semantic field of lofty male importance that can be related to Gurov...and this scene heralds his initial seduction of Anna Sergeyevna. The *"damy"*—ladies—resonate with the *"dama"* of the story's title, and here the characteristic is reversal—not the substance of the scene (i.e., elderly ladies dressed to look young), but the idea of switching position. Just after this, the steamship arrives at the quay and, before pulling in, "took a long time turning around" (S 10:131). The story is about a turn around in a life (or lives). Like the steamship, and like most change in human consciousness, Gurov changes position slowly.

The scene in Oreanda following their first sexual encounter, when the lovers sit on a bench amid nature's splendor, presents the dichotomy between the high and the low in natural imagery. The motif of height we have encountered so far leads to an interpretation here that goes against the grain of conventional readings. Few have questioned the nobility of Gurov's thoughts as he surveys the splendid landscape that stretches out before the couple in Oreanda and ruminates "that everything is beautiful in this world, everything except for what we ourselves think and do when we forget the higher goals of existence and our human dignity" (S 10:134).

The symbolic essence of the Oreanda passage occurs in the dual orientation toward the sea below and the mountains above. Although Gurov and Anna Sergeyevna look down at the sea (*smotreli vniz*), it is the narrator's voice that extols the eternal qualities of the "monotonous, lacklustre noise of the sea, coming from below" which had eternally "sounded so below" and would continue to do so; and proposes that everlasting meaning lies in "the uninterrupted movement of life on earth, uninterrupted perfection" (S 10:133). This is the first glimpse that there is value "down below," and that the value resides precisely in fluidity, in the sound and movement of water. Subsequently Gurov and Anna are to make trips to see waterfalls (*vodopady*), an image that confirms the semantic intersection of flow and depth—something that might be related to women's sexuality as well.

But unlike the narrator, Gurov's thoughts, sitting beside his beautiful young lover in Oreanda, fixate on the heights. His reflections on "the higher goals of being" relate semantically not to the sea, but to the mountaintops. At the opening of the description, "white clouds stood motionless on the mountain-tops." The mountains are characterized both by obscurity (they are covered by white clouds) and by immobility. The colour white can be associated with the white *shpitz*, linking the mountain image with the masculine "heights." It would seem, however, that Gurov's upward orientation is clouded. His sentiments concerning human dignity are lofty, indeed, but have little to do with how he leads his life. What dignity is there, after all, in a sexually promiscuous middle-aged man waxing eloquent over the glories of nature in the company of his latest conquest? In other words, I would suggest that Chekhov means Gurov's words to be understood as an intellectual abstraction derived from his faulty notion of hierarchy. What looks like a lyrical flight can in fact be read as a virtual state of mental paralysis symbolically represented by the immobile white clouds. In this scene, Gurov is exposed to the notion of movement, fluidity, and depth as bearers of value, but keeps his attention focused on the heights.

Everything about Anna Sergeyevna tacitly urges a descent from the heights. First, it is noted in the opening paragraph that she is not very tall. Although he initially fantasizes about an affair with an anonymous woman, Gurov learns her surname—i.e., part of her identity—at the desk downstairs (*vnizu*) in the hotel. Chekhov makes a point of Anna Sergeyevna affirming her family status as "Orthodox." This, along with the church by which they sit in Oreanda and the steamer they watch arriving from Feodosia (the Greek root means "gift of God"), hardly bespeak a religious orientation in the story but they do place the non-descript Anna in the company of value-laden phenomena.[7] Anna's first name, incidentally, consists of a palindrome that both represents a full turn-around (from a closed end—"An"—to an open end—"na") and draws exclusive attention to the middle.

Gurov's "journey to the middle" begins with the trip to the town of S., in the middling provinces, implicitly located between the northern (or "upper") Moscow and the southern (or "lower") Yalta. While it may

---

[7] I discuss this kind of displacement in my book, *Chekhov and Russian Religious Culture*.

not be Chekhov's thinking, we can note that his use of "S." to designate the anonymous town (rather than the conventional "N.") resonates with the words "Sergeyevna," "*seredina*" ("middle"), and "*seryi*" ("grey").

Chekhov almost heavy-handedly characterizes the hotel room in which Gurov stays with the colour grey:

> ...the whole floor was covered by grey soldier's cloth and on the table was an inkstand, grey with dust, in the figure of an equestrian on a horse whose raised hand held a hat and whose head had been knocked off [...] He sat on a bed that was covered with a cheap grey hospital blanket. (S 10: 137–8)

First, the "grey" circumstances are associated with *soldatskoe sukno*— "soldier's fabric"—a downgrading for Gurov from his earlier symbolic proximity to generals, and a sign that demotion from the heights into the realm of grey is a healthy thing, signaling something like the beginnings of humility. Of course, Gurov himself is incensed by the grey surroundings, conceiving a hatred for the grey fence that surrounds the von Dideritz house and mentally registering the impulse to flee from such a fence. Accordingly, this greyness has been read mostly as Chekhov's take on the dismal, tasteless and colourless provincial world. Chekhov was no fan of mindlessness in the provinces or anywhere else, but I would suggest that "grey" here functions in a symbolic sense: "grey" is the site of synthesis, of reconciliation of extremes, of the middle—the place Gurov needs to be.

Note the metaphor of illness: the grey bed covering is like a hospital blanket. Perhaps Gurov's metaphoric sickness is the very quotidian thinking and pedestrian worldview that automatically attaches a sense of dullness to the grey surroundings. The colour grey, of course, is the synthesis of black and white, a midpoint between the two conventional signifiers of polarization. And, of course, Anna Sergeyevna's eyes are grey, as is her "favourite grey dress" (S 10:142). It would be absolutely uncharacteristic of Chekhov to unleash one word with unrelated meanings in the same story (i.e., "bad" provincial grey and "good" Anna grey). Chekhov—himself labeled a grey writer because of texts without obvious meanings—brings them together at Gurov's moment of recognition in the theatre.

The hotel room is situated directly on the route to Gurov's realization—once in the theatre—that there is no one more important to him in the whole world than Anna Sergeyevna, the small woman sitting in the third row and holding a vulgar lorgnette. The hallmark of the hotel room scene is an equestrian with its head knocked off, symbolic of the dethroned intellect formerly lodged in the head of the body, and it is in the form of an inkstand, suggesting that Gurov may now quit repeating stale texts and begin, figuratively, to write on his own. The horseman's arm remains raised in the air holding a hat, the equivalent of a cheer, and an image linked to the messenger in the red hat who later relays to Gurov that Anna Sergeyevna has arrived in Moscow to see him.

Now we return to the theatre scene. The couple's interactions in the theatre are initially cast in terms of high and low, as if in recapitulation of a theme; Anna sits with her very tall husband and, upon seeing Gurov, tries to avoid falling (*upast'*) into a faint; they both worry about being viewed together from above (the loges). But this is not the real space of their meeting. They will "connect" with each other only outside the theatre. This location—beyond the theatrical—is important. Earlier Gurov tells Anna Sergeyevna that as a youth he trained for the opera, a "high" art form full of melodrama and fully scripted. Gurov has lived a scripted life (recall his attraction to the stories of sexual conquest in Yalta and his compulsive reading of newspapers). His Moscow life abounds in roles and card playing. No wonder he thinks that Anna Sergeyevna "is joking or playing a role" (S 10:133) when she sobs in contrition after their first sexual contact. And, of course, "Geisha"—with its connections to Anna Sergeyevna's Japanese perfume and pose as a fallen woman—is being performed *inside* the provincial theatre from which Gurov and Anna Sergeyevna exit. The move outside of the theatre, then, represents a sign of distancing from the poles of high and low, a rejection of the pretense of posing and acting, and a dismissal of the inflated status of the dramatic.

Gary Saul Morson describes the way that characters move away from the dramatic in Chekhov as a function of an essential prosaics embraced by the author whereby knowledgeable characters come to abide by low-key, everyday decencies.[8] However, Gurov and Anna Sergeyevna move not toward simplification, but toward complexity. In other words,

---

[8] Morson, "*Uncle Vanya* as Prosaic Metadrama": 214–27.

the station midway on the staircase where they land after leaving the theatre (the point with which this paper started) is not a solution or resolution: such stability of meaning belongs, rather, to the world in which high is high, and low is low. Gurov is gradually leaving that world, as suggested by the conversation he has with his daughter as he accompanies her to school on the way to a rendezvous with Anna Sergeyevna in the Moscow hotel where they regularly meet.

Gurov's conversation with his daughter has attracted relatively little attention, I suspect, because critics have not known what to do with it. As it happens, his explanation of the weather serves as a sort of apotheosis of the height motif:

> "It's now three degrees above zero, but meanwhile it's still snowing," Gurov said to his daughter. "But it's only warm on the surface of the earth; in the upper layers of the atmosphere there's a completely different temperature." (S 10:141)

The "different temperature" high up in the atmosphere clearly means cold, and coldness has been associated with Gurov's life in what we might call the "upper layers" of society: he is cold toward men, he has had affairs with "cold women," and he returns to a cold, winter Moscow from warm Yalta. The snow consists of "large wet flakes" because it is nearly grounded; the wetness ties in with the image of the sea and waterfalls encountered earlier, suggesting a gradual thaw in Gurov. And, of course, the snow is falling. Finally, the adverbial phrase *mezhdu tem*— literally "between that"—situates Gurov in the middle, between cold and hot, between black and white, between high and low.[9]

The couple's meetings take place in the *Slaviansky bazar*—a favourite hotel of Chekhov, to be sure. But more pertinently in a symbolic sense the *bazar*, or marketplace, evokes a space of non-hierarchical interaction, a concept well known from Bakhtin.[10] Here hierarchies are nonexistent and meanings compete with one another; or, as more recent commentators have put it, "only hybrid notions are appropriate to such a hybrid place."[11] The

---

[9] My thanks to Wallace Sherlock for the observation about *mezhdu tem*.
[10] This is not Bakhtin's "carnival square," but the concept derives directly from it. Bakhtin, *Problems of Dostoevsky's Poetics*: 128–29.
[11] Stallybrass and White, *The Politics and Poetics of Transgression*: 27.

hotel as stand-in for marketplace also represents a "hybrid place," a space at once commercial and domestic, public and private; and it is here that Gurov's "hybrid notions" are realized, as the high and the low meet on middle ground.

It is important to note that Chekhov shows Gurov in the process of transition, and not fully re-formed[12] (a radical gesture in itself given the Russian literary tradition): recall that the steamship in the Yalta harbor "took a long time turning around." The impulse toward hierarchy, then, still resides within Gurov even toward the end of the story. Arriving at the hotel, Gurov takes off his coat below and goes upstairs, performing a condensed form of the polarized motif. However, after he has entered the room, Anna Sergeyevna immediately "fell onto his breast." (S 10:142). This embrace has symbolic resonances in several senses, not the least of which is the location of the chest in the middle between head and abdomen, and the obvious associations between breast and heart. I believe, too, that this passing reference to "breast"—"*grud'*"—can be related to the caged birds at the story's end.

Earlier in the story, when Gurov starts to become disenchanted with the elite Moscow social world in which he circulates, he blasphemes this "tailless, wingless life" (S 10:137). The implied image of a bird soaring represents Gurov's ideal—but we can now regard the soaring bird with some suspicion, both because it valorizes height and because it is a hackneyed image that reflects Gurov's cliché mentality. This leads me to suspect that something different is going on at the end of the story when the narrator compares Gurov and Anna Sergeyevna to "two migrating birds, a male and female, which been caught and forced to live in separate cages" (S 10:143). Surely this is an image of restriction, but perhaps grounded birds are not only, or not even chiefly, a tragic metaphor for the couple's separation.

Like the birdcage (*kletka*), Gurov's chest is also a cage (*grudnaya kletka*). This is where the epigraph from Pasternak comes in, for his "What am I to do with my rib (breast) cage?" in the 1931 poem *Borisu Pilniaku* clearly queries the status of the individual's inner life in the face

---

[12] On Gurov's transformation, see Shcheglov "Dve variatsii na temu smerti i vozrozhdeniia" (*Russian Language Journal* 68:159–61), and Kirjanov, *Chekhov and the Poetics of Memory*: 144.

of a repressive society,[13] a cousin to Gurov's meditations on the difference between his overt life of lies and his covert life, where "everything important, interesting and crucial to him took place secretly from others, all of that in which he was sincere and didn't deceive himself, all that comprised the kernel of his life" (S 10:141). Could the cages which separate the two be, also, a sign of interiority and self-knowledge? This reading finds reinforcement in the reference to the enclosed birds, "*samets*" and "*samka*," literally "male and female of a species" but symbolically resonant with the root *sam*, or self.

Carl Jung might say that Gurov's move from open air to the enclosures of the narrow staircase outside the theatre and the "bird cage" is part of the process of self-knowledge: "ageing people should know that their lives are not mounting and expanding, but that an inexorable inner process enforces the contraction of life."[14] The dilemma is clear: true knowledge of self can rarely be reconciled with one's public world. But this mature dilemma is not tragic in the operatic sense; ambivalent, yes — but not tragic. Men and women in their separate cages, read as a stand-in for the "middle part" of the body, suggests a centred sense of self, but with the semantically porous open air of communication between them. Or, as Michael Finke argues, the ending of "The Lady with the Little Dog" may have to do with Chekhov's own erotic sensibilities, which Finke identifies as largely *visual* and expressive of "a concern about loss of self in union with the other."[15] One has only to think of how Chekhov and Olga Knipper conducted their marriage (Finke treats this question in depth) to understand the value Chekhov placed on autonomous selves.

This "turned-around" reading of the story, then, questions the status of the images in the story as often read. The "middle spaces" have not only to do with what Gurov comes to realize when he looks in the

---

[13] My thanks to Anna Muza for pointing me to the Pasternak poem.

[14] Jung, *Aspects of the Masculine*: 33. For an unrefined Freudian reading of this story, see Greenberg, "The Presentation of the Unconscious in Chekhov's 'Lady with a Lapdog'": 126–130.

[15] Finke, *Seeing Chekhov*: 149. Finke compares the moment in which Gurov looks in the mirror at the story's ending with one of Chekhov's own encounters, suggesting that "these two scenes share a peculiar and markedly narcissistic circumstance of seeing: both Chekhov and his character experience an access of emotion in a moment following, and arguably following from, viewing themselves in a reflective surface" (145).

mirror at the narration's end—that his grey hair is a sign of value, that real meaning does not reside in prefabricated patterns, that his story is open-ended, that indeterminancy and dialogicity proffer the only real freedom; it also has to do with what *we* realize as consumers of Chekhov's images: that we can not hook them into the neat paradigms of traditional literature—paradigms that equate a soaring bird with freedom, "the higher goals of existence" and opera singing with nobility of character, the fallen woman imagery with low self-esteem, the colour grey with bland mediocrity, birds in a cage with romantic tragedy. Such standard readings risk sounding as hackneyed as Gurov's own mistaken perceptions.

The "vast field," then, is a place, like the marketplace, of unfinalizability, a place of "creating anew." The notion that the interior space of individual selfhood might be the most hospitable territory for creating anew was indeed radical for the Russian mind. Moreover, this is as much about Chekhov "creating anew" the terms of literature as it is about the specifics of Gurov and Anna Sergeyevna, who remain in dialogue at the story's end about the unknown direction of their lives.

WORKS CITED

Bakhtin, Mikhail. *Problems of Dostoevsky's Poetics*. Ed. and trans. Caryl Emerson. Minneapolis: University of Minnesota Press, 1984.

Chekhov, Anton. "The Lady with the Little Dog," in *Stories*, trans. Richard Pevear and Larissa Volokhonsky. New York: Bantam Books, 2000.

Chudakov, Aleksandr. "Chelovek polia," in *Anton P. Čechov—Philosophische und religiöse Dimensionen im Leben und im Werk*, ed. Vladimir Kataev, Rolf-Dieter Kluge and Regine Nohejl. Munich: Otto Sagner, 1997: 301–308.

————. *Chekhov's Poetics*. Ann Arbor, MI: Ardis, 1983.

de Sherbinin, Julie W. *Chekhov and Russian Religious Culture*. Evanston, IL: Northwestern UP, 1997.

Finke, Michael C. *Seeing Chekhov: Life and Art*. Ithaca NY: Cornell UP, 2006.

Greenberg, Yael. "The Presentation of the Unconscious in Chekhov's 'Lady with a Lapdog." *The Modern Language Review* 86.1. January 1991: 126–130.

Jackson, Robert L. "Evoliutsiia v rasskaze 'Dama s sobachkoi,'" *Russian Language Journal* 171–73, 1998: 51–59.

Jung, Carl. *Aspects of the Masculine*. Trans. by R.F.C. Hull. Princeton NJ: Princeton UP, 1989.

Kataev, Vladimir. *Literaturnye sviazi Chekhova*. M.: Izd-vo Moskovskogo universiteta, 1989.

Kirjanov, Daria. *Chekhov and the Poetics of Memory*. New York: Peter Lang, 2000.

Morson, Gary Saul. "*Uncle Vanya* as Prosaic Metadrama," in: *Reading Chekhov's Text*, ed. Robert L. Jackson. Evanston, IL: Northwestern UP, 1993: 214–227.

Senderovich, Savely. "A Fragment of Semiotic Theory of Poetic Prose (The Chekhovian Type," *Essays in Poetics* 14, no. 2 (1989): 43–64.

—————. "Chekhov's Figure of Concealment," *Chekhov the Immigrant: Translating a Cultural Icon*, ed. Michael Finke and Julie de Sherbinin. Bloomington, IN: Slavica, forthcoming 2006.

—————. *Chekhov s glazu na glaz*. SPb.: Dmitrii Bulanin, 1994.

—————. "Poetics and Meaning in Chekhov's 'On the Road,'" *Anton Chekhov Rediscovered*. Ed. Savely Senderovich and Munir Sendich. East Lansing, MI: Russian Language Journal, 1987: 135–166..

Shcheglov, Iurii. "Dve variatsii na temu smerti i vozrozhdeniia," *Russian Language Journal* 68: 1994: 79–101.

Stallybrass, Peter and White, Allon. *The Politics and Poetics of Transgression*. Ithaca, NY: Cornell UP, 1986.

"A Cruel Audacity": The Poetics of Deceived Expectation

VLADIMIR KATAEV
Moscow State University

Of all the elements in the poetics of drama Chekhov attached the greatest importance to the plot endings:

> I have an interesting subject for a comedy, but have not yet thought of an ending. Whoever invents new endings for plays will open a new era. The darned endings don't work! The main character has to either get married or shoot himself, there's no other way. My future comedy is called "The Cigar Case." I won't start to write it until I've thought up an ending [...]. If I think of an ending, I can have it written in a fortnight. (Letter to A.S. Suvorin, 4 June 1892; P 5:72)

As we can see, he has in mind not finales as such, but rather denouements of the dramatic action, the working out of the collisions or conflicts depicted in the play, of what happens to the characters and the fates, the history or *Geschichte*, to use Wolf Schmid's terminology.[1]

In both versions of *Ivanov*—the comedy (1887) and the drama (1889)—the death of the main character was the denouement. In the comedy the concluding stage direction "Curtain" is preceded by the sentence: "All: Get water, a doctor, he's dead..." (S 11: 292). In the drama *Ivanov* it is the stage direction "(*Runs to the side and shoots himself.*)" (S 12: 76). In the censored version of 1889 Ivanov exclaims in the final monologue: "Oh, I know how to put an end to myself!" (S 12: 257). In the last stage direction Chekhov crossed out the words "Sasha faints. Confusion" (ibid.).

Here we can already see the search for a new type of conclusion.

---

[1] See: Schmid, *Narratologiia*: 158. We would like to make an immediate distinction between *denouements* in the given sense and the *finales* of Chekhov's plays. The denouements of different plot lines are only one of the components in the polyphonically orchestrated finales of Chekhov's plays.

Chekhov had abandoned what was the finale in his juvenile play, in which the wounded main character took several scenes to die. In the last act Platonov condemns himself to death in his monologue, but cannot bring himself to carry out the sentence; there then ensues a lengthy scene with one of the female characters; in the final scene he is shot "point-blank"; he "falls," but in the middle of the following scene "he gets up and looks around at everyone" and only then "falls and dies," while those characters present go on to comment on what has happened in different ways (S 11: 175–180).

The resolution of *Ivanov* represents a decisive break with the device of melodramatic retardation: "(*Runs off to the side and shoots himself.*) *Curtain.*" Such a resolution was like a full stop, a period placed in the necessary spot. In the denouement in *Ivanov* some have frequently perceived genuflections to the "old way," the traditional principle of "shock ending."[2] This is hardly the case. Not only does Chekhov very strikingly signal the decisive choice of the hero between the two types of ending known to world drama ("[t]he main character has to either get married or shoot himself"). In both the comedy and the drama the main hero leaves this world. However, when reworking the initial version, the author intensifies the element of activity on the part of the main character. Ivanov shoots himself on the day of his wedding. Both alternative resolutions coexist, which increases the tension of the finale; the catastrophic choice is made in favour of one of two conclusions.

The next full-length play, *The Wood Demon*, also contains the two alternative types of ending. In the third act there is the suicide of one of the main characters, but this event does not constitute the ultimate denouement. In the final fourth act two couples suddenly declare their love for each other and there is the prospect of two marriages.

In his plays of the 1890s and 1900s Chekhov replaced the methods of combining the oxymoronic possibilities of conclusion tested in *Ivanov* and *The Wood Demon* in favour of a new type of resolution. We can only infer indirectly the approach Chekhov adopted in searching for new endings—for example, by comparing them with analogous experiments in prose. He himself pointed out the link between these varieties of plot resolution early on while working on *Ivanov*: "I end each act as I do the stories; I have the act proceed peacefully and quietly, and in the end I

---

[2] See Tverdokhlebov's commentary to the play (S 11: 386).

punch the audience on the snout" (Letter to Aleksandr Chekhov of 10 or 12 October, 1887 [P 2:128]).

The change in approach to the conclusion of a work is clearly visible when we compare the two versions of the story "A Little Joke"—the text published in the magazine *Sverchok* (1886, No. 10), and the reworking of the text in 1899 for the A.F. Marks edition. In the first, totally humourous redaction the end of the story looked like this: "Creeping like a thief to the bushes, I hide in them and waiting until a gust of wind passes over me in the direction of Nadenka, say out loud: 'I love you, Nadia!'." The first-person narrator, who has teased his companion Nadia frequently and pitilessly, for the umpteenth time pronounces these words, and for the umpteenth time she tries to believe in the reality of what she has heard: "Heavens, what happens to Nadenka! She cries out, a smile covers her face, and she stretches out her arms to the wind... This was all I waiting for... I emerge from the bushes and, without giving Nadenka time to lower her arms and open her mouth in astonishment, run to her and... 'But now let me get married'" (S 5: 492).

In the final version Chekhov gives the story a completely different ending. The narrator leaves the town in which the action takes place. All the events are presented as a later sad, hopeless, and extremely lyrical reminiscence:

> That was a long time ago. Now Nadenka is already married; whether they married her off or she married of her own volition— it doesn't matter—to the secretary of the Nobleman's Trust, and now she already has three children. The fact that we used to go together sometimes to the skating rink and the time the wind carried to her the words "I love you, Nadenka" have not been forgotten; for her now that is the happiest, most touching and beautiful memory of her life...
> And now that I am older, I don't understand why I said those words, why I joked... (S 5: 24)

This is a truly Chekhovian finale—musically organized, polyphonic, denoting a layered prospect of continuation after the end of the action.[3] Of

---

[3] Much has been said on the subject of the characteristics of Che khov's finales. See, for example, Arkady Gornfeld, "Chekhovskie finaly"; Zinovii Papernyi,

course, the transition to such an ending demanded the restructuring of the entire preceding text—the tone of the narrative and the descriptions of the characters. The initial variant contained a sketch of provincial mores that was highly ironical towards the protagonists, with a successful marriage at the end. This sort of happy end was preprogrammed in the plot and the narrative, and was predetermined first of all by the need to pander to the tastes of the readers of *Sverchok*, which was a humorous magazine for family readers of the "middle class" of the time.

The refusal to pander to such readers was the deciding factor in the transition to the new type of ending. Chekhov documented this refusal in 1895 in a review of Henryk Sienkiewicz's novel *The Polaniecki Family*: "The goal of the novel is to lull the bourgeoisie in its golden dreams. Be faithful to your wife, pray with her according to the prayerbook, accumulate wealth, love sport—and it will be in the bag for you in this and the other world. The bourgeoisie adores so-called 'positive' types and novels with happy endings, since they reassure them with the thought that one can accumulate capital and keep one's innocence, be a savage and happy at the same time" (P 6: 45).

Here a question that would seem to be strictly technical—the choice of the type of conclusion for an artistic text—emerges from a much vaster context: the author's understanding of the world, his social position, value system, and so on. Chekhov's declaration is provocative and openly contemptuous of the reigning tastes of the reading public. He himself wrote no novels—neither with happy nor unhappy endings; the equivalent in his case was his four last great plays. The organization of the finale in the ultimate variant of "A Little Joke" had already been tested in the finales of both *The Seagull* and *Uncle Vanya*, which preceded it, especially in the denouements of these plays.

Many plot lines found their way from *Uncle Vanya* into *The Wood Demon*, but their *conclusions* were radically different. In the last act of *The Wood Demon* the relationship between Sonya and Khrushchov (the "Wood Demon") comes to a happy denouement. This happy end could not have taken place in the first acts, strictly speaking, because of a misunderstanding: they both love each other from the beginning, but Sonya, as she admits herself, "was bound by prejudices" (S 12: 199). She likes

---

"*Vopreki vsem pravilam...*"; Viktor Gulchenko, "Finaly poslednikh chekhovskikh p'es."

Khrushchov as a person, but at first she is a "college girl," "a miss in muslin," a professor's daughter, who sees in him a representative of another, alien class: "your democratic feelings were offended by the fact that you were our close acquaintance. [...] you are a populist. [...] you were ashamed to appear before your district doctors and lady medics" (S 12: 156–157). Although Khrushchov is extremely surprised: "Democrat, populist... [...] is it really possible to talk about that seriously and with a tremor in one's voice?"—in fact he concurs with her refusal: "That's what I need to be told: don't step out of line! Farewell!" (S 12: 157).

It is only the shock they go through in act three—Egor Petrovich Voinitsky's suicide—that forces them to stop applying social yardsticks to people and sticking labels on them. Sonya's father professor Serebriakov persists in his inability to understand others. Sonya and Khrushchov, on the other hand, recognize their error in not understanding each other, and embrace. The end of the play is comfortingly optimistic:

> *Laughter, kisses, noise.*
> Diadin. This is delightful! This is delightful!
> *Curtain* (S 12: 201)

The relationship between Sonya and Astrov in *Uncle Vanya* leads to a totally different denouement. In the play this denouement—their unrealized or even impossible union—demanded that the author change both the characters' personalities and the importance of the questions posed.

Sonya is in love with Astrov (this "everyone knows"—S 13: 92), counts the days and months till his next visit, is saddened to see him drunk, and yet in her mind he remains beautiful and unlike "ordinary people" (S 13: 84); she is ready to repeat his ideas and explain them to others. By comparison with the Sonya in *The Wood Demon* her style of life and status in the house has changed: she toils, "has worked herself to the bone" (S 13: 82). She suffers because she is not good-looking, would like Astrov to be worthy of how own exalted ideas, and consoles uncle Vanya... And yet, ponders Elena Andreyevna, he "is not in love with her—that is clear; but why should he not marry her? She is not good-looking, but for a country doctor of his age she would be a splendid wife. She is clever, and such a good and pure person..." But then she understands: "No, that's wrong, that's wrong..." (S 13: 93). Astrov's justifications are unconvincing and vague ("My time has gone... Moreover I am too busy... When could I?"), or even starkly cruel with regard to Sonya's feelings ("I cannot love her... and anyway that's not what fills my head"). *Uncle Vanya* is a play about love containing at least four love triangles. (Despite this, in productions of the play it is the collision between Vanya and Serebriakov that is most often foregrounded. Moreover, the conflict is treated as if the author of the play were Ivan Petrovich Voinitsky: always, or most frequently, it is his perspective on the proceedings that is dominant.)

The Wood Demon is also a play about love. But in the earlier play it is the "aristocratic woman versus democrat and populist" opposition that is significant. The misunderstanding is overcome in the reconciling denouement. In *Uncle Vanya* the problems of love, of liaisons inside marriage and without, are transferred from a special social level to a much broader existential level common to all humanity. The characters' relationships are subjected to a correction concerning the way "life itself" (S 13: 63) and a person's life in Russia in particular, is organized. We were acquainted and suddenly for some reason... we will never see each other again. *Everything in life is like that...*" (S 13: 110, 112; my emphasis—V.K.). Life as a whole, in general, does not offer happy endings. Bringing things to a happy denouement is deceitful. Hence the plots of Chekhov's vaudevilles with the death at the end. Evidently, the characters of his later plays are endowed with this understanding, as they escape compromise denouements—although the possibility of such endings is anticipated in the course of the play.

Sonya and Astrov are of the same blood group as far as their outlook is concerned; in their way of life they are as alike as two peas in a pod. They have the same understanding of what man is created for, what people's predestination is. But there simply cannot be a happy end for them in a play in which the matter has to do not with the relationships between separate people, but about what is happening to them all. The play has to do not only with family ruptures, but broader ones, with cases of missed connections, of losses and of betrayals for which it is useless to blame separate individuals who are more ill-intentioned than the others. No one knows the real truth. We are all to blame. Chekhov never doubted that. Marriage between Sonya and Astrov on the basis of their similar ideas and democratic way of life would be a denouement in the spirit of those brochures that that "old jackdaw *maman*" reads.

The distinctiveness of the denouements in *Three Sisters* is also clearly visible through a typological juxtaposition—for example with the "epistolary tale" of Chekhov's literary contemporary I. Yasinsky also entitled *Three Sisters*. Apart from the fact that they share the same title, one can see in the tale elements that closely, almost directly, anticipate Chekhov's play. Olga, Sofia and Zinaida Tumanov are left as orphans: their father, a Kiev architect, dies shortly after their mother. Olga, the eldest, is the most energetic and active of the sisters. She keeps talking "about women's labour and wants to enter university"; they find for her a post of director in some provincial high school. The words from the letter of another of the sisters, Sofia, sound like the refrain to certain monologues of the Prozorov sisters: "After some twenty or fifty years have gone by who will remember our father? Who remembers those who have lived and suffered before us..."[4] Yasinsky concluded his tale *Three Sisters* in the spirit of his philosophy of practical action and optimism about life (as expounded in his tract "The Ethics of Everyday Life"). Olga, having experienced a series of difficulties and blows of fate, received a proposal from a friend of their family. The tale ends with her letter to him: "...on the table the samovar boils, the room is decorated with flowers, the candles burn brightly. Your, your Olga."[5] The moral that follows from Yasinsky's *Three Sisters* is completely optimistic: despite all the adversities of life you should not despair; you must remain active, and in the end success will smile for you.

Chekhov began his *Three Sisters* where Yasinsky ended his tale: there is a brightly lit, flower bedecked room and a cosily boiling samovar... But the entire plot of Chekhov's play and its concluding denouements seem a direct challenge to the falsely optimistic philosophy of the author of the tale. In "The Ethics of Everyday Life" and in his fiction Yasinsky addressed his contemporaries, laying out definite "life rules": fulfil the requirements of hygiene, observe moderation in eating, give preference to respectable forms of amusement—in short, "make demands on life that are commensurate with one's abilities." And then, "I am convinced that humanity can be happy even with contemporary forms, and even without fail if one retains them."[6] This is that same apology for bourgeois existence, well-fed prosperity and cheap optimism that Chek-

---

[4] *Russkoe obozrenie*: 460.

[5] Ibid: 497.

[6] Iasinsky, *Etika obydennoi zhizni*: 39, 51–52.

hov saw in *The Polaniecki Family* and other works of Russian and European literature and which he rejected contemptuously. Neither "positive" types nor happy endings that lull the reader are possible in Chekhov's works.

One of the main features of Chekhov's plays is the *rejection of happy denouements*. In the finales of his plays there are not tragic denouements (resulting from a fatal chain of events), but precisely the rejection of the possibility of ending the action with a happy denouement, even if it might seem that everything is tending towards it and even if the bases for it are built into each of the plays. Thus, in *Ivanov* it might seem possible that everything will end with the marriage of Ivanova and Sasha, and in *The Seagull* with the joining of Nina and Kostya after all their tribulations. In *Uncle Vanya* such a happy result might be the shaming of Serebriakov, the union of uncle Vanya and Elena, or, at least, Astrov and Sonya; in *Three Sisters*, the driving out of Natasha, the union of Irina and Tuzenbakh, of Masha with Vershinin, Olga with Kulygin maybe, and the long-awaited departure for Moscow…

More frequently than not this is what playwrights do: they take their characters through all sorts of trials and reward them and the audience with a happy ending, or at least a partly happy one. "What normally happens is that a young man wants a young woman, that his desire is resisted by some opposition, usually paternal, and that near the end of the play some twist in the plot enables the hero to have his will."[7] This is how Northrop Frye defines the structural principle of traditional comedy. Chekhov, by contrast, in the finales to his play pitilessly rejects any of the happy conclusions that are expected in the course of the action. *Not simply an unhappy end, but precisely the rejection of a happy end, this is the general denouement of all Chekhov's late plays.*

Vladimir Nemirovich-Danchenko wrote about Chekhov's "cruel audacity"[8] when defining the structure of the final act of *The Cherry Orchard*. To be sure the orchard has been sold (end of act three), but before act four some hope seems to have been left for the traditional expectations of reader and audience. There is, for example, the hope shared by everyone in the play regarding Lopakhin and Varia. In how many hundreds of preceding plays (and novels) the author kept in reserve "some

---

Frye, *Anatomy of Criticism*: 63.

[8] Nemirovich-Danchenko, *Ezhegodnik Moskovskogo Khudozhestvennogo teatre*: 161.

twist of fate" that would lead to a comforting and situation-saving denouement: either there is a reconciliation between the characters, or feelings heretofore hidden burst through, or desires are satisfied, or seemingly insurmountable obstacles are removed... But behind the unrealized happy end of Lopakhin's proposal of marriage to Varia there stands the same cruel truth that in *Uncle Vanya* frustrated prospects of a marriage between Sonya and Astrov ("I cannot love her... and anyway that's not what fills my head"). Sonya puts off the moment of truth for one more act; Varia "sobs quietly"...

Chekhov needed an absolutely uncompromising belief in the rightness of his decisions in order to refuse to such a degree to cede to the expectations of his characters and audiences. The definition "cruel audacity" is applicable to all Chekhov's denouements; as the author himself put it: "in the end I punch the audience on the snout." However, this refusal to compromise as regards denouements, audacious to the point of cruelty as it was, is only part of Chekhov's playwriting strategy. The story that is narrated in each play does not and cannot end happily. Chekhov uses this powerful device in combination with others, including elements in his authorial strategy that are not directly linked to the sequence of events.

The denouements in Chekhov's plays astonished and shocked his contemporaries. Critics, audiences and readers protested against the pitilessness of *Three Sisters* and the absence in it of any ray of consolation or reconciliation. Though breaking sharply with the traditional expectations of readers and audiences, Chekhov did not, however, "kill hope" (as Lev Shestov put it); instead he shattered illusions by pointing out the real complexity of the problems of human existence. Chekhov did not simply write plays with unhappy denouements; he traced the paths that lead people to unhappiness. "...Everyone is right in his own way; everyone goes wherever his inclinations take him. This is why everyone suffers: because everyone in his own way is right" (S 13: 263). In *Three Sisters*, as in *Uncle Vanya* and *The Seagull*, the author is merciless towards illusions and towards the way everyone makes his own "truths" absolute, but he is neither indifferent nor pitiless towards people. His goal is to show the deep causes of unhappiness, which usually go unnoticed, and hence reveal new ways to comprehend, surmount, and eliminate them.

The conversations of his characters about the future, the meaning of life and the necessity of believing are in sharp contrast to the absurdity of their real position and their day-to-day behaviour; they find themselves at cross-purposes with the real course of events and with the unfolding of their individual fates. In their dreams and the demands they make on life they clearly do not want to think about the "commensurateness" of their desires and whether these correspond with their abilities and are truly achievable. Happiness, "given contemporary forms," is impossible for them, unlike Sienkiewicz and Yasinsky's characters; their gaze is fixed on remote distances of space and time, which they will clearly not attain themselves. In spite of everything they "want to live dammit" (S 13: 163); "one has to live" (S 13: 187); "and I want to live!" (S 13: 187). The effect of the finales in Chekhov's plays is based on the indissoluble combination of denouements without compromise, their "cruel audacity" and this escape beyond the limits of everyday time and space.

The question of the method of denouement, i.e., the conclusion of the series of events in the plays, is linked with the issue of their genre. Douglas Clayton talks about the "avoidance of comedy as one of the specific features of Russian literature, from *Evgeny Onegin* right up to *Uncle Vanya*."[9] "...in the works of Russian realism we find case after case in which the syntagm 'love at first sight / obstacles overcome / happy ending' is rejected, following the pattern of *Eugene Onegin*."[10] The classical, traditional model of comedy, beginning from ancient Greek examples right to the present day, is described by Northrop Frye.[11] In all the innumerable variations of this model, in the beginning some young couple is confronted with opponents who block their coming together. More often than not the opponents are representatives of the older generation who possess a certain power over them. The young protagonists struggle for their happiness, overcome all obstacles, and are finally united in the end. The happy denouement is an indispensable structural element in traditional comedy; frequently it conceals a hidden meaning that transcends the limits of the given plot, signifying the necessity of reconstructing society according to the demands of the younger generation. Such a literary model reflects the idea of the priority of individual happiness and a pattern of societal development typical for the West.

This is not the case in Russian literature. Following Pushkin Rus-

---

[9] Clayton, "*Eugene Onegin*: 83–95.
[10] Ibid.: 91.
[11] Frye: 163–186.

sian writers, starting from the same initial situation, at the end of their works abandon the expected happy denouements. Tatiana in *Eugene Onegin* marries, not the man she loves, but the one her mother "begged" her to wed, and, while keeping alive in her heart and memory her love for Onegin, chooses for herself traditional family morality. In the text of the novel Pushkin indicates the possibility of another, happy ending for the pair ("...the torments of woeful jealousy, / separation, tears of reconciliation, / I'll make them quarrel again, and finally / I'll bring them together under the wedding wreath"). But the two are not united, and happiness in love remains an unrealized possibility in *Eugene Onegin*. In Turgenev's *Rudin* the hero turns out completely incapable of assuring personal happiness for himself and Natalia. The same unwillingness or inability to struggle with the obstacles on the path to personal happiness marks the characters in Chekhov's *Uncle Vanya*. In all these works we find a rejection of the conclusive structural element of classical comedy.

Clayton's work contains more than a few valuable and perceptive observations on the topic under discussion. Even if considering the fact that Russian realism contains several comedies of the classical type, with a happy denouement, whether it be Ostrovsky's *Forest* or *Truth is Good, but Happiness Better*, or Tolstoy's *Fruits of Enlightenment*, one cannot help but agree that in the examples Clayton adduces we find a deliberate rejection by Russian authors of the standard pattern of western literature, its deformation or inversion or parody. The suggestion that *Eugene Onegin* played a programmatic role in this is also important and useful.

In *Uncle Vanya* Clayton sees "Chekhov's brilliant modulation of the comic situation." Voinitsky, a forty-seven year old bachelor, can only appear as a parody of the traditional romantic lover of comedy. Astrov too, though the twist of his fate is dramatic rather than farcical, is also incapable of achieving personal happiness for himself and the woman who loves him. At the end of the play it is not the young lovers that triumph, but the old man Serebriakov, who is remote from them all. *Uncle Vanya* turns out to be a "comedy of impotence and frustration rather than fulfillment and happiness."[12]

One might say that the play discussed by Clayton is not the only Chekhov play in which the heroes do not achieve happiness in the end and there is an avoidance of the traditional comedic denouement. It is

---

[12] Clayton: 93.

equally true of *The Seagull, Three Sisters* and *The Cherry Orchard*. At the same time, Chekhov stubbornly designated his plays comedies — evidently, while realizing that he was veering from the norm of comedy in the traditional sense. Can we still consider is plays comedies, given the fact that there is an indubitable "avoidance of comedy" in them? Yes we can. However, the comic in these plays is based on different structural models from those described by Frye. Of course, in Chekhov's plays there are numerous traditional sources of laughter — from ridiculous phrases and actions to characters that invoke general laughter. But the onset of the "new era" in dramatic art was marked by previously unheard-of structural innovations, and in particular the organization of the conflict in the play. The basis of the comic in Chekhov lies not in the traditional *opposition* of one group of characters to another (for example, young and old, victims and oppressors, dissidents and their environment, etc.), but in the hidden commonality between characters who do not want to see it and do not even guess at its existence.

"We are all to blame." Each makes his own contribution to the disaster that occurs at the end of each play. This does not happen because some are given the role of victims and others the role of destroying their happiness. Practically every character is both victim and destroyer of someone's happiness. This is most frequently because while he is in an equal state of passive dependence on life, at the same time he makes absolute his "truth" (his temporary view of things, his false idea), and is not able to understand and accept another's truth. Again "…Everyone is right in his own way; everyone goes wherever his inclinations take him. This is why everyone suffers: because everyone in his own way is right" (S 13: 263). "We all stick our noses in the air before others, but look out! life is passing" (S 13: 246).

Chekhov developed a type of comedy in which the avoidance, the rejection of a happy ending is a variety of the "irony of life." It is existential irony that dominates in Chekhov's late works. "A slight shift of perspective, a different tinge in the emotional colouring and the solid earth becomes an intolerable horror,"[13] writes Northrop Frye, and, speaking of *Three Sisters*, he writes: "we are coming about as close to pure irony as the stage can get."[14]

---

[13] Frye: 235.
[14] Ibid.: 285.

One should not forget that Chekhov does not simply represent his characters as parodies of traditional lovers or marriage breakers. His characters are not just comical in their inability to attain a happiness that (as in *Eugene Onegin*) "was so close, so possible." Each of them is in his own way worthy of happiness; evoking sympathy with their situation, their dreams and their hopes is part of the playwright's strategy. Their ultimate failures are not simply the mockery of the fate that has fallen to their lot. They are a conscious device of the author as he strives to shatter the reader's and audience's false ideas about the real causes that lead to misfortune and to raise individual fates to an existential level. Every time his cruel audacity is triumphant in the choice of conclusion of the plot. The audience is "punched on the snout"—that audience that is expecting a pleasant denouement that will lull one and calm one's conscience. But the finales of Chekhov's plays bring a catharsis for those who are able to hear the true voice of the author.

Translated from the Russian by J. Douglas Clayton.

WORKS CITED

Clayton, J. Douglas. "*Eugene Onegin* and the Avoidance of Comedy in Russian Literature," *Wave and Stone: Essays on the poetry and prose of Alexander Pushkin*. Ottawa: The Slavic Research Group at the University of Ottawa, 2000: 83–95.

Frye, Northrop. *Anatomy of Criticism*. Princeton: Princeton University Press, 1970.

Gornfeld, Arkady. "Chekhovskie finaly," *Krasnaia nov'*. 1939, nos. 8–9.

Gulchenko, Viktor. "Finaly poslednikh chekhovskikh p'es," *Drama i teatr: sb. nauchnykh trudov*, II. Tver: Tverskoi gosudarstvennyi universitet, 2001: 72–87.

Nemirovich-Danchenko, Vladimir. *Ezhegodnik Moskovskogo khudozhestvennogo teatra*, 1944, I, M.: 1946.

Papernyi, Zinovii. "*Vopreki vsem pravilam*": *P'esy i vodevili Chekhova*. M.: Isskustvo, 1982.

Schmid, Wolf. *Narratologiia*. M.: Iazyki slavianskoi kul'tury, 2003.

Yasinsky, Ieronim. *Russkoe obozrenie*, 1891, No. 10.

————. *Etika obydennoi zhizni*, 2nd ed. SPb: V. S. Balashev, 1898.

Three Degrees Of Defamiliarization: Rhythm and Action In Anton Chekhov's Drama

YANA MEERZON
University of Ottawa

V sevolod Meyerhold was the first to recognize that the rhythmically organized patterns of letters and punctuation marks in Anton Chekhov's texts were forms of estrangement. In his widely quoted 1904 letter to the playwright, Meyerhold described the climactic scene of *The Cherry Orchard* (Act 3) as an example of pictorially encoded musicality and grotesque poeticity: "In the third act, against a background of the stupid stamping of feet [...] enters Horror, completely unnoticed by the guests. 'The cherry orchard is sold.' They dance on. 'Sold.' Still they dance. And so on to the end."[1] To Meyerhold, it is the sound of rhythmical "variations upon themes, all of which contribute to the weakening of the dependence of the work upon outside referents, inner rhymes, repetitions, parallels and symmetries"[2] that the director must grasp and work with when staging Chekhov's plays.[3]

In what follows, I propose to use Meyerhold's line of argument and discuss three degrees of defamiliarization in Chekhov's dramatic works that are transmitted through the *ironic channel of communication*. This channel is employed in drama to convey the dialectics of the relationship between the fictional or characters' world and the author's "adequate conception of the plot."[4] The discrepancy between the two creates *theatrical irony*, which is expressed through direct and indirect communication between the stage and the audience. In Chekhov's dramatic writings it is through these three types of foregrounding that the

---

[1] *Meyerhold on Theatre*: 34.
[2] Winner, "Syncretism in Chekhov's Art": 163.
[3] *Meyerhold on Theatre*: 34.
[4] Rozik, "Theatrical Irony": 137.

author's objective vision of the characters is revealed. This article examines first Chekhov's use of semantic juxtaposition of the characters' discourses as a device leading to generic estrangement from tragedy to farce. It then explores Chekhov's use of dramatic *skaz* (a character's verbal idiosyncrasies expressed through syntactic and lexical choices in his/her utterances). And finally, it discusses Chekhov's punctuation in monologic speech as the graphic representation of the paradox of estrangement similar to Vladimir Mayakovsky's pictorial poetic estrangement. In effect, I shall argue that the collision between Chekhov's rhythmical design of the implied action and its graphic appearance is comparable to Labanotation, a pictographic representation of dance movements.[5] This statement can be illustrated best through an account of Michael Chekhov's theatrical adaptations of his uncle's short stories as a paradigm of estrangement in performance.

According to Anne Ubersfeld, a dramatic text contains several dramatic voices: that of the scriptor or the initiator of the communication (always the author of the text) and that of the speaker—any character involved in a dialogic situation.[6] Ubersfeld contends that "if the discourse of the scriptor takes on meaning only in terms of theatricality, there is nothing to stop us from also considering it, at least provisionally, as a 'total poem,' to be approached through textual analysis alone—indeed through 'infinite poetic analysis'."[7] Ubersfeld finds four voices involved in every theatrical discourse: that of the creative author of the play (the scriptor), that of the character (the speaker), the biographical I of the scriptor as such, and finally, the subjectless discourse of the theatrical narrative as such, because "theatrical discourse is the discourse of a subject–scriptor, it is the discourse of a subject that is immediately stripped of his or her I, the discourse of a subject that denies his or her

---

[5] "Labanotation is a system of analyzing and recording of human movement. The original inventor is the (Austro-) Hungarian Rudolf von Laban (1879–1958) [...]. He published this notation first 1928 as 'Kinetographie' in the first issue of *Schrifttanz*. [...] In Labanotation, it is possible to record every kind of human motion. Labanotation is not connected to a singular, specific style of dance [...]. The basis is natural human motion, and every change from this natural human motion [...] has to be specifically written down in the notation." Christian Griesbeck, 1996. *Labanonotation*. 6 Dec. 2004.

[6] Ubersfeld, *Reading Theatre*: 66.

[7] Ibid.: 166.

subjecthood, that declares himself or herself to be speaking through the voice of another, or several others, to be speaking without being a subject: theatrical discourse is a discourse without a subject."[8]

Peter Brook describes the rhythms of Chekhov's action and the alienation effect they create in *Three Sisters* in the following way: "The vase of flowers that overturns, the fire-engine that passes at just the right moment; the word, the entrance, the farewell—touch by touch, they create through the language of illusions an overall illusion of a slice of life. This series of impressions is equally a series of alienations; each rupture is a subtle provocation and a call of thought."[9] Brook comments on how the poeticity of Chekhov's world embraces both the solemnity of everyday life and its humour. He underlines the representational nature of Chekhov's verbal act which, according to Jakobson, "is determined by its slant, its emotional content, the audience it is addressed to, the preliminary 'censorship' it undergoes, [and] the supply of ready-made patterns it draws from, stylizes and transforms the event it depicts."[10] Jakobson defines poeticity in the following way:

> The poetic function, poeticity, is, as the "formalists" stressed, an element *sui generis*, one that cannot be mechanically reduced to other elements. [...] Poeticity is only a part of a complex structure, but it is a part that necessarily transforms the other elements and determines with them the nature of the whole. [...] Poeticity is present when the world is felt as a word and not a mere representation of the object being named or an outburst of emotion, when words and their composition, their meaning, their external and inner form, acquire a weight and value of their own instead of referring indifferently to reality.[11]

In fact, it is Chekhov's fastidiousness regarding the sentimentality of the linguistic utterance that penetrates his speech codes and causes the excess of patterns of estrangement in his plays. For instance, the rhythmical and semantic juxtaposition of Olga's recollection of her father's funeral with Chebutykin and Tuzenbakh's remarks in the background at the be-

---

[8] Ubersfeld: 167.
[9] Brook, *The Empty Space*: 89.
[10] Jakobson, "What is Poetry": 374.
[11] Ibid.: 378.

ginning of *Three Sisters* (read as a solitary text or a poetic stanza with *the voice of the author as the scriptor* and *the voice of the character as the speaker*, in Ubersfeld's vocabulary) not only creates theatrical irony but also anticipates the futuristic techniques of poetic expression exemplified in the works of Khlebnikov and Mayakovsky.

In the Chekhovian scene the juxtaposition of the characters' speeches not only destroys the communication between them but also disrupts the implied dramatic genre. For instance, at the beginning of *Three Sisters*, by cutting short Olga's intimate moment with a burst of laughter in the background, Chekhov manipulates the audience's reaction. He frustrates the spectators' expectations and breaks the magic barrier between the stage and the audience. However, unlike Meyerhold or Brecht, Chekhov does not employ the actor to achieve this effect. He simply violates the rhythmical patterns of a dramatic speech, thus emphasizing the mechanisms of the utterance's construction and foregrounding the genre conventions. Therefore, the primary type of defamiliarization employed in Chekhov's dramatic writing functions through the *inversion of meaning*.[12] The playwright *prestructures* the plot from the viewpoint of the spectator (the outside onlooker),[13] who observes the semantics of the scene in its syntheses not merely from the perspective of a single character. It embraces two types of messages, one created for the characters and the other intended for the spectators:

> Olga … Eleven years have passed, but I remember everything there as if we'd left yesterday. My God! I woke up this morning, saw the sunshine everywhere, saw the spring, and I felt happiness stirring in my heart, I wanted to go home so much.
> Chebutykin. Like hell you will!
> Tuzenbakh. Nonsense, of course.
> *Masha, deep in thought over her book, whistles a song to herself* (Act 1, Sc.1).[14]

One simply needs to omit the names of the characters in the recitation of the passage for its implied rhythmical design to emerge based on the

---

[12] Rozik: 136.

[13] Ibid.: 136.

[14] This and subsequent translations from *Three Sisters* are my own.

mixture of utterances and sounds meant to be spoken and a pause intended to be acted out. The disagreement between the verbal communication and its implied action creates an ironic semantics, characteristic for this type of defamiliarization. It is the paradox of various verbal and audio signs juxtaposed with each other that constitutes the contrast between the intended meaning of the speech (Olga's sincerity) and the actual reaction it generates (the cynical comment). Using the same principles of dramatic composition as Eisenstein's montage in film, Chekhov in his plays makes the intra-diegetic and extra-diegetic utterances and sounds intersect:

> Olga. Don't whistle, Masha. How can you! (*Pause*). I spend the whole day at school, and then tutor until night, so I get constant headaches and such thoughts as if I were already old. Honestly, all these four years of working in school I've felt drained of my youth and strength, drop by drop. There's only this one dream that grows stronger and stronger...
> Irina. Off to Moscow. Sell the house, leave it all, and off to Moscow...
> Olga. Yes! As soon as we can, off to Moscow.
> *Chebutykin and Tuzenbakh laugh.* (Act 1, Sc. 1)

This segment contains a single pause and several ellipsis marks (three dots) that either interrupt Olga's speech or indicate a full stop before Irina's line. Both the pictographic image (three dots) and the stage direction—"*Chebutykin and Tuzenbakh laugh*"—function here as indexical signs, pointing at a psycho-physical action implied by the author. Chebutykin's laughter mocks the nostalgic atmosphere of the scene created by the sisters' exchange. By weaving the background noises and sounds into the primary text, Chekhov creates rhythmical cacophonies, or *oratorical dissonance*. As Meyerhold comments:

> Similar instances of dissonant notes emerging fleetingly from the background and encroaching on the act's leitmotiv are: the stationmaster reading poetry; Yepikhodov breaking his billiard cue; Trofimov falling downstairs; and note how closely and subtly Chekhov interweaves the leitmotiv and the accompaniment:
> Anya (*agitatedly*). And just now someone said that the cherry orchard was sold today.

Ranevskaya. Sold to whom?
Anya. He didn't say who: he's gone now (*Dances with Trofimov*).[15]

By emphasizing the interaction between the intra-diegetic and extra-diegetic noises, Chekhov focuses the attention of the spectator on the device itself, as described by Shklovsky in his definition of literary de-familiarization. The goal is reached. The stage/audience communication is broken and reestablished anew. Interestingly, looking at the rhythmical design of a Shakespearean character, it is possible to discover the same patterns of characterization as exist in Chekhov's texts. An actor playing in Shakespeare's tragedies is forced to follow both the rhythm of the poetic expression and the images it evokes. Chekhov's texts are full of reminiscences of Shakespeare, which may suggest Chekhov's unconscious adoption of some of his rhetorical techniques.

In his critique of Stanislavsky's theatrical interpretation of Chekhov's plays, Meyerhold states that the director destroys the grotesque harmony of the text by utilizing "various bits and pieces of equipment"[16] in order to thoroughly illustrate the characters' emotions. He makes scenes too long and too complex rhythmically, so that "he loses the act's leitmotiv."[17] To Meyerhold, Stanislavsky destroys the potentialities of vaudeville or farce in Chekhov's texts. He overlooks the various alienation techniques in the rhythmic structure or poeticity of beats in Chekhov's texts which reflect Bergsonian processes of automatization and mechanization. Meyerhold goes on to say: "*Time* is a very precious element on stage. If a scene visualized by the author as incidental lasts longer then necessary, it casts a burden on to the next scene which the author may well intend as most significant."[18] That is to say, any modification of Chekhov's rhythmical design disrupts the implied vaudeville composition based on metrically and semantically paradoxical resolutions of its conflicts.

The genre defamiliarization found in Chekhov's texts is based on the inversion of meaning and is a type of comic automatization translated into forms of theatrical irony:

---

[15] *Meyerhold on Theatre*: 28–29.
[16] Ibid.: 29.
[17] Ibid.
[18] Ibid.: 28.

> One recalls how the overall harmony was disturbed in Moscow Art
> [Theatre] interpretation of Act Three of *The Cherry Orchard*. The au-
> thor intended the act's leitmotiv to be Ranevskaya's premonition of
> an approaching storm (the sale of the cherry orchard). [...] The fol-
> lowing harmony is established in the act: on the one hand, the lam-
> entations of Ranevskaya with her presentiment of approaching dis-
> aster [...]; on the other hand, the puppet show [...]. Translated into
> musical terms, this is one movement of symphony. It contains the
> basic elegiac melody with alternating moods in pianissimo, out-
> bursts of forte [...], and the dissonant accompaniment of the mo-
> notonous cacophony of the distant band and the dance of the living
> corpses.[19]

Stanislavsky's directorial explication of *Three Sisters* can serve to illustrate this statement. Stanislavsky brings into Chekhov's complex text
various audio-visual details that muffle the humour of the scenes and
hide the sarcasm of the author. For example, Chekhov constructs one of
the most sexually intense moments in the play, the scene between Masha
and Vershinin in Act Two, using a number of repeated verbal interrup-
tions and delayed actions. The successive use of mutually exclusive lines
(non-sequiturs) and sounds functions here as another form of genre defamiliarization technique:

> Masha. You are a bit moody today.
> Vershinin. Perhaps. I haven't had dinner today, haven't eaten at all
> since morning. My daughter is a little sick, and when my girls are
> sick, anxiety takes over me, my conscience torments me because
> they have such a mother. [...] (*Pause*). I never speak about it, and
> it's strange, but I complain only to you. (*Kisses her hand*). Don't be
> angry with me. I don't have anyone but you, no one ... (*Pause*).
> Masha. What a noise in the chimney. (Act 2, Sc.2)

The only indication of an extra-diegetic sound here is Masha's mention
of the noise in the chimney. This noise can be read, of course, either as an
indexical sign—there is indeed some humming in the chimney; or as an
implied action of the character—Masha is hiding her pleasure and confusion when listening to Vershinin's words. Stanislavsky, as his explication

---

[19] *Meyerhold on Theatre*: 28.

demonstrates, orchestrates the dialogue with an excessive number of extra-diegetic details, thus losing its ambiguity. The humming chimney not only accompanies the entire dialogue but is also reinforced by Andrey's violin and some sort of sawing in the background. Moreover, the "mouse" game is invented to go with Vershinin's speech about his sick wife. The game begins with the sound of a mouse scraping the floor under the sofa. "Masha pounds the sofa with her hand to chase it away [...] The mouse is gone."[20] It is repeated several times, and the director wonders, "How do you create the noise a mouse makes? Take a boxful of goose-feather toothpicks and brush them."[21] Synchronically, backstage or in the other room, "Andrey moves a chair abruptly. He sighs, walks about and starts playing an awfully plaintive tune on his violin,"[22] while on the front stage "Vershinin sits closer to Masha during the pause. The maid brings a lighted lamp into the dining-room and leaves. It's light in the dining-room."[23] Finally, the climactic moment of the scene—the kiss—takes place against the following background:

> Anfisa exits and takes away the boiled milk or a medicine; drops the glass in the doorway leading to the corridor and breaks it; screams and exits. A sawing sound is heard from Andrei's room (the door is closed)—he's sawing or carving something. He must be all restless from ennui in there, taking up several things at once and dropping them; he can't focus on anything.[24]

As a result, Chekhov's poeticity, his interest in the ironic concurrences between an object and a sign, in the clash between a word and an action expressed only through rhythmically constructed patterns, is destroyed. According to Jakobson, the process of distraction indicates a discrepancy between the linguistic sign and its referent:

> It means the sign does not fall together with the object because, besides the direct awareness of the identity between sign and object

---

[20] Stanislavskii, *Rezhisserskie ekzempliary K.S. Stanislavskogo*: 147. This and subsequent translations from Stanislavskii's prompt-book are my own.
[21] Stanislavskii: 147.
[22] Ibid.
[23] Ibid.
[24] Ibid.: 149.

(A is A1), there is a necessity for the direct awareness of the inadequacy of that identity (A is not A1). The reason this antinomy is essential is that without contradiction there is no mobility of concepts, no mobility of signs, and the relationship between concept and sign becomes automatized. Activity comes to a halt, and the awareness of reality dies out.[25]

In his article on the sound qualities of the dramatic text, Veltruský argues that Stanislavsky's inability to memorize his lines properly, his reliance on the visual images and the spatial metaphors in his productions, reflected his deafness to the implied rhythmicality, poeticity and irony of Chekhov's texts. Stanislavsky was insensitive to the rhythmical structure of a text and "transformed the contradiction between his delivery and the sound shape of the text into a structural feature of his acting."[26] In addition, Stanislavsky's misuse of physical actions visually representing characters' emotions on stage in a super-realistic manner replaces and thus extinguishes the grotesque potentialities of the text.

It was Vladimir Nemirovich-Danchenko, a very sensitive literary critic and reader of Chekhov's plays, who, when working with Stanislavsky's mise-en-scène of *Seagull* and trying to help actors to understand the text and the blocking better, hesitated to accept all the realistic details proposed by Stanislavsky. Nemirovich-Danchenko felt that Stanislavsky's suggestion to incorporate "the frogs' croak" during the presentation of Treplev's drama would disturb the audience's reception and was inappropriate given the play's genre. As he wrote, "On the contrary, I want complete mysterious silence. A bell tolling somewhere in a cemetery would be a different story all together. Sometimes one must not divert the audience's attention, or distract it with minute realistic details."[27]

Both in his prose and in his plays, Chekhov employs various techniques of defamiliarization in the verbal portrayal of his characters. The organizing principles of monologic utterances in the dialogic dramatic communication create an illusion of *skaz*, the semantic and linguistic ex-

---

[25] Jakobson, "What is Poetry": 378.
[26] Veltruský, "Sound Qualities of the Text...": 250.
[27] Nemirovich-Danchenko, *Izbrannye pis'ma*: 146.

pression of each character's behaviour.[28] It is the idiosyncratic syntax and the curious choice of the characters' vocabulary that generate Chekhov's theatrical irony. By giving his characters' speeches obscure patterns, Chekhov not only distances plot but also exhibits his attitude toward a particular character. At the same time, although his characters are always unique, Chekhov gives each of them certain easily recognizable archetypal characteristics that transcend these speech patterns.

In *Three Sisters* it is the verbal idiosyncrasy of Vershinin, his linguistic inadequacy, through which the author's irony is felt. Vershinin, the former "lovesick major," is cast in the play in the role of a Prince Charming. He has up his sleeve the adjective *wonderful* to describe his vision of the future and the words *magnificent* and *stunning* to talk about his love for Masha: "In two or three hundred years, life on Earth will be unimaginably wonderful, amazing" (Act 1); "You are a magnificent, stunning woman. Magnificent, stunning!", "I love, I love, I love… I love your eyes, I see your movements in my dreams… Magnificent, stunning woman!" (Act 2). Chekhov's choice of Vershinin's linguistic patterns creates an image of a most ordinary man bored to tears with his sick wife, little daughters and the life on the move in an apartment with no flowers. "I am thirsty. I'd like some tea," Vershinin says to Masha in reply to her praise of the army officers, the most educated, noble and dignified people. The character's verbal habit emphasizes the emptiness and dullness of his thoughts and ideas. Vershinin's emotions, the ways he seduces Masha and the outcomes of this affair are unexciting, predictable, and conventional.[29] The only originality present in his *skaz* is the rhythmical combination of words, the way they are put together. His recurring dinner-related inquiries during his "love scene" with Masha create another form of inversion of meaning, indicating a gap between the speech and its implied signification.[30] Chekhov's fastidious attention to the

---

[28] For a discussion of *skaz*, see Boris Eikhenbaum, "How Gogol's *Overcoat* is Made": 269.

[29] The only other example of sexual activity in the play is the marriage of Natasha and Andrei. However, Natasha is the only one who possesses the ability to reproduce. She not only bears children but also has an affair with Protopopov that eventually leads to Andrei's depression and even alcoholism. Otherwise, *Three Sisters* represents a world of asexual, amorphous and frigid people for whom the rhythm and act of speaking are a substitute for physical sensuality.

[30] Rozik: 134.

characters' verbal idiosyncrasies is revealed in his commentaries addressed to the Moscow Art Theatre company as they prepared to rehearse *The Cherry Orchard*. In his 1903 letter to Nemirovich-Danchenko, Chekhov specifies that in his new play, for example, "Sharlotta speaks not in a broken but grammatically correct Russian; she should every now and then end a word with a hard consonant instead of a soft one, and mix up feminine and masculine endings of her adjectives."[31] His awareness of and concentration on the rhythmical patterns of Russian language as it is used by each particular figure in a play or a short story, and his meticulous structuring of the dramatic *langue* as the background for each singular character's *parole*, are exposed in his letters to a certain Argutinsky-Dolgorukov who was traveling at that moment in Europe and sent the famous writer some samples of his literary exercises. On April 28, 1897 Chekhov writes, "I envy you, my dear Vladimir Nikolaevich, [...] you are in England and speaking English. [...] I liked your short story, but it's not your own work, it is a translation from English, there isn't a single Russian phrase—not a single one!"[32] As this quote demonstrates, Chekhov is not only able to explore the possibilities for rhythmical idiosyncrasy of his characters, but also to detect and emphasize the discrepancy between certain natural, authentic intonations and rhythms of the Russian language and the incursion of the rhythms and intonations of another language (English in this case) in a literary text. In *The Cherry Orchard* Sharlotta's idiolect has a slightly foreign accent that any native speaker of Russian is able to hear and which colours her dramatic and psychological characterization. Sharlotta's otherness, displacement and nostalgia for some lost referent, some lost country (whether the real one of her parents or the metaphorical one of her childhood) is expressed not necessarily directly in the semantics of her speeches but in the manner she pronounces them.

Thus, Chekhov's sensitivity to the rhythmical idiosyncrasy of his characters can be pointed out as another area of defamiliarization that the playwright explores. For instance, Tuzenbakh's *skaz* suggests his somewhat clownish position in the play. Chekhov gives him a self-reflexive discourse and stresses his insecurity by having him constantly interrupted and overlooked. He depicts Tuzenbakh in the psychological

---

[31] Chekhov, *Perepiska…*: 110.
[32] Chekhov, *Sbornik dokumentov i materialov*: 30.

costume of Pierrot, in contrast with the confident Solyony who takes the role of Harlequin or Lermontov's villain. Tuzenbakh's self-effacing statements ("I have three surnames. I am Baron Tuzenbakh-Krohne-Altschauer, but I am Russian, Orthodox, just like you. There's hardly anything German left in me" [Act 2]); and his ambivalent position in the house of the Prozorovs ("Every single day I'm going to come to the telegraph and walk you home, for ten, twenty years, until you send me away" [Act 2]) make him the best candidate to die in this play.

In addition, Chekhov creates theatrical irony by employing *the direct channel of communication*.[33] Chekhov alienates the elements of plot: "You've got to be thinking: the German is getting all sentimental. But, honestly, I'm Russian, and I don't even speak German. My father is Orthodox" (Act 1). However, Chekhov was about to present even such a tragic event as Tuzenbakh's death in a farcical manner. The original version of the play closed with Chekhov's stage directions featuring a background procession carrying Tuzenbakh's body while Olga finishes her final monologue: "We will live! The music is playing so cheerfully, so happily," and Chebutykin sings "Tara... ra... boom-dee-ay" (Act 4). Stanislavsky worried about the depth of the Moscow Art Theatre's stage, wondering how he could squeeze both the sisters with their monologues and the funeral procession onto it.[34] In a letter to Nemirovich-Danchenko, Chekhov expressed his anxiety about the final mise-en-scène as it was designed by Stanislavsky. He suggested keeping the staging as minimalist as possible: "it is awkward to carry Tuzenbakh's body across your stage, but Alekseyev [Stanislavsky] kept insisting that the body is indispensable. I wrote to him not to have the body carried across."[35] As a result, Chekhov cut the direction "a commotion in the back of the stage; a crowd watches as the baron, who has been killed in the duel, is carried off,"[36] which, in my opinion, potentially contained another moment of alienation in the play, foregrounding not only the audience's anticipations but also containing an implied reference to Shakespeare's tragedies and their closing funeral processions.

Chekhov was also attentive to the artificiality of the exchange on

[33] Rozik: 138.
[34] Stanislavskii: 288.
[35] Chekhov, *Perepiska*: 197.
[36] Stanislavskii: 288.

the dramatic external-communication level (the level of author–reader or author–spectator communication) established in the type of realistic drama contemporary to his theatre (from Ibsen to Hauptmann). The essence of Chekhov's dramatic irony lies not only in his introduction of the so-called "dialogue of the deaf" that will become the trademark of Beckett's drama, but also in his launching of various types of direct author-spectator communicative devices. This communication between the author and the reader happening "over the heads of the characters," was very much explored later in the dramatic works of Pirandello and in the directorial experiments of Meyerhold and Brecht. The sheer fact of calling the audience's attention to the dramatic device itself, making the familiar, the automatic theatrical communication distant and estranged, is one of the major devices of dramatic irony employed in Chekhov's plays. In *The Seagull*, it is the star of the provincial stage, Arkadina, who gives lessons in the theatricality of life to Masha, who is hopelessly in love with her son, Treplev. In *Three Sisters*, the theme of the impossibility of privacy between lovers or friends, and the necessity of one's feelings being constantly exposed to the scrutiny of others (for example, Andrey and Natasha's kiss in the first act, or Masha's public mourning for the departing officers in the very last one) signals the dramatist's awareness of and sensibility to the paradox of theatrical communication: what is most private and sincere is at the same time the most public and deceitful.

Punctuation, the use of dots and exclamation marks in Chekhov's dramatic texts, constitutes a third type of defamiliarization. As Mukařovský points out, the author's choice of graphic devices can indicate "the impulse of emotion […] not expressed in words, […] [and] a sudden change in the direction of thought from one sentence to the next."[37] Thus, punctuation (the dash in Čapek's writing or the three dot ellipsis in Chekhov's) functions as another type of indexical sign pointing at the psycho-physical experience of the character. In *Three Sisters*, Irina's verbal eccentricity with its famous sudden changes of tempo is a good example of Chekhov's representation of theatrical irony through the graphics of punctuation. In one of her opening speeches, Irina reflects on the meaningfulness of the worker's life, with which she is certainly familiar by reading some sort of progressive magazines. Her fascination with the

---

[37] Mukařovský, "Čapek's Prose as Lyrical…": 135.

beauty of being an ox or a horse, who works "by the sweat of his brow," is contrasted with the image of a young woman "who gets up at noon, has coffee in bed, and takes two hours to get dressed" (Act 1). Visually, the sentence finishes with three dots that are followed by the words: "how awful! You get thirsty on a hot day the way I thirst for work" (Act 1). Here the author's irony comes across through the utilization of the pause just before "how awful." It is followed by the sentence expressing the character's desire to be punished for not working and not getting up early, and by being refused the friendship of Chebutykin, an old admirer of her mother and herself.

By reinforcing the poetic potentialities of the text, Chekhov emphasizes in this monologue the obvious comical difference between Irina's life experience and the reality outside of it. In Osip Brik's words, the language of verse is regulated "by the laws of rhythmic syntax [...] in which the usual syntactic laws are complicated by rhythmic requirements. [...] The [character's] line is the primary rhythmico-syntactic unit; therefore, a study of the rhythmico-syntactic configuration of verse should begin with the line."[38] Brik goes on to write:

> Depriving the line of semantics, we go beyond the limits of poetic language; further variations of this line will be conditioned not only by its verbal composition, but by its tonality. In particular, the systems of stress and intonation will be independent of the stress and intonation of ordinary speech and will imitate the stress and intonation of a musical phrase. In other words, by depriving the line of its semantic meaning, we transfer it from the domain of language to a new domain—that of music. The poetic line thus ceases to be verbal fact.[39]

This idea of the rhythmico-syntactic configuration of the line or a *rhythmeme* as the basis of a poetic utterance and as a pictorial sign corresponds to Mayakovsky's vision of the graphics of verse. In his article "How to Make Verse," Mayakovsky writes:

> Having written a poem that's going to be published, you need to consider how the printed version will be perceived as printed text.

---

[38] Brik, "Contributions to the Study of Verse Language": 123.
[39] Ibid.: 124.

[…] Our regular punctuation with its full stops, commas, question marks and exclamation points is quite meager and flat. […] If you break the line into halves, there won't be any semantic or rhythmical confusion.[40]

Chekhov's use of three dots and the implied pause is similar to Mayakovsky's breaking up lines in a poetic utterance. Although the function of the pause as a device of making strange in Chekhov's plays has been studied,[41] a review of Chekhov's dramatic discourse as a form of a poetic utterance has yet to be done. As Yury Lotman notes,

> The rhythmicality of verse is the cyclical repetition of different elements in identical positions in order to bring together unequal things and to reveal congruence in the different; or it may be the repetition of the identical in order to reveal the false nature of this sameness, to establish the difference in the congruent. Rhythm in verse is a semantically significant element; when they become part of a rhythmical structure, even those linguistic elements that in normal use have none, acquire a semantic significance.[42]

Chekhov's three dots, if not as radical as Mayakovsky's pictographic representation, still demonstrate the implied rhythm and semantics of a dramatic utterance. They are quite experimental in regard to the norms of verbal construction in his time. The only other Russian writer famous for his peculiar punctuation was Maxim Gorky, who utilized the dash to express, if not all, then the majority of his characters' actions and emotions.

Chekhov's responsiveness to punctuation as the manifestation of rhythm in drama was in step with Andrey Bely's theory of rhythm in poetry and prose and Michael Chekhov's use of rhythm in acting. Chekhov employed the device of onomatopoeia as another form of rhythmical estrangement, emphasizing the irony of the message and making it possible for the spectator to observe the characters once more from a distance, from the outside. In his letter to Olga Knipper, in January 1901,

---

[40] Maiakovskii, "Kak delat' stikhi": 496. The translation is mine.
[41] See Strelkov, "Zvukopodrazhatel'nye mezhdometiia v iazyke Chekhova"; Borisova, "Pauzy i antipauzy v dramaturgii A. P. Chekhova."
[42] Lotman, Analiz poeticheskogo teksta: 45.

Chekhov wrote: "Vershinin says 'tram–tram–tram' as a question, and you as an answer, and you imagine this to be such an original joke that you pronounce this 'tram–tram' with a smile.... You pronounce this 'tram–tram' and then you laugh, but not very loudly, just so [...] Remember you are given to laughter, yet irascible."[43]

In fact, it was left to Michael Chekhov, an actor, director and theatre pedagogue, to create an acting theory embodying a distance between the actor's "I" and the character's "I" as the paradigm of estrangement in performance, thus reinforcing his uncle's dramatic devices of defamiliarization in his own performative practice. Michael Chekhov recognized the actor's function on stage as the originator of the action and its receiver. He defined the product of the actor's activity—the stage mask—as an aesthetic object. In his rhythmical stage designs, Michael Chekhov employed elements of theatrical irony similar to those found in Anton Chekhov's writings. Unfortunately, Michael Chekhov had never had a chance to play any significant role in Anton Chekhov's drama. In 1913 Stanislavsky worked with him ineffectively on the role of Epikhodov (played by Moskvin at the opening night), and in 1917 he cast the young actor as Treplev in his new version of Seagull that, however, was never finished. The only true encounters the two Chekhovs had were the First Studio's staging of the short story The Witch (Vedma, 1916) with Michael Chekhov in the role of an old deacon whose beautiful wife cheats on him; and An Evening of One-Act Plays and Sketches by Chekhov (Vecher odnoaktnykh pyes i rasskazov Chekhova) that consisted of several vaudevilles and a short story I Forgot (Zabyl), the highlights of the actor's repertoire in exile. Chekhov played I Forgot both in Russian—for various émigré audiences in Europe and America—and in English in 1942 at the Barbizon Plaza Theatre, New York.[44]

Michael Chekhov's directorial attention to the preservation and presentation of the dramatic rhythms in performance revealed itself through his view of the actor's psychophysical presence onstage. In the role of the old deacon in the staging of The Witch, Michael Chekhov demonstrated the mixed feelings of outraged love and insulted pride as analyzed by Stanislavsky for the students. The audience laughed at the

---

[43] Chekhov, Perepiska A.P. Chekhova: 196.
[44] In 1944 Michael Chekhov played I Forgot at a charity-concert of the Russian-American Society of Hollywood Actors.

character's attempts to put his wife to shame and cried at his tenderness. The tied woman has fallen asleep, and the deacon sits down beside her. Chekhov keeps looking at his motionless partner and then starts to stroke her shoulder with very short and uneven gestures. In *I Forgot* Chekhov practiced his talent for improvisation, creating a theatrical mise-en-scene—equivalent to the rhythm of the literary original. He composed a sort of invisible rhythmical score interweaving words with gestures and sounds with movements. As Zhdanoff (Chekhov's stage partner, colleague and a co-founder of his American acting studio in Ridgefield) recollects, "during the rehearsals Chekhov asked me that the packages I was handing to him were be cued to certain words to a pause, and that I do it very precisely to make sure that a certain package goes into either left or right hand.[45] In fact, Chekhov's approach to his uncle's text demonstrates the *author-reader* type of theatrical recitation that respects the rhythmical requirements of the text, its diverse forms of foregrounding, theatrical irony, and "the sound shape […] rooted in the author's own kinesthetic make-up."[46]

In conclusion, I would like to go back to the three degrees of defamiliarization found in Anton Chekhov's texts, that is to say, genre estrangement, character *skaz* and punctuation. As Vershinin had predicted, it has already taken a hundred years and will take another hundred for theatre makers to agree on how to bring the theatrical irony in Chekhov's plays to the stage. It is still up to some new Stanislavsky to come and to re-stage Chekhov's *Three Sisters* in all its nostalgia, bitterness and humor:

> Tuzenbakh. In many years, you say, life on Earth will be wonderful and amazing. This is true. But in order to share in it now, even from a distance, one must prepare for it, one must work...
> Vershinin (*stands up*). Yes. But what a lot of flowers you've got there! (*Looking around*) And the apartment is wonderful too. (Act 1)

WORKS CITED

Borisova, L. M.. "Pauzy i antipauzy v dramaturgii A. P. Chekhova." *Russkaia*

---

[45] Zhdanoff quoted in Bykling, *Mikhail Chekhov v zapadnom teatre i kino*: 374.
[46] Veltruský, "Dramatic Text as a Component of Theatre": 251.

Rech': Nauchno-populiarnyi zhurnal. Jan–Feb (2001) 1: 11–18.

Brik, Osip. "Contributions to the Study of Verse Language." *Readings in Russian Poetics. Formalist and Structuralist Views.* Ed. Matejka, Ladislav. Ann Arbor: Michigan University Press, 1978: 117–125.

Brook, Peter. *The Empty Space.* Victoria: Penguin, 1972.

Bykling, Liisa. *Mikhail Chekhov v zapadnom teatre i kino,* SPb.: Akademicheski Proekt, 2000.

Chekhov, Anton. *Sbornik dokumentov i materialov.* M.: GIKHL, 1947.

Chekhov, Anton. *Perepiska A.P. Chekhova v trekh tomakh.* Ed. V.B. Kataev. M.: Nasledie. 3: 1996.

Eikhenbaum, Boris. "How Gogol's *Overcoat* is Made." *Gogol from the Twentieth Century: Eleven Essays.* Ed. Maguire Robert A. Princeton: Princeton UP, 1974: 269–291.

Elsworth, John. "The Concept of Rhythm in Bely's Aesthetic Thought." *Andrei Bely Centenary Papers.* Ed. Christa, Boris. Amsterdam: Hakkert. 1980: 68–80.

Griesbeck, Christian 1996. *Labanonotation.* 6 Dec. 2004
< http://www.uni-frankfurt.de/~griesbec/LABANE.HTML>

Jakobson, Roman. "What is Poetry." *Language in Literature.* Ed. Pomorska Kristina. Cambridge: Harvard University Press, 1997: 368–379.

Lotman, Iurii. *Analiz poeticheskogo teksta: struktura stikha.* L.: Prosveshchenie, 1972.

Maiakovskii, Vladimir. "Kak delat' stikhi." *Sochineniia.* Moscow: Khudozhestvennaia literatura. 2. 1970: 465–503.

Meyerhold, Vsevolod. "Naturalisticheskii teatr i teatr nastroeniia (1906)." *Stat'i, pis'ma, rechi, besedy, 1891–1917.* Moscow: Iskusstvo, 1968: 118.

Meyerhold on Theatre. Ed., trans. Braun, Edward. London: Methuen, 1969.

Mukařovský, Jan. "Čapek's Prose as Lyrical Melody and as Dialogue." *A Prague School Reader on Esthetics, Literary Structure and Style.* Ed. Garvin, Paul. Washington: Georgetown University Press, 1964: 133–149.

Nemirovich–Danchenko, Vladimir. *Izbrannye pis'ma.* Moscow: Iskusstvo, 1: 1979.

Rozik, Eli. "Theatrical Irony," *Theatre Research International.* 11 (2) Summer (1986): 132–151.

Stanislavskii, Konstantin. *Rezhisserskie ekzempliary K.S. Stanislavskogo. Tom tretii 1901–1904.* Moscow: Iskusstvo, 1983.

Strelkov, P. "Zvukopodrazhatel'nye mezhdometiia v iazyke Chekhova," in *Tvorchestvo A.P. Chekhova.* Ed. Trofimov, I. Moscow: GUPI, 1956: 240–300.

Veltruský, Jiřy. "Dramatic Text as a Coponent of Theatre." *Semiotics of A* Ed. Matejka, Ladislav; Titunik, Irwin. Cambridge: The MIT Press,1977: 74–94.

————. "Sound Qualities of the Text and the Actor's Performance." *Drama und Theater. Theorie-Methode-Geschichte.* Ed. Schmid, Herta; Kroll, Hedwig. München: Verlag Otto Sagner, 1991: 238–255.

Winner, Thomas. "Syncretism in Chekhov's Art: A Study of Polystructural Texts." *Chekhov's Art of Writing*. Ed. Debreczeny, Paul; Eekman, Thomas. Columbus: Slavica Publishers, 1977:153–167.

Ubersfeld, Anne. *Reading Theatre*. Trans. Collins Frank. Toronto: U of T Press, 1999.

On Calculability and Incalculability in *The Three Sisters*

WASILIJ SZCZUKIN
Jagiellonian University

In the vast literature on Chekhov's plays it has been frequently asserted that the texts of his plays only come to life on the stage, and that outside theatrical incarnations they lose the true multiplicity of meanings they contain.[1] There is some truth to this view. Yet at the same time the language of Chekhov the playwright still apparently remains that of a prose writer.[2] It is only a close reading that reveals a whole series of striking signals and signs quite intentionally inserted in the text to give it a particular, hidden meaning. This is despite the fact that the members of the audience in the theatre are not able to grasp this "meta-meaning": a meaning which surely escapes them unnoticed, or at best is able to exert a special influence on the subconscious, subliminal centres of their psychological perception, and creates at the same time that much discussed general mood that characterizes all Chekhov's plays.

We shall attempt to demonstrate this assertion on the basis of *The Three Sisters*, one of the most attractive of Chekhov's plays. We shall examine the role of numerals and a whole chain of hidden meanings that are added through them, and which serve to enrich what is already a complex semantics in the text. Having seen this play on the stage, the viewer cannot help but notice and retain at least two important numerals. First, he will surely remember that there were three sisters, and that Vershinin and Tuzenbakh argued all the time about how life will be in two or three hundred years. Second, many spectators, though probably not all, will likewise recall that Vershinin had two daughters. These numerals do indeed incise themselves in the memory—at least to a greater extent than does the self-evident act upon which the author insists: the

---

[1] See, for example, Iuri Domanskii, "Finaly chekhovskikh p'es: drama versus teatr?": 16.

[2] Gitovich, Irina, "Dramaturgiia prozaika, ili Genial'nye nep'esy Chekhova" : 22.

drama has four acts, each of which is separated from the other by a significant distance of time. After all, in contemporary productions with one intermission the fact that the story of the three sisters and their family goes through four phases of development may even slip the viewer's memory completely. Other numerals the spectator of *The Three Sisters* may not as a rule remember.

And yet the text of the play is overrun with numerical markers—both cardinal and ordinal. This is evident in the first five pages. The first act begins with Olga's words as she recalls that their father had died exactly a year (*one* year) ago, on the *fifth* of May, on Irina's nameday, and that the clock struck then too (whereupon onstage the clock strikes twelve times). Further on, Olga talks about how their father left Moscow with them *eleven* years ago, and that she had begun to want very much to return there. In reply we hear Chebutykin's remark: "Like hell!" [In Russian: *Cherta s dva*—"*Two* devils!"]—although Chebutykin says this not in connection with Olga's words, but in answer to another of Solyony's nonsensical assertions, which is not given in the text and which the audience thus does not hear. The sisters continue to dream about Moscow, talking about the joyful feeling in their hearts, and for about a minute the flow of numerals ceases. But then it occurs to Olga to talk about how unfortunate it is that their brother has put on weight, and how she herself has grown old, and the numerals return to the stage: "I am *twenty-eight*," she says, and almost immediately after Tuzenbakh, who has just come in, announces to the sisters that they are about to have a visit today from the new battery commander Vershinin, that (in reply to Irina's question) he is *forty* to *forty-five*, married for the *second* time, and that he has *two* daughters. There then ensues the baron's unflattering opinion about his commander's wife, followed by a uniquely Chekhovian dialogue at cross-purposes:

> Solyony (*coming into the living-room from the hall with Chebutykin*). With *one* hand I can lift only *one and a half* poods, but with *two* I can lift *five*, even *six* poods. From this I conclude that *two* men are stronger than *one* not *two* but *three* times, or even more...
> Chebutykin (*reading a newspaper as he walks*). In the case of hair loss... *two* zolotniks of naphthalene to a *half* bottle of alcohol... dissolve and apply daily... (*Writes in a notebook.*) Let's note that, sir! (*To Solyony.*) So you see, a cork is inserted in the bottle, and through

the middle there is a little glass tube... Then you take a pinch of common or garden alum... (S 13: 122).

Then we suddenly hear Irina's voice:

Irina. Ivan Romanych, dear Ivan Romanych!
Chebutykin. What, my little one, my joy?
Irina. Tell me, how come I am so happy today? It's as if I am in full sail, over me there is a broad, blue sky, and big white birds are flying. How come? How come?
Chebutykin (*kissing both her hands, tenderly*). My white bird... (S 13: 122–123)

And this comes right after talk of two zolotniks of naphthaline and a pinch of alum...

It seems to Irina that for her everything in this world is clear and that she knows how to live (NB: in the final scene Olga several times repeats quite the opposite: "If only we knew, if only we knew!). The youngest sister's knowledge is gradually transformed into figures: she is in horror at the thought of the fate of a young woman getting up at *twelve* noon, and then drinking coffee and getting dressed at *two* o'clock. Olga's reply is ironical: "Father taught us to get up at seven o'clock. Now Irina wakes up at *seven* and lies there until at least *nine* and thinks about something. And she has such a serious expression" (S 13: 123). In reply the name-day girl reminds her that she is already *twenty*. A yearning for work is close to Tuzenbakh's heart also, as he muses that in *twenty-five* or *thirty* years everybody will work. Solyony jealously tells the baron that in *twenty-five* years he will not be alive, because in *two* or *three* years he will have a fit and die, or be shot by Solyony himself. Masha, in a melancholic mood ("melanchondry") recalls that when their father was alive *thirty* or *forty* officers would come to their house for a name-day celebration, but today only *one and a half* had come "and it's as quiet as a desert" (S 13: 124).

These examples could be expanded upon. The flow of numerals mentioned (including fractions: *a quarter, a half, one and a half*) or ordinal numerals (*first, second* etc.) sometimes drops off, and then increases. One thing, however, is certain: there are a great many numerals. To be sure, I have not conducted a statistical count of all the numerals used in the text of *Three Sisters* and in Chekhov's other works; therefore, my observations can only claim relative accuracy. Nevertheless, even a cursory comparison of the play I have chosen with other Chekhov plays suggests that Chekhov was always inclined to mention numerals with relative frequency. Thus, for example, in the middle of the last act of *The Seagull*, the tragedy of life is played out against the backdrop of a game of lotto (a game which consists of the uninterrupted naming of numerals).[3] The denizens and guests of Sorin's estate constantly cry out "ninety," "twenty-seven," "eighty-eight," and so on. They discuss Treplev's prose and, as it were, rationally weigh its virtues and shortcomings in the balance while he himself all the while performs something incalculable on the piano—a melancholic waltz (S 13: 53–55). In the other acts of *The Seagull*, by contrast, the waves of numerals are noticeable to a lesser extent. They make their presence much more felt in *Uncle Vanya* and, what is more striking, in *The Cherry Orchard*. However, no other play of Chekhov's contains such a quantity and such a flow of numerals pouring over the spectator or reader than *Three Sisters*. Recognition of this fact leads us to surmise that the rhythmical flows of numerals in this play do not appear by chance: they bear a not insignificant meaning, the understanding of which will bring us closer to grasping the many hidden meanings of this complex "drama in four acts"—the only dramatic work of Chekhov's that contains a numeral in the very title.

Reading the text of the play again and again, I asked myself whether, in this case, one might talk about the symbolism of specific numerals in that quite definite sense: as they occur in, for example, Dante's *Divine Comedy* or in Blok's poem *The Twelve*. After lengthy consideration and analysis I came to answer this question in the negative. Of course, one might point out the obvious link between the number of sisters and the images of the three graces or three maidens of the fairy tale. One might also link the number of acts in *Three Sisters* (as in all the other "classical" plays by Chekhov) with the archetypical proportions of nature, including human psychology: the four points of the compass, the four seasons and the four divisions of the day, the four psychological functions according to Jung and the four rhythmical units of musical

---

[3] A parallel might be drawn between the game of lotto in *The Seagull* and that in the story "Children" (1886). In the latter unconsciously cruel children are playing, while in the former it is unconsciously cruel adults.

harmony. However, these sorts of analogy are too universal and applicable to many other authors and works. Decisively, there is no secret, symbolic meaning contained in the fact that the clock at the beginning of the first act strikes twelve, that it is seven minutes fast (as Kulygin informs us); that in the game of patience in the second act the eight falls on the two of spades, or that in St Petersburg, according to the watchman Ferapont there had been two hundred degrees of frost. Quite simply, Masha's husband is a pedant, and the game of patience did not work out because the sisters are not going to return to Moscow. There is, however, a slight hint that the spiritual world in which the three main heroines exist is a few minutes ahead of the time according to which this provincial town exists.

And yet the author does not scatter the numerals around in *Three Sisters* at random, in some kind of anarchic disorder.[4] A close reading of the text allows one to penetrate not only concrete meanings, but also those internal emotional and spiritual states that arise from a layering of meanings one on top of another. On the emotional level *Three Sisters* is constructed, so to say, according to a female rather than a male logic. The conversations about schoolbooks, medicines and the humdrum train of days can suddenly be interrupted by joyfulness and inspiration, which can in turn give way as quickly as lightning to tears and melancholy as a result of some carelessly uttered words or apparently chance events and coincidences; this melancholy can very quickly be supplanted by a feeling of the fullness of life, of love, and birdlike flight. Thus it continues, endlessly, rhythmically and in wave-like fashion, as in nature or in music. This is the way the weather often changes, or a mood—especially a woman's. For this reason *Three Sisters* is, apart from everything else, a play about the nature of the female soul.

A great deal has been written about the musico-lyrical composition

---

[4] The complete absence of "intentionality," the unpredictably chance choice of words, physical details, images and episodes was seen by Aleksandr Chudakov as a principal feature of Chekhov's poetics (see Chudakov, *Poetika Chekhova*). In actual fact the *visibility* of the anarchic unpredictability and "lack of intention" functions as a fully thought through device of Chekhov's, the intention of which was evidently to give the text a Pushkinian *nonchalance*—an aristocratic negligence, casualness and elegance.

of Chekhov's plays. [5] They are constructed according to laws of harmony that approximate those of music. But if this is the case, their ideational and emotional "score" must have been carefully thought through and, what is more, calculated. The task is to find the devices used to convey the natural, "feminine" rhythmicality of the shifting moods. Chekhov scholarship has yet to explore these ideas.

Further, it may be assumed that one of the means used by Chekhov to organize the rhythm of the emotional organization of the text is precisely the numerals, or rather the abundance of numerals: the *numerality* and the *accountability* of the depicted world, and its periodical opposition to the unquantifiable, unaccountable nature of some of its aspects. If one takes the trouble to trace the intensity of the occurrence of numerals in *Three Sisters*, it is easy to ascertain that this parameter is subordinated to the laws of a rhythmical and, in a certain sense, even *musical* organization of the action onstage: now the characters begin to count and enumerate different things, now suddenly as if on command (all at once, or only some of those onstage) they seem to forget numbers. The successive waves of *numerality* and *accountability* of different existential phenomena alternate with waves of heightened lyrical and emotional exaltation—after which numbers are forgotten, at least for a moment.

Another important circumstance that is directly linked to the semantics of numbers in *Three Sisters* lies in the fact that, according to my calculations (which, though not quite precise, nevertheless reflect a definite tendency), between 75% and 80% of the numbers mentioned in the play denote measures of *time*—a number of minutes, hours, weeks, months or years.[6] In general images expressing time are among the most important and significant elements in the semantic structure of the play; they are worth a separate investigation. It is customary to count and measure time, and mechanical clocks symbolize the measurability of

---

[5] See, for example, Shakh-Azizova, *Chekhov i zapadnoevropeiskaia drama ego vremeni*; Papernyi, *Vopreki vsem pravilam...*; Zingerman, *Teatr Chekhova i ego mirovoe znachenie*.

[6] The shortest period of time mentioned in the text of *Three Sisters* is the seven minutes by which the clock in the Prozorov's house is fast (S 13: 134). The longest is one million years in Tuzenbakh's monologue in act two ("Not just in two hundred or three hundred years, but even in a million years life will remain as it has been" [S 13: 147]).

time and hence the measured, rhythmical, predictable, ordered nature of existential processes. Humanity living in the New Time, at the dawn of which mechanical clocks appeared, became used to associating time with numbers and hands of clocks, and not with the height of the sun over the horizon and not with the ringing of a bell in the neighbouring monastery that called to mind the unearthly, immeasurable and eternal.[7] Subsequently "clock watching" became such a habitual activity for Europeans that their image of the world was reminiscent of a big clock. Newton and Descartes constructed a rational, mechanistic model of the world, which for centuries on end became obligatory for all school programmes. Not just the pupils of Olga Prozorova, but their grandchildren too studied this model in mathematics and physics classes.

Returning to *Three Sisters*, we should note what an important role is played in it by clocks. In the first and second acts it is the clock in the drawing room that is seven minutes fast, and that various characters keep looking at: Natasha, for example, counts out the time in such a way that she manages to go for a spin with Protopopov "for a quarter of an hour" (S 13: 155). During the fire in the third act there is a different clock—the porcelain one that belonged to the sisters' late mother: it stands in Olga and Irina's room, and is unexpectedly broken by Chebutykin. The fire is extinguished, but the broken clock is fortunately not the main thing in the house, and a real catastrophe does not occur in the play: even Tuzenbakh's death is not perceived as tragically as it would be if Irina loved him. However, the old, relatively passive rhythm of life of the three sisters is nevertheless broken, and the breaking point coincides with the fire, with the confession of Masha, who has fallen in love and been unfaithful to her husband—and with the destruction of the porcelain clock. Even in the concluding act, in the garden, although no clock is to be seen, everybody still talks about time: they count the hours and minutes until the military leave, until Tuzenbakh's duel with Solyony and until the ultimate parting of the ways. Of course, the time scale of the action contrasts with the image of a larger one, or rather, as in *King Lear* or in Chekhov's story "The Student," with the linkages between different timeframes—an idealized past, an idealized and unclear future, and the "cursed" present, full of suffering, which already soon

---

[7] Interestingly, in act three a knell is tolled offstage because of the fire.

will become the idealized past.[8]

The fact that Chebutykin breaks the porcelain clock that belonged to the mother of the sisters is not only a minor catastrophe or a foreshadowing of future catastrophes. In the context of the pulsing flows of numbers that surreptitiously exhaust the spectator or reader, the symbol of the broken clock—which is to say the loss of count of time—can turn into a circumstance that, if it is not gratifying, is at least, in a paradoxical way, an inspiration of hope. As the saying has it, "happy people don't watch the clock." The three sisters and the kind military men are not only in search of lost time; they try to peek into the future which no clock can measure, but which one can sense in one's heart.

A third important comment has to do with specific numerals which seem to yield a concrete meaning.

If we assume that from the moment of the fire (which took place in the summer) to the moment when the artillery battalions are transferred to another location (which takes place in the spring) ten or eleven months have passed, then it turns out that the action of *Three Sisters* takes exactly four years. This is easy to calculate, since in the first act Irina is twenty, while in the third she is twenty-four. There are four acts over four years, and the four seasons—spring, winter, summer and autumn—make a complete cycle of one year. The circularity and natural completeness of events is underlined through the fact that both the first and last acts begin as the clock strikes noon: the entire action lasts, as it were, four years and two hours. However, the distant future is denoted in the characters' speeches in round figures: twenty-five, thirty, fifty, two hundred, three hundred, a thousand and a million years, which is quite natural. Another important date creates a certain dissonance. Eleven years have gone by from the moment when the sisters were obliged to leave their beloved Moscow to the moment when the action of the first act begins—but this means that the leave-taking of the departing officers occurs fifteen years after the sisters' departure from Moscow. Why precisely the

---

[8] Compare also the following from "The Steppe": "From this conversation Egorushka understood that his new acquaintances, whatever the different in age and character, all had one thing in common and that made them resemble each other: they all had a wonderful past and a very disagreeable present; they all to the last one talked about their past with delight, while they viewed the present almost with disdain. A Russian loves to remember, but hates to live..." (S 7: 64).

numbers eleven and fifteen? I would venture to suggest that the action of *Three Sisters* ends at the moment when the idea of the play occurred to Chekhov (1898–1899), and that if we count back fifteen years we come to important years in the life of Chekhov himself—1883–1884—his last year in university: his youth; his life in Moscow; the years of his first literary successes and the beginning of his fame. "Eleven to fifteen years ago" is associated in the writer's mind, as it is in the minds of the three sisters, with youth, health and happiness. This, however, ends the list of concretely significant numbers in the play. Let us now trace and illustrate the above in greater detail, taking each of the four acts in turn.

The first act begins, as has been said, with a flow of numbers that is interrupted literally for a minute when it seems to Irina in her happiness that she is in full sail, and that above her there is a broad blue sky and large birds (S 13: 122). The stream of numbers then begins again to flow from the mouths of the characters with renewed force, until the nurse Anfisa and the watchman Ferapont bring the name-day cake into the living room, whereupon animation and joy reign onstage for several minutes. Few numbers are mentioned here: Chebutykin says that he will soon be sixty, and when Vershinin arrives he declares that he recalls the three sisters being three little girls in colonel Prozorov's house on Malaya Basmannaya Street. Further pleasant reminiscences ensue, including a few rare mentions of numbers; these tend to evoke unpleasant or sad facts that create a dissonance on the background of the general mellow feelings: Vershinin will soon be forty-two; eleven long years have gone by since the sisters saw Moscow (although by the autumn they will have moved there…); the station is a long way from the town—twenty versts. Then, however, for quite a long time numbers are not mentioned at all: there is a moment of philosophizing and arguments about the present and the future between the most noble characters in the play—Vershinin and Tuzenbakh. True, Solyony and Chebutykin somewhat undermine and parody the intellectual conversation, but they also do not count anything. A carefree atmosphere reigns onstage which the strict precision of hard numbers would serve to disrupt. The bright and serene motif of being in love intervenes: Vershinin had once been called the love-sick major, and now Andrei is the love-sick violinist or love-sick professor. But then at the height of the general merriment it is precisely from Andrei's mouth that numerals again begin to be heard. At first they are joyful in content: out of love he didn't sleep till four, and saw the early dawn. Then they become much more prosaic: after their father's death he began to put on weight and within a year had become fat. And then it is as if the sluice-gates had opened: Masha complains that knowing three languages in this town is an unnecessary luxury, like having a sixth finger. Vershinin disagrees, evoking the prospect of a happy future, but his monologue, unlike his preceding speeches on this topic, is loaded with numbers (S 13: 131). From exalted topics the colonel gradually moves to every-day details and we hear what we should have heard from him long before: he has a sick wife with a difficult character and two little girls, and if he could begin life again, he would not have married.

Kulygin enters in his official tail-coat and gives Irina his history of the high-school for the past fifty years, which he had already given her at Easter. From that moment almost to the end of the first act numbers may not exactly wash over the spectator, but they make their presence felt in the speeches of different characters. There will be no more inspired speeches: the characters talk about time and the clock ("Masha, at four o'clock we have to be at the director's"; "Your clock is seven minutes fast"; "yesterday I worked from morning until eleven in the evening" [S 13: 133, 134]) and about how old different people are. "You get a mark of C [in Russian three] minus for behaviour" (S 13: 136), Kulygin declares to Masha, who has become slightly tipsy and merry (after being down in the dumps and wanting to go home at the beginning of the act). Fedotik photographs those present: "One! Hold it a little... Two!" (S 13: 137). It then turns out that thirteen are sitting at the table; this is bad—a "devil's dozen." But at the same time there is a good omen: there are lovers present... In a word, life, normal, down to earth, *measurable* and *calculable* life asserts itself. Only at the very end of the act, when Andrei declares his love to Natasha, are there no numbers. Say what you like, but there *is* love...

The juxtaposition of the everyday world of numbers and the "exalted" world of incalculable essences is fundamental to the score of the entire play. In fact, it is that very problem mentioned by Vershinin in the second act, and which is so difficult to resolve: "Exalted forms of thought are typical in the highest degree for Russians, but tell me, why do they stoop so low in life itself?" (S 13: 143). Evidently, it is because in geographic and social situations that would be so unimaginably difficult for inhabitants of Western Europe (as represented in, for example, "The Steppe," "Peasants" and "In the Ravine") it is much easier to think in an exalted fashion than to make ends meet, to make one's apartment pleasant to live in, to bring up the children and keep on the right side of relatives and neighbours. Everyday life was always the Great Russian's Achilles heel, and as long as daily life is not organized, no legal norms will enter the flesh and blood of the nation, nor will it be possible to speak of a civil society. One wonders whether we understand, some hundred-odd years later, that Chekhov's three sisters appeared in Russian literature (and hence in the Russian cultural consciousness) in order to make a heroic attempt to make pleasant and ennoble not the sphere of ideas and utopian ambitions, but everyday life itself with its hours and minutes, its versts and poods. Not to abolish or overcome it, but precisely to assimilate and ennoble it. And this they managed to accomplish—better than all those characters who came before and after in our literature.

Let us then return to the play. At the beginning of the second act Chekhov, without forcing it on us, depicts the contrast between two contiguous worlds and two types of life. On the one hand, it is eight o'clock, or rather a quarter past eight; the same wall-clock is hanging in the room as hung there in the first act; Andrei and Natasha are discussing various everyday cares, as well as what time the mummers promised to come. But at the same time, "offstage in the street one barely can hear an accordion being played" (S 13 : 139), and an *accordion* (*garmonika*) in the system of Chekhov's motifs denotes something joyful—the memory of happy minutes, beauty, *harmony*, and perhaps what Chekhov called the God of living man.[9] How are these two worlds to be reconciled? No, it doesn't happen: here is Vershinin talking about his sick daughter and an argument with his wife; unavoidably he reverts to cold figures (they argued from seven to nine in the morning). But then he suddenly declares his love to Masha, and although the wailing in the stove foreshadows a sad

---

[9] In "A Dreary Story" there is a passage where Nikolai Stepanovich tells Katia about the happiest minutes of his youth: "It happened that I would be walking in the garden of our seminary. [...] The wind would carry to me from some distant tavern the squeal of an accordion and a song, or a troika with bells on it would race past the fence of the seminary, and that was quite enough for a feeling of happiness to invade not only my breast, but even my stomach, my legs and arms..."(S 7: 283). Curiously, in this passage the accordion is heard from afar, "offstage," as in *Three Sisters*.

end to their affair, the illusion of happiness takes over: the lovers do not once mention numbers and do not think of calculations. The more pragmatic but no less noble Tuzenbakh talks about his love differently: "And every evening I will come by the telegraph and accompany you home; I'll do it for ten or twenty years, until you chase me away..." (S 13: 144). But Irina, who is tired from her work and does not love the Baron, doesn't listen to him; she is taken up with life's problems... and with figures: Two weeks ago Andrei lost two hundred rubles gambling; how long will it be until they leave for Moscow?—one, two, three, six months, and Chebutykin has not paid for his apartment for the last eight...

Vershinin is thinking about something completely different, and not for nothing does he ask for tea ("Half my life for a glass of tea!" [S 13: 145]). In the Russian tradition tea is a "philosophical" drink, stimulating the intellect and the utopian imagination: not for nothing was it the favourite drink of the idealists of the 1840s, and the nihilists of the 1860s, and the populist terrorists of the 1870s—we have only to recall Dostoevsky's *Devils* or the famous painting "The Soirée" by Vladimir Makovsky. Vershinin and Tuzenbakh's "historiosophical" dialogue does not appear as esoteric as this: it is peppered with figures. True, these are not mere numbers, but "beautiful" signifiers of time, almost eons: two hundred, three hundred years, a million years. Irina's complaints about her demanding job are completely forgotten, and onstage there reigns an atmosphere of high culture and a particular lyrical intimacy. Can it be that here the world of calculable everyday reality (after all the figures are still present) has fused somewhat with the world of noble dreaming and readiness for glorious deeds? Perhaps it has; in any case, in Chekhov the two worlds coexist side by side, in parallel, and the boundary between them is unstable and easily penetrated. This would seem to be a bad thing, since noble dreams can too easily fall victim to the difficulties of life, the paralyzing "slime of petty details" (to use Saltykov-Shchedrin's expression). But it is also a good thing, since there is something "refreshing and envigorating"[10] in the fact that the characters in *Three Sisters* are able to make such an easy transition from Andrei's losing two hundred rubles to the search for their own faith or to dreams of ennobling work. At this point the numbers start to sound not depressing, but amusing: Chebutykin says that he is thirty-two, and then a few minutes later

---

[10] An expression of Nikolai Dobroliubov's ("The ray of light in a dark realm").

Masha reminds him that he is exactly sixty years old.

But not everything is so simple and easy. In the game of patience the eight falls on the two of spades, the patience does not work out, and again the sisters will not go to Moscow. The two worlds, the two semantic fields again become agitated, as it were, and come into conflict: Solyony would fry and eat Bobik; Vershinin's wife tries to poison herself; the lovesick colonel will not get to drink his tea, and everyone is on the point of falling out with each other... but then Tuzenbakh goes to Solyony with a bottle of cognac in order to make things up. He drinks, and sings along with Andrei and Chebutykin. Sometimes the numbers attack, and sometimes they retreat a step: the mummers had promised to come by nine, but Natasha gave orders to send them away; Solyony asserts stubbornly that there are two universities in Moscow, while Tuzenbakh, by now tipsy, has decided finally to retire ("I've been thinking about it for five years" [S 13: 131]) and plays a waltz on the piano ... the fog and melancholy of life slowly win out, however, and the wave of sadness and hopelessness grows. The final "numerical" note in act two is when Protopopov invites Natasha for a ride in his troika, and she is prepared for "quarter of an hour" (S 13:155), but in the end she tells the maid that she will be home "in half an hour" (S 13: 156). Olga has a headache; Irina pines for Moscow; and Kulygin, regretting that the party has been a failure, declares, using the exclamatory accusative: "*O fallacem hominum spem!..*" (Oh false hope of men! [S 13: 156]). And indeed it is false—or perhaps not?

Act three is organized in a similar manner. Twice the "mouse-like scampering of life" dominates onstage, accompanied by the mention of numeric parameters, most of which denote segments of time or years: the nurse Anfisa is over eighty-one; she has been in service with the Prozorovs for thirty years; in that night Olga "has aged ten years" (S 13: 159); Chebutykin has not had a drink for two years, but now he ups and gets drunk; Masha has not played on the piano for three or four years and has forgotten everything; Kulygin and Masha have been married for seven years, but it seems to him that it was only yesterday. Irina is twenty-three), but there is also "Andrei Sergeich, I have told you ten times" (S 13: 169), and the sum of money (Andrei Sergeich has thirty-five thousand in gambling debts, and he has mortgaged the house, which belongs to all four of them). However, almost all the characters are capable of abstracting themselves for a time in their thoughts and feelings from this vanity of vanities that is controlled by the pitiless movement of the hands of the clock. The wave of lyricism would seem to sweep over them without any motivation; it suddenly happens a few seconds after Chebutykin smashes the porcelain clock (truly "the happy do not watch clocks"). At this moment of general distress and embarrassment the guilty apology for a doctor already manages to announce (evidently in order to draw attention from the smashed clock of their mother) that "Natasha is having a fling with Protopopov" (S 13: 162), whereupon Vershinin, who has arrived shortly before from the fire and is wrapped in his thoughts, suddenly laughs and utters the "transitional" line ("How strange this all is in essence!" [S 13: 162]). Then, after a short pause we hear his monologue about his little girls standing on the threshold of the house in their underwear and about the astonishing, indeed strange link of the times and the progressive movement of historical time.

The monologue of the philosophizing colonel also contains numbers: either years—two hundred, three hundred years (the characters in the play really do talk more than anything about years)—or... three sisters. Evidently, according to Chekhov's plan, it is precisely with the three sisters that there begins the timid, careful, but nevertheless perceptible movement towards a possible future happiness (possible, but not inevitable):

> Vershinin. [...] And when my little girls were standing on the threshold dressed only in their underwear, bare-foot, and the street was red from the fire and there was a terrible roar, I thought that something similar must have happened many years ago, when an enemy suddenly attacked and pillaged and burned... By the way, basically what a difference between things now and what used to happen! And a little more time will go by, two or three hundred years or so, and people also will look back at our life now with horror and amusement, and all our present life will seem awkward and difficult and very inconvenient and strange. Oh what a life there will probably be, what a life! (*Laughs.*) [...] Right now there are only three people like you in the town, but in the generations to come there will be more, more and more, and the time will come when everybody will change and be the way you are, and they will live the way you do, and then you will become out of date, and people will be born who will be better than you are... (*Laughs.*) I am in some sort of strange mood today. I want to go a little wild...

(*Sings.*) To love all ages must surrender, [tram-tam-tam] ... its impulses are beneficial... (*Laughs.*)
Masha. Tram-tam-tam...
Vershinin. Tram-tam ... (S 13: 163)

Thus the author "transports" the consciousness of his characters from numbers denoting the measurable and calculable problems of life, first into "exalted" numbers (two or three hundred years, three sisters) and then into lyrical incalculability. Vershinin laughs several times and once sings of love to which "all ages must surrender," and we are reminded that it is about age that the characters in the play complain every time they have the chance. However, when they make declarations of love, when they laugh, and when they sing, they never count anything. Laughter is immeasurable, and music, like lyricism, on the one hand is subordinate to mathematical rules of harmony, but on the other hand it contains structural levels that cannot be expressed just in numbers or words. Apparently normal, good people (and such are the majority in *Three Sisters*) are not capable of talking all the time about passing years, lost hours or money spent. There comes a moment when the word turns to laughter, lyricism or song. This kind of substance can be neither counted nor expressed with unequivocal logic. Not for nothing do Masha and Vershinin express their love not in complete lexemes, but through onomatopoeia, akin to children's babble.[11] Chekhov as it were agrees with the romantics who declared that language is incapable of expressing the beauty of the universe and the unrepeatable delight of human feeling, for apart from what can be logically represented and calculated in the world there is the inexpressible (*das Unaussprechliche*).[12] And it is no doubt for this reason that, when after Vershinin's monologue an atmosphere of general love reigns onstage for a certain time, none of the characters men-

---

[11] According to Aleksandr Kugel', this was the way a certain enamoured actress (probably Lidia Iavorskaia), who was later to play Masha, explained herself in Chekhov's presence (Aleksandr Kugel' [Homo Novus], *List'ia s dereva: vospominaniia*: 68).

[12] This term probably first appeared in the works of Wilhelm-Hermann Wackenroder, and then in Tieck and Schelling. See: Grigorii Gukovskii, *Pushkin i russkie romantiki*: 46; Vladimir Toporov, "Iz issledovanii v oblasti poetiki Zhukovskogo," *Slavica Hierosolymitana*, 1977: 41; Efim Etkind, "'Vnutrennii chelovek' i vneshniaia rech'": 19–21.

tions any numbers. It is not for nothing that towards the end of act three, when the characters manage to overcome the second wave of concrete detail and "melanchondry," Masha admits to her sisters that she loves the colonel, and then seems to try and free herself of the necessity of expressing things discretely and intelligently with logically ordered speech, preferring silence and even "madness": "I've confessed to you. Now I'll be silent... Now I shall be like Gogol's madman... silence, silence..." (S 13: 169). However, when they are silent, they cry out: her silence signifies her immersion in a galaxy of the inexpressible, a galaxy maximally saturated with insights, emotions and "silent" meanings.

Yet the involvement of the characters in the "expressible" and "calculable" in life keeps returning to replace lyrical withdrawal and charming children's babble. In all probability, man cannot remain constantly immersed either in the pragmatics of life or in the sweet lyrical twilight of the inexpressible. And so numbers return to the stage as imperceptibly as they disappeared several minutes ago. It is as hard to live without arithmetic and clocks as it is without faith, hope and love. And in this consists one more of those truths that Chekhov offers his audiences and readers in *Three Sisters*—a not impeccable truth, but one worth thinking about.

The fourth and final act is dominated by the autumnal atmosphere of leave-taking and ... tripling. Today three batteries are leaving, tomorrow another three—and the three sisters will remain. Solyony, who likens himself to Lermontov, will fight a duel for the third time. And immediately after his shot the clean-shaven Kulygin, in an attempt to cheer up Masha, who is crying, puts on a dress-up moustache and beard that he has confiscated from a third year high-school pupil. In the fourth act triads are distributed in those places that bear a special semantic load. But in order to make the construction less obvious, Chekhov introduces a certain variety into the numerical algorhythm: a certain Kozyrev was excluded from the fifth year because of the *ut consecutivum*; Kulygin has the order of Stanislav Second Class; Vershinin's wife and daughter will remain in the town another two months; the batteries will leave not at three, but one o'clock. The characters consult the watches even more frequently and more tensely than in the preceding acts, and are too late to get somewhere. Nevertheless, the wave-like alternation of moods between a pragmatic concern with petty details and a lyrical melting into something exalted and inexpressible and then back again is still present. Thus, a serious Andrei recalls that the town has existed for two hundred years, but no religious figure has ever lived there; Ferapont apparently apropos of nothing conveys the latest news from the administration building, that in St Petersburg in the winter there had been two hundred degrees of frost.

The last act differs from the others inasmuch as it contains a little more music—wordless music, like the distant playing on the accordion in act two. Yet the triadic principle still remains in force, for onstage three melodies are heard in turn—a solo, a duet, and an orchestral piece.[13] The first of them is a popular tune of the time, "The Maiden's Prayer," that comes from an open window: Natasha is playing it on the piano for her Protopopov. In the world of the three sisters and Chekhov himself this kind of music was looked down on as the epitome of vulgarity. A few minutes later "someone far away can be heard playing on the harp and violin" (S 13: 177). No one notices this, since all are absorbed in their thoughts and cares. But the melody continues to be heard and then, apparently, falls silent for a long time (there is no corresponding stage direction). At the same time Tuzenbakh goes to his duel with Solyony; Vershinin cannot wait to see Masha; and Andrei walks the pram with the baby... The power of the inexpressible suddenly makes itself felt:

> Natasha (*behind the window*). Bobik, what is Mummy's name? Darling, darling! And who is this? It's Auntie Olia. Say hello Olia to your auntie!
> (*Itinerant musicians, a man and a woman, play on the violin and harp; Vershinin, Olga and Anfisa come out of the house and listen for a moment in silence; Irina approaches.*)
> Olga. Our garden is like a thoroughfare; people walk and even drive through it. Nanny, give the musicians something!..
> Anfisa (*giving money to the musicians*). God be with you, good people. (*The musicians bow and go off.*) Miserable people. You don't start playing if you're well-fed. (S 13: 183)

The musicians seem to be in the way, and in general the music results, not from happiness (from being "well-fed"), but onstage, where time is strictly calculated, the harp and violin are heard for a whole minute, and everyone "listens in silence." After, when the musicians have been asked

---

[13] The Chekhov scholar Anatolii Sobennikov first drew my attention to this fact. I hereby express my deep appreciation.

to leave, Vershinin nervously looks at his watch: it is time to say farewell forever. And again, but now for the last time, we hear numerals onstage: Vershinin's wife and little girls will live there for another two months; tomorrow there won't be one military man in the town; and—already after Solyony's shot—Kuligin confiscates from someone in the third year a moustache and beard.

From this point until the end of the play no further numbers are mentioned. Masha cries. Natasha plans to move the children to the room that Irina is about to vacate, to cut down the fir grove and plant nice little flowers everywhere. Her speech is interrupted by the third melody to be heard in this final act: the departing military play a march,[14] and will not stop playing until the curtain falls. The musical triad thus works in the following way: in the perception of the audience there is a sequential transition from the vulgar "Maiden's Prayer" through the pensive lyrical melody on the harp and violin to a sort of synthesis of the two—a lively march, in which, as in life itself, one can find both vulgarity, and genuine joy, and a "farewell" melancholy.

The concluding episodes of the play, which was conceived of as an argument between the calculability of everyday life and the inexpressibility of the spirit, are filled with not only "just music," but the musical mumblings of Chebutykin, for whom it's "all the same,"[15] and also the sisters' thoughts about the beauty of life (despite everything that has and will happen) and about the impenetrable, immeasurable "large-scale time," which it is impossible to recognize and "calculate." "If only one could know, if only one could know!" repeats Olga, and in her words one hears the natural desire for a person of the New Time to know and express the hidden and intimate in simple and comprehensible formulae— best of all in numbers. After all, in the world there should be space for natural numbers. But even for the incalculable there should be space.

I shall now try to sum up my observations. It seems to me that the text of *Three Sisters* was not consciously thought up, but gradually felt through by Chekhov as a sort of musical, or more precisely an emotional-

---

[14] According to a verbal comment of the director Viktor Gul'chenko, in all productions of *Three Sisters* it is "Proshchanie slavianki" (The Slavic Girl's Farewell) by Vasily Agapkin that is played.

[15] Chebutykin (*Sings quietly*). Tara... ra... boom-de-ay... sitting on a stump today..." (*Reads a newspaper.*) It's all the same! It's all the same!" (S 13: 188).

lyrical score in which it is not the visual but the acoustic parameters that dominate. It is based on the opposition of two semantic fields. One of these is a positivistic picture of the world, the realm of arithmetical and mechanical comprehensibility, of the divisibility of being, including time, into discrete elements that can be counted and enumerated. It is from such representations of the world, from a Cartesian model of the universe as being like an immense clockwork mechanism, that New Time began. The ability to subject life to analysis, multiplied by pragmatism and distrust of utopias, facilitated the rational organization of life. This permitted Vershinin to declare with complete justification in act three that in comparison with times when "the enemy arrived unexpectedly, pillaged and burned" (S 13: 163), life has become much more civilized. But the humanitarian sphere, which is inhabited not by discrete elements but by living people: people saying intelligent things and stupidities; people crying, falling hopelessly in love; people singing and playing the accordion—this sphere is not susceptible to Cartesian or positivist analysis: harmony cannot be tested with algebra, and even less with arithmetic and mechanics. And so man is attracted to the opposite semantic pole—to the inexpressible, to amorphous and by no means always rational feelings, to the unfathomable and the unpredictable. This field Chekhov expresses not through numbers, but with a musical-lyrical aura of integral, non-discrete "meta-objectivity." By the same token the author of *Three Sisters* becomes a unifying link between romanticism[16] with its search for the inexpressible and modernism, which discovered beauty and harmony in what seemed to the ordinary positivist consciousness to be irrational and even ridiculous.

In contemporary mathematics discrete calculation stands in opposition not to madness, but to analogic thought. The three sisters and their noble companions subconsciously feel the necessity, but also the limitation of a numerical image of the world, and therefore, keeping a certain amount of skeptical circumspection, they more and more boldly acquire

---

[16] Among Chekhov's Russian predecessors Turgenev occupies a special place. He was a late romantic, and at the same time a person of the enlightenment and a rationalist, who valued highly certain aspects of positivism, but nevertheless as an artist was in thrall to impressionist visions and fantasies.

the complex ability to see and hear beyond objects, measures, and numbers.

Translated from the Russian by J. Douglas Clayton.

WORKS CITED

Chudakov, Aleksandr. *Poetika Chekhova*. M.: Nauka, 1971.

Domanskii, Iuri. "Finaly chekhovskikh p'es: drama versus teatr?" *Drittes Internationales Čechov-Symposium in Badenweiler im 100. Todesjahr des Schriftstellers veranstattet vom Slavischen Seminar der Universität Tübingen. Anton P. Čechov als Dramatiker. Zusammenfassungen.* Tübingen: 2004: 16.

Etkind, Efim. *"Vnutrennii chelovek" i vneshniaia rech': Ocherki psikhopoetiki russkoi literatury XVIII–XIX vv.* M.: Iazyki russkoi kul'tury, 1998.

Gitovich, Irina. "Dramaturgiia prozaika, ili Genial'nye nep'esy Chekhova." *Drittes Internationales Čechov-Symposium in Badenweiler im 100. Todesjahr des Schriftstellers veranstattet vom Slavischen Seminar der Universität Tübingen. Anton P. Čechov als Dramatiker. Zusammenfassungen.* Tübingen: 2004.

Gukovskii, Grigorii. *Pushkin i russkie romantiki.* M.: Khudozhestvennaia literatura, 1965.

Kugel', Aleksandr. (Homo Novus) *List'ia s dereva: vospominaniia.* L.: Vremia, 1926.

Papernyi, Zinovii. *Vopreki vsem pravilam... P'esy i vodevili Chekhova.* M.: Iskusstvo, 1982.

Shakh-Azizova, Tatiana. *Chekhov i zapadnoevropeiskaia drama ego vremeni.* M.: Nauka, 1966.

Toporov, Vladimir. "Iz issledovanii v oblasti poetiki Zhukovskogo," *Slavica Hierosolymitana*, 1977: 51–77.

Zingerman, Boris. *Teatr Chekhova i ego mirovoe znachenie.* M.: Nauka, 1988.

The Flora and Fauna In
The Cherry Orchard

NATALIA VESSELOVA
University of Ottawa

Nature in its various manifestations is a constant presence in Chekhov's works. Moreover, his view of nature is characterized by a certain duality: on the one hand there is the combination of practical ideas and the dispassionate eye of the natural scientist, and on the other the admiration of the connoisseur and even aesthetic appreciation. This ambivalence may originate in the interaction of Chekhov's interests in science and art, as well as being an inherited characteristic. Emma Polotskaya writes:

> Chekhov was a true son of his father Pavel Egorovich Chekhov, whose record of the Chekhov family's life in Melikhovo was full of abundant observations of a phenological character, and inherited his eye for nature—partly practical, partly lyrical. Pavel Egorovich observed the opening of each bud of the violets and peonies, the blossoming of the jasmine and hyacinths, and the song of the nightingales and starlings. [...] All this comprised a disingenuous and disinterested admiration of nature. But his famous laconic statement: "The rye is looking beautiful" is surely the precursor of Lopakhin's delight at the purchase of the estate [...] and his words about the poppy harvest that brought him "forty thousand clear."[1]

Lopakhin's pragmatic attitude towards nature is echoed in the story "Ariadne": "It's just like farming: the beauty of nature is one thing, but the income from the forests and fields is something else" (S 9: 14).

The special place occupied by nature in his writings would justify speaking of an idiosyncratic Chekhovian philosophy of nature. Valentine T. Bill goes so far as to assert that this philosophy is based on ideas of the unity of nature and man. He writes: "Chekhov adhered to this basic view

---

[1] Polotskaia, *O poetike Chekhova*: 75–76.

of the unity of all living things and of a disturbed harmony in nature to the end of his life."[2] Bill goes on to say: "To Chekhov, Man and Nature are one and neither is more important than the other. Trees, grass, flowers, birds, clouds—each particle, large or small, of life on this earth leads its own individual existence and at the same time is integrated into the universal process of life."[3] In his article Bill examines the short fiction; however, he also makes reference to several of Chekhov's dramatic works, in particular, *The Seagull, The Wood Demon* and *Uncle Vanya. The Cherry Orchard* is a surprising exception, for in that play the importance of the theme of nature is already signalled in the very title. The only oblique reference to the play is in the strange concluding paragraph, which contradicts the content of the article: "So, Chekhov's vision of life on this earth was one of a cherry orchard in bloom, be it fifty, one hundred, two hundred or perhaps even one thousand years away."[4] All this suggests that an analysis of the mentions of flora and fauna in Chekhov's works can be extremely productive, in particular for determining the psychological make-up of his characters through their attitude towards nature.

The action of *The Cherry Orchard* takes place in the country, in direct proximity to nature. A natural feature—the cherry orchard—plays the role of a sort of eponymous character in the play. The question then arises as to the relationship of the characters to living nature. A close reading of the text reveals a significant number of mentions of items of flora and fauna encountered in the speech of the characters and in the stage directions. The following is an exhaustive list of the instances of naming of objects of flora or fauna in the text, whether they are mentioned directly, or used in a metaphorical sense, including idiomatic expressions. These mentions fall into several groups: plants; insects, fish and reptiles; birds; and mammals. We shall examine each in turn.

Plants

> Sharlotta. My dog even eats **nuts**.
> Pishchik. (*Surprised.*) Fancy that!

---

[2] Bill, "Nature in Chekhov's Fiction": 153.
[3] Bill: 154.
[4] Ibid.: 166.

It's already May. The **cherry trees** are in flower.

Epikhodov enters with a **bouquet** *[...] drops the* **bouquet** *[...] picks up the* **bouquet**. Look what the gardener sent. He says to put it in the dining room. (*Passes the* **bouquet** *to Dunyasha.*)

Epikhodov. There's a morning frost right now. It's three below, but the **cherry trees** are all in flower.

Yasha (*to Dunyasha*). Hmn... there's a nice little **cucumber**!

Sharlotta. [...] (*Pulls a* **cucumber** *out of her pocket and eats it.*)

Gaev. It smells of **patchouli** here.

Lopakhin. [...] **Cherry trees** bear fruit once every two years, but even then we have nowhere to put it, nobody buys it.

Firs. In the olden days, about forty or fifty years ago, the **cherries** were dried, soaked, marinated, turned into jam, and time was ... [...] and time was, the dried **cherries** would be shipped by the cartload to Moscow and Khar'kov. The money there was! Back then the dried **cherries** were soft, juicy, sweet, scented.

Firs (*about Pishchik*). Hizonner was here for Holy Week, went through half a bucket of **cucumbers**.

Varya (*quietly*). Anya is asleep. (*Quietly opens the window.*) The sun's come up already. It's not cold. Look, mummy: what marvellous **trees**!

Liubov Andreyevna. [...] There's no one there, it just seemed like it. To the right, on the turn-off towards the summer-house, a **little white tree** has bent over. Looks like a woman [About her mother's ghost]. What an amazing orchard! White masses of **blossoms**, a pale-blue sky...

Varya. [...] Only I hear they've put around a rumour that I gave the order to feed them just **peas**.

[Beginning of act two.] [...] *The road is visible that leads to Gayev's estate. To one side tower some dark* **poplars**: *this is where the* **cherry** *or-*

chard begins.

Yasha (*kissing her* [Dunyasha].) A nice little **cucumber**!

Liubov Andreyevna. [...] My poor Varya to save money feeds everybody milk soup. All they serve the old folks in the kitchen is **peas**. [...]

Petya. [...] you mean you can't see human beings looking at you from every **cherry** tree in the garden, from every last **leaf**, from every **trunk** [...]

*Somewhere near the **poplars** Varya is looking for Anya and calling to her* [...]

Dunyasha. You, he says, are like a **flower**.
Yasha (*yawning*). Ignorance personified. (*Exits.*)
Dunyasha. Like a **flower**... I am such a delicate girl, I adore tender words [...]

Lopakhin. In spring I sowed ten thousand *desyatinas* of **poppies** and now I've made forty thousand clear. And when my **poppies** were in flower, what a sight it was! [...]

*In the distance can be heard an axe chopping at a **tree**.*

*[...] Amid the silence one can hear the muffled chopping of the axe against a **tree**.*

*Silence falls, and only an axe can be heard somewhere far off in the garden chopping at a **tree**.*

These mentions of plants constitute numerically the largest group. This is not surprising, since it is precisely the orchard that is the "eponymous hero" of the play. However, our attention is drawn to the fact that the plants that are mentioned are almost exclusively edible (peas, cucumbers, nuts, cherries and poppy seed), or have a practical value and bring a profit (dried cherries and poppy seed). Any aesthetic view of plants is absent on the characters' part. Thus, Yasha's likening of Dunyasha to a flower is a pure formality and is rather a vulgar comparison than any admiration of beauty. And when Ranevskaya seems to be sharing

Varya's delight at the sight of the orchard, she is seeing in the cherry trees a projection of her memories of her mother ("a **little white tree** has bent over. Looks like a woman") or an element of landscape ("What an amazing orchard! White masses of **blossoms,** a pale-blue sky..."), but not the beauty of the trees themselves. Even when a person is described through a comparison with a plant, it is the edibility of the plant that is stressed (when Yasha calls Dunyasha a "little cucumber"). More often than not the plants mentioned in the play are dead, taken by man from nature and used by him for his own consumption: either gathered in the bouquet that Epikhodov brings in, or used to produce perfume ("it smells of patchouli"), or cooked for food (the peas), or dried or soaked for sale (the cherries). To be sure, the living cherry trees do evoke emotions not connected with the use of the fruit as food or for sale, but nevertheless, in the finale, the trees themselves become an object of commercial exploitation and fall victim to the axe. The only exception is perhaps the poplar trees, about the destruction of which nothing is said. But they too appear not so much as living trees, but rather as markers of space: *"To one side tower some dark **poplars**: this is where the **cherry** orchard begins."* *"Somewhere near the **poplars** Varya is looking for Anya and calling to her."*

Insects

> [Varya to Anya] Your brooch looks like a **little bee.**
> Anya (*sadly*). Mama bought it for me.

> Epikhodov. [...] for what reason then this morning do I wake up, for example, so to say, and I look, and on my chest there is a **spider** of fearful dimensions... One like this (*stretching out both arms*). And also you take a drink of kvass to quench your thirst, and there, you look, and there is something to the highest degree disagreeable in it, of the nature of a **beetle.**

> Petya. [...] the workers eat disgustingly, sleep without pillows, everywhere there are **bedbugs**, a stench, damp and a lack of moral purity.

> Epikhodov. You, Avdotya Fedorovna, do not desire to see me...as if I were some sort of **insect** [...]

The variety of insects in the world of *The Cherry Orchard* is not great. Moreover, exclusively unpleasant insects are mentioned: a spider, a beetle and bedbugs. They are repulsive by definition (cf. Epikhodov's line "You, Avdotya Fedorovna, do not desire to see me...as if I were some sort of **insect**"). The only pleasant insect is the little bee, that is to say, Anya's brooch in the form of a little bee, but it evokes sadness in her, an emotion one could hardly describe as positive. For Anya the bee-brooch is probably one more frivolous, unnecessary purchase by her ruined mother. It should be noted that all the insects in the play are imagined: the spider figures in Epikhodov's dream; the beetle is mentioned, also by Epikhodov, for rhetorical purposes; the bedbugs are invoked by Petya in his passionate description of the difficult conditions of the life of the workers; and the little bee is a brooch, an imitation of nature, and hence in essence also imaginary.

Birds

> Anya. **Birds** are singing in the orchard. What time is in now?
>
> Varya (*quietly*). Anya is asleep. (*Quietly opens the window.*) The sun's come up already. It's not cold. Look, mummy: what marvellous **trees**! Heavens, what air! The **starlings** are singing.
>
> Gayev [apropos the sound of the "broken string"] Maybe it's some sort of **bird**... a kind of **heron**.
> Trofimov. Or an **eagle owl**...
> Liubov Andreyevna (*shivers*). Sort of unpleasant. *Pause.*
> Firs. I happened before the bad time too: the **owl** was wailing, and the samovar was roaring nonstop.
>
> Gayev. [...] (*To Yasha.*) Move away, my good man, you smell of **chicken**.

This group stands out from the others by the fact that the birds mentioned (starlings, a heron, an eagle owl and an owl) are of many varieties and do not perform any household function or have a commercial value, belonging to wild nature that is not subordinate to humankind. The only exception is the chicken that Yasha has eaten on the sly: "Gayev. [...] (*To Yasha.*) Move away, my good man, you smell of **chicken**." Birds facilitate the shaping of the emotional state of the characters ("Varya. Heavens, what air! The **starlings** are singing."), and even act as precursors of the future: "Gayev [apropos the sound of the "broken string"]. Maybe it's some sort of **bird**... a kind of **heron**. Trofimov. Or an **eagle owl**... Liubov Andreyevna (*shivers*). Sort of unpleasant. *Pause*. Firs. I happened before the bad time too: the **owl** was wailing, and the samovar was roaring nonstop." What is striking is the inability of the characters to distinguish the cries of the birds: the same sound is attributed now to a heron, now to an eagle owl, now to an owl, and yet the cries of these birds are quite different. We may take this to be a quite significant trait, since the ability to recognize birds' cries was important for Chekhov—one has only to recall the subtle orchestration of bird calls in the tale "The Steppe," all those lapwings and snipe and *spliuks*, etc. Moreover, the noise the characters are talking about is described in the stage directions as the "sound of a breaking string," i.e., not a natural sound, nor one produced by a living creature. In this way it becomes clear that the characters of *The Cherry Orchard* have lost all connection with nature.

Fish and reptiles.

> Pishchik (*to Liubov Andreyevna*): What's going on in Paris? Eh? Did you eat **frogs**?
> Liubov Andreyevna. I ate **crocodiles**!
> Pishchik. Just fancy!

> Gayev (*doesn't answer anything, only gives a wave of disgust; in tears to Firs*). Here take this... There are **anchovies** and Kerch **herrings**...

> Gayev (*looking at Yasha*). Who's this smells of **herring**!

> Liubov Andreyevna. My second cause for grief is Varya. She has become used to getting up early and working, and now without work she's like a **fish** out of water.

Fish and reptiles appear as food products, objects of consumption for humans, who are capable of making a dish not only out of frogs, but even crocodiles ("Pishchik (*to Liubov Andreyevna*): What's going on in

Paris? Eh? Did you eat **frogs**? Liubov Andreyevna. I ate **crocodiles**! Pish-chik. Just fancy!" In the case of the reference to crocodiles, there seems, however to be a hidden literary association. We would venture to suggest that the crocodile ended up in *The Cherry Orchard* via *Hamlet*: "Woo't weep, woo't fight, woo't fast, woo't tear thyself? / Woo't drink up eisel, eat a crocodile?" Hamlet exclaims at the end of act five scene one. Hamlet here is being ironical at the expense of affected ways of expressing grief, and also, as Mikhail Morozov and Aleksandr Parfenov write, "at the 'love vows' that were fashionable among the aristocratic youth of the time; these included, for example, drinking vinegar (eisel) or swearing to eat one of those crocodiles with which apothecaries decorated the windows of their shops."[5] If this is the case, then the meaning of the Shakespearean allusion in *The Cherry Orchard* is to be found in the fact that Liubov Andreyevna is not simply making a joking reply to Pishchik, but hinting bitterly (of course, not to Pishchik, but to herself, and moreover with a tinge of reproach) at the degree of despair that her relations with her Parisian lover had brought her to. The association with *Hamlet* is supported by the fact that it was Chekhov's favourite play. In Margarita Odesskaya's words, *The Cherry Orchard* can to some extent be read as a "paraphrase of well-known Shakespearean themes, motifs, and plot elements."[6]

The mentions of the herring that Yasha has been eating, and the anchovies and herring that Gayev has brought from the town (and which no doubt Yasha will also end up consuming) point to the main function of fish in the play, namely as an object of consumption. It is interesting to note that Varya, who, in Ranevskaya's words, when she does not have work is "like a fish out of water," is also a sort of object of consumption for those who surround her.

---

[5] Morozov and Parfenov, "Commentary": 245.

[6] Odesskaia, "Shekspirovskie motivy v *Vishnevom sade*": 497. Odesskaia points out one direct, though distorted quotation from *Hamlet* in the play (Lopakhin's line "Okhmeliia, get thee to a monastery") and reveals a system of echoes and analogies between the characters in the two plays (in particular, between Lopakhin and Hamlet, and between Ranevskaia and Hamlet). She stresses that Chekhov had Shakespeare constantly in mind, and invokes a whole series of studies on Shakespearean motifs, quotations and images in Chekhov.

Mammals

Lopakhin [about himself]. With a **pig's snout** into carriage row.

Dunyasha. The **dogs** didn't sleep all night; they can tell that the master and mistress are coming...

*Sharlotta Ivanovna with a **dog** on a chain.*

Sharlotta. My **dog** even eats **nuts**.

Firs. [...] The old master once drove to Paris... with his own **horses**...

Lopakhin [about himself]. I didn't study anything; my handwriting is atrocious; I write in such a way that I feel as ashamed in front of people as a **pig**.

Pishchik. [...] If you've fallen in with the **pack, bark or not, you wag your tail** [...] My late progenitor, a wag, may he rest in peace, used to say about our origin that supposedly our ancient line of Simyeonov-Pishchiks is supposed to be derived from that very **horse** that Caligula put in the Senate... (*sits down*) But here's the snag: there's no money! A hungry **dog** believes only in meat... (*snores and then immediately wakes up*). So I too can only go on about money.
Trofimov. Well it's true that there's something **horsey** about your countenance.
Pishchik. So what... a **horse** is a fine animal... You can sell a **horse**...
Trofimov (*slaps Pishchik on the shoulder*). What a **horse** you are.

Pishchik [...] (*to Liubov Andreyevna*) And if the rumour should reach you that my end has come, just remember this old ... **horse** [...]

*Yasha and Sharlotta go off with the **little dog**.*

The only mammals mentioned in the play are domestic animals that are subordinate to man: the horse, the pig and the dog. The pig, as we might expect, is used as a negative simile for a person; Lopakhin twice compares himself to a pig: "With a **pig's snout** into carriage row"; " I write in such a way that I feel as ashamed in front of people as a **pig**." The horse is used to characterize a crude, gluttonous, but nonetheless agreeable person about whom everyone is ready to put in a good word. The horse is a subordinate animal that man uses for his needs, both everyday (the old master) and, on occasion, political (Caligula). The horse also has commercial value as a liquid asset ("You can sell a **horse**...").

The dog is the most complex living creature (apart from man) in the context of the play. On the one hand, when the dog is used to characterize a person, it is not the most noble aspects of the animal that are emphasized. As Pishchik says about himself: "If you've fallen in with the **pack, bark or not, you wag your tail**"; and "A hungry **dog** believes only in meat." On the other hand, dogs "have the right" to their own emotions (they sense the presence of the master and mistress); to their own hierarchy of values ("A hungry **dog** believes only in meat"); and finally to eccentricities ("My **dog** even eats **nuts**.") We recall Chekhov's special attitude towards dogs and the hypothesis that Kashtanka in the story of that name is a representation of Chekhov himself.[7] Dogs are the only representatives of the animal world that are fully-fledged (albeit secondary) characters in the play: there are lines mentioning dogs, and a dog's relationship to another character (Sharlotta) is depicted. Sharlotta and her dog are inseparable; there first appearance is together, and they leave the stage for the last time together. The dog is subordinate to a person (Sharlotta leads it "on a little chain"), but at the same time is emotionally attached to that person, not an object of consumption or a mere possession.[8] Interestingly, the three varieties of mammal mentioned in *The Cherry Orchard* are not simply domestic animals, but also appear in circuses. Horses and dogs are traditional performers in the circus ring and even can be seen as emblems of the circus; pigs, too, are used in the cir-

---

[7] It is not surprising that it is precisely the dog Kashtanka, a creature on the borderline between nature and man and eponymous hero of the story of that name, who has attracted a whole series of scholarly articles. See, for example: Senderovich, "Chekhov's 'Kashtanka': Metamorphoses of Memory in the Labyrinth of Time...": 121–134; Bogomolov, "Kashtanka i Sharik": 6; Kataev, "'Kashtanka' v XX veke: iz istorii interpretatsii": 302–310.

[8] On Sharlotta as the sad clown see Goriacheva, "Fokusy Sharlotty v focuse dramaticheskogo analiza": 489. Of course, circus animals (i.e., animals subordinate to man) do not entirely belong to the natural sphere, but rather occupy a middle position between nature and man.

cus, for example, Khavronia Ivanovna in Chekhov's story "Kashtanka." Thus these animals are linked to the circus motif in the play represented by Sharlotta with her circus past, her tricks and her image of a sad clown.

Valentine Bill writes: "In the post-Sakhalin period Chekhov increasingly uses attitudes and behaviour toward nature as a measure of the character and moral stature of individuals and groups. Indifference or thoughtlessness or cruelty to nature is seen as evidence of character and moral deficiency." [9] Our analysis suggests that the characters of the play live outside nature, despite being seemingly surrounded by it. They do not perceive nature in a discrete fashion: everything is generalized as "birds," "trees," etc. Nature in itself does not evoke any interest or aesthetic reaction. Any comments they make about nature are in the form of abstract, high-flown rhetoric:

> Lopakhin. Lord, you gave us huge forests, immense fields, endless horizons, and living here we ourselves ought to be true giants...
> Gayev (*in a low voice, as if giving a speech*). [...] O nature, wondrous one, thou shinest with an eternal radiance, beautiful and indifferent, thou, whom we call our mother, containest within thee existence and death, thou livest and thou destroyest...
> Varya (*imploringly*). Uncle, please!

The characters' attitude towards nature is that of a consumer; most frequently the objects of flora and fauna are eaten or sold. Even the orchard itself is an object of consumption (for Lopakhin commercial and for the others emotional). They take from the orchard and give nothing in return. The sale and subsequent felling of the cherry orchard are ultimately acts of suicide, if we consider that Chekhov makes a clear parallel between the fate of people and that of trees in another play, as Bill points out: "Chekhov [...] strengthens and underscores the parallel between people and trees in *Uncle Vanya*. The survival of trees and the survival of sensitive, self-effacing, humble people like Uncle Vanya and Sonya merge into one. Both are two sides of the same theme: beauty—moral and natural—and its senseless destruction."[10] The only exception is Sharlotta with her little dog, but for her the dog is endowed with anthropo-

---

[9] Bill: 159.
[10] Ibid.: 162.

morphic traits and serves as a substitute for a family, i.e., it is more a part of human society than a part of nature. Indifference towards, and incomprehension of, nature is a by no means positive characteristic of the characters in the play. As Aleksandr Chudakov wrote, "For Chekhov man's attitude towards nature lies in the ethical sphere."[11] We may venture to suppose that in the context of Chekhov's oeuvre and his own opinions, separation from nature should be viewed as one of the signs of, and perhaps even reasons for, the doomed world of the characters in *The Cherry Orchard*.

WORKS CITED

Bill, Valentine. "Nature in Chekhov's Fiction," *Russian Review*, 33, 2 [Apr., 1974] :153-166.

Bogomolov, Yuri. "Kashtanka i Sharik," *A.P. Chekhov v kul'ture XX veka: tezisy dokladov konferentsii*. M.: Nauka, 1990: 6.

Chudakov, Aleksandr. *Poetika Chekhova*. M.: Nauka, 1971.

Goriacheva, Margarita."Fokusy Sharlotty v focuse dramaticheskogo analiza," *Chekhoviana: "Zvuk lopnuvshei struny: K 100-letiiu p'esy Vishnevyi sad."* M.: Nauka, 2005: 479–494.

Kataev, Vladimir. "'Kashtanka' v XX veke: iz istorii interpretatsii," V.B. Kataev, *Chekhov plius… Predshestvenniki, sovremenniki, preemniki*. M.: Iazyki Slavianskoi Kultury, 2004: 302–310.

Morozov, Mikhail and Parfenov, Aleksandr. "Kommentarii," U. Shekspir, *Dve tragedii (Gamlet, Makbet)*. M.: Vysshaia shkola, 1985: 188–276.

Odesskaia, Margarita M. "Shekspirovskie motivy v 'Vishnevom sade'," *Chekhoviana: "Zvuk lopnuvshei struny: K 100-letiiu p'esy Vishnevyi sad."* M.: Nauka, 2005: 494–505.

Polotskaia, Emma A. *O poetike Chekhova*. M.: 2002.

Senderovich, Marena. "Chekhov's 'Kashtanka': Metamorphoses of Memory in the Labyrinth of Time (A Structural-Phenomenological Essay)," *Russian Language Journal*, 39 (1985, Nos.132–134): 63–75.

---

[11] Chudakov, *Poetika Chekhova*: 271.

The Cherry Orchard and Fathers and Sons

NICHOLAS G. ŽEKULIN
University of Calgary

T he question of the role played by the works of Ivan Turgenev in Anton Chekhov's œuvre has long attracted the attention of scholars. Several studies have been devoted to "Turgenev" elements in Chekhov's prose works as well as to the issue of the extent to which Turgenev's plays, and in particular *A Month in the Country*, foreshadow Chekhov's theatre.[1] Some fifty years ago the Russian scholar Maria Semanova proposed the following definition for the relationship between the works of these two writers "Chekhov did not blindly imitate [...], but rather introduced 'Turgenevian' themes that would have been recognized by his readers, in a creative manner, that was sometimes even at odds with the original, and that gave them a new [...] perspective."[2] In other words, by invoking in his reader's (or audience member's) memory some Turgenev work, character or situation, which he simultaneously repeated and modified, Chekhov provided his take on the current development of a Turgenev theme.[3]

At first glance any juxtaposition of Turgenev's *Fathers and Sons* and Chekhov's *The Cherry Orchard* might seem surprising and even capricious. A closer examination, however, yields some interesting parallels between the protagonists in these works, and especially between the servants. A remarkable picture emerges when we apply Turgenev's descriptions of Prokofich, Petr and Dunyasha to the three servants in *The Cherry Orchard*, Firs, Yasha and Dunyasha:

---

[1] For a survey of the literature on this topic, see Elena V. Tiukhova, *Turgenev — Dostoevskii — Chekhov*: 45–57 and Nicholas G. Žekulin,"Chekhov and Turgenev. The Case of Nature Description."

[2] Semanova, "Chekhov and Turgenev": 179.

[3] See Mariia L. Semanova, "'Rasskaz neizvestnogo cheloveka' A. P. Chekhova ...": 222.

Firs is "alive and hasn't changed in the least. He grumbles just as he did before."[4] He "... has white hair, is thin and has a dark complexion, wears a brown frock coat with bronze buttons and a pink foulard round his neck" (Turgenev 7: 18); " in his own way [he] is ... an aristocrat no less than his master" (Turgenev 7: 44)

Yakov is "a young fellow with heavy jowls, a whitish down on his chin and small, lustreless eyes" (Turgenev 7: 7) "Everything [about him]: the turquoise earring in his ear, the pomaded vari-coloured hair and his deferential body movements, everything in a word, reveals a person of the newest, most refined, generation, with a condescending look about him ..." (Turgenev 7: 7); he is "is extremely egotistical and stupid with a continually furrowed brow, a person whose sole merit lies in the fact that he has a courteous look about him, reads haltingly and often cleans his frock coat with a brush ..." (Turgenev 7: 44)

Dunyasha is "a girl who is very serious when on duty and a giggler when off" (Turgenev 7: 42). She "giggles easily and quickly and flashes a meaningful sideways glance as she rushes by with dance-like steps" (Turgenev 7: 44). "Without realizing it, [he] had become the *cruel tyrant* of her heart" (Turgenev 7: 135) and "she had [...] to run away into the grove of trees in order to hide her emotion" (Turgenev 7: 150).

The quotations extracted from Turgenev's text could easily pass for unknown drafts by Chekhov for *The Cherry Orchard*, or for newly discovered notes by Stanislavsky for a production of the play. Nor are the parallels limited to the ones cited. After the duel between Pavel Petrovich and Bazarov, Prokofich declares: that "in his time also gentlemen fought, except that 'it was only gentlemen of quality with each other, and they would have ordered knaves like that thrashed in the stables for their vulgarity'" (Turgenev 7: 150). One inevitably recalls the words of Firs about the guests at Lyubov Andreyevna's ball: "In the old days, generals, barons, admirals danced at our balls, and now we send for postal clerks and the station master, and even they only come reluctantly" (S 13: 235).

---

[4] Turgenev, I. S. *Polnoe sobranie socheninenii i pisem*: 7, 14. Future references to this work are provided directly in the text with Turgenev's name (to differentiate them from the Chekhov citations), volume and page number.

Individual similarities might be just coincidental, but similarities in a series of protagonists, especially when those protagonists are all of the same social class, cannot be considered accidental. Two questions immediately arise from this. Firstly, are the coincidences confined to protagonists from one and the same social class, or are there other notable parallels? Secondly, what is the significance of such conspicuous parallels between Chekhov's play and Turgenev's novel?

A broader juxtaposition of the protagonists of these two works reveals a remarkable number of links and references. Although they are not as obvious and striking as the links between the servants, there are many subtle connections, which, in the context of those close parallels, cannot easily be ignored.

In Turgenev's novel, the principal protagonists from among the landed gentry are two brothers; in Chekhov's play we also have a pair of siblings, a brother and sister. One of Turgenev's brothers is a bachelor; so is Chekhov's Leonid Gayev. Nikolai Kirsanov has two sons by two different mothers and the social origin of the mother of the younger one, Mitya, is rather ambiguous; Lyubov Ranevskaya has two daughters and we know nothing at all about the origins of the older, adoptive, daughter. The story of Pavel Kirsanov's romance with Princess R. is remarkably similar to the story of Lyubov Ranevskaya and her French lover. Turgenev provides a description of Pavel Kirsanov in the years he spent abroad "sometimes chasing after her, at other times deliberately letting her disappear from view; he was ashamed of himself, he was annoyed at his pusillanimity ... but nothing helped. The image of her, that incomprehensible, seemingly meaningless, but enchanting image had penetrated too deeply into his soul" (Turgenev 7: 32). This could well serve as a description of the condition of Lyubov Ranevskaya, with the only difference being that whereas the Princess R. dies and at the end of the novel Pavel Kirsanov leaves for Dresden and a lonely life as an expatriate, Lyubov Andreyevna's lover recovers from his serious illness and at the end of the play she leaves for Paris, presumably to take up with him again.

It is often suggested that in his works Chekhov was depicting the end of an era. For a variety of reasons, most often socio-political, the era in question is usually identified as the "era of the Russian land-owning gentry" (dvoryanstvo). I would like to suggest that the link between The Cherry Orchard and Fathers and Sons provides a more specific time frame.

Turgenev's novel was published in 1862 and is set in the period immediately before the emancipation of the serfs. *Fathers and Sons* can thus be viewed as marking the beginning of the "post-emancipation" period in Russian literature and consequently, through its link with this novel, *The Cherry Orchard* marks the end of the post-emancipation time frame.[5] Through his references to *Fathers and Sons* Chekhov turns our attention to the changes undergone by Russian society over the previous forty years. And it is the image of Nature—a comparison of the natural environment in which the protagonists of the two works find themselves— that serves as a metaphor for these changes.

In Turgenev's novel, after the division of his lands with the peasants, Nikolai Petrovich had to begin building his estate from scratch on a rather unprepossessing, flat and bare piece of land. "He built a house, the service and farm buildings, laid out a garden, dug a pond and two wells; but the young trees took poorly, only a very little water accumulated in the pond, and the water in the wells had a rather salty taste. The only thing that flourished was a bower of lilacs and acacias: they sometimes took tea or dined there" (Turgenev 7: 21). Only at the very end of the novel, in what is effectively its epilogue, we are told that: "Their affairs are beginning to improve. Arkady has become a keen owner and 'the farm' has begun to bring in a fairly sizeable income" (Turgenev 7: 186). In Chekhov's play, forty years later, the income from the cherry orchard has shrivelled to nothing. Firs reminisces: "In former times dried cherries were shipped by the wagon load to Moscow and Kharkov. There was so much money! ... They knew how to do it then ... [Now] they have forgotten how. Nobody remembers" (S 13: 206). At the beginning of this period ornamental trees were barely able to provide shade, and a steady income from the estate was just a dream; at the end commercial trees had become purely ornamental. The time had come for a different type of enterprise—leisure property: "The location is wonderful, the river is deep. The only thing is, of course, that it will need to be tidied up, cleared ... to knock down all the buildings, for example ... cut down the old cherry orchard..." says Lopakhin (S 13: 205).

---

[5] It is perhaps interesting that for many historians there is indeed a significant break point in Russian history, marked by military defeat in the Russo-Japanese War and the "first revolution" of 1905; events that Chekhov, of course, did not live to see, but that some may consider his last play to foreshadow.

When making comparisons, differences are no less important than similarities. There is one protagonist in Turgenev's novel, and a central one at that, who at first glance seems to be absent from Chekhov's play: namely the main hero, Evgeny Bazarov. This is indeed the case, if one thinks of Bazarov from the perspective of the evolution of that character in subsequent Russian literature, as a representative of the nihilists, who later became the radical youth pursuing revolution. (This was the perceived evolution, regardless of whether one supported or decried it). But what if one were to consider Bazarov outside of this tradition and, taking as a starting point how he is actually depicted in Turgenev's novel, imagine that as a future for him? Bazarov then emerges as a student who never completed his studies, someone who spends more time dreaming about abstract theories than about his practical medical studies. Forty years later, Trofimov is still a perpetual student dreaming about a bright future that he is incapable of either defining or implementing. I would suggest that in Trofimov, now very much a subsidiary character, Chekhov is pointedly rejecting the Bazarov tradition in Russian literature and arguing that the path represented by this tradition is a dead end and that the direction that Russia should be pursuing lies with a protagonist, who is not to be (and could not have been) found—indeed, could scarcely have been imagined—at the time of Turgenev's novel, namely with Lopakhin. Significantly, this new central character is a mature man who has already achieved much and promises to achieve more.

The contention that Chekhov's *The Cherry Orchard* represents the end of one era (that of landed gentry), and the beginning of another and that, in his view, the future belonged not to the intelligentsia, but to clever peasants, is hardly new. On the contrary, it is more of a confirmation of a widely held traditional view, albeit with some substantive refinements. Set against Turgenev's *Fathers and Sons*, the historical context is made more specific by defining more precisely the chronological parameters; *The Cherry Orchard* marks the end of the post-emancipation period of Russian history, the beginning of which is marked by Turgenev's novel. At the same time, Chekhov is also taking sharp issue with the radical tradition that had developed in Russian literature out of Turgenev's seminal novel. The point is not that the hopes of the landed gentry who had tried to adapt to the post-emancipation economic order, were doomed. Nor is the point that the future did not belong to the Bazarov type, whom Chekhov depicts here as an eternal student (and elsewhere in his works as the cynical country doctor). Despite the general mood in this play of decay and collapse that it has become traditional to emphasize ever since Stanislavsky's original production, placing *The Cherry Orchard* in the context of *Fathers and Sons* clearly suggests that the central theme of the play lies in Chekhov's assertion that the future belongs to the grandchildren of the peasants whom Nikolai and Arkady Kirsanov encountered heading for the local drinking den at the beginning of the novel (Turgenev 7: 13). It is no accident that Chekhov had Stanislavsky in mind for the role of Lopakhin, not Gayev (the role Stanislavsky chose for himself).[6]

In the context of *Fathers and Sons*, *The Cherry Orchard* can therefore be seen as Chekhov's attempt to provide an alternative reading of the evolution of Russian society since the emancipation of the serfs in 1861. A comparison of the characters of Ranevskaya, Gayev, Trofimov and Lopakhin with the protagonists in *Fathers and Sons* would thus confirm Semanova's view that Chekhov used and adapted Turgenev's works as a means of providing a commentary or a corrective to Turgenev's themes. However, the marked similarities between the three servants in the two works thereby become even more intriguing. After all, the conditions in which these servants lived had changed fundamentally, their juridical and social status had changed more than that of any of the protagonists from other social classes, and yet it is these servants whom Chekhov depicts in virtually identical terms to the ones given by Turgenev on the eve of the emancipation.

In deliberately and pointedly echoing Turgenev's servants in a play in which he emphasizes social changes, Chekhov is asserting his belief in the immutability of basic human nature. External circumstances and conditions may change, may even change beyond recognition, but fundamental human character traits remain the same. One continues to find the conservative, endlessly complaining about all changes and unwilling to adapt to new circumstances. Similarly, one continues to find the vacuous young egotist, for whom rudeness and ignorance are essential character traits and not some political statement. One continues to find the flighty young girl, who is ready to fall for the first unsuitable

---

[6] See the notes to this play in S 13: 496.

young man she encounters. Petya Trofimov envisages a happy bright future in which "new people" will live in some fundamentally new way. The repetition in *The Cherry Orchard* of the servant characters in *Fathers and Sons* asserts that even when circumstances change, basic human characteristics remain unchanged. The changed circumstances in Russia made it possible for a Lopakhin to appear, but not every peasant is destined to become a Lopakhin. For Lopakhin himself became Lopakhin not because he is a peasant, but because of the native intelligence, enterprise and hard work that are his essential character traits. Similarities—the focus, in other words, on what has *not* changed—thus assume no less important a role for our understanding of the way in which Chekhov uses Turgenev's works in his own to present a changing world peopled by familiar human characters.

WORKS CITED

Semanova, Mariia Leont'evna. "Chekhov and Turgenev." *Uchenye zapiski Leningradskogo gos. ped. instituta*, 134 (1957).

————. "'Rasskaz neizvestnogo cheloveka' A.P. Chekhova: K voprosu o turgenevskikh traditsiiakh v tvorchestve Chekhova." *Uchenye zapiski Leningradskogo gos. ped. instituta*, 170 (1958).

Tiukhova, Elena Vasil'evna. *Turgenev—Dostoevskii—Chekhov: problemy izucheniia tvorcheskikh sviazei pisatelei.* Orel: OGPI, 1994.

Turgenev, Ivan Sergeevich. *Polnoe sobranie socheninenii i pisem.* 2nd ed. Sochineniia v 12 tt., vol. 7. M.: 1981.

Žekulin, Nicholas G. "Chekhov and Turgenev. The Case of Nature Description." In Rolf-Dieter Kluge, ed., *Anton P. Čechov—Werk und Wirkung.* II. Wiesbaden: Harrassowitz, Opera Slavica N.F. 18, 1990: 688–713.

Postmodernism Revisited: *The Seagull* by Boris Akunin

VOLHA ISAKAVA
University of Alberta

Anton Chekhov was one of the fortunate—or unfortunate—authors of the turn of the twentieth century whose canonized works have received close attention from the Russian literati at the turn of the twenty-first century. Besides contemporary productions of his famous plays, which provide new, often experimental visions, the literary appropriation of Chekhov's oeuvres seems to be a growing tendency as well. These appropriations include, to mention just a few, Liudmila Petrushevskaya's play *Three Girls in Blue* (1988) and Vladimir Sorokin's experiments with the literary Canon (*Blue Lard*, 1999). The work I will concentrate on is *The Seagull* (1999) by B. Akunin (or Boris Akunin), a contemporary appropriation, interpretation and continuation of the canonical *Seagull* by Anton Chekhov.

In recent years Russian culture has produced a great number of works in the vein of what is called postmodern literature, concentrating on the appropriation of the classics. The authority of the Canon has always been especially strong in the Russian cultural discourse, which is attested to by the conception of the "poet as a prophet" and in the last century strengthened by the Soviet system of education that had a very definite standard of literary works that do or do not sow the seeds of that which is "reasonable, good, and eternal." That authority, however, has been shattered since the days of the Soviet dissident underground art, which includes conceptual poetry (Dmitry Prigov, Timur Kibirov) and prose by semi-censured authors such as Andrei Bitov or their émigré counterparts such as Sasha Sokolov. With the breakdown of the Soviet Union and the "re-evaluation of all values" in the post-Soviet era, the Canon itself as a concept of cultural heritage has been reconsidered. In the beginning of glasnost it was promisingly enlarged by authors who had been excluded from the Soviet Canon, then, with the rise of what could be called postmodern literature, the Canon was rejected as a valid foundation for the advancement of literature.

Russian literary postmodernism is an issue too controversial and complex in itself to be included in the present discussion.[1] However, it is worth mentioning a few major literary trends that identify themselves with postmodernism. First, of course, there is the formerly dissident, now-flourishing movement of conceptualism, the strategy of which since the underground days of sots-art has been deconstruction of the official language (propaganda) and subversion of the dominant discursive practices such as Socialist Realism. Second, there is eclectic literature that incorporates intertextual allusions and ironic pastiche, and which has rejected the messianic status so commonly assigned to the status of an author in Russia.[2] I have in mind the self-reflective metafictional prose of Viktor Erofeyev, Viacheslav Pietsukh and Tatiana Tolstaya. Obviously, both tendencies have a negative or at least ambiguous relation to the Canon, either deconstructive and subversive, such as conceptualism, or one that engages canonical works in an ironic play of styles and allusions, parodying and lowering their high status.

Critics continue to argue about the nature and specifics of the Russian postmodern condition. For the immediate purposes of this essay I propose the application of Jean-Francois Lyotard's notion of "postmodern" in relation to Russian contemporary literature and how this fiction attempts to revisit and reconsider the Canon. Jean-Francois Lyotard introduces the notion of "metanarrative," a dominant discourse that legitimises knowledge distribution and establishes the hierarchy of values in the society. The specifics of the "postmodern condition," Lyotard suggests, lies in the rejection of metanarratives, giving priority to "small narratives" and plurality of discursive practices.[3] Thus, the new forms of knowledge in postmodern culture are dispersed combinations of heterogeneous language rather than stable discursive structures for cultural representation like the literary Canon. The incredulity of metanarratives

---

[1] For different opinions on the nature and roots of Russian postmodernism, see the critical works of Mikhail Epstein, Mark Lipovetskii, Viacheslav Kuritsyn.

[2] The article by Viktor Erofeev "Soviet Literature: In Memoriam" could be regarded as a manifesto of that tendency. In Berry and Miller-Progacar ed. *Reentering the Sign: Articulating New Russian Culture*: 147–155.

[3] Lyotard, *The Postmodern Condition*.

gives rise to the subversion of the dominant discourse, destroying the Canon and leaving a cultural void, or ironically incorporating the Canon into the pluralistic multiplicity of "language games."

Boris Akunin, whose *Seagull* I will examine, is a figure of the Russian literary scene who is somewhat different from the radical conceptualists or ironic "pastichists." Akunin is a best-selling contemporary Russian author primarily known for his series of crime novels set in the nineteenth century. Boris Akunin initially should be pronounced or read as B. Akunin, being a written pun on the name of the famous revolutionary anarchist Alexander Bakunin. It is the pseudonym of Grigory Chkhartishvili, a literary critic and a co-editor of *Innostrannaya Literatura*, the thick journal that publishes contemporary foreign literature.

In Russian criticism Akunin has been highly praised for producing renditions of the genre-based story fit for mass consumption but which also incorporate an elitist style and sophistication. It is believed that Akunin's texts entertain their audiences through carefully constructed detective plots just as much as they engage the sophisticated reader through complex intertextual play with the Russian historical and literary tradition and masterful imitation of the language and daily milieu of nineteenth-century Russia.

> Such different novels. But from all of them there is such an attractive perfume of great Russian literature. They all develop dynamically, according to the best western standards. They are all at a single high level as regards the control of the material, both historical and literary. And the highest level means not just the abundance of historical detail and literary allusions, but also their appropriateness and the absence of anything superfluous.[4]

Needless to say, it is also common to place Akunin in the vast category of literary postmodernism. The mass popularity of his texts, which transgress the boundaries of carefully constructed and stylistically elaborate parody and enter the domain of popular literature, corresponds to the postmodern tendency to appropriate and even out all cultural productions (popular and elitist) in order to produce true polysemy and the subversion of metanarrative cultural restrictions. Thus, Akunin's works

---

[4] Verbieva, "Ellinizm detektivnogo zhanra."

feature one of the core characteristics of postmodern poetics, namely, the blurred boundaries between high and low cultures, as examined by Leslie Fiedler (*What Was Literature*, 1982). It seems likely that Akunin is the first writer in Russia to fully enjoy mass popularity and elitist acclaim in the way Umberto Eco enjoyed success with his *The Name of the Rose*. In this way Akunin stays separate from the figures of Russian Postmodernism that are clearly bred from high culture, be it either the aesthetes of pluralistic poetics or the avant-garde radicals of deconstructive poetics. The works of the latter also happen to be an object of mass popularity, i.e. the conceptual writer Vladimir Sorokin, who became widely known and read in the late 1990s. However, his works, belonging to the taboo-breaking literature of shock, enjoy popularity inspired by scandal, which recalls the blasphemous fame of the avant-garde.

The Seagull is the first instance in which Akunin explicitly plays with the Canon, ambitiously undertaking the project of creating a detective sequel to Chekhov's play. For the present study I would like to focus on two aspects: first, how and why Akunin's version of *The Seagull* is postmodern and which specific postmodern techniques Akunin uses to interpret Chekhov; second, I will examine the theoretical perspective of the "open" and "closed" narrative (as conceptualized by Umberto Eco in *The Open Work* [1962]) in relation to both texts. I will provide a textual analysis of both *Seagulls* on the levels of structure, form and language and I will attempt to show how the concept of narrative closure is as essential for understanding Chekhov's poetics as it is crucial for postmodern aesthetics and specifically Boris Akunin's oeuvre. The open and closed narrative constructions interest me firstly because the "openness" of a postmodern work of art is often taken for granted as an inseparable part of any given text that demonstrates or exploits the poetics of postmodernism. The Canon as a legitimizing "grand narrative," therefore, represents an essentially closed structural hierarchy and the ultimate point of reference, undermined by the pluralistic visions of postmodern aesthetics.

To introduce the notion of narrative openness/closure I would like to start with Umberto Eco's concept of "open work". According to Eco, an "open work" is a work of art that produces multiple interpretations on the level of performance and perception. That means that an open work is intentionally structurally incomplete, so that performance and perception (the act of reading implies both) can be interpreted in multiple ways, by which multiple networks of meaning and references become apparent. Eco states:

> "Open" works, insofar as they are *in movement*, are characterized by the invitation to *make the work* together with the author [...]. On a wider level (as a subgenus in the species "work in movement" [characterized by "indeterminacy and discontinuity"] there exist works which though organically completed are "open" to a continuous generation of internal relations which the addressee must uncover and select in his act of perceiving [...].[5]

To provide another example from contemporary literary theory, the notion of "open work" is similar to Roland Barthes's concept of "Text" in "From Work to Text" (1971). Being a "methodological field," Text is a not an object but a ceaseless production of polysemy, by reading the Text the reader engages in an interpretive effort that is infinitely deferred:

> Text does not stop at (good) Literature: it cannot be contained in a hierarchy, even in a simple division of genres. What constitutes the Text is...its subversive force in respect to the old classifications...The text practices the infinite deferment of the signified, is dilatory... [and] the generation of the perpetual signifier.[6]

Thus, Barthes asserts that the Text subverts any discursive inscription of meaning as a fixed entity. On the contrary, the multiplicity of the interpretations produced by the Text is not a hierarchy or taxonomy but rather an infinite play, in which no fixed meaning could be assigned and no structure could be stabilized:

> The Text is plural. Which is not simply to say that it has several meanings, but that it accomplishes the plural of meaning: an *irreducible* [...] plural. The Text is not a co-existence of meanings but a passage, an overcrossing [...].[7]

Both Umberto Eco and Roland Barthes refer to contemporary art as a phenomenon that exemplifies the notion of openness.

---

[5] Eco, *The Open Work*: 21.
[6] Barthes, "From Work to Text": 157–158.
[7] Ibid.: 159.

I suggest that the openness of a work of art operates on two levels: first, as in avant-garde productions, it strives to deceive the reader by failing her/his genre-generated expectations and introducing a labyrinth-like narrative with interpretive layers of meaning. A few examples of avant-garde openness are literary works by James Joyce, or, in the Russian context, Vladimir Nabokov. Second, as in a postmodern text, the openness functions as an indeterminacy and equality of plural interpretations (as exemplified by Lyotard). The text is a rhizome-like creation, driven by intertextuality that shifts and decentralizes the meaning. For example, Milorad Pavić's works and, in the Russian context, oeuvres by authors like Venedict Erofeyev, Sasha Sokolov or the Moscow conceptualists, more or less fit the description. Therefore, the "open narrative" is essentially based on a multiplicity of interpretations: the reader either does not know how to decipher the text (failed expectations), or the reader can decipher the text in different directions, and the further s/he goes the more interpretations arise (intertextuality).

It should be noted that a multiplicity of interpretations does not equal "an open work." Eco mentions that a medieval text also generates multiple interpretations (allegorical, anagogical, moral and literal). Yet a medieval text will never be an open work, because all its interpretations are geared towards the discursive closure of a theological hierarchy. Furthermore, the reader knows exactly how to decode and relate the text to the cultural semiosis (discursive hierarchy) of correspondence to the heavenly and earthly order. That example defines the border between narrative openness and narrative closure. Consequently, a "closed" work of art features the following: it guides the reader's interpretation to the extent that the narration becomes self-explanatory. Interpretation of such a text exemplifies a stable discourse structure; therefore, it produces a symptomatic reading; it also projects a strong author-like point of narration (which could be the dominant Canon and not necessarily a subject-author). To use Barthes's notions, the "closed" work corresponds to his concept of "work" as opposed to "Text":

> The work is caught up in a process of filiation. Are postulated: a *determination* of the work by the world (by race, then by History), a

consecution of works amongst themselves. And a *conformity* of the work to the author...[8]

My intention here is to examine the notions of "openness" and "closure" of both *Seagulls*, as described by Eco and Barthes, and to determine the importance of those notions for contemporary readings of Chekhov as well as contemporary visions of postmodernism.

Akunin starts his play at the end of the last act of Chekhov's *Seagull*: the point when Treplev shoots himself. Akunin's play is presented as an investigation conducted by Dorn, who discovers that Treplev was killed. As in a conventional detective story, Dorn puts all the suspects into one room and then uncovers the murderer along with other dirty family secrets. However, Akunin's play is structured in a series of "takes," when the investigation starts all over and eventually everyone is proven to have killed Treplev.

The very idea of completion of the canonical work suggests twofold intention: it is a postmodernist deconstructivist effort to revisit the Canon and subvert it; it also aims to trivialize the Canon, namely by blending its high elite status with mass-culture effects. Akunin takes a "high" canonized work by Chekhov and writes a "low" detective story as a sequel of the original work, obviously conscious about the fact that the notion of sequel is a mass-culture attribute too.

Akunin introduces different elements associated with pulp fiction: for example, the unpleasant description of Treplev's guts and brains is reiterated over and over by different characters:

> Sorin. Someone shot Kostya in the ear and split his head open, and knocked out an eye... (Take 1)
> Dorn. When I came into the room after the bang, the body was warm. Blood was bubbling out of the body, and the blown-out brains were still running down the wall.(Take 5).[9]

Akunin also uses ironic parody, namely ironic repetition. He starts the play with the last scene of the fourth act of *The Seagull*. Retaining all of Chekhov's dialogue, Akunin introduces different remarks into the scene,

---

[8] Barthes: 160–161.

[9] A. Chekhov / B. Akunin *Chaika. Komediia i ee prodolzhenie*: 119, 140.

thus, Treplev is obsessively playing with a gun, and Nina recites her lines as if reading a part in a pompous play:

> Treplev. ...Nina, what for? For heaven's sake, Nina... (There is a threat in his voice, and he raises his hand with the revolver in it.)
> Nina (in a trembling voice). My horses are waiting at the gate. Don't see me out. I'll get there by myself... (Loses self-control. Nervous tears.) G-give me some water.

Or:

> Nina (puts away the glass decisively and, sighing deeply, says in a put-on, stage voice): Why do you say that they kissed the ground on which I walked? I should be killed. (Leans dramatically over the table... raises her head, watches his reaction).[10]

Akunin repeats Chekhov with ironic detachment. Chekhov's dialogue is subverted by the actions of the characters as suggested in the stage directions, which also appear to have more referential power for the viewer because they play upon contemporary allusions. For example, Treplev's obsessive attachment to the gun alludes to the psychotic undertones common in the detective novels or gangster films. Finally, the most absurd reference is made to Greenpeace and ecology. In the final culmination of the play Dorn confesses that he killed Treplev out of ecological sentiment for the innocent seagull murdered by the deceased writer. The theatrical pathos with which Dorn pronounces the final words ironically contrasts with the absurd reasoning behind his actions.

> Dorn. I ought to have put an end to this bloody bacchanalia. The innocent victims have demanded revenge. (He points to the stuffed animals.) And it all started with that bird there—it was the first victim. (Stretches his hand out to the seagull.) I have avenged you, you poor seagull![11]

The use of contrast between deliberate and "high style" theatrical speech and the false, cynical or bizarre reasons that provide motivation, constitute another discrepancy in the narrative that subverts the original

---

[10] *Chaika. Komediia...*: 99–100.
[11] *Chaika. Komediia...*: 158.

Chekhovian work. Thus, Akunin's play represents a postmodern collage of different discourses and ironic references.

The choice of the detective story genre appears to be a postmodern guise as much as an ambitious desire to complete the classic work. Umberto Eco writes:

> I believe people like thrillers not because there are corpses or because there is a final celebratory triumph of order (intellectual, social, legal, and moral) over the disorder of evil. The fact is that the crime novel represents a kind of conjecture, pure and simple.[12]

The point of conjecture is exactly the point where Akunin's play turns into a pseudo-detective story. The serial structure proves every character to be a murderer, making it impossible to complete the picture, to draw a logical conclusion. The completeness does not need to be restored. *Au contraire*, the most bizarre version of Dorn killing Treplev functions as an apotheosis of the eclectic play of takes. Furthermore, Dorn, assuming the role of a private detective, does not prove anything through logical argument; on the contrary, the slightest hint of suspicion triggers a hysterical or cynical confessional monologue from each character.

Akunin's *Seagull* subverts Chekhov's canonical play by introducing pop culture elements, the pseudo-detective genre, ironic detachment and repetition. The subversion, however, does not bear any apparent satirical or ridiculing intention. Being a postmodern work of art, Akunin's *The Seagull* represents instead what Linda Hutcheon calls parody:

> Parody, then, in its ironic "trans-contextualization" and inversion, is repetition with difference. A critical distance is implied between the backgrounded text being parodied and the new incorporating work, a distance usually signalled by irony. But this irony can be playful as well as belittling; it can be critically constructive as well as destructive. The pleasure of parody's irony comes not from humour in particular but from the degree of engagement of the reader in the intertextual "bouncing" (to use E. M. Forster's famous term) between complicity and distance.[13]

---

[12] Eco, *PostScript to the Name of the Rose*: 54.
[13] Hutcheon, *A Theory of Parody*: 32.

Akunin's *Seagull*, therefore, is an ironic parody, that takes Chekhov's play and re-contextualizes it through the lense of pulp culture and the crime story. However, as Hutcheon points out, the parodic vision does not necessarily entail destructive subversion or downplay, but functions through intertextual engagement with the reader, which allows the parodical work to stand on its own, conceptualizing the critical distance through metafictional references. Akunin is engaged in a play of self-reflexivity rather than in scornful deconstruction. The subversion of the Canon bears the playful character of a metafictional exercise.

Thus, Akunin's *Seagull* contains a specific reference to Chekhov's *Lady with the Little Dog*, when Nina mockingly calls Trigorin Arkadina's lap dog, stating that "it is almost like in Chekhov's *Lady with the Dog*."[14] Another example of the metafictional ironic interplay is the reference to *Uncle Vanya*. The naturalist obsessions of Dr. Dorn echo the naturalist pathos of Dr. Astrov in that play. Moreover, Akunin introduces a reference to himself and his crime novels about adventures of the detective Fandorin:

> Dorn. My ancestors, the von Dorns, moved to Russia under tsar Alexis Mikhailovich; they quickly became russified and multiplied terribly. Some turned into the Fondornovs, others into the *Fandorins* [my italics—V.I.], while our branch was simply reduced to Dorn.[15]

However, with the prevailing generic characteristics of postmodern parody, Akunin also ambiguously leaves space for possible interpretations of *The Seagull* as: a deconstruction of the canonical work and subversion of former ideals; a sequel, updating Chekhov (or completing Chekhov) to correspond with common generic expectations; a travesty in the form of bringing the Chekhovian work down to the level of pulp culture; or an eclectic metafictional narrative that playfully alludes to "high" culture (Canon), "low" culture (crime story) and to its own creator (the reference to Fandorin).

Those multiple connotations of the generic nature of the work seem to fit almost all possible literary means of dealing with the Canon

---

[14] *Chaika. Komediia…*: 121.
[15] *Chaika. Komediia…*: 113.

present on the Russian literary scene (subversion, downplay, intertextual metafiction). However, these multi-faceted devices also exhaust all possible versions of the Canon-oriented postmodern text and by the same token refer the reader to them as to the conventional choices for constructing a postmodern narrative. In this way, Akunin's text embraces not ambiguity or indeterminacy but rather a taxonomy that classifies all possible versions of postmodern play with the Canon. Therefore, the reader is presented with the paradox of multiple interpretations fixed within a structure that could be called *postmodern textual taxonomy*, however much it may sound like a contradiction in terms. In addition to the generic paradoxical openness/closure solutions, the play itself has difficulty fitting into the notion of "open narrative" customarily attributed to postmodern texts.

On the level of structure the two *Seagulls* differ significantly. It is worth mentioning that Akunin, in his own words, was prompted to write *The Seagull* out of dissatisfaction with the incompleteness of Chekhov's work. It is often said that the plot structure in Chekhov's plays and stories is essentially open-ended. The tragic shot ends the comedy on an ambiguous note: indeed, why did Treplev shoot himself? Was it the conflict with his mother, the failed romance with Nina, literary impotence, unexplained restlessness and depression, a feeling of the futility of all his efforts or all of these things at once? The conflicts presented by Chekhov never reach the point of an explicit conflict; there is no catharsis in terms of conflict resolution. The reader witnesses no repentance or redemption: the play ends before the viewer *can* experience catharsis. What is left are interpretive possibilities that make us wonder. That fact led Chekhov's contemporaries to call his theatre a theatre of "mood" and "atmosphere," [16] subverting nineteenth-century didactic theatre.

This way Chekhov presents the reader with an open structure of multiple interpretations and deceived expectations. Chekhov's plays are characterized by a certain ambiguity, when nothing happens in terms of action or even dialogue. With regards to these peculiarities of the structure of the Chekhovian story, Dmitry Chizhevsky attributes an "impressionist" style of writing to Chekhov:

In respect to outer form: 1) vagueness of the total picture, and 2) [...]

---

[16] See Meyerkhold, "Naturalistic Theatre and Theatre of Mood": 62–69.

the prominence of details and trivia [...]. The content of the impressionistic literary works reveals those further traits: 3) the renunciation of the formulation of thoughts [...], which are supposed to communicate to the reader the intent, the "tendency" of the work; 4) the creation of the "general mood" through which, if need be, certain results of the artistic presentation may be suggested to the feelings of the reader, to the capacity to feel if not to the intellect. However, 5) certain small features, lines, particularities, details, speak to the feeling of the reader—these are the bearers of the soft and gentle shadings, the "differentials of mood."[17]

The ambiguity of plot structure and the absence of conflict resolution provide Akunin with the material with which to construct his work. The fact that every character in Akunin's *Seagull* gets a chance to be the murderer gives Akunin's play a serial structure of multiple solutions to the multiple conflicts embedded in Chekhov's play but that are never played out as conflicts. The series of takes presents the confession-monologues of the characters. That is obviously a postmodernist solution (remembering the fact that postmodern art frequently adopts the serial form of reinventing or reshaping events, as in Tom Tykwer's film *Run Lola Run*). Akunin brings the Chekhovian conflicts to their logical resolution, introducing a murder—the highest manifestation of conflict. A certain excessiveness of this "detective catharsis" (too many murderers for one corpse) points to postmodern ironic detachment.

However, analogous to medieval exegesis, the multiplicity of postmodern "takes" does not mean multiplicity of interpretations or open and infinite polysemy of the text. The serial structure is aimed, first, at the resolution of conflicts and, second, at the creation of an eclectic postmodern text. The resolution of the conflict (Treplev is killed) is juxtaposed with the postmodern statement that it is irrelevant who killed Treplev. By using the serial structure Akunin exemplifies and guides the reader through the "Canon" of Postmodernism, or more precisely, how one should read a postmodern appropriation of a classic work. This way, Akunin's oeuvre fits with both fundamental aspects of the "closed" work: the play finishes and completes the open structure of Chekhov's play and refers this work to the general paradigm of Postmodernism, educating the public about how "it has to be done," provoking a symp-

---

[17] Chizhevsky, "Chekhov in the Development of Russian Literature": 54.

tomatic reading. This way the serial structure represents a finite number of solutions and interpretations, as well as a finite and precise "package" of postmodern devices.

The narrative closure is especially evident in the way Akunin treats the characters. Akunin's characters are shrouded in the subnarrative of confessional monologues, which serve as an additional means of narrative closure. Arkadina, in Chekhov's *Seagull*, embodies the qualities of a caring, yet careless mother, ambitious passionate actress, somewhat petty *meshchanka* [petty bourgeois] and an aging woman afraid to lose her lover. She combines pragmatism with naiveté and optimism. Akunin's Arkadina is a Medea, who is cold-blooded rather than impassioned by her murderous love; she kills her son to keep her lover by her side and is quite cynical about it. Compare these two passages:

Chekhov's *Seagull* (during the fight between Treplev and Arkadina):

> Arkadina. I have never played in such plays. Leave me! You couldn't even write a wretched vaudeville. Kievan bourgois! Hanger on!
> Treplev. Tightwad!
> Arkadina. Ragamuffin! Nonentity! (Pacing up and down in excitement.) Don't cry. You shouldn't cry... (Cries.) Don't... (Kisses him on the forehead, cheeks, and head.) My dear child, forgive me... Forgive your sinful, unhappy mother. Forgive me... (S 13: 40)

Akunin's *Seagull*. After she learns about Treplev's death:

> Arkadina. Stop that. How can you at such a time... (Looks at the closed door.) This must be unbearable—red on green. Why did he have to shoot himself on a green carpet? All his life there was pretentiousness and lack of taste.[18]

The characters from the original *Seagull* are trivialized into archetypes that bear several cliché features like murderous passion (Arkadina), or shameful homosexuality (Trigorin), or the rebellion of the humble man (Medvedenko). Those are predictable iconic images of common intertextual knowledge. The closing structure functions on the level of archetypal images and on the level of ironic intertextual play upon those images.

---

[18] *Chaika. Komediia...*: 108.

Akunin employs the same methods on the level of language as well. The language of Akunin is the language of mass-media and sensational tabloids. The speech style of the characters fluctuates between contemporary and nineteenth-century style, which is presented as an archaic, pretentious language. Thus, Arkadina's speech combines melodramatic rhetoric with cynicism typical for the sensational 'yellow' press:

> Arkadina. Oh my God. And I, a mother who has just lost her only, endlessly beloved son, have to participate in this farce! Let me be, gentlemen. Leave me alone with my grief. (Gets up majestically.) Boris, take me into some remote corner where I might just wail, like a wounded she-wolf.

> Arkadina (to Trigorin). Don't look at her like that. She has played this entire scene just to pluck at your heartstrings—believe me, I understand these tricks very well indeed. There's no reason to take pity on her. She will act the seagull like that in front of the jury—and they will acquit her. They'll even ignore the trick with the ether. And why not—she's young, cute, and in love. She'll get so much publicity from this business! Enough to make you jealous. And she'll get a good contract. The public will go to her performances in crowds.[19]

Chekhov's language is characterized by stylistic contrast through creating a peculiar recognizable language for certain characters. This way Medvedenko's language comically combines a teacher's didactic vocabulary with constant lamenting about the financial difficulties that teachers have to face.

> Medvedenko. No one has any justification for separating the spirit from matter since the spirit itself may be the totality of the material atoms. (*Animatedly, to Trigorin.*) You know what, someone should describe in a play and then show onstage how we school teachers live. It's a hard, hard life! (S 13: 15)

Chekhov's use of language suggests an elaborate reading, penetrating different levels of style and speech effects; it is a multi-layered stylistic construction. Akunin's use of language is unified by contemporary me-

---

[19] *Chaika. Komediia...*: 116, 123.

dia discourse. In fact, one can hardly perceive any difference between the speech styles of different characters.

The last aspect I would like to touch upon is the formal characteristics of both works. Nils Åke Nilsson points to the importance in Chekhovian poetics of "non-significant" elements that constitute digressions from the general plotline [20]. To my mind, those elements could be classified as: fixated speech (like "I'm a seagull... No, that's wrong... " in *The Seagull* or "Bank the yellow to the centre..." in *The Cherry Orchard*); sheer nonsense ("Tarara-boom-de-ay, sitting on a stump today..." in *The Three Sisters*); or digressions to unrelated matters ("Masha's leg has gone to sleep" in *The Seagull*).

Those elements repeatedly appear in the text, seemingly without any particular significance. Thus, in *The Seagull* a type of such digression is presented by Dr. Dorn, who murmurs song lines in many crucial moments of the play. Consider the following example:

> Sorin. If you found it necessary to summon my sister, I must be dangerously ill, and yet I am not given any medicines.
> Dorn. So what would you like? Valerian drops? Soda? Quinine?
> Sorin. Thank you very much.
> Dorn (*bursts into* song). "The moon is sailing through the heavens of the night... "
> Sorin. I'd like to suggest a story topic to Kostia. It ought to be called "The Man Who Wanted." (S 13: 48)

The digressions appear to fill in the gaps when there is nothing more to say. At those points Chekhov introduces Dorn singing: seemingly meaningless digressive song lines signify the communication gaps that Chekhovian characters suffer from, the inevitability and irreversibility of misunderstanding. The dialogue cited above is not really a dialogue but rather speech existing in a void, which allows no possibility for communication. Sorin is going to die, dissatisfied with his life and there can be no consolation for him and no words or drugs that could improve that

---

[20] Nilsson, "Intonation and Rhythm in Chekhov's Plays": 161–174. Similar observations on the importance of elements that are deviating or irrelevant to the storyline were made by other critics; for example, see Dmitry Chizhevsky and V. Ermilov in the same volume.

condition. The digressions are those important subtleties that constitute indeterminacy and a mood of hopelessness in all of Chekhov's plays.

Another important example of that digression is the fact that Dorn murmurs a line from a song right after he discovers Treplev's body. Treplev is dead and there is nothing that can change this situation or restore mutual understanding to the members of a disjointed family, the frustrations of which are manifested by activities devoid of clear meaning or immediate response to the situation. Nils Åke Nilsson points out that the words (like song lines) in those moments function as a backdrop for the emotional key:

> There are several types of indifferent remarks in Chekhov's plays. Let us begin with Gaev's billiard terms in *The Cherry Orchard*. The real meaning of the words has no relevance in the context where they are used. Gaev resorts to them on occasions when he is disturbed or embarrassed and does not know what to say [...]. Thus the semantic content is of no interest here; what matters is the intonation: it reveals the emotional state of mind behind the words.[21]

Digressions represent metonymical shifts of meaning, which deviates from the patterns of literal or symbolical representation. Here I understand metonymy in the psychoanalytical sense of displacement and guise, the deferral of meaning that prompts the reader's interpretive effort (the theory of correlation between metonymy and displacement and metaphor and condensation is developed by Jacques Lacan). Thus, Sigmund Freud described the displacement (metonymy) in dreams or in slips of the tongue as a "de-centralized situation," when interpretation is misguided by misplaced and shifted accentuations.[22] The displacement shifts and disguises the symptom in order to point it out, i.e. the repressed contents can show themselves only in the deviated form of metonymic dream-work, as both a diversion and a digression.

Thus, digressions in Chekhov's play relate metonymically to the content of the text by displacing and shifting the accent to the insignificant elements (like song lines), thereby pointing out the narrative subtexts. Metonymy is a rhetorical trope, and digressions constitute the elaborate formal system of Chekhov's play, which deviates and escapes

---

[21] Nilsson: 168.
[22] See Freud, *The Interpretation of Dreams*.

direct reference, confusing the interpretational effort and shifting the meaning.

Akunin also makes his Dorn sing; however, those digressions bear a different formal significance:

> Dorn. What a strange activity—bandaging a corpse. But I've had to do even weirder things. [Дорн: Странное занятие—бинтовать покойника.] (*Goes off into the next room, singing: "A poor steed fell in the field"*).[23]

Here Akunin transforms digression into a direct reference to the sad event of Treplev's death. The displacing "insignificant" language of the metonymy becomes a content-oriented explanatory mechanism in Akunin's work. From the semiotic point of view I would call it an emblematic reference. Christian Metz suggests that unlike symbol or metaphor, emblem does not condense, converge or displace meaning but rather appeals to common knowledge.[24] That knowledge in Akunin's case is a reference to postmodern culture and aesthetics, that indexes Dorn's singing as a clever intertextual matching of common knowledge (the popular song) with events in the play.

Thus, to summarize the present analysis: in Akunin's *Seagull* the reader is dealing with an obviously postmodern work, characterized by a mix of genres, high and low culture and an abundance of intertextual references. However, just like medieval exegesis, postmodern interpretation limits itself to its common culture of ironic subversive discourse. Chekhov's play leaves more room for the use of interpretive strategies through subtle characteristics and "indeterminacy and discontinuity" within the story line. Akunin produces a closed narrative with a determined interpretational set and stable referential structure, providing the reader with what could be called a "postmodern taxonomy" of different gestures indicating its relation to the Canon. This way we as readers are faced with a puzzle: either postmodernism could be quite different from its agenda of pluralistic polysemy of the text based on the chain of signifiers and refusal to subscribe to any dominant or pervasive discourse. Or,

---

[23] *Chaika. Komediia...*: 108.
[24] Metz, *Psychoanalysis and Cinema*.

there is the provocative possibility that postmodernism itself has become Canon. Therefore, intending to revisit Chekhov, Akunin also revisits postmodernism, consciously or unconsciously questioning its main premise: that postmodern text is always an "open" plural narrative, generating endless interpretation in the "methodological field" of the text.

NOTES

I would like to gratefully acknowledge the support and critical input of Professor Elena Siemens of the University of Alberta, whose help and consideration made the present work possible.

WORKS CITED

Barthes, Roland. "From Work to Text." In *Image—Music—Text*. Essays selected and translated by Stephen Heath. New York: Hill and Wang, 1977.

Berry, Ellen E. and Miller-Progacar, Anesa eds. *Re-entering the Sign: Articulating New Russian Culture*. Ann Arbor: The University of Michigan Press, 1995.

Chekhov, A. / Akunin, B. *Chaika. Komediia i ee prodolzhenie*. M.: Mosty Kultury, 2000; Ierusalim: Gesharim, 5760.

Chizhevsky, Dmitri. "Chekhov in the Development of Russian Literature." In Jackson, Robert Louis ed. *Chekhov: Collection of Critical Essays*. New Jersey: Prentice-Hall Inc., 1967: 49–61.

Eco, Umberto. *PostScript to the Name of the Rose*. New York: Harcourt, Brace, Jovanovich Publishers, 1984.

———. *The Open Work*. Cambridge: Harvard University Press, 1989.

Freud, Sigmund. *The Interpretation of Dreams*. New York: The Macmillan Company, 1913.

———. *Psychopathology of Everyday Life*. London: Adelphi Terrace, 1914.

Hutcheon, Linda. *A Theory of Parody: The Teachings of Twentieth-Century Art Forms*. New York: Methuen, 1985.

Lyotard, Jean-Francois. *The Postmodern Condition: A Report on Knowledge*. Minneapolis: University of Minnesota Press: 1984.

Metz, Christian. *Psychoanalysis and Cinema. The Imaginary Signifier*. London: The Macmillan Press, 1982.

Meyerkhold, Vsevolod. "Naturalistic Theatre and Theatre of Mood." In Jackson, Robert Louis ed. *Chekhov: Collection of Critical Essays*. New Jersey: Prentice-Hall Inc., 1967: 62–69.

Nilsson, Nils Åke. "Intonation and Rhythm in Chekhov's Plays." In Jackson, Robert Louis ed. *Chekhov: Collection of Critical Essays*. New Jersey: Prentice-Hall Inc., 1967: 161–174.

Verbieva, Anna. "Ellinizm detektivnogo zhanra." *Nezavisimaia Gazeta*, Ex Libris, 15.04.1999 [Анна Вербиева "Эллинизм детективного жанра." *Независимая Газета*, Ex Libris, 15.04.1999].

Seagulls over Trubnaya Square

ELENA SIEMENS
University of Alberta

On my last trip to Moscow I attended an unusual adaptation of Anton Chekhov's *Seagull* that boldly transformed Chekhov's iconic play into a "classical operetta." The old, unassuming building of the School of Contemporary Play Theatre on Trubnaya Square, where the show was performed, was decorated prominently with large Chekhov posters that in addition to the operetta, advertised the theatre's two other *Seagull* productions, the original play and Boris Akunin's postmodern adaptation of *The Seagull* as a detective story. The impression was that Trubnaya was an important Chekhov address, which seemed rather puzzling. To a contemporary spectator, the primary Chekhov destination, where one expects to find a proliferation of Chekhov ads, is Kamergersky Lane, the site of the venerable Moscow Art Theatre. As for Trubnaya, until just a few years ago it was perceived as a cultural wasteland and, as poet Evgeny Rein aptly described it, an architectural blunder (*oploshnost*).[1]

This essay examines recent changes in the theatrical, and more precisely Chekhovian, geography of Moscow. In particular, I will discuss the historical Trubnaya Square with its School of Contemporary Play Theatre as a new theatrical destination aggressively staking its claim on Chekhov. I will argue that the three *Seagull* productions currently offered by the theatre contribute to restoring a number of aspects of Chekhov's work, as well as his biography, that received little or no attention in the Soviet period. I will further argue that the theatre's innovative repertoire helps to rediscover the lost culture of Moscow's boulevards. In this connection, the paper will address the Soviet concept of leisure and the changes it has undergone since the demise of the Soviet Union.

Before turning to the *Seagull* productions, I will first consider the theatre's unusual building, as well as the area around it. As pointed out by Marvin Carlson, the author of *Places of Performance: the Semiotics of*

---

[1] Rein, *Golubaya Laguna: Antologiia noveishei russkoi poezii* , 2: 236.

Theatre Architecture, our perception of a play "is not governed solely by what happens on the stage."[2] Theatre buildings and their locations, writes Carlson, "generate social and cultural meanings of their own which in turn help to structure the meaning of the entire theatre experience."[3] Carlson argues as well that since their meaning will change "as the society that interprets them changes," places of performance should be analyzed not only synchronically, but also diachronically.[4] In the case of Trubnaya Square diachronic analysis proves to be highly productive. Among other things, an investigation of the history of this area reveals that its connection to Chekhov may not be as coincidental as it appears today.

The historical building currently occupied by the School of Contemporary Play Theatre initially housed the celebrated Hermitage restaurant. Founded by merchant Yakov Pegov and French chef Lucien Olivier, the Hermitage first opened in 1864. As reported by Vladimir Gilyarovsky, the author of *Moskva i moskvichi* (Moscow and Muscovites), the Hermitage was popular with theatregoers, as well as important artists and authors. Chekhov, who was also known to drop by, invented a neologism *"proermitazhit"* translated loosely as "to spend a night of eating and drinking" at the Hermitage.[5] In addition to offering impromptu concerts by such luminaries as Fedor Shaliapin, the Hermitage hosted a number of high-profile cultural events, notably the Day of Saint Tatyana, a gathering of the Moscow University professors, and the Days of Pushkin, an annual celebration attended by Dostoevsky and other prominent figures.

While welcoming artists and intellectuals, the Hermitage catered above all to rich merchants, who by and large had little appreciation for either the cultural gatherings or the sophisticated French cuisine. As described by Gilyarovsky, upon arriving at the Hermitage, the merchants headed directly to private rooms, where they drank copiously and dined on caviar served in silver buckets. The most legendary of the private rooms was the Red Room, where on one occasion a group of merrymakers consumed a circus pig abducted from Tanti the clown who per-

---

[2] Carlson, *Places of Performance: The Semiotics of Theatre Architecture*: 2.

[3] Ibid.

[4] Ibid.: 9.

[5] Nilsson, *Chekhov's Great Plays: A Critical Anthology*: 253.

formed at the nearby circus on Tsvetnoy Boulevard. Gilyarovsky writes that in fear of stumbling upon their superiors, the police rarely showed up at the Hermitage and as a rule turned a blind eye on the wild pranks and debauchery that went on there.[6]

Chekhov, who in the 1880s wrote a column entitled "Fragments of Moscow Life" for the Petersburg magazine *Oskolki*, also recorded the incident with Tanti's pig cruelly consumed at the Hermitage. In an installment dating from 1885, he writes that Moscow was "terribly addicted to swinishness," and that when the merchants "gobbled up" Tanti's pig, another animal was immediately trained to replace it, so as to take "the mournful Muscovites' minds off the deceased."[7] Chekhov goes on to describe the new pig's routine, which provided the audience "with the greatest of aesthetic pleasures." In addition to dancing and grunting on command, the pig read newspapers and was particularly fond of the pulp publication the *Moscow Leaflet*.

The Hermitage was shut down in 1917. It briefly reopened during the NEP era, at which time it went back to serving French-inspired cuisine. Gilyarovsky writes that the Pompadour and Marie Louise cutlets were now tough as leather. Among cultural celebrities who frequented the restaurant during the NEP years was renowned actor Mikhail Sadovsky, who came here to observe the nouveaux riches, so as to portray them faithfully on stage. In the early 1920s, the Hermitage closed down for good and was renamed the House of Peasants (*Dom krestyanina*). In subsequent years, it accommodated a succession of administrative offices, as well as housing a dental clinic and a bank outlet.

The closure of the Hermitage drastically changed the image of Trubnaya Square, which in the past was perceived as one of Moscow's most flamboyant destinations. In 1924 the square also lost its thriving pet market, which served as another important landmark of this area. Chekhov, who rented his first Moscow flat in this neighbourhood, enthusiastically described the market in a short piece entitled "*V Moskve na Trubnoy ploshchadi*" ("On Trubnaya Square in Moscow"). With its detailed account of the market crowd, the story is reminiscent of the "physiological sketch," a genre advocated by Belinsky and designed to chronicle the

---

[6] Gilyarovskii, *Moskva i moskvichi*: 120–33.

[7] Quoted in L. Gavrilenko, "Chekhov and the Circus," in *Soviet Circus: A Collection of Articles*: 195–96.

everyday life of the lower classes. Following the lead of Belinsky and his fellow members of the "natural school," Chekhov provides individual portraits of several "types," among them "a post-office official in a faded overcoat," and an old man in a "fur cap, iron-rimmed spectacles and galoshes that look like two dread-noughts."[8] While maintaining a matter-of-fact tone, as was expected of the "physiological sketch," Chekhov's narrative ends with a poetic tribute to the market as a special place with its unique atmosphere and customs that mystified an outsider.

Chekhov also described Trubnaya Square and its surroundings at night, when this area doubled as the city's red-light district. In the story entitled "A Nervous Breakdown," an emotional law student Vasilyev and his two friends take a "joint expedition" to side streets around Trubnaya populated by "rows of houses with brightly lit windows and wide open doors."[9] Vasilyev finds it odd that "cabbies sat on their boxes as calmly and unconcernedly" as anywhere else. He notices as well that "no one hurried, no one hid his face in his coat collar, no one shook his head reproachfully." The overall atmosphere resembled that of "slave markets in the old days," where there was "just the same sort of bustle and high spirits, with people's faces and walk expressing just the same off-handedness." Having reluctantly visited several brothels, Vasilyev confronts his carefree friends, telling them that they too were responsible for destroying those "foolish, hungry" women, who die well before their time from entertaining hundreds of men. Following this confrontation that takes place on Trubnaya, Vasilyev abandons his friends and later that night suffers a severe attack of nerves.

With the closure of the Hermitage and the pet market, the only prominent landmark that remained in this area was the Old Circus on Tsvetnoy Boulevard, where the public once admired performances by Tanti and his unfortunate pig. The circus was nationalized in 1919 and subsequently underwent a number of important reforms that aimed to free it from the "the old style of clowning." In contrast to the customary buffoon, the Soviet clown was a "lively, natural man," who appeared "in

---

[8] Anton Chekhov, "The Bird Market," in Constance Garnett, ed., *The Cook's Wedding and Other Stories*, <http:// www.gutenberg.org.dirs/>. For the original text, see A. P. Chekhov, "V Moskve na Trubnoi ploshchadi" (S 2: 245–48).

[9] Anton Chekhov, "A Nervous Breakdown" (*The Oxford Chekhov*, vol. 4: 159–79). For the original text, see A. P. Chekhov, "Pripadok" (S 2: 199–221).

a realistic guise that would not in itself be a cause for laughter."[10] In his book *Almost Serious*, the celebrated Soviet clown Yury Nikulin recalls how in his early days he was criticized for his oversized shoes with long pointed toes. Nikulin writes that upon seeing those shoes, a zealous colleague warned him that "cosmopolitanism" had no place in Soviet art and that it was high time he renounced the old customs derived from the West.[11]

As pointed out by Nikulin, the popularity of a circus often depends on its location. He writes that in the past "owners built circuses near markets, train stations, and in city parks," as these were the places with the most concentration of people.[12] In the Soviet era, the construction of circuses did not appear to observe this rule. The new circus in Moscow was built on Vernadsky Avenue, a location removed from the city's centre and dominated by the Moscow State University campus. Rather than only entertaining the audience, the Soviet-era circus, as was the case with theatre at large, served the function of education. Nikulin writes that the circus on Vernadsky was big and impersonal and could not compare with the Old Circus on Tsvetnoy Boulevard. Quoting his fellow clown Karandash, he says that the new circus was designed for spectacles, whereas the old one was a place conducive to creating genuine art.

Although it remained popular, the Old Circus alone could not prevent the decline of Trubnaya Square and the surrounding boulevards. The diminishing significance of this area serves as a good illustration of the overall attitude to boulevard culture in the Soviet period, when even the word "boulevard" acquired negative connotations and was often used in a derogatory sense. In her study *Common Places: Mythologies of Everyday Life in Russia*, Svetlana Boym points out that in the early years of the Bolshevik Revolution, the boulevard attracted avant-garde artists, who aspired to liberate the "art of good taste" from the confines of palaces and take it to the streets and boulevards. Boym reports that by the late 1920s "the emphasis shifts from the unruly streets to the 'organized outdoors' in the Parks of Culture and Rest and in sport stadiums."[13] With

---

[10] Popov, *Soviet Circus*: 54–5.

[11] Nikulin, *Pochti ser'ezno*: 312.

[12] Ibid.: 424.

[13] Boym, *Common Places: Mythologies of Everyday Life in Russia*: 126–7.

its "dynamism of the early avant-garde and its foreign accent," the boulevard begins to be perceived as a hostile territory and eventually is excluded from the "Soviet urban iconography."

"Bolshevism has abolished private life," Walter Benjamin wrote famously after visiting Moscow in 1926.[14] With their lives consumed by meetings at factories and offices, people no longer had any free time to pursue their individual interests. Private space also came in short supply. Benjamin comments that apartments "that earlier accommodated single families in their five to eight rooms now often lodge eight." Moreover, every effort was made to expel "coziness" and any trace of the "petty-bourgeois interior." With their cushions and ornaments, bourgeois living quarters were turned into "battlefields over which the attack of commodity capital has advanced victoriously." This attack spread out to other spaces, notably the cafes. "Free trade and free intellect have been abolished," and as a consequence of this, the cafes were "deprived of their public." Even for private affairs, writes Benjamin, there remained only the office and the workers' club.

Mikhail Bulgakov, who experienced first-hand the housing crisis of the 1920s, writes mockingly that Muscovites "have lost even the understanding of the word 'apartment' by naively applying it to everything."[15] In *Moscow in the Twenties*, Bulgakov describes his visit with his journalist friend, whose apartment was "like a pit, divided by plywood partitions into five compartments, appearing to me like large oblong hatboxes." Bulgakov says that every "whisper, the sound of a match dropping to the floor, was audible in all the boxes," and that since his friend's "box" was in the middle, it was virtually impossible to conduct any conversation in it without hearing the next door neighbours. Following this visit, the distressed Bulgakov found a renewed appreciation for his own place, a communal flat he shared with a drunkard Vasily Ivanovich and his wife. If nothing else, it gave him the gift of silence, "a gift of God and paradise."

Unlike Bulgakov, who mocked it and agonized over it, Vladimir Mayakovsky attempted to embrace the new order of things. In his poetry, as well as his personal correspondence, Mayakovsky continually speaks about his struggle with his conventional self, that "terrible dou-

---

[14] Benjamin, *One Way Street and Other Writings*: 187–89.
[15] Bulgakov, *Russian Literature Triquarterly*, No. 15: 11–13.

ble" who formed "an emotional attachment to a securely selfish and stable life."[16] One revealing document testifying to this ongoing struggle is his 1923 letter-diary composed during his two-month separation from Lily Brik. In a segment entitled "What to do with 'the old'," Mayakovsky writes, "I, who for a year threw even the mattress, even the bench out of my room, I, who three times have led such a 'not quite ordinary' life as today—how could I have, how did I dare be so moth-eaten by a flat?"[17] He now denounces soft mattresses and tea drinking, and says that in the future there "will never be anything routine about anything" in either his own life or his relationship with Lily.

Another interesting document concerning his struggle with "the old routine" is Mayakovsky's essay on Chekhov. Entitled "Two Chekhovs," it argues that in addition to the popular Chekhov, the author of lyrical stories from the "twilight Russia," there is Chekhov the innovator and precursor of the Futurist art. Mayakovsky writes that before Chekhov, Russian literature resembled "a greenhouse at a sumptuous noble estate."[18] Its heroes were aristocrats Onegin, Lensky, and Balkonsky, and the language it used was also like a "faded photograph of a rich and tranquil estate." By contrast, Chekhov populated his work with a motley crowd of estate managers and store clerks, who bore unattractive surnames like Kuritsyn and Kozulin. Mayakovsky points out that Chekhov was first to introduce "coarse objects" and give them "coarse names." To the sound of axes chopping down cherry orchards, the old notion of beauty crumbled into pieces as well.

While presenting a highly innovative argument, Mayakovsky's essay neglects to mention that in Chekhov's work, the idle life at a country estate is described as a source of both torture and pleasure. A case in point is Chekhov's story "The House with the Mansard," in which the protagonist, a landscape painter, bemoans his life of idleness at a provincial country estate, and, at the same time, finds a "special charm" in it.[19] The Volchaninov sisters also contribute to developing this ambiguity. Lida, the elder sister, leads an active life and despises the painter for "not

---

[16] Jakobson, *Verbal Art, Verbal Sign, Verbal Time*: 116.

[17] Vladimir Mayakovsky, letter to Lily Brik from 1–27 February 1923, in. *Love is the Heart of Everything*: 125–6.

[18] Mayakovsky, *Sobranie sochinenii v dvenadtsati tomakh*: tom 11: 22–29.

[19] Chekhov, *Anton Chekhov's Short Stories*: 143–58.

trying to show the needs of people" in his art. By contrast, the younger sister Missuse passes "the time in complete idleness," reading and taking leisurely walks with the painter. The story does not suggest a clear answer as to who is right. The painter chooses Missuse, but the two are soon discovered by Lida and their relationship comes to an abrupt end.

In its Soviet incarnation, the concept of leisure left little room for ambiguity. It defined leisure as an active pursuit, as well as stressing "the collective rather than the private nature of the consumption of leisure."[20] In commenting on this concept, economist William Moskoff writes that it implies that "people should engage in more collective activities, i. e. consuming leisure not as an individual, but participating jointly in organized, group activities." Another, equally important aspect is "the idea that there are social obligations and what one does during non-working time should be consistent with those responsibilities." Moskoff goes on to say that the control over the consumption of leisure was "highly imperfect," and that ultimately individuals were able to make some "free choices." However, the resources devoted to recreation were insufficient, and as a result those "free choices" were rather limited.

An insightful critique of the Soviet attitude to leisure and spaces of leisure can be found in Ilya Kabakov's *Three Green Paintings*, a conceptual installation that symbolically represents the relaxation zone of the Sokolniki region in Moscow. The relaxation zone, as the viewer learns from the wall label (*doska-ob"iasnenie*), "is a specially selected big piece of land in the suburbs in the so called 'Green Zone,' with a forest, pond and a river."[21] The wall label also states that such "zones" surrounded every large city, and that the number of these "zones" corresponded to the number of the city's districts. On weekends, urban dwellers were encouraged to travel to their specially designated "zone," where they attended various recreational activities. While visiting such a "zone," people observed certain rules of conduct. The inscription on one green painting reads as follows, "Where are you throwing the peels? Put everything on the paper!"

The formal properties of Kabakov's installation also suggest that in the Soviet Union leisure was a highly regulated and disciplined affair. In describing the genre of his work, Kabakov says that the green paint-

---

[20] Moskoff, *Labour and Leisure in the Soviet Union*: xiii–xv.
[21] Kabakov, *Ilya Kabakov: 1969–1998*: 43–5.

ings resemble "functional, technical stands" that decorated Soviet medical and technical institutions and factory offices. Like those stands, his paintings are meant to signify "unimaginable boredom and sadness." The green colour, writes Kabakov, "was well known in the 1950's—60's to any Soviet citizen" and followed people throughout their lives, "from the maternity room to the last hospital." Metaphysically, green represents nature, and like brown, the colour of earth, it tends to make everything "disappear, dissolve and drown." Accordingly, the labels with small fragments of vacationers' dialogues appear in the corners of Kabakov's paintings. Dissolved in the vast green expanse, Kabakov's interlocutors fail to hear and understand each other.[22]

Similar contradictions marked other Soviet spaces of leisure. Particularly interesting in this regard was the fate of the boulevard, an inherently polysemic space, sharing characteristics of both a street and a park. In Moscow, as was the case in other European capitals, boulevards were constructed in place of old fortification walls. As pointed out by the architectural historian Viacheslav Glazychev, the boulevard was initially designed for royal processions that gathered large crowds of spectators. As a privileged destination exempt from traffic, the boulevard was separated from trivial everyday pursuits. Its primary function was to provide people with an opportunity to indulge in the act of looking, or gawking (*glazet'*), as Glazychev puts it. Alluding to the work of Gogol and Pushkin, Glazychev writes that the boulevard served as a meeting place of the "entire society," and that as a "sacral" space reserved strictly for walkers, it gave rise to unique rituals.[23]

By the middle of the nineteenth century, with a rapid growth of urban population, boulevards began to multiply. In addition to a primary circle of boulevards, cities often included several additional boulevard circles. At this juncture, reports Glazychev, many boulevards opened to traffic and functioned as regular streets. As a result, the old rituals associated with the boulevard gradually became a thing of the

---

[22] In this respect, Kabakov's interlocutors share the fate of many Chekhov's characters. Significantly, Kabakov selects Chekhov as his preferred writer and includes an excerpt from Chekhov's "Steppe" in the chapter "Artist's Choice," see *Ilya Kabakov* (London, 1998).

[23] V. L. Glazychev, "Bul'var i ego okresnosti," in *Lektsionnyi kurs "Proektnye formy kreativnogo myshleniia,"* < www.glazychev.ru>.

past and survived only in novels and films. Transformed into a "mythological" space, the boulevard no longer encouraged the art of looking for the sake of looking. It now acquired a "purely lyrical" function, serving as a site of amorous rendezvous. Deprived of its original functions, comments Glazychev, the boulevard eventually gave way to the arcade, which in turn was replaced by the arcade's modern incarnation, the shopping mall.

In the Soviet Union, the evolution of the boulevard exhibited several unique traits. Following the Bolshevik revolution, boulevards no longer served commercial purposes, as was the case in the past, when they housed numerous hotels, restaurants and shops. Instead, Soviet boulevards were made to serve the function of propaganda and were decorated with Socialist Realist statues. Unlike squares and main streets, boulevards featured mostly statues of writers and artists, rather than those of politicians and military leaders. Nevertheless, a boulevard statue was also expected to observe faithfully the Socialist Realist conventions and render its subject in an optimistic and straightforward manner. Because it was deemed too gloomy, the 1909 statue of Gogol by Nikolai Andreyev was moved to a secluded courtyard of the house on Nikitsky Boulevard where Gogol lived briefly before his death in 1852. In place of Andreyev's pensive statue that depicted Gogol in a seated position and shrouded by a large overcoat, Gogolevsky Boulevard acquired a life-affirming monument by Nikolai Tomsky that represented the author of *Dead Souls* in an upright position with his head held high.

While receiving some attention, the Soviet boulevard was looked upon as a rather marginal territory. Entertainment venues located on and around the boulevards were often awarded to young and inexperienced troupes, as was the case with the Sovremennik Theatre that was given a building on Chistoprudny Boulevard, a location far removed from Moscow's traditional theatrical routes. Boulevard theatres also accommodated problematic and unwanted directors. The unconventional director Anatoly Efros spent many years working at the Malaya Bronnaya Theatre, a modest structure tacked away in the maze of back streets behind Tverskoy Boulevard. Ironically, this policy of exclusion often produced the opposite result. The limitations of their second-order geography notwithstanding, both the Malaya Bronnaya and the Sovremennik were highly popular and attracted many dedicated spectators.

As a result of its marginal status, the Soviet boulevard ceased to perform most of its inherent functions. Those functions that still prevailed, notably the "lyrical function," were perceived in a negative light. A popular Brezhnev-era film *Moscow Doesn't Believe in Tears* includes two key scenes depicting amorous meetings that take place on a Moscow boulevard. In both instances, the boulevard is represented as a space that divides the characters, rather than bringing them together. Moreover, the intimate meeting is portrayed as an incongruous activity that contradicts the overall joyous and wholesome atmosphere of the Soviet boulevard. In the film, the boulevard is populated mostly by pensioners and children, who are represented as indigenous to the boulevard culture. For their part, the lovers are clearly out of place here, and their presence on the boulevard is depicted as purely coincidental.[24]

Having transformed into an extended playground for children, the Soviet boulevard no longer served as a site of any significant rituals and failed to accommodate both intimate meetings and large gatherings. With its unique location at the intersection of four prominent boulevards, Trubnaya Square remained largely a neglected territory throughout the Soviet era. The most prominent event that took place here in the Soviet period was a tragic gathering of Muscovites attending Stalin's funeral in March of 1953. As described by poet Evgeny Evtushenko, the crowd of mourners comprised tens of thousands of people, who were "caught between the walls of houses on one side and a row of army trucks on the other."[25] Evtushenko writes that he was saved by his height, and that short people "were smothered alive, falling and perishing." Because they were given no direct orders, police officers refused to move the trucks so as to give more space to the crowd and prevent further deaths. Following this tragedy, Trubnaya Square became known as *"Trupnaia ploshchad',"* or the Square of Corpses.

Trubnaya Square maintained this rather gloomy reputation more or less until the post-Soviet era, when its image gradually began to change. In the early 1990s, the square acquired a prominent new monument dedicated to Moscow's security officers. With regard to its subject matter, the Trubnaya monument differs significantly from other recent

---

[24] For an account of *Moscow Doesn't Believe in Tears* that briefly touches on the film's tendency to idealize urban environments, see Lawton, *Kinoglasnost:* 17–19.

[25] Evtushenko, *A Precocious Autobiography:* 84–7.

boulevard statues, most of which continue to portray prominent artists.[26] While failing to comply thematically with the traditions of the boulevard culture, the monument has greatly contributed to upgrading the square's overall image. Shaped as an obelisk and crowned with a statue of Saint George, the patron saint of Moscow, it transformed Trubnaya Square into a more polished and well-defined space. As argued by the architectural critic Grigory Revzin, obelisks bring attention to the artistic significance of their surroundings. Resembling an exclamation mark, writes Revzin, an obelisk encourages the passerby to perceive a square as a phenomenon of artistic and metaphysical, rather than only physical, reality.[27]

The new Trubnaya monument also reveals an important change in the attitude of the state towards the boulevard culture. Particularly significant in this regard is the figure of Saint George on the monument's top designed by sculptor Anatoly Bichukov. In recent years, statues of Saint George have appeared in many locations throughout Moscow, notably in the Victory Park on Poklonnaya Gora (Hill of Greetings), where Saint George is represented as a slayer of the Nazi dragon. Statues of Saint George now decorate attractive new stands with theatre ads that can be found practically near every Moscow theatre, as well as elsewhere in the centre of the city. His image also appears on new Russian monetary coins. As is the case elsewhere, the statue of Saint George on Trubnaya Square plays an important symbolical role. Serving as an official seal of approval, it transforms the square from a second-rate marginal territory into a legitimate part of Russia's new capital.

The Old Circus on Tsvetnoy Boulevard has also received a new statue. Placed near the entrance to the circus, it commemorates the celebrated clown Yury Nikulin. Designed by Aleksandr Rukavishnikov, the playful statue depicts Nikulin smiling and waving his hand, as he exits an old-fashioned cabriolet. He wears his usual stage costume, including those famous oversized shoes that once got him into trouble with his conservative colleague. Since its very inauguration soon after Nikulin's death in 1997, the statue has been very popular with Muscovites, and in

---

[26] Boulevard statues dating from the post-Soviet era often portray previously prohibited or semi-prohibited cultural figures, among them Vladimir Vysotsky and Sergei Rakhmaninov (both on Strastnoi Boulevard).

[27] Revzin, *Ocherki po filosofii arkhitekturnoi formy*: 64–5.

particular with children, who like to climb inside the big bronze car and take imaginary journeys. In this respect, the Nikulin statue is quite different from the Trubnaya monument that attracts worshippers only on special occasions, most of them celebrating security forces and the army.

One of the most prominent and well-attended rituals conducted today in this area is the annual celebration of the singer/songwriter Bulat Okudzhava, Moscow's beloved bard. Staged by the School of Contemporary Play Theatre, the event coincides with Okudzhava's birthday on May 9th and takes place both inside and outside the theatre. In the early afternoon, crowds of spectators attend an outdoor concert held near the theatre on Tsvetnoy Boulevard. Later on, the crowd relocates to Trubnaya Square to watch singers perform from the theatre's outdoor balcony. The celebration ends in the evening with a big indoor concert featuring major music stars and famous actors. It is unclear why Okudzhava's birthday is celebrated on Trubnaya, rather than on Arbat, an area associated most closely with him. Most likely, the reason for this is that the School of Contemporary Play Theatre sees itself as Moscow's foremost venue defending the cause of Russian contemporary art.

With its high-profile Okudzhava celebration and a flamboyant contemporary repertoire, the School of Contemporary Play Theatre has played a crucial role in turning Trubnaya Square and its surroundings into an exciting cultural destination. While focusing primarily on contemporary material, the theatre's repertoire includes three adaptations of Chekhov's *Seagull*. Following Chekhov's original play that appeared in their repertoire "almost by accident," the theatre staged Boris Akunin's postmodern adaptation of *The Seagull* as a detective story. When asked how it coincided with their contemporary agenda, the chief artistic director Joseph Raikhelgauz replied that the original *Seagull* served as "the first part" of Akunin's play.[28] Raikhelgauz said as well that there was nothing wrong with reworking and updating the classics. He pointed out that this was a common practice in theatre, citing as an example Rodion Shchedrin's opera *Carmen*, a reworking of Bizet's original composition.

Raikhelgauz's observation regarding a liberal attitude towards the

---

[28] Quoted in Tatyana Nagornaya, "Akunin ubil 'Chaiku' i vzialsia za 'Gamleta'," in *Vladivostok News*, No 1192 (03. 07. 2002), <www.Vladnews.ru/magazin.php?id=Vladnews>.

classics should be taken with a grain of salt. Until recently, the Russian theatre was expected to treat the classics with the utmost respect and remain faithful to their work at all times. Traces of this restrictive approach can still be found even in the most provocative post-Soviet adaptations. A case in point is Akunin's *Seagull*, a work that only extends Chekhov, rather than reworking his play in its entirety. Featuring the original cast of characters, Akunin's adaptation begins with faithfully reproducing the final portion of Chekhov's play. In what follows, Doctor Dorn, who now assumes the role of a detective, conducts a thorough investigation into Treplev's sudden death. Dorn's series of individual interrogations reveal that rather than dying from his own hand, Treplev may have been murdered, and that everyone present, including Dorn himself, had a motive to kill him.

Curiously, Akunin's postmodern adaptation is also more conservative than the original play. As Mayakovsky points out astutely, Chekhov "does not need a suicide to get things moving on the stage."[29] Instead, he employs the resources of language, or, as Mayakovsky puts it, "simple gray words," to generate "the highest dramatic intensity." By contrast, Akunin's play is plot driven and revolves entirely around Treplev's death. In this regard, Akunin follows more closely the conventions of traditional drama, in which death and marriage aid in generating action. As evidenced from the rather uniform vocabulary and syntax used by his characters, Akunin pays only a secondary attention to matters of language. In his case, language by and large serves as a means of communication and rarely performs any additional function.

The most daring aspect of Akunin's work is that it transforms Chekhov's play into a detective story. In her article on Russian detective fiction, Catherine Theimer Nepomnyashchy reports that in the Soviet Union the detective story belonged to the realm of the "objectionable 'boulevard' literature" and was largely suppressed.[30] In the eyes of Soviet political rulers, writes Theimer Nepomnyashchy, "literature considered escapist distracted readers from more serious ideological concerns, and the detective novel in particular seemed to incarnate harmful values." She goes on to say that according to the "Soviet socialist utopian

---

[29] Quoted in Nils Ake Nilsson, "Two Chekhovs: Mayakovsky on Chekhov's 'Futurism'": 256.

[30] Theimer Nepomnyashchy, *Consuming Russia:* 161–91.

ideology," crime was not "a universal aspect of human nature," as it was depicted in the traditional Western detective fiction. Rather, its origins were "social, and therefore 'curable'." Moreover, as perceived in the Soviet Union, crime derived from "the injustices of the very capitalist system upheld by Sherlock Holmes and his confreres."

With the arrival of glasnost and perestroika, detective fiction became one of the most popular genres in Russia. Following the lead of some researchers, Theimer Nepomnyashchy links its renaissance with "the wholesale social displacement of the cult of high culture." In this respect, Boris Akunin (pseudonym of Grigory Chkhartishvili) represents a special case. A graduate of the Moscow State University, he has authored several important scholarly works, including a book-length study entitled *The Writer and Suicide*. He also served as an associate chief editor of the highbrow magazine *Inostrannaia Literatura* (Foreign Literature), as well as editing a twenty-volume anthology of Japanese literature. His best-selling detective fiction reveals Akunin's sophisticated scholarly background and his fascination with high art. Containing numerous allusions to the classics of Russian and Western literature, his work stands in sharp contrast to most crime literature produced in Russia today.

With regard to *The Seagull*, Akunin also pursues a philosophical objective, aiming to resolve the enigma of this strange comedy that ends with a suicide. As he said in one interview, he wanted to figure out why Chekhov identified his work as a comedy, because after all the play featured death, and this was not very funny.[31] For his part, Akunin subtitles his *Seagull* as "The End of the Comedy in the Genre of a Detective Story."[32] While it is undertaken in the name of a lofty intellectual objective, this change of genre draws attention to the connection between Chekhov and lowbrow culture, and in so doing significantly undermines the elevated status of Chekhov's iconic play. A largely neglected area of inquiry in the Soviet period, Chekhov's association with low culture, and the genre of detective fiction in particular, continues to be perceived with mild outrage even today.[33] When describing Akunin's production, re-

---

[31] Interview with Boris Akunin, in *Komsomolskaia pravda* (6 oktiabria, 2000): 6–7.
[32] Boris Akunin, *Chaika*. Featuring a unique format, this attractive edition includes both Akunin's *Seagull* and Chekhov's original play.
[33] Aleksandr Chudakov, one of few critics who analyzed in detail the connection between Chekhov and the low culture, writes that his early association with

viewers tend to use such adjectives as *"epatazhnaia"* (shocking) and *"neodnoznachnaia"* (ambiguous).[34]

More recently, the School of Contemporary Play Theatre staged another provocative adaptation of Chekhov's *Seagull*, this time a "classical operetta." Unlike detective fiction, the operetta was a highly popular genre in the Soviet era. Musical comedy theatres that specialized in operetta were recognized as an important component of the Soviet entertainment industry and were found in every major city. The reason why the authorities supported it was that in contrast to crime novels that focused on negative aspects, the operetta promoted a bright and cheerful atmosphere. As described by Valery Kichin in his article on the prominent Yekaterinburg (formerly Sverdlovsk) Musical Comedy Theatre, the operetta "distracted people from the hardship of everyday life and transported them into the world of a sumptuous fairytale."[35] Kichin points out that in this regard the Soviet operetta can be compared to the 1930s Hollywood musicals designed to perform the same function.

While enjoying the support of the state, the operetta was looked upon as a middlebrow genre. As a consequence of this, musical comedy theatres were precluded from staging any serious material, let alone the classics. Chekhov's plays, including his vaudevilles, were performed mostly at drama theatres. The only high-profile musical adaptation of *The Seagull* dating from the Soviet era was Rodion Shchedrin's 1980 ballet staged at the Bolshoi Theatre. In analyzing this production, critic Emma Polotskaya discusses the numerous challenges of translating Chekhov's play into the language of ballet. Among other things, she points out that Chekhov "opposed any expressiveness" in depicting the emotions of his characters. According to Chekhov, even suffering "should be expressed as it is in life, i.e., not with the legs and arms, but by the tone of voice, by a look, not through gesticulation, but through a

---

lowbrow magazines allowed Chekhov to experiment with "new styles," and that the "artistic principles" he developed "remained constant for the rest of his career." See Chudakov, "Dr Chekhov: a biographical essay (29 January 1860–15 July 1904).

[34] See, for instance, Tatyana Nagornaya, "Akunin ubil 'Chaiku' i vzialsia za 'Gamleta'," and Interview with Boris Akunin, in *Komsomolskaya Pravda*.

[35] Kichin, *Teatr*: No. 3: 26–37.

graceful gesture."[36] As reported by Polotskaya, despite its rich expressiveness and the inevitable use of "legs and arms," the Bolshoi show succeeded in maintaining the "restraint and understatement characteristic of Chekhov."

For its part, the production of the School of Contemporary Play Theatre pursues a less daunting task. When compared to ballet, the operetta, a genre that combines words and music, has more in common with drama. As staged by Raikhelgauz, the distinction between the operetta and drama is further undermined. The show's subtitle, "A Classical Operetta for Drama Actors," instructs spectators to bear in mind that they are still at a drama theatre that only happens to stage an operetta. The subtitle also implicitly juxtaposes the "classical operetta" and the musical, a highly fashionable genre that more or less has decimated the old-fashioned operetta in post-Soviet Moscow. As pointed out by Kichin, because of its exceptional flexibility, the musical is capable of addressing a more complex subject matter, and musically it is closer to opera. By contrast, the operetta is highly formulaic, both with regard to the story it narrates and its musical score. Kichin writes that this explains why Russian spectators have experienced considerable difficulty in making the transition from the operetta to the musical.

In staging a "classical operetta," Raikhelgauz appeals to the nostalgia for uncomplicated, old-style entertainment. Rather than focusing on its darker aspects, the show overtly emphasizes the more playful and carefree side of Chekhov's play. As its epigraph the operetta production takes an episode from Chekhov, in which upon seeing a dead seagull, Trigorin jots a few lines in his notebook. When Nina asks him what he is writing, Trigorin replies, "Oh, making some notes... A subject crossed my mind just now... [Pocketing his notebook.] A subject for a short story."[37] In taking this exchange as their point of departure, Raikhelgauz and his team interpret the entire play as just a "subject for a short story" ("*siuzhet dlia nebol'shogo rasskaza*"). They leave it to "some other theatre in the vicinity" (most likely, an allusion to the Moscow Art Theatre) to deal with rifles and death.[38]

---

[36] Polotskaia, *Chekhov Then and Now*: 239–58.

[37] Chekhov, *Anton Chekhov's Play*: 28.

[38] Quoted from the programme notes for *The Seagull: A Classical Operetta for Drama Actors*.

Although it significantly reduces the overall impact of the original play, this cheerful production nevertheless offers a legitimate reading of Chekhov, who identifies his work as a comedy. The operetta is also one of the three *Seagull* productions offered by the theatre, and this too justifies the limitations of its scope. Designed to complement the two other shows, the operetta addresses an important but often neglected dimension of Chekhov's dramatic work. It encourages the viewer to acknowledge that, like his vaudevilles, Chekhov's major plays contain elements of light-hearted romance and melodrama. In this respect, the show takes a radical detour from most adaptations of Chekhov produced in the Soviet period, an era when no one was allowed to trifle with him and was more or less expected to follow the lead of the great Stanislavsky.

Each in its own way, the theatre's three *Seagull* productions provide a fresh take on Chekhov. When performed at the School of Contemporary Play Theatre, even the original *Seagull* acquires a new meaning. The experience of watching it on Trubnaya Square differs greatly from that of seeing it on Kamergersky Lane, the site of the Moscow Art Theatre, where most of Chekhov's plays were performed for the first time. Although it premiered at another location, *The Seagull* was their key production, with which the Art Theatre acquired its first critical and commercial success. In commemoration of this, the theatre decorated its curtain with an emblem of a seagull. The same emblem was also used to decorate the building's facade. Another factor contributing to this theatre's legendary status is that Chekhov visited it in person. As documented by Konstantin Stanislavsky, the theatre's founding director, in the fall of 1903 Chekhov came here to participate in several rehearsals of *The Cherry Orchard*.[39] In January of 1904 the gravely ill Chekhov attended the play's premiere. In conjunction with the show, actors and staff staged a lavish jubilee celebrating their number-one author.

For its part, the School of Contemporary Play Theatre brings forth a very different set of associations. In the eyes of the contemporary spectator, this area is connected at best with the Old Circus on Tsvetnoy Boulevard. Its ties with Chekhov have remained largely unexplored as well. In the Soviet period, few people were aware that the rundown administrative building on Trubnaya Square once housed the exciting Hermitage Restaurant visited by numerous cultural celebrities, including

---

[39] Stanislavsky, *My Life in Art*: 415–25.

Chekhov. Moreover, the School of Contemporary Play Theatre is a relative newcomer to the Moscow theatre scene. Founded in the late 1980s, it lacks the clout of the old, well-established theatrical institutions, such as the Moscow Art Theatre. When staged here, Chekhov's *Seagull* inevitably loses its cultural and historical gravity. However, by the same token, the play opens itself to a variety of new interpretive possibilities, an advantage eagerly pursued by Raikhelgauz and his team.

In addition to drawing attention to a number of neglected aspects of Chekhov's work and biography, the theatre's three *Seagull* productions contribute to revitalizing the stagnant culture of Moscow's boulevards. In the Soviet era, because of their marginal geography, boulevard theatres gave shelter to unconventional troupes and directors, and as a result were able to stage a more experimental repertoire. However, by and large those productions appealed primarily to the intellectual spectator. In offering three highly diverse adaptations of Chekhov's *Seagull*, the School of Contemporary Play Theatre reestablishes the boulevard as a vibrant and semiotically complex destination capable of accommodating a classical drama, as well as a light-hearted operetta and a postmodern detective story.

The theatre's provocative adaptations of Chekhov also help this area to regain its commercial significance. Particularly important in this regard is Akunin's *Seagull*, a show that employs conventions of detective fiction, currently one of Russia's most popular and commercially lucrative genres. Akunin's own immense popularity also contributes to attracting large crowds of spectators, many of them avid readers of his detective novels. Ironically, contemporary Muscovites appear to privilege Akunin's adaptation over the original *Seagull*. As reported by Raikhelgauz, when, due to an actor's illness, the theatre had to replace Akunin with Chekhov, some people demanded to have their money back. As one disappointed spectator put it, "For this price, I can watch Chekhov's *Seagull* anywhere I want." Whether or not Chekhov has lost the battle with Akunin, comments Raikhelgauz, the theatre "must take into account that Akunin is a fashionable and popular author."[40]

In the Soviet era, the boulevard offered little in terms of visual stimulation, save occasional Socialist Realist statues and children's playgrounds. Back then, leisure was defined as an active pursuit, and conse-

---

[40] Quoted in Tat'iana Nagornaia, "Akunin ubil 'Chaiku' i vzialsia za 'Gamleta'."

quently "gawking" was looked upon with disdain. As demonstrated by the example of Trubnaya Square, in recent years the attitude to leisure and spaces of leisure has undergone a significant transformation. After years of neglect, the historical neighbourhood around Trubnaya Square now features a number of prominent architectural landmarks. Together with other new monuments and statues, the School of Contemporary Play Theatre contributes to upgrading this area's visual appeal. Generously decorated with bold ads and oversized photographs of its three *Seagull* productions, the theatre helps Muscovites to rediscover the pleasure of looking, and in so doing restores the defining function of the boulevard culture.

WORKS CITED

Akunin, Boris. *Chaika*. Sankt-Peterburg: Neva, 2000.

Benjamin, Walter. "Moscow," in *One Way Street and Other Writings*. London: Verso, 1985.

Boym, Svetlana. *Common Places: Mythologies of Everyday Life in Russia*. Cambridge: Harvard University Press, 1994.

Bulgakov, Mikhail. "Moscow in the Twenties," in *Russian Literature Triquarterly*. Ann Arbor: Ardis, 1978: No.15, 11–13.

Carlson, Marvin. *Places of Performance: The Semiotics of Theatre Architecture*. Ithaca: Cornell University Press, 1992.

Chekhov, Anton. "The Bird Market," in Constance Garentt ed., *The Cook's Wedding and Other Stories*, http:// www.gutenberg.org.dirs/.

————. "A Nervous Breakdown," in Ronald Hingley trans. and ed., *The Oxford Chekhov*. Oxford: Oxford University Press, 1980.

————. "The House with the Mansard," in Ralph E. Matlaw sel. and ed., *Anton Chekhov's Short Stories: Texts of the Stories, Background, Criticism*. New York: Norton, 1979.

————. *The Seagull*, in Eugene K. Bristow trans. and ed., *Anton Chekhov's Plays*. New York: Norton, 1977.

Chudakov, Alexander. "Dr Chekhov: a biographical essay (29 January 1860–15 July 1904), in Vera Gottlieb and Paul Allain eds., *The Cambridge Companion to Chekhov*. Cambridge: Cambridge University Press, 2000: 3–16.

Gavrilenko, L. "Chekhov and the Circus," in *Soviet Circus: A Collection of Articles*. Moscow: Progress Publishers, 1967: 194–197.

Giliarovskii, Vladimir . "Na Trube," in *Moskva i Moskvichi*. M.: Pravda, 1979: 123–135.

Glazychev, V. L. "Bul'var i ego okresnosti," in *Lektsionnyi kurs "Proektnye formy kreativnogo myshleniia,"* www.glazychev.ru.

Interview with Boris Akunin, in *Komsomolskaya Pravda*.October, 6 2000.

Jakobson, Roman. "On a Generation that Squandered Its Poets," in Krystyna Pomorska and Stephen Rudy eds., *Verbal Art, Verbal Sign, Verbal Time*. Minneapolis: University of Minnesota Press, 1985: 111–132.

Kabakov, Ilya. *Ilya Kabakov: 1969–1998*. New York: Annandale, 2001.

Kichin, Valery. "Veselaia vdova: Ekaterinburgskaia muzkomediia vchera, segodnia, zavtra," *Teatr*. Moskva, 2003: 3, 26–37.

Lawton, Anna. *Kinoglasnost: Soviet Cinema in Our Time*. Cambridge: Cambridge University Press, 1992.

MacAndrew, Andrew R. and Yevgeny Yevtushenko, *A Precocious Autobiography*. New York: Dutton, 1963.

Mayakovsky, Vladimir letter to Lily Brik from 1–27 February 1923, in Bengt Jangfeldt ed., and Julian Graffy trans., *Love is the Heart of Everything: Correspondence of Vladimir Mayakovsky and Lily Brik: 1915–1930*. Edinburgh: Polygon Books, 1986: 125–126.

—————. "Dva Chekhova," in *Sobranie sochinenii v dvenadtsati tomakh*. M.: Pravda, 1978: 11, 22–29.

Moskoff, William. *Labour and Leisure in the Soviet Union: The Conflict between Public and Private Decision-Making in a Planned Economy*. London: Macmillan, 1984.

Nagornaya, Tatyana. "Akunin ubil 'Chaiku' i vzialsia za 'Gamleta'." *Vladivostok News*, No 1192 (03. 07. 2002), www.Vladnews.ru/magazin.php?id=Vladnews.

Nepomnyashchy, Catherine Theimer. "Markets, Mirrors, and Mayhem: Aleksandra Marinina and the Rise of the New Russian *Detectiv*," in Adele Marie Barker ed., *Consuming Russia: Popular Culture, Sex, and Society Since Gorbachev*. Durham: Duke University Press, 1999: 161–191.

Nikulin, Yury. *Pochti Ser'ezno*. M.: Vagrius, 1998.

Nilsson, Nils Ake. "Two Chekhovs: Mayakovsky on Chekhov's 'Futurism'," in Jean-Pierre Barricelli ed., *Chekhov's Great Plays: a Critical Anthology*. New York: New York University Press, 1981: 251–261.

Polotskaia, Emma. "Chekhov in the language of ballet: The Seagull at the Bolshoi Theatre," in J. Douglas Clayton ed., *Chekhov Then and Now: The Reception of Chekhov in World Culture*. New York: Peter Lang, 1997: 239–258.

Popov, Oleg. "My Hero." *Soviet Circus: A Collection of Articles*. Moscow: Progress Publishers, 1967: 39–59.

Rein, Evgeny. "Sretenka," in K. Kuzminskii, Gr. Kovalev. *Golubaya Laguna: Antologiia noveishei russkoi poezii*. Texas: Newtonville, 1980: 2, 236.

Revzin, Grigory."K semantike obeliska," *Ocherki po filosofii arkhitekturnoi formy*. M.: O.G.I., 2002.

Stanislavsky, Konstantin. *My Life in Art*. New York: Theatre Arts Books, 1952.

Index

MEMBER OF SCABRINI GROUP

Québec, Canada
2006